Korea
in the World Economy

IL SAKONG

WITHDRAWN

Korea
in the World Economy

INSTITUTE FOR INTERNATIONAL ECONOMICS
Washington, DC
January 1993

AOS 0579- 6/3

Il SaKong, a *Visiting Fellow* at the Institute for International Economics, has been a Special Consultant to the International Monetary Fund since 1989. He was formerly Minister of Finance (1987–1988), Senior Secretary to the President for Economic Affairs of the Republic of Korea (1983–1987) President of the Korea Institute for Industrial Economics and Trade (1983), Senior Counsellor to the Minister of the Economic Planning Board (1982), Senior Economist of the Presidential Council on Economic and Scientific Affairs of the Republic of Korea (1979–1980), Vice President and Senior Fellow at Korea Development Institute (1973–1983). He is the coauthor of *Government, Business, and Entrepreneurship: The Korean Case* (1980) and the editor of *Macroeconomic Policy and Industrial Issues* (1987) and *Human Resources and Social Development Issues* (1987).

INSTITUTE FOR INTERNATIONAL ECONOMICS
11 Dupont Circle, NW
Washington, DC 20036-1207
(202) 328-9000   FAX: (202) 328-5432

C. Fred Bergsten, *Director*

The views expressed in this publication are those of the author. This publication is part of the overall program of the Institute, as endorsed by its Board of Directors, but does not necessarily reflect the views of individual members of the Board or the Advisory Committee.

Marketed and Distributed outside the USA and Canada by Longman Group UK Limited, London

Printed in the United States of America
94 93 92   3 2 1

Library of Congress Cataloging-in-Publication Data

SaKong, Il.
    Korea in the world economy / Il SaKong.
        p.   cm.
    Includes bibliographical references and index.

    1. Korea (South)—Economic conditions—1960–   2. Korea (South)—Economic policy—1960–
    3. Korea (South)—Foreign economic relations. I. Title
    HC467.S225   1993
    337.5195—dc20   92-37855
                                     CIP

ISBN 0-88132-184-2 (cloth)
ISBN 0-88132-183-4 (paper)

To My Parents

Contents

Preface

South Korea is one of the world's great economic success stories. Devastated by two brutal wars and mired in deep poverty until the early 1960s, it is now the world's 15th largest economy and 11th largest trading nation. Since 1962, Korea has enjoyed annual growth of 9 percent. Per capita income has grown eight-fold. Korea stands on the brink of becoming a major world economic power and could join the ranks of "industrial countries"—and the OECD, the key institutional symbol thereof—in the near future.

There is great interest around the world in the Korean economic miracle. Its remarkable success to date has important implications for other countries and for the international economic system. Moreover, Korea now stands at a crucial juncture: it must manage the dual transition toward a more democratic society and toward an advanced industrial economy. The world is watching to see if the Korean success story will continue.

We are delighted to publish this study on *Korea in the World Economy* by Dr. Il SaKong. Dr. SaKong, who was Minister of Finance (1987–88) and Senior Secretary to the President for Economic Affairs of the Republic of Korea (1983–87), is one of his country's most distinguished and influential economists. He joined the Institute as a Visiting Fellow in 1991–92 to write the story of Korea's economic development and future prospects, from the unique perspective of an eminent economist who has played an influential policy role in the country for many years. Dr. SaKong's goal is two-fold: to draw lessons from the Korean experience that are relevant to other countries, and to help Koreans think about how to accomplish the current transition to a democratic industrial society with global responsibilities.

Korea in the World Economy is particularly notable and valuable because of Dr. SaKong's unvarnished assessment of Korea's past successes and failures. Among the many factors that contributed to those successes were the government's consistent commitment to growth and its outward-oriented policies. The government played an activist role, but mistakes were sometimes made. Dr. SaKong is particularly critical of the heavy and chemical industry campaign of the early 1970s, where the government tried to pick industrial winners. The result was severe resource misallocation, concentration of economic power and labor abuses.

Another important feature of the book is Dr. SaKong's emphasis on Korea's emerging global role. It is gratifying to hear a leading Korean economist argue that his country has important responsibilities toward the world economy. Korea has benefited enormously from the open international economic system of the postwar period, and SaKong suggests that his nation's economic interest, and duty, is to promote future trade liberalization and the growth of other developing countries, particularly its North Asian neighbors.

In publishing this book, we hope to make a contribution to continued success in Korea and to benefit other countries seeking lessons from the Korean experience. The road ahead for many developing and emerging market economies is not easy, but Korea demonstrates that even the most poverty-stricken, resource-poor countries can achieve remarkable growth with the correct policies.

The Institute for International Economics is a private nonprofit institution for the study and discussion of international economic policy. Its purpose is to analyze important issues in that area, and to develop and communicate practical new approaches for dealing with them. The Institute is completely nonpartisan.

The Institute is funded largely by philanthropic foundations. Major institutional grants are now being received from the German Marshall Fund of the United States, which created the Institute with a generous commitment of funds in 1981, and from the Ford Foundation, the William and Flora Hewlett Foundation, the William M. Keck, Jr. Foundation, the C. V. Starr Foundation, and the United States-Japan Foundation. A number of other foundations and private corporations also contribute to the highly diversified financial resources of the Institute. About 14 percent of the Institute's resources in our latest fiscal year were provided by contributors outside the United States, including about 6 percent from Japan and 2½ percent from Korea. Korean contributions support the general operations of the Institute and were not used to fund this study.

The Board of Directors bears overall responsibility for the Institute and gives general guidance and approval to its research program—including identification of topics that are likely to become important to international economic policymakers over the medium run (generally, one to three years), and which thus should be addressed by the Institute. The Director, working closely with the staff and outside Advisory Committee, is responsible for the development of particular projects and makes the final decision to publish an individual study.

The Institute hopes that its studies and other activities will contribute to building a stronger foundation for international economic policy around the world. We invite readers of these publications to let us know how they think we can best accomplish this objective.

C. FRED BERGSTEN
Director
December 1992

Oct 21

Ackn

I have been indebted to many people in the course of writing this book.

Special thanks are due to C. Fred Bergsten, who not only inspired me to engage in this endeavor but also provided me with the valuable intellectual and logistical support of IIE. I am also grateful to IIE colleagues and other participants to IIE working sessions for earlier drafts of this book. I have benefited greatly from their stimulating comments and encouragement.

I am especially thankful to C. Fred Bergsten and Marc Noland of IIE, Richard Cooper of Harvard University, Leroy Jones of Boston University, Lawrence Krause of University of California at San Diego, Dong-Kil Yoo of Soong Sil University, and Danny Leipziger of the World Bank for reading earlier drafts of this book and providing numerous suggestions for improvement. Thomas O. Bayard and Jeffrey Schott of IIE and Chong-Hyun Nam of Korea University are also appreciated for their insightful comments. I am particularly indebted to Scot Kalb of Smith Barney, who was always available for reading earlier versions of this book for both substantive and editorial improvement.

Valuable assistance in gathering and tabulating data was offered by many Korean government officials, central bank staff, and research fellows of the Korea Development Institute (KDI) and Korea International Economic Policy Institute (KIEP) in their private capacity. Without acknowledging all individually, I express my sincere gratitude for their contributions. Young Kee Lee of KDI was more than willing to offer his time to coordinate data gathering services in Seoul. Chin Kyu Chang in Seoul and Debby Crowell and Regina Rupke at IIE were especially helpful with research assistance.

My special thanks are reserved fcr the competent and efficient editorial staff of IIE, Linda Griffin Kean and Valerie Norville in particular. They contributed greatly to the expository quality of the book.

Despite all their valuable contributions, they are not responsible for any remaining errors and controversial points made in the book.

Il SaKong

Introduction

By any measure, the performance of the Korean economy during the last three decades has been outstanding. From 1962 to 1991 the Korean economy grew at an average annual rate of nearly 9 percent in real terms. In the span of roughly one generation, Korea has achieved the kind of economic development, (albeit under a different environment), that today's advanced nations took almost a century to achieve from a similar stage of development.

Korea in the early 1960s was a typical developing nation caught in a vicious circle of underdevelopment. With a per capita GNP of less than $100, domestic savings were negligible, and accordingly, foreign aid financed well over 50 percent of the nation's investment. Unemployment and underemployment were widespread; urban unemployment in particular reached as high as 20 percent. Over 40 percent of the nation's population was suffering from absolute poverty. At the same time, as a resource-poor nation, Korea had no significant exports ($55 million in 1962), and the balance of payments had shown a chronic deficit since 1945.

Today, the Korean economic scene is totally different. With total trading volume of $153.4 billion in 1991, up from $477 million in 1962, Korea currently is the 11th largest trading nation in the world.[1] Korea's per capita income in 1990 surpassed the $5,000 mark ($6,498 in 1991), a big leap from the meager $87 recorded in 1962. The nation's unemployment rate consistently remains below 3 percent, and absolute poverty has nearly disappeared. Indeed, Korea is on the threshold of joining the

1. This ranking excludes the former Soviet Union and all of Eastern Europe.

ranks of industrially advanced nations, and it may become the first nation from the developing world to achieve such status since World War II. Korea has come a long way since those bleak days of the early 1960s.

The metamorphosis of the Korean economy raises many interesting questions. How can this outstanding performance be explained? To what extent can this performance be attributed to the development strategies and policies of the government? How relevant is the policy of "getting prices right"? If indeed strategies and policies are important, how could Korea successfully adopt and effectively implement them? What was the role of the government in Korean development? Were cultural factors important in explaining Korea's success? Can other developing nations learn from and emulate the Korean experience?

Another question relates to the future of the Korean economy. Does Korea's outstanding past performance ensure continued progress toward industrially advanced status in the near future? Korea today is at a critical juncture. Having overcome widespread unemployment/underemployment and absolute poverty, Koreans now have to face different challenges, demanding new strategies and new economic policy priorities. In addition, with its status as a major trading partner equipped with first-hand experience of development, Korea has new roles to play. Indeed, the international community expects Korea to play an active role, particularly in the field of international economic cooperation.

The changed domestic and external backdrop for economic policy, complicated by rapid domestic political changes, demand new policy priorities and strategies. Obviously, a critical question to be asked is whether the Korean people can once again adapt to a new and challenging environment.

Proper exploration of these issues would serve not only academic and policy analysts in both developing and developed nations but also business communities all over the world. At the same time, policy recommendations emerging from these explorations could serve the Koreans as well.

This book has four main purposes: to shed light on major contributing factors for the "Korean Miracle," to address the question of what lessons one can draw from the Korean experience, to discuss new policy priorities and strategies for Korea, and finally, to discuss the role Korea should play—particularly in the field of international economic cooperation in the coming years.

The book consists of eight chapters. A brief historical background of the Korean economy is presented in the first chapter. Chapter 2 examines Korea's growth performance and structural change since the early 1960s, when the nation began its phenomenal growth. Major development strategies and policy implementations in Korea during the 1960s and 1970s are discussed in Chapter 3. The role of government, Korea's five-year planning, and interactions of market and nonmarket factors, including the cultural aspect in implementation of chosen strategies, are all presented in this chapter.

Chapter 4 is devoted to discussions of development strategy of the 1980s. The Korean government's stabilization policies, structural adjustment efforts, and related economic reforms are discussed here to show how Korea adapted itself to the changing economic environment.

Chapters 5 and 6 discuss international factors and the Korean economy. Chapter 5, however, deals primarily with what has happened with regard to such factors as foreign aid, borrowing, foreign direct investment, and technology imports in Korea. The role of multilateral institutions such as the World Bank and the International Monetary Fund (IMF) and the recent bilateral trade disputes with the United States are briefly discussed. Chapter 6 primarily considers a new role for Korea, in the world as well as the regional economy, that is commensurate with Korea's elevated status. Since discussion of Korea's neighboring Asian economies cannot be meaningfully presented without referring to the role of Japan, this chapter reviews Japan's leadership role in the region.

Chapter 7 is devoted first to presenting the changed domestic and international settings for today's Korean economy and second, to discussing major challenges facing the nation, its policy priorities, and its agenda for future. The last chapter is reserved for summary and conclusions.

The Korean Economy in Historical Perspective

*An art collector will naturally be drawn to Florence, a
mountain climber to the Himalayas. In very much the same way
a social scientist interested in modernization will have his
attention fixed on East Asia. . . .* —Peter L. Berger (1988)

As a background for discussions on the Korean economy in the following
chapters, a brief overview of it in historical perspective will be useful.

Throughout its long history, Korea was secluded from the outside
world, particularly the Western world. The country was often described
as the Hermit Kingdom of the Orient. This changed in the latter part of
the 19th century, when Korea was forced to open its doors to Japan and
the Western powers.[1]

Korea was almost entirely an agrarian economy before the Japanese
colonization of 1910. During the colonial era of 1910 to 1945, the Korean
economy experienced rapid structural transformation. The structural
pattern of this development was largely determined by the Japanese
colonial regime. During the first two decades of colonization, the colonial
power pursued an "agriculture first" policy to ensure that Korea served
as a supply base for foodstuffs. As Japanese war preparations and ex-
pansionist aspirations heightened in the 1930s, the emphasis changed,
and Korea was viewed primarily as a supplier of producer goods for
Japanese industry. As a result, the Korean economy experienced what
is known as "colonial enclave" industrialization. During this period, the
share of manufactures in net commodity-product grew from less than
4 percent to over 20 percent.

Japanese colonial rule ended in 1945 with the conclusion of World
War II. The nation's liberation in 1945 was marred by the partition of

---

1. In 1876 Japan forced Korea to open its ports to Japan by a treaty of "friendship."
Between 1876 and 1886 Korea signed treaties of a similar nature with the US, Russia,
Germany, Great Britain, France, Italy and China.

Korea into two parts, North and South. South Korea was occupied by US military forces until 1948 when the government of the Republic of Korea was established. Between 1945 and 1950 Korea was in a rather chaotic situation. Economically, the partition had crippled the nation. The South was primarily agricultural while the North possessed most of the natural resources and the heavy industry established by the Japanese. For example, North Korea produced 90 percent of the nation's electricity and accounted for almost 80 percent of mining output. Between 80 and 90 percent of chemicals and metal products were produced in the North.

The withdrawal of Japanese manpower, particularly skilled manpower, was another detrimental factor for the Korean economy immediately after liberation. In addition to the colonial-enclave industrial structure, Japanese workers had been employed to fill most of the managerial, technical, and even some labor positions during the colonial period. Almost one-fifth of total manufacturing employment was Japanese; worse yet, the Japanese constituted over 80 percent of technicians and engineers in 1943.

Negative political and administrative factors worsened the situation. The sudden opening of a political vacuum created turmoil on all fronts. The US military government that existed during 1945–48 was not fully prepared, and consequently it was not helpful in improving the situation.[2]

The Korean War that followed (1950–53)[3] was devastating. It destroyed almost two-thirds of the nation's productive capacity, and almost 1 million civilians were killed. Total industrial production in 1953 was estimated to be not much more than one-third of the production level of 1940 (Frank et al. 1975, 9).

The South Korean economy began a solid recovery immediately following the devastating war. During 1953–57, GNP in real terms grew at about 5 percent per year. During this period, foreign aid was an important factor in the nation's economic growth.[4] In fact, foreign aid at this time reached its peak both in absolute terms and as a proportion of total resources available.[5] The relatively high economic growth during 1953–57, however, was accompanied by rapid inflation. The wholesale price index increased at an average annual rate of 20 to 30 percent for the period.

---

2. For a detailed discussion on the colonial heritage, see Jones and SaKong (1980).

3. The Korean War began 25 June 1950, and ended on 27 July 1953, the day the Korean Armistice took effect.

4. The aid at the time was primarily bilateral aid from the United States. See chapter 5 for further discussion.

5. For a detailed discussion, see Krueger (1979, 41-81).

The Korean government and the US aid mission in Korea agreed to implement a stabilization program in 1957. This program was partly responsible for stagnant growth rates during the 1958–60 period. The average annual growth rate for the period was less than 4 percent. Particularly, the mining and manufacturing sector grew much more slowly than in the 1953–57 period.

Korea had been under the leadership of President Syngman Rhee since the inception of the republic in 1948. Syngman Rhee devoted his leadership energy primarily to solidifying the new nation and rehabilitating the Korean economy until he was ousted by the national student revolt in 1960. However, under his leadership, Korea laid a foundation for successful outward-oriented economic growth by investing in education, introducing land reform, and completing the first stage of import substitution.

A military coup led by General Park Chung Hee toppled the short-lived Chang Myon government in May 1961, and the nation witnessed the emergence of a political leadership committed to economic development. This commitment was translated into economic actions and policies such as the adoption of an outward-looking development strategy, active inducement of foreign capital, and various institutional reforms.

Korea had no significant foreign borrowing in the 1950s. As mentioned earlier, foreign aid was the major source of financing from abroad. As will be discussed in chapter 5, imports financed with foreign aid contributed nearly 80 percent of the total resources available for the nation's capital formation during the 1953–62 period. The relative importance of foreign aid diminished rapidly during the early 1960s, as Korea started to rely heavily on foreign borrowing. At the same time, the share of total investment financed by foreign savings declined steadily from 75 percent in 1962 to 26 percent in 1979. The Korean economy recorded a remarkable performance throughout the 1960s and 1970s. The average annual growth rate for the 1962–79 period was 9.8 percent. Exports grew at an average annual rate of 40 percent during the same period. As a result, commodity exports rose from $54.8 million in 1962 to $15.1 billion in 1979.

During this period, the Korean economy also experienced rapid structural changes. The proportion of GNP originating from the mining and manufacturing sector increased from 16.3 percent in 1962 to 28 percent in 1979. Meanwhile, the share of primary products in total exports decreased steadily as exports of manufactured goods came to dominate the picture.

Most importantly, the standard of living improved greatly during this period. Real per capita GNP tripled, and the proportion of the population in absolute poverty declined from over 40 percent in 1965 to less than 10 percent in 1980. Nonagricultural unemployment rates decreased from 16.3 percent in 1963 to 5.6 percent in late 1979.

During this period, however, inflation was a continuous threat to the Korean economy. The promotion of heavy and chemical industries from the early 1970s, combined with the Middle East construction boom after the first oil shock, contributed to an overheating of the economy, lasting from 1976–78. With an average annual growth rate of nearly 11 percent for the period, the Korean economy had to face worsening inflationary pressures.

The effectiveness of heavy government intervention in the nation's resource allocation process varied at different stages of development. The government's involvement may well have been more effective in the earlier period, when the Korean economy was rather small in size and simple in structure. As time went on, however, the Korean economy became much more complicated and more open internationally, and the cost-benefit ratio of government involvement worsened rapidly toward the middle 1970s.

Accordingly, the government's decision to invest in heavy and chemical industries in the late 1970s resulted in serious structural imbalances in the economy. The second oil shock, a disastrous domestic agricultural harvest in 1979, and political uncertainty following the assassination of President Park dealt additional serious blows to the Korean economy. As a result, in 1980 the Korean economy registered negative GNP growth in real terms for the first time since the 1950s; inflation soared, and the current account showed a deficit of $5.3 billion.

In the midst of these difficult economic conditions, a new government was established. Leadership commitment to economic development and continuous promotion of the outward-oriented development strategy became the hallmarks of the new government headed by President Chun Doo Hwan. In managing the economy, the new government had to shift gears toward private initiatives and away from government intervention while reforming the nation's economic structural abnormalities. Stabilization and liberalization programs were implemented simultaneously with strong leadership initiatives.

Coming into the 1980s the government implemented wide-ranging economic reforms. During the early 1980s inflation was successfully brought under control, and stable growth was achieved. By 1986 the Korean economy was firing on all cylinders: GNP expanded 12.9 percent, consumer prices rose only 2.8 percent, and the nation recorded a current account surplus—about $4.6 billion—for the first time in its modern history.[6] From 1986 GNP growth continued to be in double digits, inflation remained moderate, and the nation continued to record a surplus in its current accounts, amounting to $14.2 billion in 1988. At the end

---

6. In 1977 Korea had a nominal current account surplus of $12 million for the first time in recent history. However, this was primarily due to temporary Middle East construction remittances in that particular year.

of 1988 per capita GNP stood at $4,127. Optimism about development was pervasive throughout the Korean society. Most Koreans, politicians in particular, seemed to take good economic performance for granted, and the economic reality was outpaced by impatiently growing expectations.

The year 1988 is a significant milestone for Korea. The Korean government was peacefully replaced by the popularly elected new government, the first time political power was transferred in this way in modern Korean history. Korea successfully hosted the 24th Olympiad, boosting its international image and self-confidence. For the first time in many years, however, the political leadership's commitment to economic growth and development was substantially weakened. As an obvious result, insatiable political demands overpowered economic logic that was politically rather unpopular. Korea's favorable work ethic and worker-management relationship began to erode rapidly. Real wage increases started to outstrip productivity gains. Korea began to lose its competitive edge in many industrial sectors.

Growth momentum in the economy stalled in 1989. The average annual growth rate was nearly 13 percent between 1986 and 1988; the GNP growth rate halved to 6.8 percent in 1989. Obviously, Korea could not have continued to grow annually at a two-digit level for many years. The problem, however, was that the slowdown primarily resulted from a negative growth in Korea's exports. Exports in volume terms were reduced by 5 percent in 1989 for the first time in many years.[7] Instead, rapidly increasing private consumption and construction were major contributing factors for the growth in that year. The average inflation rate, in terms of consumer prices, was 3.5 percent between 1983 and 1988. In contrast, however, consumer prices went up by 5.7 percent while the current account surplus fell sharply from $14.2 billion in 1988 to $5.1 billion in 1989 and turned negative in 1990. The current account deficit was $2.2 billion in 1990 and grew to $8.7 billion in 1991.

In summary, the outstanding performance of the Korean economy that began in the early 1960s has lifted the country to a new plateau and a new stage of economic development. Now the Korean people face an entirely new set of challenges. Political changes only add a new, complicated dimension to these challenges.

Absolute poverty and widespread unemployment are issues of the past; Korea now has to deal with "relative poverty" issues, striking a proper balance between efficiency, growth and equity. At the same time, with changed factor endowments and a different international competitive environment, Korea must implement appropriate structural adjustments. In addition, elimination of widespread unemployment and underemployment brings Korea face to face with the challenge of es-

---

7. Not on a customs clearance basis.

tablishing a new, productive worker-management relationship. Moreover, as a major trading partner in the world, Korea must continuously harmonize domestic policy initiatives with greater internationalization and globalization. Simultaneously, Korea has to redefine its role in the international economic arena.

Korea is at a critically important crossroads. Appropriate policy responses to current challenges will be necessary if Korea is to be successful in making the leap from developing to developed nation status.

2

The Recent Korean Development
Experience: An Overview

*Add successively as many mail coaches as you please, you will
never get a railway engine thereby.* —Joseph A. Schumpeter
(1934)

During 1962–91, the Korean economy expanded at an average annual
rate of nearly 9 percent (see table 2.1). Nominal per capita GNP during
the period grew from $87 in 1962 to $6,498 in 1991, with real per capita
GNP increasing nearly eightfold. At the same time, the proportion of
GDP originating from the mining and manufacturing sector increased
from 16.4 percent in 1962 to 27.9 percent in 1991. Commodity exports
rose from $54.8 million in 1962 to $71.9 billion in 1991, making Korea
one of the world's major trading partners.

Absolute poverty was uprooted for the most part, and nearly full
employment was achieved. The standard of living was also substantially
improved during this period. For example, people's life expectancy increased from 54 in 1960 to 72 in 1991. Income distribution improved as
well, with the exception of the late 1970s (table 2.5).

This chapter provides an overview of the recent Korean development
experience in aggregated quantitative terms that will serve as a foundation for discussions on development strategies and emerging challenges presented in the following chapters.

Initial Conditions for Development

Korea's rapid development began in the early 1960s, while the country
was suffering from all the ills associated with a typical developing nation.
Widespread unemployment, underemployment, and absolute poverty
plagued the country. Savings were negligible, and dwindling foreign
aid, mostly from the United States, primarily financed what little in-

Table 2.1 Economic structure of Korea, 1962–91

	1962	1967	1972	1977	1982	1987	1991[e]
GNP							
Billions of dollars (current)	2.3	4.3	10.7	36.8	71.3	128.9	280.9
Billions of Korean won (1985 constant)	11,215.8	13,864.2	28,504.7	46,135.4	59,322.2	99,611.6	141,602.4
Population (millions)	26.5	30.1	33.5	36.4	39.2	41.6	43.3
Per capita income							
Dollars (current)	87	142	319	1,012	1,824	3,110	6,498
Thousands of Korean won (1985 constant)	423	568	850	1,269	1,516	2,403	3,273
Gross investment (percentages of GNDI)	9.9	17.0	17.7	28.4	25.2	32.3	36.2
Gross savings (percentages of GNDI)	11.0	15.4	17.2	27.6	24.2	36.2	36.1
Export (millions of current dollars)	54.8	320.2	1,624.1	10,046.5	21,853.4	47,280.9	71,870.1
Export (percentages of GNP)	2.4	7.4	15.0	27.2	30.7	36.7	25.6
Import (millions of dollars, current)	421.8	996.2	2,522.0	10,810.5	24,250.8	41,019.8	81,524.9
Import (percentages of GNP)	18.3	23.3	23.6	29.4	34.0	31.8	29.0
Industrial structure (percentages)							
Agriculture, forestry and fishing	37.0	30.6	26.8	22.4	14.7	10.5	8.1
Mining and manufacturing	16.4	21.0	23.5	28.9	30.4	33.0	27.9
Other	46.6	48.4	49.7	48.7	54.9	56.5	64.0
Heavy industry in manufacturing (percentages)	28.6	34.7	36.1	49.2	452.8	57.0	64.9
Heavy industrial goods in exports (percentages)	n.a.	8.7	21.3	32.8	50.8	52.9	57.7
Employment structure (percentages)							
Agriculture, forestry and fishing	63.1[a]	55.2	50.6	41.8	32.1	21.9	16.7
Mining and manufacturing	8.7	12.8	14.2	22.4	21.9	28.1	26.9
Other				35.8	46.0	50.0	56.4
Unemployment (percentages)				3.8	4.4	3.1	2.3
Nonagricultural unemployment (percentages)				5.8	6.0	3.8	2.6
Absolute poverty (percentages)				14.8[c]	9.8[d]	n.a.	n.a.

GNDI = gross national disposable income.
n.a. = not available
a. 1963 data
b. 1965 data
c. 1976 data
d. 1980 data
e. Most figures for 1991 are preliminary.

Sources: Economic Planning Board. 1980. *Handbook of Korean Economy;* Economic Planning Board. *Major Statistics of the Korean Economy,* various issues; Bank of Korea. *National Accounts,* various issues; Bank of Korea. *Economic Statistics Yearbook,* various issues.

vestment there was. Exports were almost nonexistent because Korea, unlike some resource-rich developing nations, did not have resource-based exportable goods. Worst of all, there was no significant industrial base, as agriculture dominated the economy. However, the foundation for the first stage of import-substitution, or the domestic production basis for basic consumer products, was established during the reconstruction period of the late 1950s.

Korea did have significant advantages that contributed to the nation's economic take-off in the early 1960s. For one thing, even though the nation's economic development was not the top priority of the Korean political leadership in the 1950s, the Korean economy by the early 1960s was fully recovered from the devastating Korean War.

For another, Korea is blessed with a rich historical and cultural heritage. Unlike many nations in the developing world formed after the Second World War, Korea had been a single, unified, independent nation from the seventh century until 1910, when the nation was taken over by the Japanese. Koreans spoke the same language and ethnically and culturally were perhaps one of the most homogeneous people in the world (true to this day). Culturally, strong Confucian traditions, which put great value on education, social harmony, and cooperation, helped to lay a firm base for future development. Moreover, Korea's high level of general education and literacy were greatly facilitated by the Korean phonetic alphabet, which was relatively easy to learn and unique among Asian nations.

Social and cultural development far exceeded economic development even in the early 1960s, setting Korea apart from most other developing nations. According to Adelman and Morris' study (1967) of social, political, and economic characteristics of developing nations, Korea in 1961 ranked 60th on a per capita income scale, while it ranked 14th among 74 countries included in the study on a composite scale of sociocultural development factors. The sociocultural development indicator included variables such as extent of literacy, character of basic social organization, importance of the indigenous middle class, extent of social mobility, and degree of cultural and ethnic homogeneity.

As previously noted, in the early 1960s Korea witnessed new political leadership fully committed to economic development. Under this leadership, the nation's first five-year development plan was introduced in 1962, characterized by an outward-oriented development strategy. The importance of having such leadership in place, to guide and nurture Korea's economy through the early, critical stages of development, cannot be underestimated. In fact, Adelman and Morris' study (1967, 246) suggests that leadership commitment is a critical factor or catalyst for economic development, particularly in countries such as Korea with favorable sociocultural standards.

Savings, Investment, and Per Capita Income

Savings and Investment

One of the distinctive characteristics of Korea's nearly 13-fold increase in real GNP during 1962–91 was the high level of investment maintained throughout. A good part of this investment was financed by foreign savings in the earlier years (table 2.2). Korea attracted foreign savings mostly in the form of loans; consequently, Korea gradually became a major indebted developing nation.

In recent years, Korea has paid off a substantial amount of this outstanding foreign debt with its newly generated current account surplus. This aspect of Korean development will be discussed in chapter 5 in detail. It is worth noting at this point, however, that a key factor behind Korea's successful management of its foreign debt was its tendency to channel borrowed funds into productive investment projects.

Per Capita GNP and Purchasing Power–Adjusted Real Income

As indicated, Korea's GNP grew at an annual rate of nearly 9 percent in real terms between 1962 and 1991. Because the Korean population has also grown—albeit at a decreasing rate over time—per capita income has increased at a real average annual rate of 7.1 percent over the same period. Taking the increase in per capita income as a proxy for improvement in the standard of living, the average Korean's economic condition has improved over sevenfold during this 30-year period (table 2.3).

How does the Korean record compare with other nations, and how well off are Koreans as compared with people in other developed and developing nations? The purchasing power–adjusted real income for comparable nations can be used to shed light on these questions. Summers and Heston (1991) provide the purchasing power–adjusted real GDP for 130 countries.

Korea's real per capita GDP was $5,156 in 1988, up from $958 in 1962; this amounts to more than a fivefold increase (see appendix, table A.1). During the same period, most advanced nations fell short of doubling their real per capita GDP, with the exception of Japan, where real per capita GDP nearly quadrupled. On the other hand, most developing nations did not perform well. The Philippines, Thailand, and Sri Lanka started with their per capita GDP higher than that for Korea in 1962. By the late 1960s, however, Korea had the higher per capita GDP, and the real income gap between Korea and these countries continued to widen substantially. Most Latin American countries began this period with more than two to three times higher per capita GDP than Korea's, yet this trend was also reversed in late 1980s.

Table 2.2 Gross domestic investment and its finance, 1962–91

Five-year plan periods	Gross domestic investment (billions of current won)	Gross domestic savings		Foreign savings	
		In billions of current won	As percentage of gross domestic investment	In billions of current won	As percentage of gross domestic investment
1962–66	582	300	51.6	279	47.9
1967–71	2,869	1,744	60.8	1,134	39.5
1972–76	10,913	8,016	73.5	2,692	24.7
1977–81	49,070	36,050	73.5	12,625	25.7
1982–86	101,264	92,419	91.3	8,953	8.8
1987–91[a]	263,751	277,258	105.1	−13,507	−5.1

a. Preliminary figures.

Source: Economic Planning Board. *Major Statistics of the Korean Economy* and *The 6th Five-Year Plan: Overview.* Various issues.

ual GNP and population growth rates, 1962–91
centages)

	GNP	Per Capita GNP[a]	Population
	2.2	−0.5	2.9
63	9.1	6.1	2.8
64	9.6	7.1	2.6
65	5.8	3.3	2.6
66	12.7	9.5	2.5
Average 1962–66	**7.9**	**5.1**	**2.7**
67	6.6	4.4	2.4
68	11.3	8.8	2.3
69	13.8	11.3	2.3
70	7.6	8.3	2.2
71	8.6	11.0	2.0
Average 1967–71	**9.6**	**8.7**	**2.2**
72	5.1	3.0	1.9
73	13.2	11.0	1.8
74	8.1	6.2	1.7
75	6.4	5.0	1.7
76	13.1	11.4	1.6
Average 1972–76	**9.2**	**7.3**	**1.7**
77	9.8	8.0	1.6
78	9.8	8.2	1.6
79	7.2	5.7	1.6
80	−3.7	−5.1	1.6
81	5.9	4.4	1.6
Average 1977–81	**5.8**	**4.2**	**1.6**
82	7.2	5.5	1.6
83	12.6	10.9	1.5
84	9.3	7.7	1.2
85	7.0	5.5	1.0
86	12.9	12.4	0.9
Average 82–86	**9.8**	**8.4**	**1.2**
87	13.0	11.9	0.9
88	12.4	11.3	1.0
89	6.8	5.7	1.0
90	9.3	8.0	0.9
91[b]	8.4	7.5	0.9
Average 1987–91	**9.9**	**8.9**	**0.9**

a. Based on 1985 constant prices.
b. Preliminary figures.

Sources: National Statistical Office. 1992. *Major Statistics of the Korean Economy*; Bank of Korea. 1991. *National Accounts*, various issues.

To the extent that real growth in Korea has been greater than that of most of these nations since 1988, the real per capita GDP gap between Korea and these nations may have been further widened. As most Koreans are likely to observe, however, there is still far to go before Korea closes the gap between itself and advanced nations.

Structural Transformation

As Schumpeter's train analogy illustrates, economic development is very different from simple economic growth. Economic development must be accompanied by qualitative changes reflected in the structure of the economy. Economic development requires continuous structural change, and for developing economies, the essence of structural change is industrialization.

According to Kuznets (1966), today's advanced nations were industrialized 1 to 6 percentage points per decade during their eras of modern economic growth.[1] Industry's share of GDP in Korea (consistent with Kuznets' classification of industry) increased about 10 percentage points per decade during the 1960s and 1970s (see appendix, table A.2). In 1960 industry's share of GDP was 20.1 percent. By 1970 it was 29.2 percent, and by 1980 it reached 41.3 percent. After 1980, however, the industrialization process slowed, reaching 43 percent in 1987. This is a natural development, as it seems that the manufacturing sector's share of a nation's GDP grows to a certain level—that is, 30 to 40 percent—and then slowly declines. This is evident in the pattern of industrialization in certain advanced and developing nations. Some countries manage to reach a greater proportion of manufacturing in GDP than others, but the trend toward peaking out at a certain level is clear. German industry, for example, maintained a much higher share of GDP throughout the period than that of the United States or the United Kingdom. A declining industrial share of GDP in recent years, or deindustrialization, is recorded in virtually all of today's developed nations. It remains to be seen how soon Korea will start to experience it.

All else being equal, Korea, being a natural resource–poor nation, would be expected to have a relatively higher manufacturing share at its earlier stage of development.[2] Even though the Korean manufacturing share is in fact higher than most resource-rich developing nations, Korean planners expect the share to go up a bit higher. For example, they expect the share to reach 32 percent in 1996, the last year of the nation's

1. Notice that Kuznets' industry classification includes not only mining and manufacturing but also the construction, light and power, gas, water, transportation, and communication sectors. The agricultural sector also includes forestry and fisheries, etc. See Kuznets (1966, 92).

2. For a good discussion, see Noland (1990, chapter 4).

seventh five-year development plan. As a nation's industrial structure changes in terms of the composition of value added, its employment structure also changes. Consider the trend in Korea's primary sector—encompassing agriculture, fisheries, and forestry—and its secondary sector, mining and manufacturing. In 1963 the shares of employment in the primary and secondary sectors were 63.1 percent and 8.7 percent, respectively. As industrialization proceeded, the share of employment in the secondary sector increased gradually. By 1977, the initial year of the fourth five-year plan, the share of employment in the secondary sector reached 22.4 percent, about half the level of the primary sector, which was 41.8 percent.

Korea shows the typical employment pattern experienced by most developed nations: a decline in agricultural employment following the decline in the sector's value added, but with a time lag. In addition, the increase in employment in the secondary sector was smaller than the decline in agricultural employment, indicating that more workers found employment in the service sector. From 1963 to 1987 the rise in employment in the secondary sector accounted for only half of the decline in employment in the agricultural sector.

Table 2.4 presents the contributions of sectoral growth to the economy's overall growth rate. The highest growth contribution throughout the period came primarily from the secondary and tertiary sectors. In particular, the contribution is highest from manufacturing and the tertiary sector, which includes the social overhead capital (SOC) sector (also see table A.3, which includes sectoral growth rates).

Export and Import Structure

Korea's total trading volume in 1962 was only $477 million, but it reached $153.4 billion by 1991 to make Korea the 11th largest trading nation in the world. Korean exports and imports grew at an annual average rate of about 30.3 percent and 22.1 percent, respectively, between 1962 and 1990. In fact, Korean exports grew much faster than world export growth, and consequently, the share of Korean exports in the world gradually increased over the period, from a meager 0.04 percent in 1962 to 2.23 percent by 1990 (appendix, tables A.4 through A.6).

As the trade sector grew faster than the economy as a whole, trade dependency, or the ratio of total trading volume to GNP, increased dramatically. The Korean economy's trade dependency, particularly export dependency, had increased rapidly throughout the 1960s and 1970s, rising from 2.4 percent in 1962 to 11.6 percent in 1971. In the 1980s this ratio reached and stayed well over 30 percent. At the same time, the five-year averages for the imports-to-GNP ratio remained at over 30

Table 2.4 Average sectoral contribution to GNP growth, 1962–91 (percentages)

	1962–66	1967–71	1972–76	1977–81	1982–86	1987–91	Average 1962–91[a]
Agriculture, forestry and fishing	32.1	4.5	15.7	–5.1	6.5	–1.4	8.8
Mining and manufacturing	20.5	33.8	43.7	47.2	39.8	34.0	36.7
manufacturing only	n.a.	n.a.	n.a.	32.7	38.5	30.8	n.a.
Other	47.4	61.7	40.6	57.9	53.7	67.4	54.5

n.a. = not available
a. Data for 1991 are preliminary.

Source: Economic Planning Board. *Major Statistics of Korean Economy*, various issues.

percent throughout the 1970s and 1980s. The nation's total trade dependency ratio increased from about 20 percent in the 1960s to as high as 71 percent in 1981 before declining.

Similarly, the share of primary products in total exports decreased steadily as exports of manufactured goods came to dominate the picture (table A.7). The proportion of heavy industrial products in total exports has also steadily increased, reflecting the nation's industrial transformation.

The composition of the top 10 exports also illustrates the transformation in Korea's industrial structure (table A.8). In 1961 Korea's top 10 exports, constituting 62 percent of the total, were composed entirely of raw materials, minerals, lumber, agricultural, and fishery goods. By 1970 41 percent of Korea's exports were composed of textiles and garments, reflecting the nation's push into light industry. By 1980 electronic products, steel products, and footwear together made up 27 percent of exports while textiles declined to 29 percent and raw materials virtually disappeared from the top 10. In 1991 electronic goods were Korea's single largest export sector (28 percent) as the nation moved more firmly into higher-value-added production. Total exports had risen to $72 billion from $41 million in 1961.

The geographical distribution of Korea's exports and imports has also changed markedly (appendix, tables A.9 and A.10). In the 1960s and early 1970s, 70 to 75 percent of exports went to Korea's two major trading partners: the United States and Japan. While these two countries are still Korea's major trading partners today, the share of exports going to them has decreased steadily as Korea has successfully diversified exports to Europe, the Middle East, and other Asian countries. Korea's import share of these two major trading partners dropped from nearly 80 percent in 1965 to around 60 percent in the mid-1970s and still remains around 50 percent.

Korea wisely chose an outward-looking development strategy—that is, providing incentives for export activities—in the early 1960s. It chose this strategy at a time when it was not universally recognized that world trade was growing fast (Lewis 1980) and when inward-looking strategies, prescribed by economic development theories of the 1950s and 1960s, were still popular among most developing nations. With its chosen strategy, Korea was successful beyond everyone's best expectations, and it obviously benefited from rapidly growing world trade. It is important, however, to recognize that Korea's success in diversifying manufactured goods and regions for exports was another factor for the success.[3]

---

3. Riedel (1984, 56–73) suggests that the changing composition of developing nations' exports weakened the external constraint on their exports.

Table 2.5 Household income distribution, 1965–88 (percentages)

	1965	1970	1976	1980	1985	1988
Upper 10 percent	25.8	25.4	27.5	29.5	28.3	27.6
Upper 20 percent	41.8	41.6	45.3	45.4	42.7	42.2
Lower 40 percent	19.3	19.6	19.9	16.1	18.9	19.7
Lower 20 percent	5.9	7.3	5.7	5.1	6.1	6.4
Gini coefficient	0.344	0.332	0.391	0.389	0.345	0.336

Source: Economic Planning Board. 1990. *Major Statistics of the Korean Economy.*

Income Distribution and Other Social Development Indices

Korea's household income distribution has been recognized as one of the most equitable among developing nations. Korean income distribution is nearly comparable to or even better than that of some of today's developed nations. The income distribution picture is certainly much better than in most developing nations. In this connection, it is worth pointing out that Korea's early land reform positively contributed to this effect.

As an economy is industrialized, its income distribution is usually affected. However, it is not necessarily improved. According to Kuznets' U-curve hypothesis (1955), during the course of a nation's development, income distribution actually gets worse before it gets better. Table 2.5 shows household income distribution during Korea's rapid economic development period. According to the table, income distribution actually improved over most of the period. The ratio of the income of the lower 40 percent and the upper 20 percent to total income in 1965 was 19.3 and 41.8 percent, respectively.

Household income distribution improved gradually during the 1960s, but it deteriorated during the 1970s. The ratio of the income of the lower 40 percent to total income declined to 16.1 and that of the upper 20 percent increased to 45.4 percent in 1980. During the 1980s, income distribution gradually improved, but it is still worse than it was during the 1960s. The ratio of the income of the lower 40 percent and the upper 20 percent to total income was 19.7 and 42.2 percent, respectively, in 1988. The Gini coefficient was 0.389 in 1980 and dropped to 0.336 in 1988, indicating that income distribution improved in the 1980s, at least through 1988.[4]

Various plausible explanations have been provided to account for these developments in income distribution. During the earlier development

---

4. A recent study (Choo 1992) shows that the trend of improvement in Korea's income distribution continued throughout the 1980s. According to Choo, the Gini coefficient was 0.323 in 1990. It was 0.337 in 1986 and 0.357 in 1982.

period of the 1960s, when unemployment and underemployment were prevalent and absolute poverty was the major problem in Korea, the Korean government adopted an outward-looking development strategy to promote primarily labor-intensive manufacturing industries. This strategy naturally boosted income earned from wages and salaries more so than income from properties (table 2.6). To the extent that income from labor is distributed more equitably than income from property, income distribution improved during the period.

However, when heavy and chemical industries were promoted in the 1970s, the situation changed substantially. The promotion of these industries included new measures: tax subsidies, policy loans with negative real interest rates, and credit rationing, which primarily favored large, well-established business groups. These factors contributed toward worsened income distribution. In addition, inflation accelerated during this period, aggravating income distribution even further. Consumer price inflation for the 1974–79 period was close to 20 percent, compared with an annual average inflation rate between 1962 and 1973 of about 10 percent.

Coming into the 1980s, the government took steps to correct this situation by eliminating various subsidies and preferential policy loans and by bringing the nation's rampant inflation under control. These factors reversed the deterioration experienced in income distribution in the 1970s. During this period urban income distribution in particular improved as the wage gap between workers with different educational backgrounds narrowed in response to the emerging shortage of less-educated blue-collar workers in Korea. This is evident from unemployment patterns illustrated in table 2.7. During the 1980s, total unemployment was cut in half, from 5.2 percent in 1980 to 2.3 percent in 1991. At the same time, the unemployment rate for primary, middle, and high school graduates declined by an even wider margin: 78 percent, 73 percent, and 66 percent, respectively.

Despite these apparent improvements, income distribution issues are still raised in Korea. This may have to do with a gap between actual and perceived income distribution, or perhaps between statistics and reality. Such matters will be discussed in more detail in chapter 7.

Social Development and Quality of Life

During the rapid development years, the Korean people's general welfare and quality of life improved substantially. Life expectancy increased dramatically and at a faster rate than in most countries. Improvements can also be seen in such indicators as daily calorie supply, per capita physicians and nurses, and infant mortality rates (table A.11).

Education trends are also important, as they indicate the ability of citizens to improve their living standard in the future. Rapid progress

Table 2.6 Compositional distribution of national disposable income at current factor cost, 1962–91
(percentages)

National disposable income	1962	1967	1972	1977	1982	1987	1989	1991
Compensation of employees	28.9	30.2	33.9	35.2	39.9	40.4	44.3	47.5
Operating surplus	51.3	52.0	49.9	44.8	35.8	36.1	33.6	31.3
Consumption of fixed capital	4.9	5.8	6.5	7.4	8.8	10.2	10.3	9.8
Indirect taxes (less) subsidies	6.9	7.5	8.0	10.4	12.4	11.6	11.4	11.3
Current transfers from the rest of the world, net	8.0	4.5	1.7	2.2	3.1	1.6	0.4	0.2

a. Figures for 1962 and 1967 are based on 1975 constant prices and the rest on 1985 constant prices.

Source: Bank of Korea. *National Accounts,* various issues.

Table 2.7 Unemployment rate by level of education, 1980–91
(percentages)

Level of education	1980	1985	1991
Primary school graduates	2.7	1.5	0.6
Middle school graduates	6.3	4.1	1.7
High school graduates	9.3	5.9	3.2
College graduates	6.2	6.6	3.6
Overall	5.2	4.0	2.3

Source: Economic Planning Board. 1992. *Social Indicators in Korea.*

has been made in the education sector in Korea during the last three decades (table A.12). The country started from the same low level as other developing countries in 1960, but while progress has been recorded in all the developing countries shown, Korea has done even better. In fact, school enrollment in Korea is now on a par with most developed nations. It is also worth mentioning that, even though tertiary school enrollment is still relatively high in Korea, this ratio has been attained despite the government's strict restrictions on expanding tertiary school enrollment.[5]

Korean Economy in the World

The Korean peninsula as a whole has a total landmass of about 220,000 square kilometers, approximately the size of the state of Utah. It is currently partitioned into two parts, and the Republic of Korea has a total land area of about 99,000 square kilometers, about the size of the state of Indiana. As of 1988 the Republic of Korea ranked 23rd in terms of population, recording 42.8 million people in 1990. In terms of economic size, as measured by its GNP, Korea ranked 17th in 1988, while in per capita income terms, Korea stood at 40th among all nations in the world (table 2.8).[6]

As previously discussed, Korea was the Hermit Kingdom of the Orient until the late 19th century, when it was forced to open its doors involuntarily to outsiders. It was colonized for almost 36 years by the Japanese and then liberated in 1945. Consequently, the nation's history of international exposure and trade is rather short. The adoption of the outward-looking development strategy in the early 1960s put Korea on the fast track toward its becoming what it is today—a major trading nation.

As a major player in the international economic arena, Korea must take on new roles. Particularly as a nation that has succeeded under

5. For an international comparison of human indicators, see Noland (1990).

6. These rankings exclude the former Soviet Union and all of Eastern Europe.

Table 2.8 Korea in the world econo   𝒸𝓁𝓁𝓁𝓁𝓁
1988 (ranks)

		8
Total trade[a]		1
Export		1
Import		4
Population		3
Area		4
Population density		5
Total GNP[a]	34	17
Per capita GNP	56	40
Per capita export	120	29
Per capita import	103	37

a. The trade and GNP rankings exclude the former USSR and all of Eastern Europe.
b. 1962 GNP data for several countries are not available. China and Japan data are based on national income; for Fiji, Kenya, and Zimbabwe, 1963 data are used.

Source: International Monetary Fund. 1990 and 1991. *International Financial Statistics*; United Nations, Statistical Division, Department of Economic and Social Development. 1990. *Statistical Yearbook*; World Bank. *World Development Report 1990*. Data for these tables used with permission.

favorable international trade conditions, Korea has both an obligation to promote a freer trade environment and a vested interest in doing so. At the same time, Korea has valuable first-hand experience of development that can be shared with other developing nations via bilateral arrangements or multilateral institutions. These topics will be discussed in chapter 7.

Conclusions

In this chapter, we examined Korea's growth performance and its structural change. Korea made a successful transition to a newly industrializing economy from an agrarian economy in a relatively short period of time. Korea did have some favorable initial conditions for development. Among them are the relatively high sociocultural development standard, the literate and motivated work force, and plenty of latent entrepreneurial energies. Undoubtedly, these strengths were enhanced by the political leadership commitment to economic development and by the choice of an outward-looking development strategy.

Korea may become the first nation from the developing world, with the possible exception of Taiwan and Singapore, to join the ranks of industrially advanced nations since the Second World War.[7] After ana-

7. There are different opinions regarding the date that Japan achieved advanced nation status. Some argue it was in the middle 1950s, or specifically, in 1954 (Chenery, Shishido, and Watanabe 1962). Others argue it was in 1963 (Klein 1986), and still others contend it was in 1970 (Chenery and Syrquin 1986). Refer also to Song (1990, 112–13). However, Japan was never really considered part of the Third World after the Second World War.

lyzing modern growth performances of many nations, Kuznets (1971, 28–29) commented on the potential for a nation's achieving advanced status:

> It follows that the failure to reach per capita product (and related structure) that would put a nation in the developed class, may have resulted from too low an initial per capita product despite a high growth rate over a sufficiently long period or from too low a growth rate despite a fairly adequate initial level of per capita product—and this rate may have been too low *continuously* through the long period, or may have accelerated only relatively recently.

Since Korea's initial per capita product was not considered too low, the question for Korea is how long it can continue to maintain high growth and thereby achieve the status of advanced nation. Obviously, the answer lies in Korea's adaptability to the changing environment, both internal and external, and Korea's ability to face emerging challenges. This matter will be discussed in following chapters.

3

Development Strategies, Economic Planning, and Policy Implementation

When doctors don't know what caused an illness, they call it psychosomatic; when economists cannot explain a phenomenon, they call it social or cultural. —Paul Rosenstein-Rodan[1]

While getting prices right is not the end of development, getting prices wrong often is. —C. Peter Timmer (1973)

The last chapter surveyed the impressive economic growth performance and structural transformation of the Korean economy over a short period. Korea had advantages related to being a "later developer," particularly in that it did not have to go through the long process of technology development (Gerschenkron 1962; Woronoff 1986). At the same time, it was easier for Korea to close the savings gap—via transfers of foreign capital—than for earlier developing countries. However, many other developing nations, under the same conditions and with similar advantages, did not do as well as Korea did. Students of development economics and policymakers in developing nations in particular have been keenly interested in discovering the major factors behind Korea's success.

There are already many books and articles written on the Korean economy and on the Asian newly industrializing economies (NIEs), including Korea.[2] Since the Asian NIEs share a common heritage of Confucianism, this cultural factor is often emphasized in explanations of their successes (Kahn 1979). Their successes have sometimes been explained only in the context of pure neoclassical theories. Still others (Hofheinz and Calder 1982) have emphasized institutional factors, such as political structures, while some have pointed to the government's ability to guide markets and thereby reduce risk for the private sector (Wade 1988, 129–163). All these factors must have played a role in pro-

---

1. Quoted in Papanek (1988, 27).

2. For excellent surveys, see Hicks (1989) and Noland (1990).

ducing the Korean success story. What is important is to understand the interaction of these factors.

The primary purpose of this chapter is to analyze not only Korea's selection of strategy, but also its implementation, because both are important factors in Korea's outstanding performance. At the same time, there are other factors that played a critical role in enhancing and facilitating implementation of the strategy.

A nation's development strategy can be characterized in various ways. It is often described as "outward-looking" or "export-led" versus "inward-oriented" or "import-substitution driven." If its primary emphasis is on sectoral growth, it is sometimes categorized as "industry-led" or as slanted toward "agriculture-first." From a growth versus equity point of view, development strategy can be characterized as either "growth-first" or "equity-first." Sometimes, the "growth-first" characterization is made to emphasize that the weight of the nation's strategy is put toward "growth maximization" rather than "economic stabilization." Depending on the way the chosen strategy is implemented, the pattern of a nation's development can be described as either "government-led" or "private sector–led." Clearly, there are many possible directions to choose from when deciding upon a development strategy.

Korea's strategy is most often characterized as "outward-looking industrialization." The implementation of this strategy is also characterized as primarily "government-led." The next section will examine Korea's development strategy in the 1960s and 1970s, focusing on these characteristics first.

Leadership Commitment and the Government-Led Strategy

In human life, economics precedes politics or culture.
—Park Chung Hee (1970)

In the late 1950s President Syngman Rhee had no choice but to devote most of his energy to consolidating and solidifying the newly independent nation and then to rehabilitating the economy after the devastating Korean War of 1950–53.

Maintaining the people's current consumption level was the top priority of President Rhee's government, which put aside forward-looking economic development objectives. The president believed that the nation's development efforts—for example, introducing intermediate-range plans—should be postponed until national unification was achieved, which was foreseen as occurring in the "near future." At the same time, Syngman Rhee, the renowned independence fighter and patriot, never considered Japan as a viable partner for trade or economic cooperation.

Nevertheless, President Rhee's administration laid important groundwork for future outward-looking economic development. The first stage of import-substitution, regarding basic consumer products, was completed toward the end of the 1950s, and that made the later adoption of an outward-looking strategy easier, given the size of the domestic market.[3] Investments in education, assisted by US aid authorities, and land reform, first initiated by the US-occupied government in 1945 and completed by the administration in 1953, became critical bases for future growth with more equitable income distribution.[4] Korea relied heavily on foreign aid during this period, as will be discussed in detail in chapter 5. Toward the latter part of the 1950s, however, foreign aid—primarily from the US—started to decline, and it was expected to continue to decline and then to be discontinued.

President Syngman Rhee was ousted by a nationwide student revolt in April 1960. A democratically elected regime came to power briefly following the revolt, but it was weak and riven by factionalism. It lasted only nine months. In May 1961 a military coup led by General Park Chung Hee toppled this regime.

The newly emerged leadership wasted no time in committing itself to economic development, putting it at the top of the nation's policy priority list.[5] Unlike President Syngman Rhee, President Park Chung Hee saw economic development as a means toward national unification and political progress. President Park's commitment to economic development and his pragmatic approach to the subject are characterized by the following quotes:

> The focal point in politics in developing nations such as Korea is above all economic construction. As our old saying goes, no matter how wise one may be, he has to eat. Likewise, economic construction in developing nations, sufficient for people not to worry about food and clothing, is an absolutely basic requirement for democratic development. (Remarks at a press conference, 1972)

> Not only meaningful progress toward democracy but also promotion of national might to overcome communism and to unify the nation ultimately depend upon the success or failure of economic construction. (August Fifteenth Liberation Day Address, 1964)

> Since the nation's unification depends on the nation's modernization and the modernization in turn depends on economic self-support, a self-supporting economy is the first step toward unification. (New Year's Presidential Message to the National Assembly, 1966)

These thoughts were translated into action. President Park religiously attended the monthly economic activity briefings and the export pro-

---

3. For detailed discussions, see Balassa (1988) and Krueger (1979).

4. For detailed discussions regarding these aspects of Korea's development, see Mason et al. (1980), especially chapters 7 and 10.

5. For good discussions on these issues, see Lee (1968) and Cole and Lyman (1971).

motion meetings and showed keen interest in the proceedings. His time was mostly devoted to economic affairs—visiting economic sites such as plants and industrial parks, attending tape-cutting ceremonies for minor or major economic projects, and chairing and presiding over meetings related to economic affairs.

Korea's strong Confucian cultural heritage, based on hierarchical respect and loyalty, placed great weight on the chief executive's personal commitment. It undoubtedly was highly significant for civil servants in particular and contributed toward ensuring efficient policy implementation.[6] In fact, the results-oriented pragmatism of Korean bureaucrats and their ability to show nonideological flexibility in implementing policy very likely emanated from this cultural heritage.

In terms of President Park's policy initiatives, important institutional reform measures were introduced beginning in the early 1960s. The most important institutional innovation was the creation of the powerful Economic Planning Board in 1961. The head of the board was made deputy prime minister,[7] signifying the importance attached to economic policy coordination. Second on the list of important institutional changes was the establishment of a National Taxation Administration Office in 1965, created in an effort to mobilize domestic resources.

The third institutional rearrangement had to do with the nation's financial system. At that time, commercial banks were made into de facto public enterprises by legally limiting private voting rights. In addition, various state-owned special banks were established, and existing special banks were expanded specifically to accommodate development. Finally, the government introduced the nation's first serious intermediate-term economic plan in 1962.[8]

Government-Led Development Strategy

This foundation of strong leadership commitment was instrumental in bringing about Korea's government-led, or state-led, development strategy. However, the term government-led is used in different ways. It sometimes refers to a general government activism in economic development; it also may refer to prevalent government intervention in the market. In any case, such a strategy is manifested in government's involvement in resource allocation and investment activities in particular.

---

6. In the Confucian tradition, civil service is highly valued. Certainly, the tradition itself has been changing. Nonetheless, the tendency remains in Korea.

7. There was only one deputy prime minister under the prime minister in Korea until 1990, when an additional deputy prime minister in charge of national unification was appointed.

8. There were some planning efforts under the earlier regimes, but they were either paper plans never implemented or formally adopted by the government. For a detailed discussion, see Jones and SaKong (1980, 44–47).

The government's direct involvement in investment takes place through public enterprises. Yet just as importantly in market-oriented economies, the government influences private investment by providing incentives to the private sector. Let us discuss the characteristics of Korea's development strategy from this perspective in the following.

As can be seen from table 3.1, the share of public sector investment in total investment averaged about 35 percent over the period from 1963 to 1979. Table 3.2 shows the importance of public investment and loans in the government's annual budget and the nation's total investment. More than one-third of the government's annual budget was allocated for investment purposes, and it was equivalent to more than 27 percent of gross domestic fixed capital formation for the period of 1962–80.

The composition of fiscal funds for public investment and loans in terms of sectoral distribution can be seen in table 3.3. It shows that the social overhead capital (SOC) sector received close to two-thirds of total fiscal funds for public investment and loans. Interestingly enough, it also shows that the agriculture, forestry, and fisheries sectors received a substantial proportion of government funds. This was primarily for enhancing productivity through the building of farming roads, bridges, reservoirs, and dams.

A downward trend in allocations to the mining and manufacturing sector is noticeable. During the earlier stages of development, the private sector was not prepared to undertake big projects involving large amounts of investment capital and considerable risk. However, as the economy developed, the necessity of government's direct involvement in these sectors decreased. The downward trend is, therefore, a reflection of the Korean government's pragmatic and flexible approach to determining the appropriate level of involvement in investment activities.

The Government as Entrepreneur-Manager

A government's most visible intervention instrument is public enterprise. From the early 1960s on, the Korean government actively used this tool, either by establishing new public enterprises or expanding existing ones. During 1963–77, value added in the public enterprise sector increased at an annual rate of 10 percent. Table 3.4 gives the sector's value added as a share of GDP. One might be surprised by these figures, as the proportion is almost as high as in countries such as India or Pakistan where "socialist goals were well pronounced" (Jones and SaKong 1980; SaKong 1980).[9] Does this then indicate that

---

9. The public enterprise share in GDP and nonagricultural GDP for India averaged around 7 to 8 percent and 12 to 15 percent, respectively, for the period of 1965–1970. For Pakistan, they were around 6 to 7 percent and 8 to 10 percent, respectively, for the same period.

Table 3.1 **Public sector share of gross domestic investment, 1963–79** (billions of current won, except where noted)

Year	Gross domestic investment (A)	General government (B)	Public sector investment Departmental enterprises (C)	Government invested enterprises (D)	Composition (B+C)/A	(B+C+D)/A (percentages)
1963	91.1	9.7	7.9	19.7	19.3	40.9
1964	100.6	8.2	15.9	18.9	24.0	42.7
1965	120.9	14.3	16.9	21.5	25.8	43.6
1966	223.9	24.9	24.4	23.8	22.0	32.6
Average 1963–66	**134.1**	**14.3**	**16.3**	**21.0**	**22.8**	**38.4**
1967	280.7	35.4	26.9	57.5	22.2	42.7
1968	427.7	71.5	34.9	43.6	24.9	35.1
1969	621.3	129.3	39.0	75.4	27.1	39.2
1970	719.1	134.7	36.5	74.7	23.8	34.2
1971	831.4	149.6	44.4	138.5	23.3	40.0
Average 1967–71	**576.0**	**104.1**	**36.3**	**77.9**	**24.4**	**37.9**
1972	873.8	156.1	63.6	214.5	25.1	49.7
1973	1,341.0	166.7	103.0	131.9	20.1	29.9
1974	2,274.3	214.5	77.8	304.6	12.9	26.2
1975	2,881.8	320.4	311.1	584.3	21.9	42.2
1976	3,378.2	429.0	228.1	580.6	19.5	36.6
Average 1972–76	**2,149.8**	**257.3**	**156.7**	**363.2**	**19.3**	**36.2**
1977	4,645.0	611.9	432.4	888.0	22.5	41.6
1978	7,137.7	852.3	409.0	1,207.6	17.7	34.6
1979	10,293.5	1,348.1	475.8	1,556.2	17.7	32.8
Average 1977–79	**7,358.7**	**937.4**	**439.1**	**1,217.3**	**18.7**	**35.2**
Overall average 1963–79	**2,131.9**	**275.1**	**138.1**	**349.5**	**19.4**	**35.8**

Source: SaKong, Il. 1981. "Development Strategy and Finance in Korea," in Korea Investment and Finance Co. (ed.). *Economic Development and Finance in Korea*, (in Korean).

Table 3.2 Investments and loans in the government budget, 1962–80 (billions of current won, except where noted)

Year	Investment and loans (A) Investment	Investment and loans (A) Loans	Investment and loans (A) Total	Annual budget (B)	Gross domestic capital formation (C)	Gross domestic fixed capital formation (D)	Composition (percentages) A/B	Composition (percentages) A/C	Composition (percentages) A/D
1962	24.9	2.3	27.2	119.9	45.5	48.6	22.7	59.8	56.0
1963	21.5	5.8	27.2	111.0	91.1	68.0	24.5	29.9	40.0
1964	18.6	5.0	23.8	120.7	100.6	81.3	19.7	23.7	29.3
1965	25.3	4.2	29.5	154.1	120.9	119.0	19.1	24.4	24.8
1966	48.5	14.1	62.6	231.0	223.9	209.8	27.1	28.0	29.8
Average 1962–66							**23.1**	**29.3**	**32.3**
1967	59.3	19.7	79.0	291.3	230.7	274.6	27.1	34.2	28.8
1968	101.7	16.2	117.6	402.9	427.7	413.6	29.2	27.5	28.4
1969	137.4	38.3	175.6	578.0	621.3	555.8	30.4	28.3	31.6
1970	155.4	28.9	184.3	597.7	719.1	654.1	30.8	25.6	28.2
1971	171.4	41.9	213.3	732.0	831.4	742.1	29.1	25.7	28.7
Average 1967–71							**29.6**	**27.2**	**29.2**
1972	263.1	34.4	309.8	963.1	873.8	828.5	32.2	35.5	37.4
1973	219.0	52.6	271.6	960.2	1,341.0	1,255.6	28.3	20.3	21.6
1974	358.3	113.6	406.2	1,428.3	2,274.3	1,870.6	28.4	17.9	21.7
1975	617.8	182.0	805.7	2,123.6	2,881.8	2,544.0	37.9	28.0	31.7
1976	794.8	225.8	1,053.2	2,895.2	3,378.2	3,152.4	36.4	31.2	33.4
Average 1972–76							**34.0**	**26.5**	**29.5**
1977	941.5	321.7	1,259.6	3,717.8	4,645.0	4,420.9	33.9	27.1	28.5
1978	1,151.3	532.2	1,679.7	4,781.6	7,137.7	7,023.1	35.1	23.5	23.9
1979	1,576.1	644.8	2,641.4	6,466.5	10,293.5	9,458.2	40.8	25.7	27.9
1980	2,168.6	773.3	2,919.3	8,647.8	10,869.8	11,094.0	33.8	26.9	26.3
Average 1977–80							**36.0**	**25.8**	**26.6**
Overall average 1962–80							**34.8**	**26.1**	**27.4**

Source: SaKong, Il. 1981. "Development Strategy and Finance in Korea," in Korea Investment and Finance Co. (ed.), *Economic Development and Finance in Korea*, (in Korean and updated).

Table 3.3   Distribution of fiscal funds for public investments and loans to industry by sector,[a] 1962–80 (percentages)

	Agriculture, fishery, and forestry	Mining and manufacturing	Social overhead and other services
1962–1966	25.7	20.8	53.5
1967–1971	25.9	13.3	60.8
1972–1976	22.7	15.6	61.7
1977–1980	15.7	8.5	75.8
Overall average	22.9	14.9	62.2

a. Fiscal investments and loans in the government's budget do not correspond directly to public-sector investments, seen in table 3.1.

Source: SaKong, Il. 1981. "Development Strategy and Finance in Korea," in Korea Investment and Finance Co. (ed.), *Economic Development and Finance in Korea* (in Korean).

Korea was also socialistic? On the contrary, this relatively high level of public enterprise activity is evidence of the Korean government's pragmatic approach, unfettered by ideology, to economic development.

Table 3.5 presents the industrial composition of the sector's value added. As can be seen from the table, the largest share of value added originated from the manufacturing sector. These were primarily projects involving large amounts of capital, long gestation periods, and high investment risks.

The importance of public enterprise sector investment is evident from its sheer magnitude. However, the strategic importance of the sector is even greater, considering the distribution of investment among critical industrial sectors. It has been shown elsewhere that Korean public enterprises as a group, particularly those established since the early 1960s, had a far higher input-output interdependence[10] compared with the Korean economy as a whole or the manufacturing sector alone (SaKong 1980, 108–12). This highlights the strategic importance of the public enterprise sector as a whole—particularly after political leadership became committed to development—and is evidence that it has an even greater impact on development than the sheer magnitude or proportion of the sector's value added to GDP alone would indicate.

Government Influence on Private Investment

As indicated earlier, on average, the nonpublic or private sector carried out nearly 65 percent of the nation's total investment. However, private

10. Input interdependence can be measured by the ratio of intermediate purchases to total value of output; output interdependence can be calculated by the ratio of intermediate sales to total value of output. A high input and output interdependence therefore indicates a sector's high degree of linkage with the rest of the economy.

Table 3.4 The size of the public enterprise sector and its share of GDP, 1963–86 (billions of dollars except where noted)

	1963	1970	1973	1975	1977	1980	1984	1986
Public enterprises value added[a]	31.4	220.8	417.5	737.5	1,191.2	3,461.0	6,707.8	9,032.9
GDP	499.1	2,769.9	5,420.3	10,302.2	18,074.1	38,041.1	72,644.3	93,425.8
Nonagricultural GDP[b]	282.0	2,029.4	4,063.9	7,731.2	14,023.0	32,363.7	63,252.2	82,697.2
Public enterprise value added as a percentage of GDP	6.3	8.0	7.7	7.2	6.6	9.1	9.2	9.7
Public enterprise value added as a percentage of nonagricultural GDP	11.1	10.9	10.3	9.5	8.5	10.7	10.6	10.9

a. Figures for 1963–77 are from SaKong, Il. 1980. "Macroeconomic Aspects of the Public Enterprise Sector," in Park, Chong K. (ed.), *Macroeconomic and Industrial Development in Korea.* Korea Development Institute. Figures for remaining years were provided by Dae Hee Song at KDI.
b. Revised GDP series. Consequently, figures are not the same as those found in the above sources.

Sources: Bank of Korea. 1982. *National Income in Korea;* Bank of Korea. 1990. *National Accounts.*

Table 3.5   Industrial distribution of public enterprises' value added, 1963–86 (percentages)

	1963	1964	1970	1971	1972	1973	1974	1975	1976	1977	1980	1984	1986
Agriculture, hunting, forestry, and fishery	1.8	1.9	1.2	1.5	1.3	0.7	0.1	0.1	0.0	0.0	0.3	0.1	0.0
Mining and quarrying	8.8	8.3	3.0	4.2	3.5	2.4	2.4	2.5	3.2	3.2	0.8	2.3	2.5
Manufacturing	30.2	34.5	39.2	38.3	36.0	42.3	49.7	46.6	37.5	39.5	37.6	31.2	15.8
Electricity, gas, and water	12.3	11.5	13.9	13.5	13.9	11.8	7.1	12.1	13.1	17.0	19.5	24.9	31.1
Construction	1.8	0.9	2.2	2.5	2.8	2.8	3.3	3.3	4.3	3.9	4.6	4.1	5.9
Wholesale and retail trade	3.0	4.1	1.6	2.0	2.2	2.3	1.8	1.9	0.6	0.9	1.3	0.1	0.1
Transportation, storage, and communication	26.5	24.5	21.6	18.6	18.8	16.6	14.6	13.1	13.9	14.9	15.6	26.2	28.9
Finance and insurance	15.4	13.9	16.2	19.0	20.8	20.4	20.1	19.2	23.6	18.1	19.1	7.0	11.2
Community, social, and personal services	0.0	0.4	1.2	0.5	0.7	0.8	1.0	1.2	3.6	2.4	1.2	4.1	4.5
Total	100.0	100.0	100.0	100.0	100.0	100.0	100.0	100.0	100.0	100.0	100.0	100.0	100.0

Sources: Figures for 1963–77 are from SaKong, Il. 1980. Macroeconomic Aspects of the Public Enterprise Sector," in Chong K. Park (ed.), *Macroeconomic and Industrial Development in Korea.* Korea Development Institute; figures for the rest of the years are provided by Dae Hee Song at KDI.

investment itself was encouraged through various measures, and the government actively influenced its distribution toward strategic areas through use of incentives.

The Korean government relied heavily on financial policy tools to induce private investment in strategic sectors.[11] Consequently, financial policy strongly influenced Korea's investment allocation, more so than the fiscal policy measures that were also used.[12]

In the early 1960s, Korea's new leadership immediately made existing commercial banks de facto public enterprises by legally limiting private shareholders' voting rights.[13] In addition, the government established a number of state-owned special banks and expanded existing specialized state-owned banks. At the same time, the Bank of Korea Act was amended in 1962 to facilitate the central bank's cooperation with the nation's long-term development efforts.

With these institutional arrangements, monetary authorities exerted a strong influence on the allocation of financial resources into strategic sectors. The chief instrument of these authorities was the "policy loan," usually earmarked for certain sectors or even specific industries. These policy loans in most cases had preferential interest rates when compared with ordinary loans. Yet even the interest rates on ordinary loans were kept lower than curb market rates or equilibrium interest rates. Table 3.6 provides nominal and real rates of interest on ordinary loans and estimates of real rates of return for the manufacturing sector in Korea. The real interest rates for ordinary loans, let alone policy loans, were for the most part much lower than the estimated average real rates of return in Korea. They were even negative in many years.

Throughout the period, the largest proportion of policy loans that deposit banks provided to the manufacturing sector went for supporting direct export activities in Korea (tables 3.7 and 3.8). Other policy loans, such as loans for export industry plants and equipment and for special plant and equipment funds, also were related to export activities. This obviously reflects the outward orientation of Korea's development strategy. Another interesting aspect of the tables is the fact that only a small proportion of policy loans were provided through fiscal funds, including foreign borrowings allocated through banks in Korea.

These financial policies, used throughout the 1960s and until the early 1970s, were selective in the sense that exports were singled out for

---

11. For a detailed discussion on the subject, see Jones and SaKong (1980, chapter 3).

12. Taxation itself was not statistically important in influencing the nation's economic development. This result is not surprising, considering the importance of the financial policy. See Trela and Whalley (1990).

13. A "temporary" law was introduced in 1961 to limit private shareholders' voting rights so the government could exercise control even without owning majority shares.

Table 3.6 Interest rates and manufacturing sector rate of return, 1954–91 (percentages)

Year	Nominal bank lending rate[a]	Curb market rate	Inflation rate[b]	Real lending rate	Rate of return of the manufacturing sector
1954	18.3	n.a.	31.8	−13.5	9–18
1955	18.3	n.a.	62.1	−43.8	"
1956	18.3	n.a.	34.0	−15.7	"
1957	18.3	n.a.	22.2	−3.9	"
1958	18.3	n.a.	−0.3	18.6	"
1959	17.9	n.a.	1.3	16.6	"
1960	17.5	n.a.	11.7	5.8	"
1961	17.5	n.a.	14.0	3.5	"
1962	16.6	n.a.	18.4	−1.8	9–26
1963	15.7	52.6	29.3	−13.6	"
1964	16.0	61.8	30.0	−14.0	"
1965	18.5	58.7	6.2	12.3	"
1966	26.0	58.7	14.5	11.5	"
1967	26.0	56.5	15.6	10.4	16–38
1968	25.8	56.0	16.1	9.7	"
1969	24.5	51.4	14.8	9.7	"
1970	24.0	49.8	15.6	8.4	"
1971	23.0	46.4	12.9	10.1	"
1972	17.8	39.0	16.3	1.5	17–40
1973	15.5	33.4	12.1	3.4	"
1974	15.5	40.6	30.4	−14.9	"
1975	15.5	41.3	24.6	−9.1	"
1976	16.5	40.5	21.2	−4.7	"
1977	17.3	38.1	16.6	0.7	n.a.
1978	17.7	39.3	22.8	−5.1	n.a.
1979	19.0	42.4	19.6	−0.6	n.a.
1980	22.0	44.9	24.0	−2.0	n.a.
1981	17.0	35.3	16.9	0.1	n.a.
1982	15.0	32.8	7.1	7.9	n.a.
1983	14.0	25.8	5.0	9.0	n.a.
1984	14.0	24.8	3.9	10.1	n.a.
1985	11.8	24.0	4.2	7.6	n.a.
1986	10.0–11.5	23.1	2.8	7.2–8.7	n.a.
1987	10.0–11.5	22.9	3.5	6.5–8.0	n.a.
1988	10.0–11.5	22.7	5.9	4.1–5.6	n.a.
1989	10.0–11.5	19.1	6.2	4.8–6.3	n.a.
1990	10.0–11.5	18.7	10.6	−0.6–0.9	n.a.
1991	10.0–11.5	21.4	10.9	−0.9–0.6	n.a.

n.a. = not available
a. Discount rate for one-year bills.
b. GNP deflator.

Sources: National Statistical Office. *Korean Economic Indicators*, various issues; SaKong, Il. 1981. "Development Strategy and Finance in Korea," in Korea Investment and Finance Co. (ed.), *Economic Development and Finance in Korea* (in Korean); Bank of Korea, *Economic Statistics Yearbook*, various issues.

Table 3.7 Policy loan shares of domestic credit based on an annual average, 1972–80 (percentages)

	1972–76	1977–80	1972–80
General loans:			
Short-term	47.7	45.3	46.5
Intermediate- to long-term	7.2	4.5	5.9
Subtotal	54.9	49.8	52.4
Total policy loans:			
Banking fund	22.6	23.0	22.8
Export support	11.7	11.1	11.4
Machinery industry Promotion	1.0	0.3	0.7
Equipment	0.6	0.5	0.6
Agriculture	3.7	2.9	3.2
Small and medium firms	2.5	3.3	2.9
Housing	3.1	4.9	4.0
Fiscal fund	4.8	3.4	4.1
Agriculture	2.3	1.7	2.0
Small and medium firms	0.6	0.1	0.3
Housing	0.3	0.1	0.2
Other	1.6	1.6	1.6
National Investment Fund	1.0	3.2	2.1
Korean Development Bank	16.2	18.3	17.2
Korean Export/Import Bank	0.5	2.3	1.4
Subtotal	45.1	50.2	47.6
Total	100.0	100.0	100.0

Source: SaKong, Il. 1981. "Development Strategy and Finance in Korea," in Korea Investment and Finance Co. (ed.), *Economic Development and Finance in Korea*, (in Korean).

favorable treatment. However, they were also general or nonselective in the sense that, within the realm of the chosen activity, i.e., exports, all industries and firms were treated equally. Rarely were the policies industry- or firm-specific. This policy regime differed markedly from that of 1973 when the drive to promote heavy and chemical industries (HCIs) was launched.[14] Specifically, the drive was implemented through industrial targeting, and accordingly, financial policy tools became industry-specific and sometimes even firm-specific.

As will be discussed in a following section, the authorities initiated the HCI promotion drive because they recognized two developments: that Korea could no longer maintain its comparative advantage in light manufacturing industries and that developed nations were raising protectionist barriers toward light manufactured commodities from the newly industrializing economies (NIEs). The government's objective, therefore, was to change the composition of Korea's exports toward more sophisticated items with higher value added to overcome rising protectionism

14. Industries to be promoted under the plan included iron and steel, nonferrous metals, shipbuilding, general machinery, chemicals, electronics, and electrical equipment.

Table 3.8 Composition of manufacturing sector policy loans on an annual average, 1962–80 (percentages)

	1962–66	1967–71	1972–76	1977–80	1962–80
Banking fund					
Export support	54.7	65.9	63.9	64.8	62.3
Machinery industry Promotion	n.a.	9.2	6.6	1.5	4.3
Export industry plants and equipment	n.a.	n.a.	8.3	3.7	3.0
Special equipment	n.a.	n.a.	1.8	2.2	1.0
Industrial restructuring	n.a.	n.a.	1.8	0.5	0.6
Subtotal	54.7	75.1	82.4	72.7	71.2
Fiscal fund					
Small and medium firms	45.1	12.8	4.0	0.6	·15.6
Other sources	0.2	12.1	7.9	7.4	6.9
Manufacturing investment fund	n.a.	n.a.	5.7	19.3	6.3
Total	100.0	100.0	100.0	100.0	100.0

n.a. = not applicable or not available

Source: SaKong, Il. 1981. "Development Strategy and Finance in Korea," in Korea Investment and Finance Co. (ed.), *Economic Development and Finance in Korea*, (in Korean).

and to make Korean exports more competitive in world markets. The new policy had a noneconomic, national-security rationale as well: defense-related industries were to be promoted.

Particularly toward the end of the 1970s, when bank loan rates in real terms were substantially negative, the proportion of policy loans going toward heavy and chemical industries increased. As table 3.7 shows, the proportion of total policy loans to total domestic credit increased from 45.1 percent for the 1972–76 period and to 50.2 percent for 1977–80. Policy loans under the National Investment Fund heading were designated for heavy and chemical industries.

It may be impossible to evaluate empirically the impact of the financial policies of the 1960s and 1970s on overall economic growth performance in Korea, as there were so many other policy changes during the period. However, toward the latter part of the 1970s, the Korean economy started to exhibit serious sectoral imbalances and structural inefficiencies. For example, capacity utilization rates for certain heavy and chemical industries fell below the 10 to 20 percent range, and the lopsided allocation of credit toward targeted industries left other sectors without much available credit.[15] In addition, the concentration of economic power toward large business groups or *chaebols*, as opposed to small and medium-

---

15. It is estimated that nearly 80 percent of all fixed investment in the manufacturing sector was in the heavy and chemical industries.

sized companies, was another undesirable side effect of these financial policies, which favored large business groups with proven track records. Furthermore, the rapid expansion of credit for the economy as a whole aggravated already chronic inflation in the latter part of the 1970s.

Discretionary Credit Allocation

Because commercial banks were made de facto public enterprises, the allocation of credit below market-clearing interest rates naturally involved the government's discretion. This discretionary credit allocation became a critical tool for influencing resource allocation. In addition, it made what Koopmans and Montias (1971) call "partial mutuality"—defined as the removal of an existing privilege or penalty for noncompliance—work in Korea.[16]

The debt-to-equity ratio of the Korean manufacturing sector as a whole was almost 400 percent throughout the 1970s. Without going into causal factors, one can imagine Korean firms' vulnerability to external shocks with such high debt-to-equity ratios (for a detailed discussion, see chapter 7). More importantly, they were vulnerable to the whims of institutional lenders, which were mostly under the control of the government. Therefore, the potential threat of losing credit lines was more detrimental for Korean firms than for their counterparts in other nations where debt-to-equity ratios were not as high, capital markets were better developed, and banks were outside the direct influence of government. This is why partial mutuality worked well in Korea. In sum, government's discretion in credit allocation served not only to influence the allocation of resources but also to increase private compliance in Korea (Jones and SaKong 1980; SaKong 1981).

Outward-Looking Development Strategy

The outward-looking development strategy usually is described as manifesting either "export promotion" or "trade liberalization" (Krueger 1979; Bhagwati 1986; Kubo, De Melo, and Robinson 1986, 165–66). An export promotion strategy gives roughly equal or at least positive incentives to both exports and import substitution. Trade liberalization, on the other hand, is characterized as giving negligible incentives to both export and import-substituting activities. Both cases inevitably consider only quantifiable market incentives or parameter manipulation.[17]

---

16. See also Jones and SaKong (1980, 82–84).

17. Parameter manipulation is intended to affect the level of payoffs from a particular course of action and thereby to induce desirable reallocation of resources. See Jones and SaKong (1980, 82–84).

More broadly defined, outward-looking development strategy should take into account other qualitative or nonpecuniary incentives and field augmentations—i.e., the expansion of information regarding existing opportunities—in addition to "getting prices right."

The outward-looking development strategy adopted since the early 1960s in Korea is well-known, and much has already been written on the subject (Krueger 1979; Balassa 1988; Papanek 1988). As will be discussed, in the Korean context, qualitative, nonprice factors were important in implementing the strategy.

Korea introduced very active export promotion schemes in the early 1960s by providing various new fiscal and financial subsidies, correcting overvaluation of the local currency,[18] allowing exporters to import export-related raw materials and capital equipment freely, and introducing generous wastage allowances for export-related production. These measures, in fact, were designed to offset the existing import-substitution biases. In essence, they were to get relative prices right rather than to get them "wrong."[19]

In addition, a very complicated multiple exchange rate system was revamped into a simpler unitary exchange rate system.[20] At the same time, a negative-list system for imports was introduced.[21] Efforts were also made to reduce windfall gains from importing restricted items by introducing special tariffs and strengthening deposit requirements for importing these items.[22]

At the same time, the government not only introduced various nonpecuniary incentives to exporters but participated actively in the promotion of exports—for example, setting export targets for individual firms by product and regional destination. On "Export Day," established in 1964 to celebrate exports reaching the $100 million mark, high export achievers received prestigious awards usually presented personally by

---

18. During the 1950s, domestic currency was mostly overvalued. Coming into the 1960s, the currency was devalued. The most drastic devaluation came in 1964 when the Korean won was devalued by almost 50 percent. However, the total return to exporters in the 1950s was already high, thanks to such schemes as the export-import link system, under which exporters were allowed to sell foreign exchange earnings with import entitlement freely to importers at a market rate.

19. For a differing view, see Amsden (1989).

20. A completely unified exchange rate system was introduced in June 1961, a multiple exchange rate system in 1963, and a unitary fluctuating system was introduced in 1965.

21. Under this system, all items except those included in the negative list may be imported automatically. Under the previous positive-list system, all items except those included in the list required prior permission for import.

22. For detailed discussions on the subject for these periods, see Frank, Kim, and Westphal (1975) and Hong (1979).

the president.[23] The Korean government was successful in creating a social atmosphere in which contributions to exports were considered to be something good for society or even patriotic.

The government's active participation in export promotion culminated in the monthly export promotion meeting, attended by the president, top government policymakers, and business and financial leaders. The meetings were held to disseminate information regarding new export markets, new products, new policies, etc. More importantly, necessary supportive measures were easily identified and appropriate bureaucratic actions facilitated through these forums.

The government's role in providing information regarding markets abroad and in helping to find new business opportunities was also important, particularly at the early stage of export promotion. The Korean government established the Korea Trade Promotion Corporation (KOTRA) and the Korea Trading Corporation (*Koryo Mu Yeuk*) to help small and medium-sized companies overcome their limited capabilities in overseas markets and increase their exports.

The government also took steps to expand the business horizons and opportunities for exporters, actions that fall into the category of "field augmentation."[24] Most important in this regard, the government normalized diplomatic relations with Japan in 1965. At the same time, it sent numerous special trade missions abroad and completed trade agreements with important potential trading partners such as West Germany, Italy, Austria, India, and Mexico (Jones and SaKong 1980; see also appendix, table A.13).

All these government efforts must have contributed to Korea's outstanding export performance, which began in the early 1960s. However, it is difficult, if not impossible, to evaluate the individual contributions of these factors in quantitative terms. Yet even without knowing the individual contributions of each factor to Korea's export performance, it does not seem correct to assert—as many have in a purely neoclassical tradition—that "getting prices right," or parameter manipulation, was the only important factor.

Rather, getting prices right explains part but not all of Korea's outstanding export performance. Consequently, the outward-looking strategy should be viewed in a broader context, encompassing price as well as nonprice factors.

It is worthwhile to recognize that there were various price incentives provided for exports even in the 1950s, although these incentives were

---

23. Interestingly, Export Day was replaced by Trade Day in 1986 to emphasize the importance of both export and import for Korea.

24. Economic policy is implemented through behavioral change of economic units. At the policy implementation level, field augmentation expands an economic unit's opportunity set. For a detailed discussion, see Jones and SaKong (1980, chapter 4).

expanded and augmented in the 1960s (see appendix, table A.14). For example, export earnings could be converted into local currency in a variety of ways, mostly at levels well above official exchange rates. Because there was substantial excess demand for foreign exchange at the official rate, the allocation mechanism became very complicated. The import-export link system illustrates this (Frank, Kim, and Westphal 1975, 25–41).

Accordingly, Korean exporters in the 1950s could earn rates of return on foreign exchange generated from exports that were almost as high, if not higher, than they could earn in the 1960s and 1970s, even though the official yield for foreign exchange in the 1950s was substantially less than in later years (Jones and SaKong 1980, 86–99). What, then, is the whole story of the outstanding export performance from the early 1960s on? Or, put another way, what made the difference between export performance in the 1950s and that of the subsequent decades?

First of all, Korea had to overcome the widespread pessimism regarding exports that existed in the early 1960s. "What do we have to export?" and "Who is going to buy what we make?" were Koreans' typical questions at the time. Consequently, changing attitudes and the general social atmosphere regarding exports was critical. These changes occurred primarily through strong leadership commitment to economic development through export. The commitment itself gave exporters confidence in the stability of export incentives and other supports. In addition, social recognition of exporters and other nonpecuniary incentives mentioned above were important contributing factors.

Second, the reform of the exchange rate system, together with exchange rate adjustments, contributed greatly to Korea's export performance by reducing the transaction costs of export. Under the old system, higher transaction costs made export less profitable. In addition, the reform also reduced the opportunity cost of export. Under the complicated multiple exchange rate system, there were abundant opportunities for windfall gains arising from the various quantitative restrictions, providing disincentives for businessmen to engage actively in export activities. Windfall gains of more than 300 percent were easily made in the distorted foreign exchange market (see appendix, table A.15). Under these circumstances, potential exporters would prefer to engage in rent-seeking activities (Krueger 1974) or zero-sum arbitrage activities rather than socially productive, positive-sum activities.[25]

The third important factor behind Korea's export performance relates to the government's efforts in field augmentation, such as expanding

---

25. Leibenstein (1963, 111–43) explains unproductive, zero-sum entrepreneurial activities this way: "What may be a source of income creation for the individual need not be a means of income creation as seen by the community at large."

diplomatic relations with important potential trading partners. In addition, the government played an important role in fostering trade-related institutions such as KOTRA, KTA, and *Koryo Mu Yeuk*, which supported Korean exporters. These supporting activities are particularly important at the early stage of export promotion, especially for small and medium-sized exporters.[26]

In sum, Korea's effort of "getting prices right" was an important and a critical factor, but it was not the only factor that mattered. Undoubtedly, getting foreign exchange rates right and providing various price incentives were necessary factors for outstanding performance. The newly introduced unified exchange rate system was also important and necessary to eliminate irregularities in the auction market and to reduce transaction costs. In addition, one should not underestimate the importance of nonpecuniary incentives as well as greater government commitment to export promotion.

Some have questioned whether Korea experienced a major change in the outward-looking strategy toward import-substitution in the 1970s. To answer this question, it is important to discuss the HCI promotion drive of 1973–79. As was discussed in the previous chapter, from the early 1960s to 1972, before the HCI promotion drive was launched, the outward-looking development strategy was implemented through extensive market and nonmarket incentives and through the government's entrepreneurial, gap-filling activities that supplemented the immature private entrepreneurs in Korea during this period.[27] These incentives and governmental activities were designed, as previously explained, to promote exports in general rather than specific commodities or industries. In other words, they treated virtually all export-related activities and industries equally.

However, the HCI drive of the 1970s is characterized as an "industrial targeting approach," in which selected industries are promoted. This new approach was chosen, first, for the important economic objective of upgrading Korea's industrial structure and thereby its export structure for the future. Koreans felt this to be necessary for two reasons. First, it was perceived (correctly) that Korea would soon lose its competitiveness in light manufacturing products to other developing nations, including China and the Southeast Asian countries, which were pursuing

---

26. Even today, only a small proportion of small and medium-sized companies engage in exports directly. For example, there were 1,271 textile and garment companies in 1967 around the Taegu area, where mostly small and medium-sized textile and garment manufacturing companies are concentrated. Only 94 companies, or 7.4 percent of the total, engaged in export activities directly at the time. As recently as 1988, this ratio was increased only to 13.2 percent, or 358 companies out of 2,722 firms.

27. For a good discussion on this concept and entrepreneurship in general, see Leibenstein (1968, 72–92) and Jones and SaKong (1980, 166–209).

outward-looking development strategies of their own. Second, it was reasoned that the negative effects of the industrialized nations' rising protectionist barriers vis-à-vis labor-intensive light manufacturing products that began after the first oil shock could be offset by exporting higher-valued-added heavy and chemical products.

There were national security reasons as well for launching the drive at that time. In the aftermath of the Vietnam War, the United States announced the Nixon doctrine, and US troops stationed in Korea were reduced by a third in 1971. The fall of South Vietnam to the Communist camp was a shock for South Koreans because they had considered the division of the Vietnamese nation to be similar to their own situation. At the same time, they saw the reduction in US ground troops stationed in Korea as the beginning of an eventual overall US troop withdrawal from the Korean peninsula. Consequently, security concerns prompted the promotion of heavy industries in particular as the foundation for a strong defense industry.

For these reasons, the earlier industry-neutral incentives for exports were replaced by industry-specific, and even sometimes firm-specific, measures targeting the promotion of specific industries. The specific industries, designated as "strategic," included iron and steel, nonferrous metals, general machinery, shipbuilding, petrochemicals, and electrical equipment. They were promoted by providing strong tax incentives and preferential credits. Real interest rates on preferential credits or policy loans made available for these sectors were mostly negative. More importantly, these industries had privileged access to bank loans during times of credit rationing. Consequently, almost 60 percent of total bank loans went to these sectors, stifling the flow of funds available to light manufacturing industries.

It was this changed emphasis on promoting target industries that has led some to question whether Korea shifted to a development strategy biased toward import substitution in the late 1970s. Ratios of both the net and gross effective exchange rates for exports to the effective exchange rate for imports remained quite stable throughout the 1960s and 1970s,[28] suggesting that outward-looking development strategy was more or less implemented continuously (see appendix, table A.16).[29]

---

28. It should be noted, however, that the effective exchange rate for imports is underestimated to the extent that tariff equivalent effects of quantitative restrictions (QRs) on imports were not taken into account. The degree of underestimation must be higher during the 1950s, when QRs were prevalent. On the other hand, the effective exchange rate for exports tends to be underestimated for later years when various nonpecuniary incentives for exports were provided that are not reflected in the calculation.

29. Greenaway and Nam (1988) classified 41 developing countries for two periods, 1963–73 and 1973–85, according to the orientation of chosen trade strategy, as determined by

In fact, during the HCI promotion drive, import restrictions on products of infant or targeted industries were intensified. The effective subsidy rate for exports and the protection rate for domestic sales of typical heavy and chemical industries—for example, machinery and transport equipment—was very high in 1978 (see appendix, table A.17). Except for agriculture, rates for these HCI sectors were highest, far above export incentives or domestic subsidies given to the manufacturing sector or other industries. Although effective protection rates increased during the period, the export bias for the manufacturing sector as a whole still remained, albeit at a reduced rate.[30]

As has been pointed out in past studies (e.g., Bhagwati 1986), the intensification of import restrictions itself does not automatically imply that the strategy of promoting exports shifted toward import substitution. Instead, it possibly indicates a switch to a less extreme export promotion strategy.

In short, Korea's trade regime was both "outward-looking on the export side and restrictive on the import side" during this period (World Bank 1987). Korean policymakers actually were continuously "encouraging exports and promoting infant industries" simultaneously (Westphal 1990). In fact, the growth of heavy and chemical industries was fueled primarily through export expansion and only modestly through import substitution factors. Consequently, "to merely characterize the HCI promotion period as a classic import substitution experiment is incorrect" (World Bank 1987, 16).

There are other general factors indicating that Korea's export orientation was very much alive during the HCI promotion drive. Such mottos as "export-first," "nation building through exports," and the general emphasis on export promotion did not disappear during this period. Considering the size of Korea's domestic market, building up heavy and chemical industries was only feasible in connection with exports.

Again, in the beginning stages of export promotion, there was widespread pessimism in Korea. Yet Korea's outward-looking development strategy succeeded beyond everyone's best expectations. Thanks to this success, one can argue that Koreans gained self-confidence and a real "can-do spirit" by the late 1960s and the early 1970s, when the nation's first two five-year development plans were successfully completed. This self-confidence was shared by both private and public sectors. Flush with this success, the government gained enough confidence in its economic management and planning capabilities to undertake daring initiatives such as the HCI drive.

---

their criteria. Korea for both periods was included in the "strongly outward-oriented" group.

30. For a detailed discussion on this topic, see Nam (1990, 165–183).

Growth-First Strategy

We cannot expect the whole draught-stricken paddy land to become evenly watered immediately after we start to water it. We ought to have the patience and wisdom to share ten bushels later rather than the impatience and ignorance to insist on sharing a package of seeds evenly now. —President Park Chung Hee (1967)

With this statement, President Park neatly illustrates the growth-first, redistribution-later strategy adopted in the early 1960s. Political leadership committed itself to economic development at a time when poverty was prevalent, unemployment widespread, and when some other developing nations were adopting socialist patterns of development.

Yet Korean bureaucrats did not attempt to introduce income redistribution schemes for distributional equity purposes, such as a social welfare system of the income-transfer type, during the early stage of development. Instead, they were more interested in creating gainful employment opportunities through rapid export-led industrial growth. Indeed, the export-led industrialization strategy of the earlier period resulted in rapid development of labor-intensive manufacturing industries, absorbing unemployed and underemployed workers. This, in turn, naturally contributed toward increasing wage and salary income, which tends to be more equitably distributed than income from property and other sources. In fact, as was discussed in chapter 2, Korea's household income distribution improved throughout the period, except during 1972–78 when the HCI promotion drive was actively implemented. In this regard, one can say that Korea's early growth-first strategy advanced the distributional goal.

It should also be noted that the Korean government, while pursuing a growth-first strategy, paid special attention to improving urban-rural income disparity (Leipziger and Petri 1989). As previously seen, public investment for improving agricultural productivity had been substantial in the 1960s and 1970s. These efforts were further intensified in the late 1960s, when a high rice price policy was adopted along with keeping fertilizer and farm machinery prices low. Undoubtedly, these agricultural support policies contributed to improving rural-urban income distribution, despite their adverse inflationary impacts on the Korean economy. In this respect, Korea's growth-first strategy was not entirely without distributional concern. It can be argued in this regard, therefore, that the characterization of Korea's strategy as growth-first is not meant to emphasize "redistribution-later" but rather "stabilization-second."

The rapid growth through export-led industrialization required high investment, which had to be supported by a rapidly growing money supply. The inevitable result was "developmental inflation." This inflation became especially serious in the 1970s when the government was pushing HCI-related investment. As will be discussed in chapter 4, the growth-first strategy has had to be softened with a "stabilization-first" policy goal since the early 1980s, when economic stabilization was emphasized as a foundation for sustained growth. In this sense, Korea's growth-first strategy is still alive today in Korea, albeit in a "stable growth–first" form.

Interactions of Market and Nonmarket Factors in Policy Implementation

In a market-oriented economy such as Korea's, policy implementation is accomplished mostly through private entrepreneurial responses. These responses are elicited in an environment where sociopolitical and cultural factors, the role of government, market incentives, and prices all come into play. These critical factors and their interactions will be discussed here, but not in quantitative terms. Instead, we attempt to illustrate how Korea implements chosen strategies in general by observing how the outward-looking development strategy in particular was implemented.

In a society in which the Confucian tradition of hierarchical loyalty is pronounced, leadership commitment to development under a strong presidential system is expected to generate stronger bureaucratic responses and devotion to results than in societies where loyalty to top leadership is less marked. In such an environment, bureaucrats will strive harder to achieve national goals set up by the leadership. To make sure that policies are implemented in such a way that they produce the desired results, bureaucrats must be flexible and pragmatic in choosing appropriate policy instruments.

As Woronoff (1986) points out, the choice of policies and the way in which they are implemented are deeply permeated by cultural values. Confucianism, being a way of life or a philosophy rather than a rigid religion, fosters a more malleable response to different situations.[31] In sum, this cultural factor does come into play at the implementation level.

Strong bureaucratic responses, however, are only the beginning of implementation. The bureaucracy has to work out an effective system of incentives (or disincentives) and create a favorable environment for maximum entrepreneurial response.

Let us now consider how the government maximized the responses of entrepreneurs. Entrepreneurial activities always involve risk and un-

---

31. O'Malley (1988) explains Confucianism as follows: Confucianism is not a religion stressing an afterlife; it is a code of ethics and conduct, meant to guide the relationships between human beings. The important relationships in Confucianism are hierarchical, between generations, within families, between ruler and ruled. The duty of the subordinate in these relationships is to show respect, loyalty, and deference; the duty of superior is to give the proper moral example, that is, to act in the way that his status requires.

certainty, and this is even more true when unknown foreign markets are explored. By helping to reduce these risks and uncertainties, governments can more readily elicit positive response from business. In particular, the government can channel existing entrepreneurial energies away from zero-sum arbitrage and other rent-seeking activities into areas with higher social productivity, such as exports (Leibenstein 1968).

When there are plenty of opportunities to make money through arbitrage, existing entrepreneurial energies will be directed toward such activities. At the same time, in a society where great value is attached to social harmony and cooperation, social recognition for entrepreneurial activities creates a favorable environment for them. Therefore, one can say that the Confucian emphasis on social harmony and cooperation facilitates maximum entrepreneurial responses.

The government also provided gap-filling functions for entrepreneurs to compensate for existing market deficiencies (Leibenstein 1968), for example, imperfections in the information market. Through KOTRA, the KTA, and sometimes directly through governmental bodies, it provided complementary entrepreneurial inputs such as new information on foreign markets.

Certainly, if all gaps are filled by the government, the entrepreneur's only remaining role will be a lenticular function.[32] As development proceeds, some of the gaps that were previously difficult to fill become easier for two reasons: first, the entrepreneur's gap-filling ability increases, and second, the missing inputs are marketed or more easily available. For this reason, the supporting role of the government in the earlier period is very useful, but it gradually becomes less important as time passes.

In sum, the reduced opportunity costs of export activities—together with government's commitment to exports, field augmentations, and nonpecuniary incentives—contributed toward increasing the supply of entrepreneurs and attracting existing entrepreneurial energies to positive-sum entrepreneurial activities, in this case, exports. Cultural factors come into the picture at the policy implementation level: first, through bureaucrats' pragmatic choice of tools for policy implementation in response to leadership commitment and second, through appeals to entrepreneurs' desire for social harmony.

Once exports become a routine practice and market deficiencies are for the most part eliminated, however, excessive governmental inter-

---

32. Many functions go into the making of an entrepreneurial bundle, such as perception of a new economic opportunity and evaluation of the profitability of a new opportunity. The entrepreneur takes ultimate responsibility for seeing that all these functions are carried out, even though he performs few or none of them himself. He is like a lens that focuses the energies of others (Jones and SaKong 1980, chapter 6).

vention can choke private entrepreneurial initiatives. Accordingly, in later stages of development, getting prices right should play a more critical role.

Thus, the government's direct field augmentations in exports may have been less important in the 1970s and 1980s than they were in the 1960s. From the early 1970s on, indirect field augmentation was used more frequently than direct gap-filling, for example, expanding business horizons via diplomatic contacts. The government's direct gap-filling was then limited to such new areas as export markets for services.

A positive aspect of field augmentation is that it reduces uncertainties and enhances business confidence in government's ability to maintain a favorable business climate. This was very important, particularly in the early 1960s, when export pessimism prevailed and inexperience made businesses unsure of themselves.

Jones and SaKong (1980, chapters 6 and 7) argue that there was already a substantial stock of entrepreneurial intent, even in the 1950s. However, it was only in the 1960s that these entrepreneurial energies were channeled into socially productive activities such as export, mostly through policy efforts of the government. The government made it easier and less costly for entrepreneurs to engage in socially productive ventures such as exports. At the same time, to the extent that there was plenty of latent entrepreneurial intent, the government's gap-filling must have helped increase effective, positive-sum entrepreneurship.

The government's use of nonpecuniary incentives was also very important. This included creating prestigious awards and positive social support for entrepreneurs engaging in exports and positive-sum entrepreneurial activities. By stressing that such activities were directly contributing to society, the government effectively augmented entrepreneurial response to pecuniary incentives. As Habakkuk (1971, 37–52) pointed out, "The entrepreneur's behavior does not depend upon his own motives alone. It depends also on the way other people in his society regard his activities, on the general climate of opinion in which he works, on the social approval given to the entrepreneur." Therefore, it made sense for the Korean government to create conditions conducive to positive-sum entrepreneurial activities by promoting social attitudes favorable to entrepreneurial achievement. These factors contributed to the successful mobilization of private entrepreneurship in the early 1960s and therefore to Korean development (Jones and SaKong 1980; Leibenstein 1968, 72–83; Hoselitz 1957, 28–41).

At the same time, through various institutional reforms in the 1960s (e.g., the unified exchange rate system) and elimination of other rent-providing opportunities (such as quantitative restrictions or extensive licensing), the high opportunity costs for positive-sum activities were reduced, and entrepreneurial energies shifted away from nonproductive rent-seeking activities. This shift, therefore, was enhanced by narrowing the gap between private and socially beneficial business pursuits and by increasing the effective return for a given volume of entrepreneurial energy.

In addition, the continuation of strong leadership commitment and bureaucratic support induced further expectations of stability, lengthened time horizons, lowered the time preference discount rate, and increased the expected return on virtually all entrepreneurial activities.

Notice, in this regard, that Confucianism is a facilitating factor but not the major contributor to Korea's success. Confucianism has been with Korea for hundreds of years, and, in fact, it has been considered an obstacle to modernizing the Korean economy because it tends to look down on business, people engaged in commerce in general, and specialists such as people engaged in manufacturing. At the same time, in Confucian tradition respect is reserved for people who read and write poems and study philosophy but are not engaged in mundane and practical things. As a matter of fact, Weber and others have used Confucianism to explain China's economic backwardness (Weber 1951).

In sum, as Hofheinz and Calder (1982, 250) are correct to say, "Confucian culture provides a background of values reinforcing respect for authority, promoting education, and rewarding diligence. But . . . such a background will not produce the desired economic results."

The Nature of Economic Planning in Korea

Korea's first five-year economic development plan was introduced in 1962. The nation's seventh plan, covering 1992–96, is being implemented. Of course, there were plans in the 1950s, but they were paper plans drawn up in order to get foreign aid. The brief Chang Myun regime did prepare an intermediate-range economic plan that became the basis for the first five-year development plan. The introduction of the first five-year development plan marked a new era in Korean economic history in the sense that, for the first time, the government provided a national economic vision and an economic program for business and the general public (Jones and SaKong 1980, 38–77; SaKong 1990a, 677–80).

The first plan was rather hastily prepared and had to be modified substantially due to crop failures in the early years of its implementation. However, it was significant in that it reflected the political leadership's commitment to development. Of course, many people did not believe in its face value at the time, but the attempt was very important.

The second five-year plan was prepared more carefully and with greater depth than the first, as Korean bureaucrats became more experienced and received advice from foreign experts. The great success of the second plan dispelled any doubts the Korean people might have had concerning the first plan and cemented their hopes and aspirations for the future. It was also significant in building the confidence and enthusiasm of government policymakers, business leaders, and the general public that has been a hallmark of Korean development over the years.

With regard to the nature of Korean planning, there have been some misconceptions. Korean planning has often been considered unfairly as imperative or prescriptive and as having a rigid relationship between intermediate-range plans and annual economic management plans and budgets.

Korean intermediate-range plans usually did not have intertemporal prescriptions. The characteristics of the Korean plan changed over time, perhaps from less indicative to more indicative. Even then, one can generally describe Korean planning as more indicative than imperative in the sense that the process of planning serves a greater purpose than the completed plans themselves. In the course of the preparation of the plans, a substantial amount of information is shared among all participants. Participants from the private sector get the opportunity to learn more about the policy direction of the government and the government's perspective on future economic environments. This in turn facilitates private planning.

In addition, throughout the planning process, different ministries, especially different economic ministries, learn about the concerns and priorities of other ministries. At the same time, they all learn more about the nation's macroeconomic goals and policies. Thus, planning has facilitated highly critical interministerial cooperation and coordination in formulating and implementing short-term economic policies, which are the real driving force of the economy.

Korean planning has been successful in its announcement or education effects. The outstanding economic performance of Korea so far has a lot to do with the government's flexible, nonideological, pragmatic attitude in dealing with short-term policy matters. Korea's economic success owes much to good intermediate-term planning and implementation but even more to short-term policies formed in response to changing domestic and international economic conditions. Korea's past economic planning can be summarized this way:

> Korean planning has been only partially successful in charting a detailed path for the economy to follow. More important, it has functioned as a sort of economic topographic survey which educated officials and allowed them to make the intelligent short-term policy decisions that really drive the economy. It has also had a major "announcement effect" articulating leadership commitment and giving the general guidelines and implicit promises of support that facilitate private planning. (Jones and SaKong 1980, 53)

Summary and Conclusion

The emergence of a new political leadership in 1962, which made economic development the nation's top priority, brought about "government-led," "outward-looking," and "growth-first" development strategies in Korea.

Korea's growth-first strategy, adopted in the early 1960s, actually contributed to the improvement of household income distribution, except for the period between 1972 and 1978 and in recent years, by rapidly absorbing unemployed and underemployed workers and increasing the share of income earned from wages and salaries. On the other hand, the nation's heavy and chemical industry promotion drive of the 1970s was implemented so that big business conglomerates, or *chaebols*, grew at a much faster rate than the economy as a whole. The large proportion of subsidized "policy loans," tax privileges, and other benefits offered to big firms participating in HCI, together with chronic inflation, undoubtedly worsened the nation's income distribution during the latter part of the 1970s. Coming into the 1980s, the Korean government introduced various reform measures and successfully arrested this inflation.

Korea's growth-first strategy was not entirely without distributional concern. The Korean government, while pursuing a growth-first strategy, did pay special attention to improving urban-rural income disparity. Published statistics show that the worsening income distribution trend was actually reversed in the 1980s.

The adoption of an outward-looking development strategy in the early 1960s was implemented in Korea through various market and nonmarket "industry-neutral" incentives. The Korean government's entrepreneurial gap-filling activities and field augmentations for all export-related industries were also important aspects of implementing the strategy. Various nonpecuniary incentives were provided to maximize entrepreneurial responses to price incentives. A critically important factor for the successful implementation of the outward-looking development strategy in the Korean context was the elimination of rent-providing opportunities through various institutional reforms, such as the unified exchange rate system. These reforms were instrumental in shifting the nation's entrepreneurial energies from zero-sum to positive-sum, export-related activities.

Concerns about Korea's loss of competitiveness in light manufacturing products, the rising protectionism in industrialized nations, the announcement of gradual withdrawal of US troops stationed in Korea, and the attendant expectations of national security problems contributed to the initiation of the industry-specific and sometimes firm-specific HCI promotion drive of the early 1970s. Even during this period, however, the outward-looking trade regime was maintained, as export incentives were continuously provided.

The strong leadership commitment to the nation's economic development naturally resulted in the Korean government's active involvement in the nation's resource allocation. The Korean government was not reluctant to use public enterprises, the most visible intervention tool, as a means to direct the nation's investable resources. Korea's frequent reliance on this tool exemplifies the Korean government's pragmatic, nonideological approach to policy implementation. However, nearly 65 percent on average of the nation's total investment was carried out by the private sector. The implementation of Korea's government-led development strategy relied heavily on financial policy tools. As a result, the Korean financial sector was "repressed."

Price and nonprice factors affected entrepreneurial responses to chosen policies and their subsequent implementation. These elements in turn interacted to produce results within the context of a social, political, and cultural environment. In explaining Korea's success, the price factor or "getting prices right," was definitely critical, but it was not the only factor that mattered. Cultural factors, such as the Confucian background of the country, also played a facilitating role, particularly at the policy implementation level.

Korea's economic success owes much to fast and flexible short-term policy responses to changing domestic and international economic conditions. Korean intermediate-term planning can generally be characterized as more indicative than imperative in the sense that the process of planning is considered more important than the plan itself. This process has been successful in its "announcement" or "education" effects, articulating leadership commitment and giving the general guidelines and implicit promises of support that facilitate private planning.

4

Changed Development Strategy of the 1980s

Broadly speaking, Korea was able to maintain an adequate balance between the demand for and the supply of available resources during most of the rapid development period of the 1960s and the early 1970s, when the work force was heavily unemployed or underemployed and the nation's development strategy was primarily based on export promotion with industry-neutral incentives. With this outward-looking strategy, the Korean economy performed well, exporting many standardized, labor-intensive manufactured products.

The situation changed substantially in the early 1970s when the ambitious heavy and chemical industry (HCI) promotion drive was launched, using highly interventionist policy instruments, to upgrade the nation's industrial export structure. In promoting heavy and chemical industries, the government directly channeled a large proportion of the nation's financial resources into well-established big business groups in targeted sectors, leaving insufficient funds for traditional light industries where most small and medium-sized firms were concentrated.

The availability of cheap sources of credit and other accompanying privileges for those firms in the targeted heavy and chemical industries resulted in sectoral imbalances between the HCIs and light industries, and between big groups and small and medium-sized firms. At the same time, chronic excess demand for bank loans was further aggravated, and the debt-to-equity ratios of big business groups became even higher.

This drive, together with the Middle East construction boom of the mid-1970s, started to put pressure on the market for skilled workers,

53

eventually pushing up the general level of wages.[1] Accordingly, real wage increases started to outstrip productivity gains. The HCI plant and equipment investment boom, accompanied by rapidly increasing housing investments that were induced by rising inflationary expectations, boosted the annual rate of total fixed investment by more than 30 percent in real terms between 1977 and 1978. In fact, real fixed investment more than doubled between 1975 and 1978. This put tremendous pressure on the real sector.

On the financial side, the expanded supply of policy loans for HCI promotion, combined with the sudden improvement in the balance of payments owing to construction industry remittances from the Middle East, caused domestic liquidity to grow very fast. The money supply expanded at an average annual rate of 36 percent from 1976 to 1978. Undoubtedly, domestic excess liquidity during this time of economic boom fueled inflationary expectations even further. To make things even worse, the government attempted to administratively suppress inflation.

With all these domestic developments and fixed exchange rates, Korea's international competitive edge was severely eroded during this period. Unit labor costs increased nearly 20 percent per year between 1976 and 1978. Combined with a stagnant and protectionist world trade environment, this decline in competitiveness led to slower Korean export growth. Export growth in volume terms became negative in 1979 for the first time in recent Korean history.

On top of these endogenous structural problems, the Korean economy had to absorb a number of other negative developments, including the world's second oil shock of 1979, a disastrous domestic rice harvest due to severe cold weather in 1980, and political uncertainty following the assassination of President Park Chung Hee in October 1979. All these factors led the Korean economy in 1980 to register negative GNP growth in real terms for the first time since the 1950s, with soaring inflation and a current account deficit of $5.3 billion.

In order to cope with this situation, coming into the 1980s the government implemented wide-ranging economic reforms. These reforms were primarily based on a policy shift away from government intervention and toward more private sector–led initiatives. At the same time, priority was put on economic stabilization, and the basic foundation for structural adjustments was established. Simultaneously, liberalization measures for both internal and external sector adjustments were widely introduced.

---

1. Bai (1982) argues that around 1975 the Korean economy passed the so-called Lewisian turning point, the point at which an unlimited labor supply is exhausted. Consequently, at this point, wages for unskilled workers go up.

The main purpose of this chapter is to discuss the contents of this new strategy, the stabilization policies, and various liberalization and reform measures introduced during the early 1980s. Together, these actions illustrate Korea's pragmatic, nonideological, flexible responses to emerging economic problems, backed by continued strong leadership commitment to economic development. Obviously, the new strategy and various reform measures of the 1980s are positive responses to problems that were the consequences of earlier development strategies and policies. It is therefore worth discussing earlier development strategies and policies first to provide the context for Korea's adoption of a new strategy.

Antecedents to a Shift in Development Strategy

As was discussed earlier, Korea adopted an outward-looking industrialization strategy in the early 1960s when new leadership came to power. In implementing this strategy, the Korean government became actively involved in resource allocation processes. This in turn resulted in the government-led development pattern of Korea. The government-led development strategy itself centered on direct involvement in financial resource allocation.

As noted in chapter 3, the government made commercial banks de facto public enterprises, established various government-invested special banks, and screened and allocated foreign loans, both private and public. Certainly, traditional fiscal incentives for promoting exports were also used. However, the government's direct control of financial resources, especially banking funds, was far more powerful in affecting the direction of resource allocation, particularly at a time when the nation's tax system was rather narrowly based and the domestic capital market was in its infancy.

Through its control of the financial sector, the government kept tight reins on interest rates throughout the 1960s and 1970s. Financial market repression became even more severe during the heavy and chemical industry promotion period. Particularly toward the end of the 1970s, policy loans with negative real interest rates accounted for more than 50 percent of all bank loans at the time. Policy loans accounted for nearly 80 percent of incremental domestic credit extended in 1978–79. During this period, interest rates on general loans too were kept at rates much lower than the market clearing rates, primarily for the benefit of highly leveraged, HCI-participating firms. As a consequence, the curb market began to grow fast again.

Policy directives mostly supplanted the bank's role of screening and evaluating projects. Korean commercial banks, therefore, were more or less reduced to serving as the government's rationing agents.

The Drive to Promote Heavy and Chemical Industries

The heavy and chemical industry promotion drive of 1973–79 and its implementation left many challenges for the Korean economy in ensuing years. In reviewing this topic, revisionist views on the HCI promotion drive, put forth in recent years, will also be briefly discussed.[2]

As was discussed in the previous chapter, from the early 1960s to 1972 when the HCI promotion drive was launched, the outward-looking development strategy was implemented by both extensive market and nonmarket incentives as well as the government's entrepreneurial gap-filling. However, it is important to recognize that incentives and government gap-filling were primarily provided for exports in general rather than exports of specific commodities or particular export industries. That is, virtually all export industries were treated equally during this period.

The HCI promotion drive, however, promoted specific industries chosen by the government. In other words, the earlier industry-neutral incentives provided for exports as a whole were replaced by the system of industry-specific or sometimes firm-specific incentives for the promotion of these industries.[3] The specific industries, designated as "strategic" industries, included steel, nonferrous metal, general machinery, shipbuilding, electronics, and chemicals.

The government promoted specific projects by providing preferential credits, both in terms of availability and cost preference; other tax incentives, including investment tax credits, accelerated depreciation allowances, and tax holidays;[4] and by constructing industrial parks, for example the Changwon Machinery Complex and the Yeochon Petrochemical Complex. In addition, HCI promotion through industrial targeting was accompanied by typical import-substitution policies, such as restricting imports of certain intermediate inputs produced by the promoted HCIs.[5]

Real interest rates on general loans, let alone preferential credits or policy loans, were negative until the early 1980s (see appendix, table A.18). Special access to these general bank loans gave rise to chronic excess demand for debt capital and high debt-to-equity ratios on the part of the HCI participating firms, which included most large business groups in Korea. The particularly high debt-to-equity ratios of HCI par-

---

2. For a detailed discussion on both conventional and revisionist views, see Suk-Chae Lee (1991, 431–71).

3. For a good discussion on Korea's incentive policies, see Leipziger and Petri (1989).

4. The effective marginal corporate tax rate of the HCI-participating firms was estimated to be about one-third of other firms (Kwack 1985).

5. This in itself is not evidence of Korea switching to an inward-looking development strategy. This issue is discussed in chapter 3.

ticipating companies made them more vulnerable to recession and to foreign competitors that were more financially sound.

The average cost of borrowing for the HCIs was much lower than that for the light manufacturing sector throughout the period (see appendix, table A.19). From 1972 to 1979, the light manufacturing sector paid on the average 292 basis points more than the heavy and chemical sector did. This gap started to narrow from the early 1980s, as preferential lending rates for policy loans were eliminated and the proportion of nonbank financing became more important in Korea's corporate finance.

As indicated, these HCIs had privileged access to bank loans even during times of credit rationing. The benefit of easy access to credit during times of tight credit rationing is difficult to estimate quantitatively, but it might very well be as important as the direct interest subsidy of preferential interest rates, if not more important.

Of course, when borrowers were rationed out of the bank credit market, they could have borrowed from the curb market at much higher cost levels. It is also likely, however, that some potential borrowers without established credit standing might not have been able to borrow at all, even in the curb market. As a result of HCIs' preferential access to bank credit, almost 60 percent of the total bank loans from 1975 to 1977 and close to 95 percent of policy loans in 1978 were accounted for by HCIs. This discriminated against light manufacturing industries and blocked their access to cheaper funds (World Bank 1987).

In fact, the light manufacturing sector suffered not only from this disadvantage in financing but also from rapid wage increases for both unskilled and skilled workers. Wages for unskilled workers were already expected to rise around this time, as the Korean economy was reaching the Lewisian turning point. Skilled workers' wages went up even faster, as a severe shortage of skilled workers appeared in the latter half of the 1970s due primarily to the HCI promotion drive and the Middle East construction boom.

As previously indicated, in implementing HCI promotion policies, the government actively encouraged large business groups with proven track records and financial capability to participate in major projects in designated industries. At the same time, some of these groups voluntarily participated in these ventures mainly to take advantage of subsidies and other privileges rather than out of immediate profit motives or enthusiasm for the particular venture. In any case, the result was rapid growth and higher debt-to-equity ratios for these groups. Undoubtedly, one important factor contributing to the fast growth of big conglomerates, or *chaebols*, in Korea was this policy of HCI promotion during the 1970s.

Toward the latter part of the 1970s, due to the way the Korean economy was managed and particularly the way the HCI promotion drive was implemented, a number of serious structural imbalances emerged in the Korean economy. First of all, the lopsided financial resource al-

Table 4.1 Investment by heavy and light industries, 1976–79 (as a share of total investment)

	1976	1977	1978	1979
Light Industries	25.8	24.6	17.5	18.1
Heavy Industries	74.2	75.4	82.5	81.9

Source: Korea Development Institute. 1981a. *Materials for Economic Stabilization Policies*, vol. 1.

Table 4.2 Capacity utilization by industry, 1978 and 1979 (percentages)

Industry	1978	1979	Rate of increase in production capacity
Light industry			
Cotton yarn	100.0	100.0	6.5
Wood	98.0	99.3	9.6
Synthetic fiber	100.0	134.7	15.1
Plywood	85.5	93.3	n.a.
Heavy industry			
Industrial machinery	61.6	60.4	47.2
Shipbuilding	21.4	21.4	44.4
Hot coil	103.8	75.0	109.4
Nonferrous metal	82.1	76.4	42.2

n.a. = not available

Source: Korea Development Institute. 1981a. *Materials for Economic Stabilization Policies*, vol. 1.

location toward the HCIs and the benign neglect of the light manufacturing industries, which were important exporters as well as producers of daily necessities, created two serious problems. Due to insufficient investment, a severe supply bottleneck emerged in daily necessities, further fueling the inflationary psychology of the time. The supply bottleneck in these sectors was aggravated by the reduced production of existing plants because of administrative price controls. In addition, lack of adequate investment in light manufacturing sectors limited the export capacity of traditional items such as textiles.

Second, at the sectoral level, HCIs' excess supply capacity and underutilization were a serious problem. Guaranteed credit extension and subsidies for investments in designated strategic industries and implicit risk bearing on the part of the government (i.e., the "socialization of private risks") in promotion of HCIs undoubtedly contributed to the problem of overinvestment in targeted industries (see tables 4.1 and 4.2). The government's direct encouragement of investment in these sectors was primarily based on supply-side considerations—for example, "optimum" plant scales—rather than realistic demand-side forecasts at the firm level that would have been scrutinized and evaluated by financial institutions.

The second oil shock and the ensuing world economic slowdown aggravated the problems of overinvestment and underutilized capacity for most firms in targeted industries from the late 1970s. Because most of the HCI participating firms were highly leveraged, it was particularly difficult to survive during this period.

In addition, the overhang problem of commercial banks' non-performing assets (NPAs), as related to the HCIs as well as to the construction and shipping industries, seriously affected the viability of commercial banks in Korea. Due primarily to this overhang problem, banks were (and still are to some extent) vulnerable to competition from other non-bank financial institutions, slowing the pace of financial sector liberalization. In fact, the alleviation of the NPAs' overhang for banks has become an important prerequisite for Korea's financial sector reform.

Up until recently, the consensus view was that the HCI drive was a total failure and was primarily responsible for the economic setback of the early 1980s (Yoo 1989). In recent years, however, as the HCI sector as a whole has started to perform satisfactorily in terms of production and exports, more positive evaluations are being presented.

The original target of the HCI promotion drive was for HCI products to account for 50 percent of total manufactured commodity exports by 1980. This original target was almost achieved by 1980 and actually exceeded by 1983. As a matter of fact, Korea's leading export items in recent years are products of the HCIs, such as electronic products, steel products, automobiles, chemical products, ships, and machineries (see appendix, table A.8). Based on these facts, and the fact that HCIs generated various positive outcomes such as skilled-worker training, it is argued that HCI promotion was worthwhile despite the undesirable side effects.

Admitting their successes, the relevant question to ask is, at what cost were the goals achieved? We have already suggested various costs associated with the HCI promotion drive. They include inflation, financial repression, concentration of economic power, and worsened income distribution. In addition, the distorted incentive system produced implicit microeconomic costs, such as static allocative inefficiency and X-inefficiencies.

Another important source of costs is the NPA overhang. As will soon be discussed, the explicit costs associated with the alleviation of the NPA overhang were substantial, such as the central bank's subsidized loans to commercial banks, lost tax revenues from tax exemptions and deductions, forgone dividend payments to bank shareholders, and so forth. To the extent that the NPA overhang problem delayed the nation's financial sector liberalization, there is an important additional implicit cost.

It would be very difficult, if not impossible, to take into consideration all these costs appropriately in the HCI evaluation. However, unless all these costs are properly brought into perspective, the revisionist view, merely based on apparent outcomes, is difficult to accept.

Korea definitely had certain advantages associated with being a late developer. There were various tested industrial technologies and ways of doing things that were readily available to Korea. As a late developer, Korea knew what had worked and what did not in other circumstances. By carefully examining other nations' industrial transformations and overall development, late developers can take shortcuts to achieve their own developmental goals. In cases where factor endowments and political and social environments are similar, attempts to replicate those successful policies can be justified.

The Japanese case has always appealed to Koreans in this regard. Through the course of Japan's industrial transformation—namely from light to heavy and chemical industries—Koreans could clearly visualize where their economy might be directed. It could and did in many cases borrow tested technologies to speed up the nation's industrialization, following the example and direction of the model developers. Nations often adopt an industrial policy to spur this industrial transformation. A critical question to ask in this connection is what kind of policy most appropriately promotes its industry.

The current industrial performance of Korea suggests that Korea's resource endowment situation has changed substantially compared with that of its early development period and that its comparative advantage today lies in the HCI sectors. For this reason, even most critics of the HCI promotion drive would not argue that the direction of the HCI promotion policy was wrong.

There are, however, many who argue that there were less costly ways to steer development in this direction. Costs could have been reduced, they argue, if the government had provided more indirect, functional incentives instead of the direct administrative commands on an unmanageable scale that created serious imbalances.

Even among currently successful HCIs, careful scrutiny shows that the picture varies case by case. Korea's electronics products are doing well abroad, but most of them, including consumer electronics and semiconductors, are not products directly related to the HCI promotion drive. The shipbuilding and machinery sectors benefited from numerous implicit and explicit subsidies and government bail-outs. The petrochemical sector has been satisfactory, thanks primarily to cheap world petroleum prices. The automobile sector also had its share of protection. Considering the technological characteristics of the industry and existing entrepreneurs' aspirations, one might argue that the automobile sector would have soon emerged in Korea even without governmental efforts.

Chaebols and the Concentration of Economic Power

In addition to industrial imbalances, the steep upward trend toward concentration of economic power was another concern. In the process of economic growth and development under a market-oriented system, some private entrepreneurs are bound to be more successful than others, and consequently, their firms are naturally expected to grow at a faster rate than those in the rest of the economy. These successful firms accumulate profits and grow or branch into new lines of business. When these firms branch into new lines of business across industries to form groups, they become conglomerates, or *chaebols*.

A *chaebol* in Korea is a group of firms owned and controlled primarily by a single entrepreneur and usually his family members (Jones and SaKong 1980; SaKong 1980a; Jones 1987 and forthcoming; Lee and Lee 1990; Young Ki Lee 1990). A *chaebol*, therefore, can be viewed as an economic group, which is defined as "a multicompany firm that transacts in different markets but which does so under common entrepreneurial and financial control" (Leff 1978). The emergence of these *chaebols* as economic groups can be considered an institutional innovation for overcoming market deficiencies and reaping their benefits, even though government policy was instrumental in creating and sustaining them.

As previously indicated, in order to promote the HCIs, well-established, large entrepreneurs with good track records were called in to launch new ventures in targeted industries. In most cases, they received various subsidies and credits in return. As a result, many *chaebols* became further diversified and grew faster—much faster, in fact, than the rest of the economy.

As seen in table 4.3, the 46 largest conglomerates grew at a average annual rate of 22.8 percent between 1973 and 1978, while the nation's GDP as a whole grew at an annual rate of 9.9 percent for the same period (see appendix for additional data on *chaebols*, tables A21–27). Consequently, these firms' share in GDP reached 17.1 percent in 1978, up from 9.8 percent in 1973 (SaKong 1980a, 2–13; Jones and SaKong 1980, chapter 8; Jones 1987, 87–192).

Nearly 60 percent of the top 46 *chaebols*' value added came from manufacturing activities in 1978. Therefore, the fast growth of *chaebols* in the Korean economy can be attributed to their rapid growth in manufacturing. While the nation's manufacturing sector as a whole grew at an average annual rate of 17.2 percent between 1973 and 1978, the top 46's value added grew at 24.4 percent per year during the same period. As a result, the 46 largest conglomerates' share of value added in manufacturing sector GDP increased from 31.8 percent in 1973 to 43.0 percent in 1978.

Also important to note is that the bigger the group, the faster it grew during this period (table 4.3). For example, the five largest conglomerates

Table 4.3 Average annual growth rate of chaebols, 1973–78
(percentages)

	Total value added	Value added in manufacturing
Top 5	30.1	35.7
Top 10	28.0	30.0
Top 20	25.9	27.5
Top 46	22.8	24.4
1 to 5	30.1	35.7
6 to 10	22.8	16.8
11 to 20	19.9	22.4
21 to 46	12.8	16.4
1 to 46	22.8	24.4
GDP	9.9	17.2

Source: SaKong, II. 1980a. "Economic Growth and Concentration of Economic Power." *Korea Development Review* (March).

grew at an annual rate of 30.1 percent, compared with 12.8 percent for the bottom 25. As a consequence, the top five's share in GDP and their share in manufacturing sector GDP during the period more than doubled, to reach 8.1 percent and 18.4 percent, respectively.

The trend of fast *chaebol* growth in terms of value-added flow continued into the 1980s. However, the trend started to taper off in the period between 1984 and 1985. These groups' proportion of total manufactured-output shipments also shows the trend leveling off somewhere around this period (see table A.22). This leveling off may very well be temporary and a reflection of cyclical fluctuations, such as lower prices for petrochemical products and a recession in the shipbuilding industry.

Without detailed study, it is difficult to determine. But one can hypothesize that the *chaebol* growth trend was checked by two important policy measures that were adopted in the 1980s. The government strengthened the system of credit supervision for large *chaebols* in 1984. The system of restricting bank credit to large *chaebols* was introduced in August 1974, primarily to help improve the financial structure of these firms and make the banking system sound, in addition to making access to banks by small and medium-sized firms easier (Jones and SaKong 1980). According to this measure, those *chaebols* with more than a given level of bank credits—5 billion won at the time—were required to get permission from their "prime bank" when they purchased real estate or invested in new lines of business. To secure permission, they were usually urged either to sell off unused land holdings or issue new equity shares.

This system of credit supervision for large *chaebols* was reinforced in February 1984 by freezing the total amount of bank credits available for the top five and setting ceilings for the top 30 based on total asset size.

With this new system, the top 30's share of bank credits as a whole (loans and loan guarantees) was lowered substantially. Their total share of credit was lowered from 23.3 percent in 1988 to 16.8 percent in 1991. Of course, large *chaebols* actually could borrow from other sources, such as nonbank financial intermediaries,[6] to offset the reduced borrowing from the banking sector. To the extent that the cost of borrowing from these sources was higher, the firms' growth must have been adversely affected.

Another important measure was introduced in 1986. This time, the existing monopoly regulation and fair trade law was amended specifically to deal with *chaebol* growth. The amendment was first to prevent cross-equity investments by *chaebols*, and second, to limit chaebols' total equity investment in their group firms.[7] The measure was intended to prevent *chaebols* from inflating their group firms' capital base and establishing new group firms without actually increasing their overall equity capital base.[8] Important motivations behind the cross-equity holding are, first, to increase the group owner's power of control, and second, to enhance the capacity for borrowing with the fictitiously improved debt-to-equity ratio of the companies involved. With this measure, the cross-equity investment of the top 30 *chaebols* was curtailed substantially, even though it still remains at a high level. The ratio of their cross-equity investment to net asset value was lowered to 32.1 percent in 1990 from 43.6 percent in 1987.

The issue the *chaebols* raise—namely, concentration of economic power—is still one of the most talked-about in Korea today. It is not only an issue of straightforward economic efficiency, however. It has distributional equity, social justice and fairness, and legitimacy aspects as well. A comprehensive discussion on the subject is presented in chapter 7.

One of the major factors in the fast growth of the big business groups in the 1970s was the government's HCI promotion drive. Of course, even in the absence of direct government intervention, it is expected that only large firms or big groups would become involved in such sectors, considering the technological economies of scale that are involved. It can be argued, however, that because of special government

---

6. The top 30 *chaebols'* share in overall nonbank financial intermediaries reached nearly 45 percent in 1991.

7. Companies of large *chaebols* were limited in their total equity investment in group companies to no more than 40 percent of their own net asset value, which is calculated by subtracting equity investment of other group companies from the company's equity. *Chaebols* to which this law applies are designated each year based on their total asset value. As of April 1990, there were 53 *chaebols* with 798 companies that were subject to the law.

8. Holding companies are legally prohibited in Korea; yet similar results have been obtained through cross-equity investments.

support, inducements, and accompanying subsidies, participation of large groups in the drive grew at a much faster rate than it would have otherwise.

Nearly 60 percent of Korean *chaebols'* value added was concentrated in the manufacturing sector, even though they were present in every level of industrial classification. Their value-added contributions were higher—greater than 30 percent—in manufacturing, construction, finance, insurance, and retail sectors (see tables A.23 and A.24). In addition, nearly 60 percent of the top 46 *chaebols'* value added was from the heavy and chemical industries. Their shares in nonmetallic minerals and machinery sectors were even higher—over 70 percent in 1978 (see tables A.25 and A.26).

Unexpectedly, however, their shares in the petrochemical sector and basic metal products sectors are relatively low. This is so because the government invested in these sectors primarily through public enterprises in the 1960s and 1970s. When the HCI promotion drive was launched, the government mostly expanded existing public enterprises in these sectors rather than relying on new private enterprises as in other sectors. Consequently, the relatively large presence of public enterprises explains the low *chaebol* share in those sectors.

Financial Sector Repression, Excessive Domestic Liquidity, Heightened Inflation

It is not an overstatement to say that Korea's government-led development was essentially built upon the government-controlled banking sector. Especially during the HCI promotion period, Korean banks acted more as rationing agents for the government than as genuine commercial banks. Consequently, ordinary monetary and credit policies could not be used when they were badly needed.

The Korean economy experienced super-high growth from 1976 to 1978. The average annual growth rate for the period was nearly 11 percent, thanks mostly to HCI-related investment activities, good export performances (the export growth rate for this period was 56 percent in 1976, 29 percent in 1977, and 27 percent in 1978) and the Middle East construction boom. Construction earnings abroad, which reached $1 billion in 1978, played a key role in reversing the chronic current account deficit in 1977, when a surplus of $12 millon was attained.

Even though the surplus was modest, this sudden reversal in the current account balance created a serious problem in controlling the money supply. Previously, when the nation's balance of payments was in deficit, the foreign sector automatically absorbed domestic liquidity. In the absence of ordinary money and credit management instruments, the rapidly improving balance of payments inevitably contributed to accelerating domestic liquidity growth. Consequently, for example, the narrowly defined money supply (or M1) increased 30.7 percent in 1976 and 40.7 percent in 1977 (table A.33), and the foreign sector was responsible for 40.5 percent and 43.2 percent of increases in the money supply, respectively.

In addition, the government sector itself contributed to the rapidly increasing money supply. In supporting the agricultural sector, for example, the government had to increase subsidies to farmers for rice and fertilizer production, resulting in even higher budget deficits. During 1975–78, budget deficits originating from these two sources accounted for almost 40 percent of the total money supply growth for the period. Credit was extended automatically to designated strategic industries and export-related activities, and as a result, it was virtually out of reach of ordinary monetary management.

The excessive supply of domestic liquidity also fueled inflationary psychology. This, together with rapidly increasing household income (including remittances from construction activities in the Middle East), and excessive corporate liquidity, led to increased speculative demands for real estate and consumer durables. From 1973 to 1978, average housing and residential land prices went up as much as 500 to 700 percent.

Under these circumstances, it is not surprising to see a substantial proportion of entrepreneurial energies absorbed in rent-seeking activities instead of concentrating on positive-sum activities. In the meantime, sales of consumer durables—items such as refrigerators, automobiles, and washing machines—quadrupled for the 1976–78 period. In addition, government reliance on frequent price controls to alleviate inflationary pressures did more harm than good by creating shortages and curtailing investment in those very sectors experiencing supply shortages.

Super-growth affected Korea's labor situation as well. The HCI drive and the construction boom in the Middle East created severe bottlenecks in the market for skilled workers, pushing skilled workers' wages up. This spilled over to affect the general wage level, which was rising faster than the rate of productivity. The wage cost increase was the primary cause of inflation in the second half of the 1970s (see appendix, table A.28). This hurt Korea's international competitiveness at a time when the world trading environment was deteriorating due to a world economic slowdown and rising protectionism. As a result, the growth rate of Korean exports slowed steadily between 1976 and 1979, and export volume actually declined in 1979.

A bottleneck in certain categories of skilled workers caused the wage gap to widen between skilled and unskilled workers, between different industries, and between workers with different education levels. The impact of the Middle East construction boom on the labor market in Korea was especially strong. At the end of 1980, there were approximately 132,000 workers in the Middle East, equivalent to 4.5 percent of all workers in Korea's manufacturing sector, or 15.7 percent of all construction workers in 1980.

Even though the growth-first development strategy and government intervention in resource allocation were in full swing, there were serious discussions during this time on reforms to help solve structural problems in the Korean economy and the way it was managed. These discussions emphasized private initiatives, less government intervention, more market mechanisms, fewer administrative controls in both domestic and external markets, and structural reforms in antitrust laws and in the financial sector as a whole. Most of these discussions were actually translated into policy action in the 1980s.

Stabilization Policies of the 1980s

As seen in the above discussions, the Korean economy in the latter part of the 1970s suffered from several difficult problems simultaneously. The nation's economic planning circle—the Economic Planning Board (EPB) and Korea Development Institute (KDI)—had considered alternative measures for stabilization since 1977 when the nation had its first current account surplus and the rapidly growing domestic liquidity was further fueling the already-overheated economy.

However, the growth-first strategy of the past was not easily abandoned by many economic policymakers, let alone the nation's president. A new consensus for stabilization was not easily obtained. Thanks to continuous efforts by stabilization advocates, however, President Park Chung Hee eventually ordered the cabinet to come up with an overall package for stabilizing the economy in March 1979.[9] This was an important turning point in reevaluating the nation's development strategy and adapting it appropriately for the future.

On 17 April 1979, a set of comprehensive stabilization measures were announced.[10] The measures included restrictive aggregate demand management through a tighter monetary and fiscal stance. Special attention was paid to improving the operation of policy loans and to necessary interest rate adjustments. The measures also recognized the necessity of making appropriate adjustments in the HCI promotion program, including readjusting the scale, contents, and timing of HCI investments. In addition, the measures facilitated the supply of daily necessities by

---

9. President Park did this only after sitting in a policy discussion forum with the deputy prime minister, the president's special assistant for economic affairs, the senior secretary for economic affairs, the chairman of the presidential council of economic and scientific affairs, the governor of the Bank of Korea, and the president of KDI. The deputy prime minister, newly appointed in December 1978, became a strong advocate of stabilization.

10. For a detailed discussion on the subject, see Nam (1991, 207–44) and Economic Planning Board (1982c).

deregulating commodity prices and improving the commodity distribution system.

Before these new measures had a chance to take full effect, they were hampered by severe internal and external shocks in 1979 and 1980, including rapid oil price increases, a sharp reduction in the nation's rice production due to cold weather, and political uncertainty following the assassination of President Park Chung Hee in October 1979.

These events aggravated domestic inflation and Korea's balance of payments[11] while deepening the already on-going recession. The new government established after President Park's death had to deal with this rather difficult economic situation. It not only had to deal with short-term stabilization problems, but structural adjustments necessary for future sustained growth.

The new government relied sometimes on moral suasion to achieve price stability while making efforts to revive the economy. For example, interest rates were lowered three times in the last two months of 1981 and again in early 1982. Knowing that it had reduced business costs, the government tried hard to persuade businesses, particularly big businesses, not to raise prices while increasing investment. Maintaining foreign exchange rates within a narrow range was also geared toward stabilization. In addition, the government strongly urged wage restraints.

One interesting aspect was the government's effort to build nationwide consensus on its stabilization policy. This was deemed important because all economic units had to share in the loss of real income caused by the deterioration of the terms of trade. This effort led to the establishment of the Economic Education Bureau in the Economic Planning Board. The nation's new president, Chun Doo Hwan, personally evaluated the education program and often sat in on economic education briefing sessions led by working-level government officials. This is further evidence of the government's strong determination to stabilize the economy.

With these efforts, Korea succeeded in quickly controlling inflation. Wholesale prices and consumer prices on a year-end basis went up as high as 42.3 percent and 38.2 percent, respectively, in 1980. These rates were brought down to 11.3 percent and 13.8 percent, respectively, in 1981. They were further decreased to 2.4 percent and 4.7 percent, respectively, in 1982. In terms of the GNP deflator, this was the first time Korean inflation had come down to the one-digit level since 1965, when the rate was 7.1 percent. Indeed, 1982 was an important turning point for the performance of the Korean economy.

---

11. The current account deficit in the balance of payments increased from about 2.3 percent of GNP in 1978 to nearly 9 percent of GNP in 1980.

Leadership Commitment to Price Stabilization

Price stability should be our foremost policy priority, to provide a stable living environment for the general public and to strengthen the international competitiveness of our industries. (presidential statement on the 1982 budget). —Chun Doo Hwan

Economic growth with price stability is only genuine growth for the people. (August 1986 press conference). —Chun Doo Hwan

One wonders in how many nations the chief executive is regularly briefed on price movements every 10 days. It was true in Korea in the early 1980s. The nation's statistics offices prepared price movements in terms of both the consumer and wholesale price indices every 10 days for internal use. These statistics in turn were reported to the president by his chief economic secretary. This, in itself, illustrates the unshakable priority placed on price stability. Price stability was emphasized for its positive effects on resource allocation, income distribution, the balance of payments, and for reducing external debt pressure by increasing international competitiveness.

Major stabilization policies included restrictive fiscal and monetary policies supported by an informal income policy. Salaries of civil servants and public enterprise employees were restrained to induce private-sector wage restraint (see appendix, table A.30). At the time, private-sector wage restraint was considered critical to achieving price stability and thereby improving Korea's international competitiveness.

According to a recent estimation, rapidly rising unit labor costs were primarily responsible for both accelerated inflation and Korea's declining international competitiveness in the late 1970s (Nam 1991). Rapidly rising unit labor costs contributed to approximately 60 percent of the rise in the level of actual prices from 1976 to 1980 (see appendix, table A.31). At the same time, Korea's international competitiveness was also drastically reduced, primarily due to the sharp increase in unit labor costs vis-à-vis competitors during the late 1970s. However, thanks primarily to the large depreciation of the Korean currency in the early 1980s, unit labor costs in dollars did not increase in the 1980s.

The Korean government tried to set an example through disciplined fiscal management. Zero-based budgeting was introduced in the early 1980s. At the same time, a strong campaign was waged promoting "burden sharing" in real income loss to absorb built-in inflationary pressures. For example, while the government restrained budgetary expansion, it urged wage earners to demand fewer wage increases, farmers to accept fewer subsidies, businesses to refrain from price hikes, and households to spend less and save more. Simultaneously, the long-run benefit of price stability was widely propagated through economic education.[12]

---

12. President Chun personally asked KDI to find the best ways to let the Korean people

At this point, it is interesting to consider Korea's exchange rate policy and interest adjustments. From the early 1980s, a floating exchange rate system was introduced in Korea. The system was based on the performance of a trade-weighted basket of currencies, as opposed to looking at only the US dollar. There was, however, some room for adjustment based on other policy considerations. From 1981 to 1983, the nominal exchange rate was gradually reduced by 5 to 6 percent a year. The Korean won had become overvalued by 2 to 9 percent until inflation was brought under control in 1983 (see appendix, table A.32). The main concern with respect to the exchange rate policy at the time was how to help reduce inflationary pressure, even though the policy was not an "exchange-rate-based anti-inflation policy" as such.

On the other hand, interest rates, which were substantially increased in early 1980, had been adjusted downward in a relatively short period beginning in 1981. The interest rate on one-year time deposits, which was raised to 24 percent from 18.6 percent in early 1980, was gradually adjusted downward to 8 percent by June 1982. Of course, because the asset market in Korea was still tightly controlled at the time, there was little possibility that a sudden inflow of capital would create a "Southern Cone Syndrome."[13] Therefore, the objective of lowering interest rates was primarily aimed at the alleviation of cost pressures, and thereby controlling inflation.

The persistent inflationary trend was broken in 1982 when inflation declined to a single digit for the first time in 20 years. However, knowing that a chronic built-in inflationary psychology was not completely eradicated, the government again took drastic and unpopular measures in 1983. It froze the budget, civil servant salaries, and rice purchase prices to help reduce the budgetary deficit. These measures not only had direct effects on inflation, but they also had important indirect effects on price stability by setting an example for the private sector and by showing the government's unwavering commitment to price stability.

The three freezes in the year before the national general election made the government's intention and commitment more credible. As the gov-

know that the world, not just Korea, was going through a difficult time and how other economies, particularly successful ones, overcame the difficulty. In cooperation with a major TV broadcasting company, the author, then vice president of KDI, produced and anchored a three-part documentary series covering the economies of the US, UK, France, Germany, and Japan. The program was nationally broadcast during prime time. In addition, at the request of President Chun, a shortened version of the program was shown to leaders from all segments of the Korean society who gathered at the New Year's Greeting of the President arranged by the Korean Chamber of Commerce.

13. By following an exchange-rate-based anti-inflation policy in the presence of a substantial interest-rate differential, countries experience a real appreciation of their currencies. Severe crisis in the export sector was the consequence in countries employing this strategy. This phenomenon has been called the Southern Cone Syndrome (Bruno 1988, 227).

ernment's stabilization package became stronger and more comprehensive, the prevailing inflationary psychology could be truly broken. These sharp and strong disinflationary measures undoubtedly contributed to shortening the period of restraint on credit and economic activities (Bruno 1988, 242).

Following these measures, the year 1983 was a good one for the Korean economy. Economic growth was robust at 12.6 percent while the rate of inflation was kept to a record low level, with CPI at 1.9 percent and WPI at minus 0.8 percent on a year-end to year-end basis. Due primarily to the US economic slowdown and rising protectionist barriers in industrialized nations, Korean exports started to become sluggish in late 1984, and economic growth slowed substantially in 1985.

At this time, confident that inflation had truly been arrested and with an optimistic outlook on the international economy, the Korean government took a number of stimulative measures for recovery in the first half of 1985.

They included a more relaxed monetary policy and a substantial depreciation of the won (about 6 percent) to encourage investment in export-related industries. A supplementary budget was introduced to stimulate demand and to allow more investments in the social overhead capital (SOC) sector as well. As previously discussed, price stability goals constrained exchange rate policy from the early 1980s until 1985, but with confidence in price stability, exchange rate policy was used to stimulate exports. It should also be pointed out that the G-5 Plaza Agreement of September 1985 and the ensuing fast depreciation of the Japanese yen boosted the Korean economy even further.

The economy started to experience unprecedented double-digit growth from 1986. More importantly, price stability was maintained, and the current account started to show a surplus for the first time in recent history.[14]

In short, Korea's growth-first strategy relied on an expansionary macroeconomic policy stance in the 1960s and 1970s. As a result, throughout the era of rapid growth, Korea was under persistent inflationary pressure. The situation was even further aggravated by the HCI promotion drive and the Middle East construction boom of the 1970s. Toward the end of the 1970s, Korea had no choice but to shift to an alternative strategy for the nation's sustained growth and development. It seemed as though the "growth at any costs" strategy first had to be changed to "stability at any costs," at least for some time to come.[15] Given the strong

---

14. As indicated earlier, Korea experienced a token surplus in 1977. It was, however, due primarily to remittances from construction activities in the Middle East.

15. During the 1960s and 1970s, as national resources were primarily allocated toward

commitment of leadership to economic development, any serious obstacles to economic progress were going to be addressed and overcome, even if it had to be through trial and error. President Park Chung Hee, who had been personally committed to HCI promotion, began the switch to a stabilization program, which was, in a way, the antithesis of the HCI drive. President Chun Doo Hwan also put priority on the nation's economic development and committed himself to short-term stabilization. With firm leadership commitment, the bureaucracy worked hard to achieve this goal.

Based on this background, one can draw a few important lessons from the Korean experience. First, persistent and chronic inflationary expectations can be broken only with credible commitment to stabilization on the part of political leadership. Drastic and painful adjustments may be necessary to establish credibility if an inflationary situation persists for a long period. As drastic measures are painful and politically difficult to sustain, it is critical and necessary for the government to make special efforts to gather a consensus and solicit cooperation. It is important to convince the public that in the long run they, too, will benefit from burden sharing.

Second, a disciplined fiscal policy stance is a critical prerequisite, not only from a purely macroeconomic adjustment perspective, but also for establishing credibility in policy direction. At the same time, it is necessary to actively solicit public cooperation in order for stabilization policies to work effectively. One distinguishing feature of the Korean experience is the successful reduction of fiscal deficits. In the early stages of the stabilization, one cannot do away with incomes policy of one sort or another. In this regard, again, the public sector has to lead. At the same time, special attention has to be paid to protecting the lowest income class, which is most vulnerable to painful adjustments.

Liberalizing the Korean Economy

Together with stabilization efforts, Koreans have introduced various liberalizing measures since the early 1980s. Some of the most important will be discussed here.

---

both directly and indirectly productive sectors—that is, manufacturing and social overhead capital sectors—to maximize growth, investments in housing got a low priority. Up until the middle of the 1970s, the ratio of housing investments to GNP remained below the 4 percent level. It was 4.8 percent for the 1970s. On the other hand, the housing investment during the 1980s had also to be put aside under the stabilization-first strategy. The same ratio for the 1980–87 period was 4.7 percent. Of course, the nation's precarious balance of payments status was another important reason for delaying housing investments throughout the period.

Domestic Economic Liberalization

Financial Sector Liberalization

As previously discussed in chapter 3, the essential part of Korea's government-led development strategy was geared toward government domination of the financial sector, or severe financial repression. Financial repression and the HCI promotion drive together were primarily responsible for serious sectoral imbalances and structural problems of the Korean economy in the latter part of the 1970s. The concentration of economic power was another undesirable side effect of these policies.

There were other tangible negative side effects of these repressive financial policies as well. The unorganized financial market started to play a more important role in channeling private saving into the business sector. Due primarily to negative real interest rates in the organized financial sector and rapid inflation, financial dualism resulted in Korea. The exact size of the informal financial market was hard to determine. In accordance with the August 3rd Emergency Measure of 1982, the reported size of this informal market at the time was equivalent to almost 90 percent of the total money supply, or 33 percent of deposit banks' loans outstanding.[16]

As discussed in the previous section on stabilization, the Korean policymakers decided to introduce economic liberalization measures in the early 1980s. Accordingly, financial sector liberalization efforts were initiated. First of all, government-held shares of all nationwide commercial banks were privatized between 1981 and 1983.[17] The Korean government still can influence these banks through other means, such as influencing the appointment of a bank's chief executive. However, privatization was the first necessary step to reduce government intervention and give banks more autonomy. Without ownership, governmental intervention in bank operations would become more visible to the public, and as a result, would also become more difficult.

At the same time, two new nationwide commercial banks were allowed to be established in 1982 and 1983. The temporary law limiting private shareholders' voting rights was repealed.[18] With regard to bank

---

16. One of the main objectives of the 1992 measure was to freeze all reported curb market loans. This measure was taken primarily to help reduce high corporate interest costs. More than 210,000 cases of curb market loans were reported, and the total amount was 350 billion Korean won.

17. The government held 20 to 30 percent of those banks before privatization.

18. According to the law, private shareholders' voting rights were limited to a maximum of 10 percent of total voting rights. In repealing the law, however, a new provision was introduced in the Banking Act to set a ceiling for any individual shareholder (and related persons) owning shares of a bank. The ceiling was set at 8 percent. This provision was introduced primarily to prevent large *chaebols* from controlling the banks.

operations, such internal managerial matters as personnel, budgeting and branching began to be relaxed, albeit gradually.

Most significantly, in 1982 the bank interest structure was made simple by unifying all bank loan rates into one, which included various preferential rates for policy loans. With this measure, remaining policy loans were reduced in kind and volume and were no longer granted at privileged rates.[19] As an effort to reduce policy loan share, export credits extended to large *chaebols* were gradually reduced and were eliminated altogether in early 1988.[20]

In addition, something akin to a prime rate system was introduced in 1984 for the first time in Korea. Banks were allowed within a limited range to charge different rates to their clients depending on their credit standing.[21]

Major interest rate deregulation, however, was not introduced in the early 1980s. One of the most important constraints was the overhang of non-performing assets (NPAs) for all commercial banks. Most NPAs were obviously inherited from the repressive financial policy regime of the past. In any case, major efforts were made to alleviate the NPA problem for commercial banks in the mid-1980s. (A detailed discussion of NPAs will follow.)

In December 1988 a major interest rate reform was introduced.[22] Many Korean policymakers were convinced that it was the most appropriate time for interest rate liberalization, though they faced strong opposing forces, arguing that interest rates would be pushed up too high.

There were various persuasive factors for the decision. First, the Korean economy had achieved macroeconomic stability, and inflationary expectations were low. Second, national savings exceeded domestic investment. As a result, interest differentials between regulated rates and free market rates were substantially narrowed. Third, commercial banks were relieved to a large extent of the heavy burden of NPAs. Fourth,

---

19. As previously indicated, the share of policy loans went over the 50 percent level in the late 1970s (table 3.7). The share declined in the early 1980s to reach less than 40 percent in the mid-1980s. Due primarily to increases in policy loans from the Korea Export-Import Bank and the Korea Development Bank and from foreign currency loans, the share went up again to nearly 48 percent during 1988–90 (Nam 1992).

20. To promote lagging exports, export credits for large firms were brought back again in 1992.

21. At the beginning, the allowed range was within 0.5 of a percentage point, but it was widened to 1.5 percentage points later as banks got used to the new system.

22. There are some who argue that the interest rate liberalization policy of 1988 was a failure. However, it is fair to say that the policy was never given a chance. The policy was not implemented as originally planned due to a cabinet reshuffle, which occurred on the very day the reform package was announced. Without the government's firm commitment (or with the possibility of reversal), no new policy can be implemented as originally intended.

with the appreciating Korean currency and growing current account surplus, there was strong pressure for capital inflow to check rising interest rates.

Korean commercial banks would have to face fierce competition from the outside soon. How could they win the competition without learning the competitive game beforehand? Also, it was urgent to foster foreign exchange markets before capital account transactions were liberalized. Without freely determining interest rates, how could it be done?

The December 1988 interest reform included the deregulation of the lending rates of most banks and nonbank intermediaries. However, deposit rates were not deregulated, with the minor exception of some long-term rates. The main concern in this regard was again the overhang of NPAs.[23]

With regard to nonbank financial intermediaries (NBFIs), both entry barriers and operational restrictions were eliminated or reduced further in the 1980s. Some important nonbank financial intermediaries, such as short-term investment and finance companies, and mutual savings and finance companies, were allowed to be established in 1972 to help induce unorganized financial activities in the organized financial sector. These institutions were less restricted by government regulations regarding their internal operations or by regulation of interest rates. In fact, these institutions were allowed to pay higher interest rates to their deposit holders from the beginning. As a result, these institutions and their deposit base have been growing much faster than bank deposits.

This differential in growth rates, however, has narrowed in recent years as the interest rate differential narrowed. In addition, the government's conscious policy to narrow the gap was another contributing factor. For example, commercial banks were allowed to introduce new financial instruments with higher interest rates than ordinary bank deposits to compete effectively against NBFIs. Nevertheless, the bank deposit share in 1991 was reduced to 34.1 percent from 65.4 percent in 1980 (see appendix, table A.33).

Competition among financial institutions has been continuously promoted by allowing different institutions to engage in similar asset markets and by lowering entry barriers. Certainly, the growing number of foreign financial institutions is becoming a significant factor in Korea's financial market development and a new competitive stimulant.[24]

---

23. Despite the low profitability of banks, they may enter into a severely competitive game of attracting deposits "to keep the bicycle rolling," with the government's efforts to help improve profitability.

24. As of the end of 1991, there were 70 foreign bank branches and 24 representative offices of foreign banks in Korea. Their share in loans, deposits, and total assets in 1991 was 6.5 percent, 1.1 percent, and 5.8 percent, respectively.

Change in Industrial Policy Stance

Along with financial sector liberalization efforts, the Korean government decided to change the nature of Korea's industrial policy in the early 1980s. Selective industrial promotion laws, oriented toward "picking winners" in such industries as electronics and petrochemicals, were replaced by a new law in 1986. This law made "rationalization" of declining industries and support for technological upgrades possible. It held as its basic principle that the government should get involved in industry in cases of obvious market failure.

Industries designated for rationalization could be supported by subsidized credit for upgrading capital equipment, and the law also allowed limiting new entries and facilitating mergers for a limited period, of two to three years. Because there still was room for ad hoc designation of industries for rationalization, the law established the Industrial Development Deliberation Council, which consists of experts from outside the government, to scrutinize the rationalization program.

Results of the program appear to be mixed. As Leipziger and Petri (1992) rightly point out, "The government has been more successful in disengaging itself from sunrise industries than from sunset industries." Obviously, the appropriate application of rationalization is the key to the success of Korea's future industrial policy.

Alleviating the Nonperforming Assets Problem

The government's direct intervention in financial resource allocation inevitably superseded the normal function of bankers. As previously indicated, one serious result has been the heavy NPA problem.[25]

There were several salient features of the NPAs of Korean commercial banks in addition to magnitude. First, to a large extent, the government was responsible for the problem. Obviously, the banks and firms involved were also partly responsible for further worsening the situation,

---

25. NPAs can be classified in different ways, according to the Bank Supervisory Board's criteria: "normal," "caution needed," "fixed," "collection doubtful," and "estimated loss." The board usually includes assets of the last two categories as NPAs. Generally speaking, they represent the part of total credits (loans, acceptances, and guarantees) that are extended to those firms with bad credit standing and that are not covered by secured collateral. The remaining part of total credits, which are covered by secured collateral, are extended to those same firms and are not treated as NPAs.

The proportion of NPAs for five nationwide banks for 1985 was as high as 7.6 percent. It was 7.2 percent in 1987, 6.3 percent in 1988, and down to 2.6 percent in 1990. Of course, if the NPAs include total credits extended to those firms with bad credit standing, regardless of collateral secured coverage, the proportion increases substantially. It was 10.9 percent in 1984, 8.4 percent in 1987, and 5.9 percent in 1989. NPAs defined this way represented only 0.65 percent for the 1973–75 period. See P.J. Kim (1990, IV-48) and Nam (1992, 33).

as the government became an implicit risk bearer. For example, if firms wanted more loans to finance even riskier projects, banks would finance these projects without serious evaluation. In addition, they would also become more lenient in monitoring indebted firms and would even extend additional loans just to finance interest payments. In other words, "to keep the bicycle running," chunks of new credit had to be extended to hopeless firms, siphoning off precious credit from areas where it was badly needed and where it would have served more productive purposes.

Second, with their weak profitability position, commercial banks themselves could not solve the problem.[26] In other words, banks could not absorb the cost of writing off the NPAs. At the same time, bankruptcies of industrywide indebted firms was to have serious international repercussions in addition to the various domestic problems, particularly because large-scale overseas construction firms and shipping industries were involved.

Third, the worsening profitability of commercial banks carried the additional risk of drastically reducing Korea's international borrowing capacity when commercial banks were still important borrowers for the nation. In addition, the commercial banks' NPA overhang became a critical obstacle to the necessary liberalization of the financial sector, as indicated earlier.

This problem compelled the government to take steps. The first important step was to help two targeted industries of the 1960s and 1970s: shipping and overseas construction industries. According to the Shipping Promotion Law of 1967 and the Overseas Construction Promotion Law of 1975, both industries were actively promoted with financial and tax privileges.

The overexpanded and overinvested shipping industry had to compete against foreign shipping firms with their governments' protectionist shields even in the 1970s. The industry was critically affected by the second oil shock and the ensuing world business slowdown. Cutthroat competition among Korean firms worsened the financial viability of most firms.

The overseas construction industry also was hard hit by the second oil shock. Most of Korea's overseas construction projects were in the Middle East. In fact, the industry prospered there in the early 1980s, backed by government support for securing foreign contracts to Korean construction firms.

Overseas construction contracts reached a peak of $13.7 billion in 1981, 85 percent of which was from the Middle East. There were 67 construc-

---

26. An indicator of commercial banks' profitability, their net profit to total assets, was down to 0.15 percent in 1985 from 0.79 in 1980. In 1989 it was improved to 0.66 (P.J. Kim 1990 IV-46).

tion firms working abroad then; there were only four such firms in 1973. Construction contracts have since dropped off. They were reduced to $6.5 billion in 1984 and $4.7 billion in 1985. Not only were contract amounts reduced, the terms of payment were worsened, and more claims occurred to seriously affect the profitability and cash flow of construction firms. In a desperate effort "to keep the bicycle running," many of these firms were awarded contracts at dumping prices, mostly taking projects away from other Korean firms—again, a moral hazard problem.

In 1984 and 1985 the government implemented "rationalization" programs for both industries.[27] The main purpose of the plans was to reduce the number of firms by facilitating mergers (and withdrawals from abroad in the case of construction) and to make remaining firms financially viable. In other words, these programs were intended primarily to restructure these industries to help solve the problem of NPAs for banks in the long run. In the short run, more financial support had to be provided to those merging and remaining firms. For example, to help relieve the financial burden of these firms, debt rescheduling, as well as additional loans, was provided.

To deal directly with the NPA overhang problem, the government in December 1985 took serious action to get the Tax Deduction and Exemption Control Law revised in the legislature. Under the revised law, banks were provided tax privileges of exemption and deduction when the collateral of NPAs was sold off. Tax privileges were also provided to those financially stricken firms and those firms taking over the failing firms, designated as "firms for rationalization" by the Industrial Policy Deliberation Council, the government's interministerial body.[28]

Yet in most cases, though tax privileges were certainly helpful, they were not enough to alleviate the basic problems of commercial banks associated with NPAs. Because of this, the Bank of Korea was allowed to provide special low-interest loans for industrial rationalization to those banks to make up for part of the losses.[29] This extra assistance was

---

27. For the shipping industry, the original program was introduced in May 1984, and additional measures were again taken in July 1985.

28. To receive tax privileges, an industry as a whole or individual firms had to be designated as an the industry or firm for rationalization by the council. Together with clauses for dealing with the NPA problem, the revised law also included clauses to provide tax privileges for firms in sunset industries to facilitate industrial restructuring. Sunset industries could receive privileges if approved by the council and could receive tax privileges when they merged with other firms in their industry or sold properties for starting new lines of business. Particular attention was paid to the small and medium-sized firms involved. Even in the case of large conglomerates, if they decided to specialize by selling firms of nonspecialty to reinvest in their lines of specialization, they could get the tax privilege as well.

29. The interest differential with ordinary rationalization funds provided from the central bank was 3 percent, that is, 3 percent special rationalization loan as compared to 6 percent

needed for the banks. Because most cases of failing firms involved negative net worth, firms taking over these firms had to receive part of an outstanding bank debt write-off, or fresh loans with low interest and a long grace period, or both.

With these measures, the NPAs, involving 78 companies altogether, were restructured between May 1986 and February 1988. They included 13 overseas construction firms and eight shipping firms, supplementing earlier rationalization efforts for these industries. The remaining 57 firms represented many industries, including general machinery, paper and pulp, iron and steel, and textiles.

Since these measures became a serious political issue in the ensuing period, let us briefly consider what alternatives were available for dealing with the NPA overhang problem. An irresponsible solution for the government would have been a hands-off policy, resulting in bankruptcy of the financially stricken firms and possibly the commercial banks involved, even though the government itself was primarily responsible for the problem. Such a solution was not feasible politically, socially, or economically. In addition to the widespread unemployment problem and nationwide financial crisis, international repercussions could have been too much to absorb.

Another possible alternative could have been to hold an open auction of troubled firms. This alternative was not adopted, as the Korean government argued at the time, because it would have exposed financial details of both the companies and banks involved to the public, possibly leading to financial and economic crisis.

The Korean government ended up opting for a "managed solution."[30] The government provided both fiscal and financial privileges to the banks involved and to firms that took over failing firms. The banks, in cooperation with the government, chose firms to take over failing companies. In most cases, these firms were from the same industry as the troubled companies and therefore had the expertise to handle the business. Of course, the prospective buyers had to have sound financial backgrounds.

In any case, the deal had to be negotiated between the bank and the prospective purchaser before approval for rationalization could be granted. The detailed contents of the deal and the amount of compensation in-

---

ordinary industrial rationalization loan. From 1985 to 1987, the central bank provided special industrial rationalization funds amounting to 1.7 trillion won. Total central bank credits to commercial banks including ordinary rationalization funds amounted to 3.0 trillion won for the period. This amount was nearly equivalent to the total increase in reserve money for the same period. The annual subsidy involved with the central bank credits for industrial rationalization was estimated to be 189 billion won, which was equivalent to 42 percent of the total annual loss of 451 billion caused by rationalization-related financial aids (Nam 1992, 31).

30. This term was suggested by Danny M. Leipziger of the World Bank.

volved were not made public, even after the take-over was completed. Political controversy over this policy lingered for some time afterward, as the firms taking over troubled companies were in most cases *chaebols*, which happened to meet the selection criteria mentioned above. To this extent, the solution adopted to handle NPAs further deepened the problem of economic power concentration.

It is beyond the scope of this study to evaluate the costs and benefits of these measures in detail. It is important, however, to reemphasize that the benefits derived from these measures include not only the benefits of avoiding widespread bankruptcies but also the social benefits gained from more efficient operations of banks and troubled firms and from reforms possible in the financial sector. At the same time, benefits of these measures also include the potential allocative efficiency gains from diverting financial resources away from wasteful uses.

One important lesson that can be drawn from this experience is that once the government becomes directly involved in resource allocation, it becomes responsible for bail-outs when things do not go right. The corollary to this is that the best way to avoid such situations is to let the market solve the problem as it arises. The government should implement appropriate macroeconomic policies and, if necessary, provide functional incentives without directly intervening at the private firm's decision-making level.

Public Enterprise Sector Reform

As previously discussed, the public enterprise sector in Korea has played an important role in both quantitative and qualitative terms. The sector's importance in terms of its contribution to GDP generation is well recognized. At the same time, its strategic importance for the economy as a whole can be seen from its high linkage with the rest of the economy. In the nation's overall fixed capital formation in particular, the sector's contribution has been substantial throughout the last three decades, as seen from table 4.4.

For these reasons, by making the public enterprise sector efficient, the economy as a whole can benefit much more than the sheer magnitude of the sector alone would indicate. According to one estimate, a 5 percent increase in the sector's efficiency could have contributed approximately 1.5 to 2 percent to 1980 GNP (SaKong and Song 1982).

Realizing the importance of the sector, the Korean government introduced major reforms for public enterprises in 1984. As economic circumstances changed, privatization has continued to be a government concern. In the meantime, however, remaining public enterprises have to be kept efficient.

As planned economies, including the former Soviet Union, began their rapid breakdown and major market-oriented reforms were introduced in these economies, the most popular subject of the reform became

Table 4.4 Public enterprise share of gross domestic fixed capital formation, 1963–86 (percentages)

	1963	1970	1975	1980	1981	1986
Public enterprises	31.7	18.9	33.2	27.6	30.7	15.6
Government	9.5	19.1	11.6	7.0	n.a	n.a.
Private enterprises	32.0	42.2	31.9	41.5	n.a.	n.a.
Individuals	26.8	19.8	23.2	23.9	n.a.	n.a.

n.a. = not available

Source: SaKong, Il. 1980b. "Macroeconomic Aspects of the Public Enterprise Sector," in Park Chong Kee (ed.), *Macroeconomic and Industrial Development in Korea.* Korea Development Institute; and data provided by Dae Hee Song at the KDI.

"privatization" of state enterprises. The subject is popular among many developing nations as well. Yet the subject of how to make the remaining public enterprises efficient is not as popular, despite the fact that all state enterprises cannot be privatized at once. Korea's public enterprise sector reform deserves a detailed discussion in this connection as well.

The essence of the reform was to give more autonomy to public enterprises and to introduce an *ex post* performance evaluation scheme with an accompanying incentive bonus system. More autonomy was provided by eliminating complicated governmental controls regarding budgeting, personnel, material purchase, and auditing.

Before getting into the contents of the reform in detail, it is worth presenting how the reform was initiated and implemented. This will illustrate how efficiently an economic reform program can be put together by coordinated efforts of the executive office, economic ministries, and national economic think-tanks when economic affairs are given national priority backed by leadership commitment.

The whole reform process began with the president, who gave attention to the issue of public enterprise profitability. President Chun was deeply impressed by the substantial profit the Korea Electricity Company, then a government-invested enterprise, made in 1980 after suffering from chronic financial losses. He apparently thought that the management and employees of the company ought to be encouraged by being awarded special bonuses. He hoped for beneficial spillover effects in other government-invested enterprises as well.

The then senior secretary to the president for economic affairs, Dr. Kim Jae Ik, contacted the Korea Development Institute (KDI), the government-funded economic policy think-tank, to work out a bonus program for government-invested enterprises along with a one-time bonus plan for the Korea Electricity Company. KDI counterproposed to the government that it would work out a more comprehensive public enterprise sector reform program, which would include an *ex post* performance evaluation and incentive bonus system. KDI persuaded the government that most public enterprises cannot be meaningfully evaluated based on market prices and convinced officials of the necessity of an overall reform. The government accepted the proposal, and a study team for public enterprise reform was formed. It consisted of KDI economists, public and business administration experts, public enterprise and bank staff, and Economic Planning Board officials.[31]

After intensive research, including several domestic and foreign case studies based on field trips and interviews, a proposal was completed, and it was directly reported to President Chun by the KDI economist who headed the team in September 1981, eight months after the study

---

31. At the time, the author of this book had been engaged in a multinational network research project on public enterprises at KDI. The author led the study team.

was first requested. With President Chun's support, major reforms were introduced by enacting new laws or amending existing ones, and finally the new system of public enterprise evaluation was set up in the government in 1984. It remains in operation.

Salient features of the reform are worth highlighting. The first important reform had to do with personnel management. Previously, middle-level managers in general lacked incentive to work hard, knowing that there were not many opportunities for advancement because higher management positions generally were filled from outside the enterprise.

Those outsiders may have been well-qualified and competent—in fact, they were in most cases—but their appointments usually hurt morale, both of the middle managers and the organization as a whole. The reform included a legal provision that made internal promotions possible for middle-level managers. The potential gains from this were expected to be substantial.

The second salient feature had to do with the *ex post* economic performance evaluation. *Ex ante* feasibility studies were done frequently for public projects. *Ex post* evaluations of public projects were also carried out in some cases. However, *ex post* evaluations were primarily concerned with managerial performances based on market prices and profits. By the very nature of public enterprises, they usually involved externalities of one sort or another and provided public goods, rather than merely maximizing profits based on market prices only. For this reason, it is important to take these factors into account in evaluating public enterprises.

The new system reflects these factors in its *ex post* economic efficiency evaluation, on which incentive bonuses are determined. In implementing the new system, it was critical to make public enterprise managers know how their performance was to be evaluated and, more specifically, what measurable criteria would be used in the evaluation. This in turn enabled public enterprise managers to set appropriate internal goals.

In sum, the main idea behind the public enterprise reform of 1984 was to make enterprises efficient in achieving given objectives by providing better incentives, a revised bonus system, promotion opportunities for middle-level managers, appropriate signals for managers to work for, and autonomy with *ex post* accountability by eliminating redundant and rigid administrative controls and regulations. Since the reforms were introduced in Korea, visible behavioral changes have taken place in public enterprise management circles; managers are very keen on achieving high evaluation scores each year because these scores affect their corporate bonus levels. Their personal reputations and tenures are also at stake, as the scores are widely publicized through the news media. This itself contributed toward improving managerial performance.

Korea's experience in reforming the public enterprise sector definitely deserves special scrutiny by many developing nations, as well as former planned economies, as they simultaneously seek to privatize and manage remaining public sector enterprises efficiently.

Deregulating Prices, Strengthening Monopoly Regulation

During the 1960s and 1970s, economic growth was such an overriding objective that the nation's macroeconomic policy was for the most part expansionary. And therefore, persistent inflation was always a problem. This inflationary problem was dealt with primarily through various administrative controls. The Temporary Law for Price Regulation of 1961 served as the basis for administrative controls during the 1960s.

According to this law, ceiling prices could be put on important items, and remaining products became subject to administrative guidance. A more concrete basis for controlling prices was provided by enactment of the Price Stabilization Act of 1973. Then in 1976, the Price Stabilization and Fair Trade Act was introduced to deal with monopolistic practices as well as to monitor price hikes of monopolistic items without prior government permission. This was the main vehicle by which administrative price controls were implemented.

This approach to price control undoubtedly created a dualistic price system and substantially distorted the distribution system. As symptoms of administratively suppressed inflation became more serious in the latter part of the 1970s, the necessity for decontrol became more widely recognized.

A new approach was taken in 1981 when, in addition to tighter fiscal and monetary policies, the Monopoly Regulation and Fair Trade Act was introduced to deal with monopolistic market structure and conduct in a more fundamental way and to promote fair competition. The main objective of the law was to move away from direct intervention, instead promoting competition and dealing with monopolistic market practices on a fair trade and antimonopoly basis. At the same time, import liberalization and tariff reduction programs were also started in an effort to promote a more competitive environment.

Korea's Industrial Relations System

Korea in recent years has been witnessing many cases of violent labor disputes and wild work stoppages. At the same time, union membership has been growing at a fast rate, unlike in some industrially developed nations today. In this regard, Korea's industrial relations system deserves special attention.

The number of disputes increased from 276 cases in 1986 to 3,749 cases in 1987. During the two months following the announcement of the June 29 Democratization Pledge[32], nearly 2,600 disputes were started, which

---

32. This announcement was made by then ruling party leader Roh Tae Woo in June 1987

is more than the total number of disputes the nation had during the previous quarter of a century. The number has been decreasing since then. It was down to 1,873 cases in 1988, 1,616 cases in 1989, 322 cases in 1990, and 234 cases in 1991.

When the Korean economy started to develop in the early 1960s, there was an unlimited pool of labor in rural areas. While the government intervened heavily in the capital market, for the most part it left the labor market to market forces. In fact, Korea is one of the few countries that did not have a minimum wage law during the early stages of development. Even though labor union movements and collective bargaining were allowed in the 1960s, the government took steps to ensure that industrial relations would not get out of hand through the selection of cooperative union leadership.

The situation changed, however, in the early 1970s, when abundant labor began to disappear and bottlenecks started to appear in certain job categories.[33] National security became the prime concern.[34] Workers' rights to bargain and strike were effectively suspended in 1971. Since then, labor unions and labor movements in general have been under the strict supervision of the government.

As previously indicated, despite limited union autonomy and the concomitant membership discontent, the statutory basic rights of workers were respected until 1971. Throughout the 1970s, however, the system of industrial relations in Korea was suppressed. One close observer of the Korean industrial relationship for many years characterized the nature of collective-bargaining relationships allowed to develop in Korea in the 1970s as "intensive government control over both collective-bargaining activities and internal union affairs," "cozy relationships between business and some union leaders," and "a union-prone work force that is frustrated by the continuing impotency of its unions and their legally constrained ability truly to present worker interest" (Bognanno 1987, 116).

---

and endorsed by then President Chun Doo Hwan on 1 July 1987. This pledge was to democratize the nation's political system further through a new constitution, among other things.

33. From 1967 to 1971, the average real wage rate for the manufacturing sector went up nearly 20 percent per year, if nominal wage for the sector is deflated by the GNP deflator. Both the shrinking pool of redundant workers and apparent bottlenecks in certain skill categories of workers rapidly increased the wage rate.

34. The Korean labor movement has existed since the Japanese colonial days. However, it was involved with the nation's independence movements, and it became involved in the ideological conflicts during the early days of President Syngman Rhee's administration. Under the leadership of President Park, basic labor rights were restricted to prevent labor unions, which had a tradition of political orientation, from undermining security or political stability. Undoubtedly, the changing labor market was also a factor affecting the decision.

Consequently, distrust has developed between union leaders and rank-and-file members. This left room for nonunion organizations, even subversive ones, to penetrate the work place. Another natural consequence was the inability to deal adequately with industrial relations issues facing labor and management bilaterally. Representatives from labor and management tended to treat bargaining forums as "nothing more than an opportunity to state 'take it or leave it' positions . . . it is the exception rather than the rule to find occasions when labor and management sit down to exchange views and information and make concessions to one another with an eye towards reaching a joint agreement" (Bognanno 1987, 116). Under the then-existing system of industrial relations, this meant more governmental intervention over labor-management disputes of any nature.

This development of the nation's industrial relations came at a time when the size of the pool of industrial workers who were potential union members grew significantly. The number of nonfarm employment or potential union members increased from 2.5 million in 1971 to 4.6 million in 1979. Furthermore, the union membership penetration ratio increased from 19.7 percent in 1971 to 23.6 percent in 1979.[35] This trend toward unionization without any forum for union's proper collective bargaining or any possibility for collective action laid groundwork for future problems.

Toward the end of the 1970s and even before the assassination of President Park, many workers, mostly from labor-intensive sectors, joined student-led, antigovernment demonstrations demanding basic labor rights and the resignation of union leaders. During the time of national confusion and political uncertainty following the assassination of President Park, the "fragility and immaturity" of the Korean system of industrial relations existing at the time inevitably led to a burst of labor disputes and strikes. According to the official count, there were 848 strikes between January and April 1980.[36] There were 105 labor disputes reported officially in 1979.

The new government that came into being in 1980 reevaluated the system of industrial relations and introduced a new system by amending

---

35. This is due primarily to the "closed-shop" or "union-shop" clauses of union membership allowed in Korea.

36. See Bognanno (1987, 161). According to the official source, there were only 407 cases of labor disputes in 1980. The discrepancy is due primarily to the fact that under existing laws, many of those disputes were illegal in nature, and if they were somehow solved bilaterally, they were not included in the official statistics. Another thing to be mentioned in this connection is that Korea experienced sudden bursts of labor disputes during times of political turmoil and change. For example, after the nation's independence in 1945 and during the student revolution of April 1960, the number of disputes jumped from fewer than 50 cases in 1959 to almost 300 cases in 1960.

existing labor laws. The amendments included the barring of "third parties" other than local unions from playing any role in organizing and bargaining and also from participating in any acts of dispute such as strikes. This aspect of the amendments reflects the government's reaction to the radicalization of the labor movement in many cases and the penetration of nonunion organizations. At the same time, these amendments made compulsory governmental arbitration easier. Union-shop clauses were abolished, and the minimum number of workers needed to organize a union was also increased. These changes together undoubtedly contributed to a decline in union penetration until 1987.

The new government liberalized many other areas of the Korean economy from its inception in 1980. As discussed above, however, these bold reform initiatives were not applied to the system of labor-management relations or industrial relations for a number of reasons. First of all, industrial relations were never fully integrated into macroeconomic policies and intermediate-term plans except in keeping wages at a reasonable level. Consequently, the Ministry of Labor was expected primarily to prevent unreasonable wage hikes and to reduce labor conflicts rather than to develop productive industrial relations and human resources in the long term. From the point of view of economic policymakers, these functions were quite acceptable at a time when a foremost economic priority was price stabilization.

The attitude of the government was exemplified in the Office of the President's organization. Labor affairs and affairs concerning the Ministry of Labor were under the supervision of the senior secretary to the president for administrative and political affairs, not to the senior secretary for economic affairs. It cannot be denied that there was a tendency to consider labor disputes and conflicts to be unfortunate accidents or isolated incidents.

National security concern was another explanation. By restricting labor movements, the government wanted to prevent "subversive" elements of political dissident groups from penetrating labor unions.

The suppressed system of industrial relations was more or less maintained until 29 June 1987 when the Democratization Pledge was announced. As previously mentioned, immediately after the announcement was made, Korea experienced an unprecedented explosion of labor disputes. Nearly 70 percent of all manufacturing firms with 10 or more employees experienced labor disputes of one kind or another in the second half of 1987. Even though labor strikes were illegal under existing laws, the government did not attempt to enforce these highly unpopular laws. As a consequence, employers themselves had to deal with workers and unions. As previously suggested, due primarily to the state of the then-existing system of industrial relations, both sides were ill-prepared to deal with the changed environment. Under the relevant laws governing the system, the government acted as mediator and arbitrator, and in many cases the government put forward compromises on both sides. Experienced private mediators or arbitrators did not exist.

The government started to amend existing labor laws in 1987, albeit hastily. Detailed recommendations for further improvements regarding these laws are well beyond the scope of this study. It is, however, more than clear that the social cost of not having an adequate industrial relations system and industrial peace is so high that adequate social investments should be made in this regard, such as training managerial personnel to handle labor affairs and union leaders to engage in collective bargaining. Both sides should learn that collective bargaining involves give and take if issues are to be reconciled for mutual benefit. Both sides should learn how to respect the rules of the game.

International Market Opening and External Liberalization

Out of necessity, Korea has been taking a gradual approach to opening markets and to external liberalization. In recent years, however, and particularly since 1983, the process has been more rapid, as the government has accelerated the liberalization of imports, foreign direct investment, current and capital account transactions, and the reduction of tariffs.

Korea joined the General Agreement on Tariffs and Trade (GATT) in 1967 and shifted to a new system of import permits. Under this new system, only import-limited or prohibited items and the restrictions on them were announced in advance; all other goods could automatically be imported. (Since 1978, the prohibited items have been totally eliminated.) This system was designed gradually to eliminate restricted import items from the list. However, the system did not much improve the import liberalization ratio (the number of goods that could be freely imported compared to the total number of goods) until the mid-1970s. It was 58.5 percent in 1967, but it was reduced to 49.1 percent in 1975.

More active import liberalization was initiated in the second half of 1977 when the balance of payments improved substantially and supply bottlenecks of certain critical items aggravated inflation. As a result, the import liberalization ratio was increased to 64.9 percent in 1978 from 52.7 percent the previous year (table 4.5). At the same time, it was not officially announced, but the government had an intermediate-term import liberalization plan. It set 1984 as the terminal year when most manufacturing products were to be liberalized. However, this ambitious plan had to be suspended due to the second oil shock and other unfavorable factors occurring in late 1979.

Liberalization was resumed in 1981 as the economy recovered from these unexpected shocks. This is significant, considering that Korea recorded a current account deficit of over $5 billion that year. The decision

Table 4.5   Import liberalization, 1977–91

Year	All Items[a]	Items with automatic approval	Automatically approved items as a share of all items
1977	1,312	691	52.7
1978	1,097	712	64.9
1979	1,010	683	67.6
1980	1,020	693	68.6
1981	7,465	5,576	74.7
1982	7,560	5,791	76.6
1983	7,560	6,078	80.4
1984	7,915	6,712	84.8
1985	7,915	6,945	87.7
1986	7,915	7,245	91.5
1987	7,911	7,408	93.6
1988	10,241	9,694	94.7
1989	10,241	9,776	95.5
1990	10,274	9,898	96.3
1991	10,274	9,991	97.2

a. 1977–80 CCCN four-digit classification, 1981–87 eight-digit classification, and since 1988 based on the harmonized system.

Source: Ministry of Trade and Industry, Korea.

to resume liberalization was based on the belief that to increase international competitiveness, import liberalization was inevitable.[37] In other words, the primary objective of import liberalization at the time was to make the domestic economy more efficient and competitive. To minimize the impact of sudden import liberalization, a preannounced schedule and an import surveillance system were implemented.

The idea of a preannounced schedule was introduced in the earlier liberalization period of the late 1970s. However, the original preannounced schedule duration was to be quite short—six months to one year. The 1979 schedule had allowed a longer period for appropriate adjustments, but this timetable was not implemented, as explained earlier.

A comprehensive competitiveness study (with the help of various research institutes and independent researchers) was conducted regarding import-limited items, and based on the results of the study, the duration of the preannounced schedule was set at one to five years. This gave import-competing firms time to adjust, either to improve their competitiveness or move into new businesses. In other words, the preannounced schedule helped to reduce uncertainty for the firms involved

---

37. Korea's voluntary import liberalization and tariff reduction program raises an important policy question for multilateral trade negotiations of the GATT system. If negotiators fail to appreciate this voluntary effort, it will be politically difficult for the Korean government to initiate such a program in the future.

and increased the credibility of government policy as liberalization proceeded.

Complying with a self-announced schedule increases international credibility and can be used to persuade trading partners to accept a gradual approach to liberalization. The gradual approach makes structural adjustment easier to deal with. For example, resources—physical, financial, or human—can be transferred to new industrial sectors more smoothly. For this reason, the adverse impacts of sudden import liberalization can be avoided (Kim 1988). At the same time, trading partners were also notified so that they could prepare themselves by finding outlets in Korea.

The 1984–86 import liberalization schedule was announced in May 1984. In November 1985 the schedule was extended to cover the period of 1986–89.

It should be mentioned that this schedule did reflect bilateral trade disputes, particularly with the United States. At the same time, monopolistic and oligopolistic products were to be liberalized as soon as possible. On the other hand, small and medium-sized company products were allowed a slower pace of liberalization. Most agricultural items were not included in the schedule.

From 1986, when the nation started to generate a balance of payments surplus, the pace of import liberalization was further accelerated (Noland 1990, 44–46). The Korean government, which was under severe external pressure from its major trading partners and was having difficulty in managing domestic liquidity, decided to liberalize completely all manufactured imports. At the same time, it decided to eliminate, through serious interministerial discussions, the import surveillance system, which was introduced in 1977 to monitor imports of newly liberalized items for special treatment. The system was abolished in 1989. Special laws that restricted imports of even liberalized items were eliminated.[38]

Along with import liberalization, a tariff reduction program was also introduced in Korea based on the preannounced schedule. In early 1983 a five-year tariff reduction program announced. In 1988 another five-year tariff reduction schedule was initiated with the objective of making Korean tariff protection comparable to that prevailing in the Organization for Economic Cooperation and Development countries by 1992.

Regulations on foreign exchange transactions were also gradually introduced, accelerating from 1986, when the nation recorded a balance of payments surplus. Korea formally announced the acceptance of full

---

38. Many rightly argued that because of these special laws, the usual import liberalization ratio overstates the degree of import liberalization in Korea. See, for example, Leudde-Neurath, (1984). Over 800 items restricted by 17 different special laws were liberalized as these laws were eliminated between 1987 and 1988.

obligations of International Monetary Fund Article VIII in November 1988. At the same time, it also decided to give up privileges of quantitative import restrictions justified under the GATT Article XVIII Section B, effective as of January 1990.[39]

The government also continuously liberalized markets for technology and foreign direct investment in the 1980s. In addition, market liberalization for services was introduced, and intellectual property rights were to be protected according to international conventions. Moreover, a five-year capital-market liberalization schedule was announced in 1988. Considering the market's infant stage of development, the government made a detailed timetable so the market could get ready for international exposure. This positive approach to market openings has many known advantages. One has to do with trade negotiation. With such a sequenced overall program, it is much easier to persuade the other side, even when some aspects of the program are not fully satisfactory to them.

Summary and Lessons

During most of the rapid growth period of the 1960s and the early 1970s, Korea maintained an adequate balance between the demand for and the supply of available resources. The situation changed substantially in the early 1970s when the ambitious HCI promotion drive was launched. The earlier industry-neutral incentives provided for exports in general were replaced by an incentive system of industry-specific or sometimes firm-specific industrial incentives for promoting HCIs. As a result, the government channeled a large proportion of the nation's financial resources into targeted strategic sectors. In the process, well-established big businesses with proven track records were always treated favorably, receiving subsidized financial resources and fiscal subsidies. The lopsided allocation of subsidies and other accompanying privileges in those targeted sectors naturally resulted in sectoral imbalances between HCIs and light manufacturing sectors and between big firms as opposed to small and medium-sized firms.

Investments related to the HCI drive and housing construction activities, together with the Middle East construction boom, put tremendous pressure on the real sector of the economy. The real wage increase started to outstrip productivity gains. As Korea's unit labor costs increased nearly 20 percent per year from 1976 to 1978, Korea's export competitiveness eroded rapidly. Export volume growth turned negative in 1979 for the first time in recent Korean history.

---

39. Existing restrictions are supposed to be phased out in two stages by January 1997, with some exceptions.

The rapidly increasing domestic liquidity, partly the result of a sudden improvement of the nation's balance of payments, fueled inflationary expectations even further. The nation's resource allocation was further worsened by efforts to suppress inflationary pressure administratively.

On top of these endogenous structural problems, the Korean economy was hit by a number of serious exogenous shocks, including the world's second oil shock of 1979, a disastrous Korean rice harvest, and political uncertainty following the death of President Park in October 1979. With all these factors, the Korean economy in 1980 had to suffer a severe setback. GNP growth became negative for the first time since the 1950s, the inflation rate soared to reach nearly 40 percent, and the current account deficit recorded $5.3 billion.

In order to cope with this situation, the government coming into the 1980s started to implement a wide range of economic reforms and necessary structural adjustments. The nation's policy priority was put on economic stabilization and economic liberalization measures for both the internal and external sectors. These changes illustrate Korea's pragmatic, nonideological, and flexible response to emerging economic problems, given a strong leadership commitment to the nation's economic development.

The government made a strenuous effort to break persistent and chronic inflationary expectations with credible commitment to stabilization on the part of the leadership. To establish credibility, drastic and painful adjustments were made. Special efforts were made to build a national consensus among all segments of the Korean society, because the loss of real income caused by the deterioration in the terms of trade had to be shared by all.

Financial repression, together with the HCI promotion drive, were primarily responsible for serious sectoral imbalances, which appeared in the latter part of the 1970s. Financial sector liberalization efforts were an important part of the nation's economic reform. Until the late 1980s, however, major interest rate liberalization measures were not taken, due primarily to the magnitude of commercial banks' non-performing assets (NPAs). Important policy measures were introduced in the mid-1980s to alleviate the overhang problem of NPAs. This effort should be viewed as a prerequisite for financial sector liberalization.

Coming into the 1980s, the orientation of Korea's industrial policy stance shifted away from the "picking winners." Instead, a more functionally oriented policy stance was adopted.

An important reform package was introduced in the public enterprise sector in the early 1980s. Along with an ongoing privatization program, the reform was aimed at making remaining public enterprises efficient by providing better incentives and appropriate signals to managers.

In 1981 the Monopoly Regulation and Fair Trade Act was introduced to deal with the monopolistic market structure and conduct and to promote fair competition. The previously existing law regarding price stabilization and fair trade was the main vehicle by which administrative price controls were implemented.

Unfortunately, no bold reform was initiated in the nation's system of labor-management relations in the early 1980s. The suppressed system of industrial relations remained intact until June 1987, when a major political reform was announced. Many violent labor disputes and wild work stoppages occurred immediately after the announcement. Both employers and workers were ill-prepared to deal with each other, because the government had acted as mediator and arbitrator until then. Korea paid a high price for this negligence. The government started to amend existing labor laws, albeit hastily.

One can draw valuable lessons from the Korean experience. Follower nations might learn from the HCI promotion drive, for instance. First, the Korean HCI promotion was implemented within the context of a broadly defined, outward-looking development strategy. Therefore, from the very beginning, it was different from import-substitution efforts made under an inward-looking strategy. Operating under an outward-looking development strategy, structural problems that were causing economic inefficiencies were bound to surface much faster than they would have under an inward-looking policy regime. This is why Korea's structural problems with the HCI promotion drive were brought to people's attention quickly, leading to an earlier reevaluation of the policy.

Second, late developers can benefit from previous development experience provided they choose the right model. More importantly, however, the nature of industrial policy should reflect the characteristics of each country and the economic environment. At the same time, the choice of policy instruments or the nature of industrial policy should be adapted appropriately to changes in the environment and to different stages of development.

Korea's stabilization and liberalization experience also is instructive. First of all, the Korean experience seems to reconfirm many earlier findings with regard to stabilization and liberalization policies. Korea in the 1980s has been successful on both fronts. One can argue that a sharp and rapid approach to reducing inflation is preferable to a gradual approach. This is so primarily because it increases the credibility of government's commitment to bring inflation under control, which in turn helps to cut inflationary expectations. A prolonged contractionary policy, resulting in high unemployment and business sluggishness, is difficult politically and cannot be sustained for long.

Another lesson to be learned from the Korean experience is that the government budget deficit must be cured first. This helps the stabilization effort by giving it credibility, by inducing cooperation in accepting reduced real income of all economic units, and by directly contributing to aggregate demand management.

With regard to external liberalization, the Korean experience confirms that it is important to have the right sequence for market openings because of the differing speeds at which asset and product markets can adjust.

Finally, it is also advisable to preannounce liberalization measures and their schedules in order to minimize the potentially adverse effects resulting from their implementation. This is particularly true for import liberalization, where sudden market openings can cause shocks to the industries concerned and to the economy as a whole.

5

International Factors in Recent Korean Development

Korea has long been heavily overpopulated, resource-poor, short of arable land, and limited in market size. Faced with these constraints, the new political leadership that emerged in the early 1960s strongly committed itself to economic development and astutely adopted an outward-oriented development strategy. Its primary objective was to find an external means of escaping the vicious circle of underdevelopment.

President Syngman Rhee had to devote most of his energy to solidifying the new nation and was primarily concerned with maintaining current consumption levels by obtaining the maximum amount of foreign aid. Subsequent leadership, under President Park Chung Hee, was highly growth-oriented, and it encouraged attracting foreign capital, primarily through external borrowing, to finance export industries and build the necessary social infrastructure.

This export-oriented strategy was successful beyond expectations. Korea today has become one of the major trading nations in the world. Until recently, Korea was ranked the fourth highest indebted nation among developing nations, yet it has managed its foreign debt well and is expected to become a net creditor in the near future.

This chapter discusses major international factors in Korea's economic development, including foreign aid and trade. Foreign direct investment (FDI) and imported technology are also discussed. Because multilateral institutions and important trading partners affected the course of Korea's development in significant ways, a brief discussion of the role of the World Bank and the International Monetary Fund (IMF) and of the US-Korea bilateral trade relationship is included in this chapter.

The Role of Foreign Aid

> *It is not considered feasible to make South Korea self-sustaining.*
> *If the United States elects to remain in South Korea, support of*
> *that area should be on a relief basis.* —Albert C. Wedemeyer[1]

The role of foreign aid is important in Korea's earlier economic development, and it deserves a detailed discussion.[2] Foreign aid was the major source of financing the nation's balance of payments deficits throughout the 1950s and continued through the early 1960s. In particular, from the nation's liberation in 1945 until the late 1950s, foreign aid was virtually the sole source of foreign capital. As can be seen from table 5.1, more than 70 percent of imports were financed by foreign aid during the reconstruction period of 1953–60, indicating how heavily dependent the Korean economy was on foreign aid.

Korea received more than 70 percent of its foreign aid between 1945 and 1960. The United States was the major source of this aid, except for a small fraction that came from the United Nations. From the late 1950s, foreign aid began to decline and was replaced by commercial borrowing. Let us first briefly review the chronological development of foreign aid in Korea and then consider its role in Korea's development.

As was discussed earlier, the period of 1945–53 was traumatic for Korea, considering the nation's liberation and partition in 1945, the brief US military rule during 1945–48, the new government established in 1948, and the devastating war of 1950–53. As a result of its close involvement, the United States was primarily responsible for the flow of foreign aid to Korea following the nation's liberation.

In fact, the first foreign aid Korea received was provided by the US Army Military Government in Korea under the assistance program known as the Government Appropriations for Relief in Occupied Areas (GARIOA). GARIOA aid had three main objectives: to prevent starvation and disease, to increase agricultural output, and to provide essential consumer goods. Consequently, over 90 percent of GARIOA aid consisted of imports of commodities in finished form. Food stuffs, agricultural supplies including chemical fertilizer, and petroleum and fuel products together accounted for more than 50 percent of GARIOA imports throughout the period. On the other hand, the proportion of investment goods imported for "economic rehabilitation" was rather low.

Considering the dire economic situation, these aid objectives seemed reasonable enough for the period. In fact, thanks to foreign aid, widespread starvation, severe malnutrition, and disease were prevented.

---

1. Quoted in US Senate (1947, 6).

2. This section draws heavily from excellent earlier studies on the subject (Krueger 1979; Koh 1975; Suh 1977).

However, the nation's industrial production capacity was not much enhanced, and inflation posed a serious problem.

The US aid program was heavily criticized in both Korea and the United States as a stop-gap approach that lacked clear-cut policy direction. Some US aid administrators argued that more aid efforts and resources should be directed toward "capital development that would result in decreasing Korea's need for extraordinary outside assistance" (McCune 1950, 130).

The United States did consider a more positive aid program to make the new republic less dependent on foreign aid in the long run, as military rule in Korea began to wind down. The Economic Cooperation Administration (ECA), which took over the US aid program in Korea in 1949, had an initial objective of administering recovery rather than relief programs with an emphasis on capital development (Brown and Opie 1953, 374).

The ECA submitted a three-year Korean recovery program to the US Congress. The main purposes of the program were, first, "to maintain in South Korea a sufficient quantity of consumer goods and raw materials to prevent excessive hardship, disease and social unrest," and second, "to lay durable foundations for the Korean economy, which, with a rapidly diminishing level of subsidy from the U.S., could become a solvent trading partner in the world economy" (US Department of State and the Economic Cooperation Administration 1950, 4).

The proposed program put emphasis on three interrelated areas of capital investment for the purpose of making South Korea an exporter of agricultural products. The three areas were the development of coal resources, the construction of thermal power generating facilities, and the expansion of fertilizer production capacities.

This recovery program never materialized due to US congressional opposition. Some in Congress at the time argued that the United States would be backing another "loser" in providing continued aid to Korea (Cho 1967, 239–44). The minority opinion accompanying the aborted Korean aid bill even stated that "there is every reason to believe that the lending of economic assistance at this time will only enhance the price to be taken by force of arms and internal intrigue" (Cho 1967, 241–42). This kind of pessimistic view regarding Korea's economic future was not confined to US political circles. Even leading development economists at the time considered Korea a "basket case."

Consequently, the ECA ended up carrying out an aid program that was similar to the earlier GARIOA aid in that a substantial proportion of funds were allocated for agricultural supply imports, particularly chemical fertilizer, raw materials, and petroleum products, while imports for investment purposes were not a major factor. If the aid agency had any intentions of supporting rehabilitation, they had to be put aside at the outbreak of the Korean War in June 1950.

The ECA mission in Korea was closed in April 1951, and its functions were transferred to the United Nations Korea Reconstruction Agency (UNKRA) in accordance with the UN General Assembly resolution of December 1950. UNKRA was originally established to help reconstruct the Korean economy as a foundation for "the political unification and independence of the country." The UNKRA program included the provision of major rehabilitation supplies, including transportation and other social overhead capital. As the Korean War intensified, UNKRA too had to concentrate on immediate relief efforts. The funds for UNKRA were to be provided by UN member nations, and the United States pledged to provide 60 percent of the total.

Under the auspices of the United Nations, the US Army initiated its own civil relief program, called Civil Relief in Korea (CRIK), immediately after the Korean War began. CRIK provided goods for civil relief amounting to $457 million, of which $420 million, or 92 percent of the total, was contributed by US CRIK aid. The aid was provided primarily to prevent civilian disease, starvation, and unrest in the noncombat rear areas.

In terms of its magnitude, CRIK aid was much more important than the aid provided by UNKRA (see appendix, table A.34). Consequently, throughout the war, CRIK aid was the primary source of foreign exchange for imports. Exports remained negligible, at 2 percent of GNP as compared with 13 percent for imports in 1953.

Shortly after the cease-fire agreement was reached in July 1953, the United States decided to administer aid to Korea bilaterally for a better-coordinated program. Accordingly, after the war, Korea received foreign aid primarily through bilateral US-Korea channels. These included the Foreign Operations Administration (FOA) in 1953, the International Cooperation Administration (ICA) in 1955, and the Agency for International Development (AID) in 1961.

The commodity composition of imports financed during this period did not change much, in the sense that consumption goods continued to dominate. From 1953 to 1960, only a little over 10 percent of the nation's imports could be classified as investment goods (Krueger 1979, 72).

Clearly, foreign aid was the most important source of vital commodity imports for Korea during this period, be they consumer or investment goods. It is easy to see that foreign aid greatly contributed to closing the nation's savings and foreign-exchange gaps. Thanks to the inflow of foreign aid, the living standard of the Korean people was maintained at a higher level than the Korean economy alone could have supported, and inflationary pressures were also substantially eased.

As pointed out earlier, however, foreign aid primarily financed the import of finished consumer goods. For this reason, the aid authorities were accused of taking a shortsighted approach rather than initiating a comprehensive program leading eventually to development. At the same time, the Korean government was often blamed for its short-term economic policy stance. To a large extent, it is true that the Korean government was more interested in the immediate objective of maintaining people's livelihoods by maximizing the inflow of foreign aid. It seemed less concerned with long-term growth and development objectives or strategies to close the nation's savings and foreign-exchange gaps.

One should not forget, however, that with financial and technical assistance provided by UNKRA, FOA, and ICA, substantial investments were made in such important sectors as coal mining, glass, cement, fertilizer, and electricity generation and transmission during the 1950s. In addition, the important contribution of these agencies to reconstructing educational and medical facilities after the war should not be underestimated. The Korean government itself provided substantial funds for these investment projects during the 1950s. These funds were either from foreign exchange held by the government or from the Counterpart Fund, generated by selling aid goods to domestic users.

During the 1950s, the Counterpart Fund financed a significant proportion of governmental expenditures. In 1957, for example, the fund generated more than 50 percent of government revenue. With this aid-related additional revenue, the Korean government was able to invest in basic industries and social infrastructure. Thus, foreign aid inflows played an indirect but critical role in development by helping to maintain a minimum consumption level for the Korean population and allowing the government to spend its own foreign exchange holdings on investment goods.

The US government also occasionally tried to use its position as the largest aid donor to influence the direction of Korean economic policies through aid negotiation. At the macroeconomic policy level, the US government sometimes used warnings of reduced aid to pressure the Korean government to adopt effective anti-inflationary measures. For example, the strong stabilization program of 1957–58 is usually attributed to aid-related foreign advice.[3]

As seen in tables 5.1 and 5.2, the relative importance of aid diminished continuously from the late 1950s. The importance of aid as a source of

3. The influence of the US AID on Korea's major economic policy decisions continued into the 1960s. At times, AID served as a source of ideas or influence and proposed important policy changes. Major economic policies were usually discussed with AID officials before being adopted, and they participated in policymaking. For example, AID economic advisers actively participated in Korea's most significant exchange rate reform, which occurred in 1964–65 (Brown 1973 and Kwang Suk Kim 1991). The influence naturally diminished as US aid itself was reduced. However, as was discussed, Korean policymakers have been always open to external advice, including AID consultations.

Table 5.1 Foreign aid and imports, 1953–60 (millions of dollars except where noted)

	1953	1954	1955	1956	1957	1958	1959	1960
Total imports[a]	354.4	243.3	341.4	386.1	442.2	378.2	303.8	343.5
Aid-financed imports	191.8	149.4	232.8	319.9	374.0	311.0	210.7	231.9
Aid-financed imports as a share of total imports	54.1	61.5	68.2	82.9	84.6	82.2	69.4	67.5
Foreign aid	194.2	153.9	236.7	326.7	382.9	321.3	222.2	245.4
Foreign aid as a share of total imports	54.8	63.3	69.3	84.6	86.6	85.0	73.1	71.4
Total imports as a share of GNP	9.8	7.4	10.0	13.2	12.0	10.8	10.3	12.7

a. Imports of goods and services.

Sources: Bank of Korea. 1955, 1974. *Economic Statistics Yearbook*; Bank of Korea. 1990. *National Accounts*; Economic Planning Board. 1961. *Korea Statistical Yearbook*.

Table 5.2 Foreign capital and imports, 1961–73 (millions of dollars except where noted)

	1961	1962	1963	1964	1965	1966	1967	1968	1969	1970	1971	1972	1973
Total imports[a]	316.1	421.8	560.9	404.4	463.4	716.4	996.2	1,462.9	1,823.0	1,984.0	2,394.3	2,522.0	4,240.3
Aid-financed imports	196.8	218.5	232.6	42.6	135.5	143.6	119.2	125.7	120.5	161.2	105.6	21.7	0.0
Aid-financed imports as a share of total imports	62.9	51.8	41.5	35.3	29.2	20.0	12.0	8.6	6.6	8.1	4.4	0.9	0.0
Imports with foreign loans	n.a.	4.5	52.1	34.6	31.5	108.4	167.3	299.6	475.7	400.2	541.4	628.6	628.4
Imports with foreign loans as a share of total imports	n.a.	1.1	9.3	8.6	6.8	15.1	16.8	20.5	26.1	20.2	22.6	24.9	14.8
Total imports as a share of GNP	14.9	16.6	15.8	13.5	15.9	20.3	22.4	25.9	26.0	24.0	26.5	25.6	33.5

n.a. = not available
a. Imports of goods and services.

Source: Bank of Korea. 1974. *Economic Statistics Yearbook.*

financing imports dropped drastically while foreign debt became more important as a source of import financing. One should also note that Korea's import-to-GNP ratio increased steadily throughout the period.

As the importance of foreign aid declined, the importance of the Counterpart Fund also diminished. This change was brought about by a shift in the direction of US foreign aid policy in the early 1960s. In accordance with the Foreign Assistance Act of 1961, the AID was created to absorb the ICA, the Development Loan Fund (DLF), and other aid activities such as that supported by PL 480. The US government decided to rely more on developmental loans than on grants-in-aid. This change in US aid policy and the realization that US aid would gradually decline must have contributed toward Korea's adoption of a new, outward-looking development strategy and a policy of greater reliance on foreign borrowing.

The Role of Foreign Borrowing

In the face of declining aid flows and meager domestic savings, Korea set out to find new channels for injecting foreign savings into the economy to support growth and development. This was particularly important for the newly emerged political leadership, which had already committed itself strongly to economic development. This set the stage for a new era in public and commercial borrowing for Korea.

Korea's first public borrowing was from the DLF, which amounted to $12 million in 1959. Korea's foreign aid up to that point had been primarily grants-in-aid rather than commercial loans. Thus, in the 1950s Korea was mostly a passive receiver of foreign capital. As this source of foreign capital started to dwindle in the latter part of the 1950s, the nation had to change its approach. In this regard, the Foreign Capital Inducement Promotion Act was enacted in 1960, even before Korea's new, growth-oriented political leadership came into power.

This law was primarily designed to facilitate foreign direct investment (FDI) from Koreans living abroad as well as from foreigners. Korea's rather precarious political situation and cloudy economic outlook at the time lowered expectations that FDI sufficient to fill the financing gap could be induced. Even if it had been possible, as will be discussed later, Koreans preferred loans to direct investment as a means of financing growth and development.

The new government recognized that the previously introduced law of 1960 was not sufficient to attract the required foreign capital, and it established a new foundation for attracting foreign funds, particularly foreign loans. First of all, the Law for Payment Guarantee of Foreign Borrowing was introduced in July 1962 to facilitate both private and public foreign borrowing by enhancing the credit standing of Korean borrowers in international financial markets.

At the same time, the government also introduced a special law to facilitate capital equipment imports on a long-term deferred payment basis. These two laws and the Foreign Capital Inducement Promotion Law of 1960 were merged into a broad new law called the Foreign Capital Inducement Law of 1966. This new law was intended not simply to integrate similar regulations and eliminate overlap but also to make foreign capital inducements more effective, to prevent "unnecessary" borrowing by improving governmental guarantee procedures for foreign loans, and to give more incentives to foreign direct investors.

This change in financing strategy coincided with Koreans' efforts to become more active participants in the international economic community. The outward-looking development strategy itself called for an active international financial strategy in the sense that export capacity had to be created mostly through foreign financing. Accordingly, Korea gradually transformed itself from passive aid receiver to active participant in the world financial community, and the Korean economy started to gain an international dimension.

The new Park government in 1961 persuaded private business leaders to make foreign capital inducement missions to the United States and Europe. At the same time, the government dispatched official economic cooperation missions to these countries. Summit meetings between Korea, the United States, and West Germany were also arranged, mostly to help facilitate public borrowing.

With this new approach to financing the nation's economic development, Korea borrowed heavily in the 1960s, 1970s, and into the mid-1980s, becoming the fourth most heavily indebted nation in the developing world. Since 1986, however, Korea's outstanding foreign debt, in both absolute and relative terms, has declined at a rapid rate.

Given Korea's successful economic performance to date, financed largely by foreign borrowing, a critical question is how Korea was able to use borrowed capital in a productive manner. The answer is definitely not a simple one, but it can be better understood through examination of the some of Korea's key policies regarding foreign debt management.

The key to successful use of foreign debt is creation of a mechanism by which the borrowed capital can be used to generate future debt servicing capacity instead of being used for current consumption. The Korean government had full control over the use of borrowed capital in different sectors and industries. The following section examines the institutional framework in which Korea's foreign debt was managed. Before turning to this subject, however, let us briefly review the magnitude of Korea's foreign debt over time and discuss factors that affected the flow of this debt.[4]

---

4. Detailed analyses are found in Economic Planning Board (1985) and Park (1986, vol. 14).

By 1985 Korea's outstanding foreign debt had reached $46.8 billion and the total debt-to-GNP ratio reached as high as 52.1 percent (see appendix, tables A.35 and A.36).

The first big surge in foreign borrowing occurred in the early 1960s, the transitional period of changing from foreign aid to loan financing. The second big jump came in the latter part of the 1960s, when Korea's ratio of total debt to GNP went above 15 percent in 1967, and then to well over 30 percent in 1971. Two more big increases occurred in the early and late 1970s, when the world suffered from the first and second oil shocks.

Several factors are responsible for the foreign debt increases. From the early 1960s, the Korean government believed that developing an outward-oriented economy, with growth as the top priority, would not only promote growth but also would lay a foundation for enhancing equity and fair income distribution. It was also believed that export-led growth and industrialization, financed by foreign debt, would eventually generate debt-servicing capacity and stimulate domestic saving. Accordingly, it was hoped that as this process unfolded, foreign debt would gradually become less important for continued growth and development.

Based on these premises, the government encouraged borrowing from abroad. One difficulty, in addition to raising the funds, was deciding the optimum amount to borrow and how to best use the debt to avoid future debt-related economic problems. At the macroeconomic policy level, the optimum amount of foreign debt can be determined within the context of a simplistic growth model, and, in fact, Korea did determine necessary annual foreign debt requirements in this fashion. Given that economic growth was to be achieved through an export-led strategy, it followed that the export sector and supporting social infrastructure had to be built and augmented through an appropriate level of investment. The appropriate amount of foreign capital was therefore equal to the existing investment-savings gap or current account deficit, according to this simplistic model. In this way, the Korean government started from a target growth rate to come up with the amount of borrowing needed in each year. This was consistent with the growth-first strategy adopted in the early 1960s.

In addition to filling this gap, however, annual borrowing from abroad augmented foreign reserves to support expanding international transactions and to provide export credit for foreign buyers. At this point, it is worth remembering that the Korean government fully controlled foreign borrowing and to a large extent the use of the borrowed capital.

The current account deficit was on average 62.3 percent of total annual borrowing (see appendix, table A.37). An average of 22.9 percent was used annually to augment foreign reserves. In recent years, Korea's net foreign debt position has declined rapidly, reflecting a sharp reduction in Korea's foreign borrowing and an increase in foreign assets.

The Korean government monitored foreign borrowing closely. There are two basic laws regarding foreign exchange transactions in Korea: the Foreign Capital Inducement Law of 1966 and the Foreign Exchange Control Law. Long-term external borrowings were regulated by the former; all other foreign exchange transactions were covered by the latter. Most of the detailed regulations and policies regarding foreign exchange are at the discretion of the Ministry of Finance (MOF).[5] As international financial market conditions changed and the nation's balance of payments situation was affected, the ministry from time to time revised foreign exchange policies.

The Foreign Capital Inducement Law concerns external borrowings with a maturity of over three years and foreign direct investment. The MOF is fully responsible for these long-term borrowings, although some responsibilities and authorities in these matters are delegated to the central bank and commercial banks.

There are four types of external borrowings, as defined by these laws: public, commercial, bank, and private-sector overseas bond issues. For developmental purposes, the first two types are important while the other two are mostly for operational liquidity of banks and business enterprises. Both public and commercial borrowings are subject to the Foreign Capital Inducement Law. Public borrowing is defined in the law as "borrowing by the government, or borrowing from a foreign government or a multilateral institution by the public sector as well as private sector." Consequently, foreign public borrowings include all borrowings by the Korean government and also all borrowings by the private sector from foreign public sources. As for foreign commercial borrowings, these were defined as borrowings by the private sector or public enterprises from foreign private sources with a maturity of over three years. However, this does not include bank borrowings or bond issues, which are treated separately.

All prospective public borrowings are reviewed by relevant ministries before their loan applications are sent to the MOF, where they are evaluated against various criteria, including the economic and technical feasibility of the project involved, the amount to be borrowed, repayment capability, and financial and managerial planning. Applications are then sent back to the relevant ministries and to the Economic Planning Board (EPB), where they are evaluated in terms of the five-year plan and annual economic priorities. The EPB also examines the projects' budgetary implications over the years. After all opinions are gathered, the MOF puts

---

5. The Finance Ministry gained this authority, which was previously held by the Economic Planning Board, in November 1981 after governmental organization changes.

together all proposed public borrowings into a package submitted to the national assembly for approval. In the case of government borrowings, the MOF carries out all the necessary negotiations. However, for public borrowings by government agencies or private entities, the government guarantees the loans contracted. All loan agreements and related contracts must be approved by the MOF in advance.

The MOF also must approve commercial borrowings in advance. "Guidelines for Commercial Borrowing," issued by the MOF, explains the conditions for commercial borrowing, including eligible projects, eligible borrowers, the usage of the loan, and repayment terms. The MOF revises these guidelines from time to time, adapting to changes in domestic economic and international financial conditions. Depending on these conditions, the eligibility criteria or borrowing terms are either tightened or made more lenient. The MOF evaluates applications according to the guidelines and solicits opinions from concerned ministries and the guaranteeing bank. The MOF refers the application to the Foreign Capital Project Review Committee for its approval. There is no legal or administrative ceiling for commercial borrowing in a given year. However, the government always tries to limit such borrowing to reasonable levels.

In general, foreign borrowing in Korea has been tightly monitored from the very beginning to make sure that borrowed capital is used productively. In this regard, the Foreign Capital Inducement Deliberation Committee was established at the EPB in 1962 to screen foreign borrowing applications in advance. At the same time, the government's approach to foreign borrowing was somewhat liberal, in that no limits were set and all appropriate applications were given consideration.

Government encouragement of foreign borrowing, particularly by giving government and bank guarantees, sometimes resulted in excessive foreign borrowing. This was especially true when Korean inflation rates and nominal interest rates were much higher than the rates of their trading partners and the foreign exchange rate was not properly adjusted to reflect this differential. There was a wide gap between domestic and foreign borrowing costs in favor of foreign borrowing throughout the 1960s and 1970s (see appendix, table A.38). Under these conditions, businesses naturally preferred to borrow from foreign sources.

Consequently, there was excess demand for foreign loans despite active government involvement. It is difficult to judge how much economic waste resulted from excessive borrowing in Korea in the past. There are many who believe that this excess did not substantially distort the allocation of resources in the 1960s, as most borrowings were allocated to labor-intensive export sectors in keeping with the outward-looking development strategy.

At the same time, one can also say that borrowed funds were generally well used in the sense that Korea's social rate of return on capital was higher than the interest rate on foreign borrowings (Krueger 1979, 198–201). It is doubtful, however, whether the same can be said for the 1970s, when the HCI promotion drive was forcefully implemented. This issue should be considered within the context of the current debate on the success or failure of the HCI promotion drive itself. (This issue was briefly touched on in chapter 4.)

In terms of foreign capital, the first five-year plan period of 1962–66 was a transitional stage for Korea during which the nation shifted from grant-in-aid to foreign borrowing, and particularly to public borrowing. The government initiated measures to make foreign borrowing attractive and easier to obtain, including favorable exchange rate policies, loan guarantees, and enhancements in access to trade-related loans. These measures, combined with other factors, such as tight domestic credit, interest rate differentials, and brighter prospects for the Korean economy, caused the first foreign borrowing, which was reasonable given the previously small base of foreign debt. Moreover, the normalization of diplomatic relations with Japan in 1965 laid the foundation for additional capital inflows.

The government became concerned about excessive foreign debt accumulation around this time and began to address the problem. As mentioned earlier, the Capital Inducement Law was introduced in 1966 to merge, improve, and make more efficient existing laws on foreign capital inducement. In addition, in December 1967, the first year of the second five-year plan, the government announced "Overall Rationalization Measures for Foreign Capital Inducement." According to these measures, a ceiling was placed on foreign borrowing to maintain the debt-service ratio at a maximum of 9 percent. Private commercial borrowing was tightened by raising the minimum domestic fund reserve to 20 percent, and limits were placed on cash loans from abroad.

Nevertheless, foreign borrowing grew rapidly in the latter part of the 1960s. The World Bank's Pearson report in 1969 expressed concern over Korea's rapid accumulation of foreign debt. For example, between 1966 and 1969, Korea's foreign borrowings increased by over 450 percent. Foreign borrowing increased from a meager $8.9 million in 1962 to $1.8 billion in 1969.

In 1968 and 1969, private commercial loans increased sharply, and the nation's total foreign debt increased from $1.2 billion to $1.8 billion. Private commercial loans increased from $255 million to $361 million while public loans increased by $32 million. In addition to the above-mentioned factors behind the surge in foreign borrowing, the interest rate reforms of 1965 were also important.

Korea's exchange rate policy at the time was broadly stable despite rapid inflation, and as a result, the real rate of interest paid for foreign debt was negative and far lower than interest paid on domestic loans. In addition to the differential between interest rates on domestic and foreign credit, domestic credit was severely rationed while export-related suppliers' credit was almost automatically extended. These factors made borrowing from abroad even more attractive.

In response to this situation, the government implemented other measures, such as introducing a commercial loan ceiling system, prohibiting cash loans with the exception of public corporations or funds coming from multilateral institutions, tightening the criteria for receiving guarantees, and initiating a mechanism to take care of insolvent firms ridden with foreign debt. At the same time, incentives and promotional policies were introduced to attract foreign direct investment. Accordingly, the policy of 1969 was meant to discourage private cash loans and to encourage both public loans and foreign direct investment. The IMF became concerned about Korea's rapidly rising foreign debt and requested that the Korean government, through a stand-by agreement, more strictly limit foreign borrowings, particularly regarding short- and intermediate-term loans.

These measures did have an appreciable impact on Korean borrowing. The nation's rising trend of foreign debt, and private loans in particular, slowed substantially during this period.

Korea's second surge in foreign borrowing occurred immediately after the first oil shock of 1972. The rapid increase was further accelerated by additional borrowings related to HCI investments beginning in the mid-1970s. Korea was (and still is) virtually 100 percent dependent on crude oil imports. When the first oil shock hit, the country could have reacted in two ways: first, it could have tried to absorb the impact through contractionary policies to minimize inflation; second, it could have continued the growth-first strategy by sacrificing price stability. Korean policymakers at the time chose the second alternative, and the growth-first strategy was not altered. This policy stance naturally called for substantially more foreign borrowings to finance rising current account deficits caused by surging oil and HCI-related imports. At the same time, the Korean won was devalued by nearly 20 percent in 1974, and export credits with preferential interest rates were extended. Bank credit was also increased by 50 percent to help finance imports.

As a result of this policy stance, in the short run the current account deficit increased dramatically, reaching 11.2 percent of GNP, the highest level ever. At the same time, the ratio of debt to GNP increased to 32.0 percent, and inflation soared to 30.5 percent (see appendix, table A.39). Due to an increase in exports, however, the debt service ratio did not deteriorate much. In fact, recovery in the world economy and the Middle East construction boom contributed to a sharp increase in exports. Korea even experienced a small current account surplus in 1977 for the first time in its history.

On the other hand, the HCI promotion drive required an increase in capital equipment imports, which were mostly financed by foreign borrowings. Consequently, foreign borrowing did not slow down. It is believed that Korea's ability to borrow abroad helped the country adapt successfully in difficult periods such as the oil shocks. The rapid resumption in exports after the first oil shock might not have been possible without this borrowing. Korea gained the ability to borrow through its good track record regarding debt service (Krueger 1979, 149–52). In addition, the commitment of political leadership to economic development and the quality of its policies lent Korea credibility in international markets, and this was another important factor enabling the country to borrow continuously during difficult times.

Inflation was administratively suppressed from 1976 on, and consequently, even though inflationary pressures were still building, the rate of inflation seemed to slow. Inflationary pressure became evident as inflation began to accelerate in 1978. The HCI promotion drive, together with the above-mentioned problems, caused serious structural adjustment problems in the early 1980s.

The third upsurge in foreign borrowing came in the aftermath of the second oil shock of 1979. The Korean economy was overheated from 1976 to 1978. The Middle East construction boom aggravated shortages of skilled labor. Lopsided resource allocation toward HCIs and credit-starved light manufacturing industries contributed to inflationary pressures. Money supply increased very rapidly in those years. All these factors produced rapid inflation from 1978, and Korean competitiveness drastically declined. Consequently, exports slowed substantially, actually decreasing in 1979 by 2.5 percent, adjusted for price changes. On top of these structural problems, President Park was assassinated in 1979, and there was an unexpected bad harvest in 1980.

Under these difficult conditions, the Korean government again had to choose an appropriate economic management strategy. This time, the situation was different from that of the first oil shock. Given the structural imbalances, rampant inflation, growing current account deficit, and future uncertainty surrounding the Korean economy, the growth-first strategy could not have been continued through foreign borrowing. Borrowing itself was not only difficult but very costly due to prevailing high international interest rates. So the new government adopted stabilization policies in January 1980 that were first introduced in April 1979.

Korea's total foreign debt nearly doubled from 1979 to 1983. As seen previously, 86 percent of the gross increase in foreign debt was to finance the current account deficit. Basically, the relatively low level of domestic saving and chronic inflation were the main reasons for the rapid increase in the current account deficit through these years. During this period, both foreign exchange reserves and deferred-payment export credits also increased. The structural imbalances and general economic inefficiency caused by the misallocation of resources in the 1970s reduced Korean export competitiveness substantially. Fast increases in unit labor costs also contributed to reducing export competitiveness.

Korea's weak industrial structure and high dependency on imports—energy imports in particular—also contributed to the third upsurge in foreign borrowing. In addition to these underlying structural causes, there were other external factors. First of all, the oil price increase itself was an important contributing factor. The average import price for crude oil in Korea increased from $13.10 per barrel in 1978 to $35.60 per barrel in 1981. Consequently, Korea suffered a $17.6 billion increase in its oil import bill from 1980 to 1984 while only $1.4 billion of this sum was due to increases in oil consumption (table 5.3).

Another external factor was persistently high international interest rates. The second oil shock brought rapidly increasing international interest rates, owing to restrictive monetary policies adopted by most industrialized nations at the time. As a result, the average three-month London Interbank Offer Rate (LIBOR) went up from 8.8 percent in 1978 to 16.8 percent in 1981. Because Korea's foreign debt was increasing rapidly due to other factors and there was a relatively high proportion of variable interest-payment debt, the country suddenly had to shoulder $5.5 billion more in payments because of the increase in interest rates (table 5.4).

Another external factor was the substantial increase in the grain import bill due to the bad rice harvest in 1980. From 1972 to 1976, the total grain import bill amounted to $2.5 billion, but it was $2.2 billion for 1981 alone.

In terms of distribution among industrial sectors, Korea's foreign debt for the first plan period went mostly to the mining and manufacturing sector; during the second plan period, the social overhead capital sector was the primary recipient.

Korea's foreign debt had been increasing rather fast, but the country never had trouble servicing the debt. More importantly, the domestic savings base increased steadily during this time. This pattern was different from other highly indebted developing countries around the world, particularly those in Latin America, whose external debt problems went from bad to worse during this period. In this regard, one can find a difference in the sequence of liberalization between Korea and other heavily indebted nations in Latin America. Some Latin American countries chose to liberalize financial and trade sectors simultaneously, and some the financial sector first, causing severe disruptions and imbalances in those economies and resulting in foreign exchange crises, heavy capital flight, increased unemployment, and runaway inflation (Bruno 1988). Korea, on the other hand, concentrated on liberalizing trade markets first and left financial liberalization for later when the economy was more mature. This sequence proved to be more effective and helped Korea to adapt during this difficult period following the second oil shock.

Table 5.3   Imports of crude oil, 1978–84

Oil imports	1978	1979	1980	1981	1982	1983	1984	Total 1980–84
Crude oil imports (millions of dollars)	2,174	3,331	5,654	6,584	6,075	5,768	5,807	29,808
Quantity (millions of barrels)	167	186	183	183	178	193	200	937
Average unit price (dollars per barrel)	13.1	18.0	30.9	35.6	34.1	29.9	29.1	
Oil bill increase								
as compared to 1978 (millions of dollars)	n.a.	1,157	3,480	4,330	3,901	3,594	3,633	18,938
Price factor (millions of dollars)	n.a.	908	3,266	4,556	3,746	3,249	3,199	17,576
Quantity factor (millions of dollars)	n.a.	249	214	214	155	345	434	1,362

n.a. = not applicable

Source: Economic Planning Board. 1985. *White Paper on Foreign Debt.*

Table 5.4 International interest payments, 1978–84

	1978	1979	1980	1981	1982	1983	1984	Total 1980–84
Interest payments (millions of dollars)	887	1,406	2,471	3,476	3,620	3,187	3,744	16,408
Total debt (millions of dollars)	14,823	20,287	27,190	32,433	37,082	40,378	43,053	n.a.
Average interest rates	6.5	8.0	10.4	11.6	10.4	8.2	9.0	n.a.
LIBOR	8.8	12.1	14.2	16.8	13.2	9.6	10.8	n.a.
Increase in interest payments as compared to 1978	n.a.	519	1,584	2,589	2,733	2,300	2,857	12,063
Price factor	n.a.	260	920	1,533	1,358	666	1,028	5,505
Quantity factor	n.a.	259	664	1,056	1,375	1,634	1,829	6,558

LIBOR = London Interbank Offer Rate
n.a. = not available or not applicable

Source: Economic Planning Board. 1985. *White Paper on Foreign Debt.*

In this regard, it is important to recognize that the speed of adjustment in the asset markets is different from that in the product market.

Unlike some Latin American countries, capital flight was never a serious problem in Korea. Many factors contributed to setting Korea apart from other nations in this regard. Chief among these is the fact that Korea was one of the world's fastest-growing economies. Other factors were the relatively clean government and its leadership, coupled with heavy penalties to individual and corporate violators of the laws on international capital transactions.

It is generally believed that Korea was able to use foreign capital productively. How was Korea able to do so when most of its counterparts in the developing world could not? Based on previous discussions, it is safe to say that the right development strategy and effective leadership commitment to economic development taken together were the most important factors in this difference. The outward-looking strategy successfully promoted exports and growth, and consequently, generated debt service capacity. This gave Korea sound credit standing in the international financial market. Continued growth and development were also expected by international lenders due to the strong commitment of Korean leadership to appropriate development goals.

At times, foreign debt was a controversial political issue in Korea. It was the hottest issue during the spring 1984 general election, when opposition parties adopted it as a main issue of their political platforms to damage the governing party. Even government party politicians became uncomfortable about the issue, despite the reassurances of the administration and economic authorities.

Many academics also expressed their concern over the debt issue, and there were foreign critics as well. However, the foreign financial community was in general optimistic regarding Korea's external debt. Articles and books written around that time prove this point. Nevertheless, sensitive to the political nature of this issue, President Chun personally ordered economic authorities to reduce the nation's foreign debt much faster than was originally planned.

When Korea successfully began to reduce its external debt in 1986, critics argued it was fortuitous and that the nation was simply benefiting from the "three lows"—low oil prices, low interest rates, and rapid depreciation of the dollar vis-à-vis the yen—rather than giving proper credit to the government's policies and strategies. Certainly, Korea did take advantage of favorable external factors prevailing at the time. However, this successful reduction was to a large extent a handsome payoff for the painful adjustments made in Korea from the early 1980s and the economic leadership's correct choice of economic policies, timing, and sequencing. It should be reemphasized that Korea's readiness to take advantage of these external developments originated from its careful and successful stabilization and structural adjustments.

At the macroeconomic level, the contribution of foreign borrowing to the economy can be estimated based on various assumptions. Based on crude marginal-capital to output ratios, the contribution of total foreign capital to national growth has been estimated at 30 to 40 percent of total growth for the 1960s (Westphal and Kim 1982). Similarly, it is estimated to be 20 to 30 percent for the period between 1972 and 1982. These estimates include FDI's contribution, but as will be discussed in the following section, FDI played only a minor role in Korea at the time, so the estimates can be considered valid for foreign borrowing.

The Role of Foreign Direct Investment

One of the main purposes of the previously mentioned Foreign Capital Inducement Promotion Law of 1960 was to make FDI more attractive by giving incentives to foreign direct investors including tax holidays, investment protection, and guaranteeing the remittance of profit and principal. However, until 1965 when the normalization of diplomatic relations with Japan was achieved and FDI from Japan started to flow into Korea, there was not much activity in this area.

The new law of 1966 also made direct investment more attractive to foreigners by giving tax incentives, eliminating remaining restrictions on profit remittance and liberalizing requirements for employing Korean workers. The Office of Investment Promotion was established at the EPB to facilitate FDI by providing pre- and postinvestment consultations as well as to help reduce red tape involved in processing FDI applications.

Despite these efforts, toward the end of the 1960s, private foreign borrowing was still increasing at a very fast rate, and there was some concern about debt service. Accordingly, the government decided to encourage FDI even more actively. It announced measures to promote foreign investment and foreign investment firms in 1969. Eligible sectors for foreign investment were broadened, and more privileges were provided. The government established the Masan free trade zone in 1970 and even introduced a special law to prevent labor union activities in foreign-invested firms. Also in 1970, the government established a one-stop service office, mostly to facilitate interministerial coordination of FDI-related matters.

In encouraging FDI, the Korean government strictly enforced export requirements and foreign equity share limits in most cases, with the exception of certain strategic sectors that needed better technology. Even in those strategic sectors, sole foreign ownership was allowed with the proviso that the owners were expected to sell their shares to local businesses in an appropriate time frame. Especially in the early 1970s when the government's HCI promotion drive was launched and Korea's vulnerability to external shocks became a major national concern, policies regarding FDI became more restrictive with respect to foreign owner-ship, export requirements, and minimum amount of investment. With respect to foreign ownership, no more than 50 percent of foreign equity was allowed in principle, and less than 50 percent was permitted in simple, labor-intensive sectors.

These restrictive policies were maintained more or less until the late 1970s. Coming into the 1980s, the Korean government adopted a new development strategy, and the policies for FDI were reformed. This reform was consistent with the general direction of market liberalization and the new development strategy, but it was motivated by two addi-tional factors. The first had to do with concern over the nation's debt-service capability, as the external debt had ballooned in the late 1970s. The second factor was the need for upgrades and restructuring of Korean industries.

Accordingly, in the early 1980s, guidelines for FDI approval were revised to allow 100 percent foreign ownership for preannounced, spec-ified sectors and to reduce the number of noneligible sectors. Another major reform measure was introduced in 1983 when the Foreign Capital Inducement Law was revised. In accordance with the revised law, guide-lines for FDI approval were also revised and became effective in July 1984. Under the new law, a negative list system for FDI approval, in which any industry not specified on the list was open to foreign in-vestment, was introduced. This represented a change from the old sys-tem, in which foreign investment was allowed only in sectors specified on the list. At the same time, existing restrictions on foreign equity participation and dividend remittance were eliminated, and administra-tive procedures for FDI approval were also simplified.

Since the 1983 FDI liberalization measure, the government has con-tinually liberalized remaining restrictions regarding FDI. For example, as can be seen from table 5.5, the FDI liberalization ratio—or, the number of FDI-eligible sectors to the total number of sectors—has increased steadily. In particular, the manufacturing sector has been opened widely to foreign investment. Currently, virtually all manufacturing sectors, with the exception of a few limited cases such as public utilities, are eligible for foreign investment.

Since the introduction of the negative list system, the list itself has been regularly reviewed for further opportunities for making it more open. In 1985 more than 100 sectors were eliminated from the list. The liberalization ratio for total industries reached 76 percent, for the man-ufacturing sector it reached 93 percent, and the number of industries open to foreign investors reached 762. In 1987 an additional 26 manu-facturing industries were opened to foreign investors, raising the lib-eralization ratio for the manufacturing sector to 97.5 percent.

Recently, service sectors, including financial services, have been opened gradually to foreign investment, primarily in response to US demands.

Table 5.5 Foreign direct investment: liberalization status, 1980–November 1992 (percentages)

Date	Liberalization ratio,[a] overall	Liberalization ratio, manufacturing
1980	49.9	
1983	60.9	80.0
July 1984	66.1	86.0
Oct. 1985	76.3	92.5
July 1987	78.9	97.5
July 1989	79.0	97.5
Jan. 1990	79.1	97.7
July 1990	79.2	97.7
Jan. 1991	79.4	97.7
Nov. 1992	81.7	97.8

a. Number of sectors eligible for foreign direct investment over the number of all industrial sectors.

Source: Ministry of Finance, Korea. Financial Statistics, various issues.

Regardless of the outcome of the Uruguay Round of trade negotiations, a more systematic approach to the liberalization of service sectors is necessary for Korea. At the same time, with the exception of a few sectors in which technological advancement via FDI is critical, special privileges provided for FDI will have to be eliminated, in accordance with the principle of national treatment, as the economy matures and becomes more open. As mentioned in chapter 3, Korea's development was keyed to a continuous, high level of investment financed primarily by foreign capital, particularly in the earlier stages of development.

As can be seen from table 5.6, the share of FDI in total long-term capital transferred to Korea throughout the period was rather small, except for recent years when Korea started to pay off outstanding loans and incoming FDI began to pick up. Throughout the 1960s and 1970s, the proportion of FDI was around 10 percent. FDI as a proportion of total fixed capital formation or gross capital formation is rather small throughout this period, at about 1 percent.

The nation's total incoming FDI approved between 1962 and 1991 (as of January 1991) amounted to a meager $8.0 billion. Out of this total, 80 percent had entered Korea since 1982, when FDI policy reforms were introduced. Over 60 percent of total FDI approved arrived during the four-year period between 1987 and 1991 (see appendix, tables A.40, A.41, and A.42).

More than 40 percent of total FDI flows, or 58 percent of the FDI cases from 1962 to 1991, came from Japan. About 30 percent of FDI originated in the United States (see appendix, tables A.41 and A.42). It is clear that FDI flows to Korea are too heavily dependent on these two important economic partners. In recent years, however, the European share of FDI has been rising as the Korean economy gradually becomes more inte-

Table 5.6 Foreign direct investment on an arrival basis, 1962–90 (millions of dollars, except where noted)

| | Foreign invest-ment | Loans | | | Capital formation | | Capital inflow[a] | Foreign investment as share of | | | |
		Public	Commercial	Total	Gross	Fixed		Total loans	Gross capital formation	Fixed capital formation	Capital inflow
1962–66	17	116	176	292	2,713	2,425	309	5.8	0.6	0.7	5.5
1967–71	96	811	1,355	2,166	9,089	8,563	2,262	4.4	1.1	1.1	4.2
1972–76	557	2,389	3,043	5,432	24,664	22,796	5,989	10.3	2.3	2.4	9.3
1977–81	1,666	5,751	7,381	13,132	88,872	86,206	14,798	12.7	1.9	1.9	11.3
1982–86	1,040	6,690	5,329	12,019	127,360	125,302	13,059	8.7	0.8	0.8	8.0
1987–90	3,228	2,907	3,436	6,343	245,527	247,682	9,571	50.9	1.3	1.3	33.7
Total 1962–90	6,604	18,664	20,720	39,384	498,225	492,974	45,988	16.8	1.3	1.3	14.4

a. Capital inflow equals foreign investment plus loan total.

Source: Economic Planning Board. 1980 and 1990. *Major Statistics of the Korean Economy;* Ministry of Finance, Korea. February 1991. *Financial Statistics.*

grated with these economies. The geographical proximity of Japan to Korea and their complementary factor endowments contribute to the high proportion of Japanese FDI in Korea. Another important factor is the more than half a million Koreans residing in Japan. According to one study, Korean residents in Japan provided as much as 16 percent of total FDI, or almost one-third of all Japanese FDI between 1962 and 1981 (Koo 1985, 182, footnote 5).

The Japanese share of Korean FDI was highest between 1972 and 1976, reaching 71.3 percent of total FDI. This reflects the Japanese policy of actively encouraging and lifting restrictions on outgoing FDI. As a matter of fact, 1972 is called *gannen* in Japan, or "the very first year" of FDI.

The *gannen* of FDI from Japan resulted from two major factors. First, as the Japanese balance of payments turned into a large surplus, the Japanese saw the necessity of industrial restructuring toward high-value-added, high-technology industries. Second, rapidly increasing Japanese domestic wage rates, coupled with a sharp appreciation of the Japanese yen vis-à-vis the dollar and the won, pushed labor-intensive Japanese industries such as textiles and electrical machinery overseas, and especially toward neighboring newly industrializing economies such as Korea. At the same time, the rapidly appreciating yen reduced the initial cost of FDI substantially, further drawing FDI from these countries (Komiya and Wakasugi 1991).

As wage rates in Korea started to increase rapidly in the latter half of the 1970s, Japanese FDI fell dramatically. From the early 1980s, Japanese FDI started to increase again while Japan's total outgoing FDI also started to increase rapidly. This time, however, Japanese FDI inflows to Korea were directed toward different sectors.

Nearly 70 percent of incoming FDI in Korea between 1962 and 1991 went to the manufacturing sector (see appendix, tables A.43 and A.44). This again reflects both the government's policy favoring FDI inflow into the manufacturing sector and the peculiar factor endowments of Korea, with its abundant, hard-working labor force and lack of significant natural resources. The distribution of FDI changed as Korea's economic environment and factor endowments changed.

In recent years, the service sector, and especially the financial sector, has seen an increasing share of FDI as Korea's capital and financial markets began to open. The period between 1982 and 1986 was exceptional in that a large proportion (46.8 percent) of FDI went into the service sector compared with total FDI. The 1986 Asian Games and the 1988 Olympic Games necessitated the construction of hotel accommodations during this period. Nearly 62 percent of Japanese FDI in Korea during 1982–86 went into this sector.

Distribution of FDI from Japan and that from the United States is somewhat different. US FDI concentrated primarily in petrochemicals, transportation equipment, and electronics sectors,[6] and Japanese investments were heavily weighted toward hotel services, electronics, petrochemicals, and textiles and garments. As previously indicated, however, the pattern of Japanese FDI changed in the 1980s. A larger proportion of Japanese FDI has begun to be channeled into electronics and electrical equipment, transportation equipment, petrochemicals, and financial services rather than such sectors as textiles and garments.[7]

The relatively minor role FDI played in Korea's development can be explained by various factors. First of all, from the suppliers' point of view, Korean policies throughout most of the period were not accommodating enough for foreign management to gain control or exercise autonomy over firms in which they invested. The general fear of foreign domination of Korean industries was too widespread for the government to be accommodating on this matter. This fear is rooted in Korea's history of Japanese colonization. Consequently, Koreans still tend to cast a suspicious eye on FDI as a means of once again exerting foreign (especially Japanese) domination of Korean industries. It is no secret that Koreans remain highly sensitive to the potential domination of Japanese industrial power within their own country.

There are other economic and policy-related factors that explain why FDI plays such a small role in Korean development. For example, it may have to do with Korea's choice of development strategy, which gave incentives to exporters in general and resulted in the promotion of labor-intensive light manufacturing industries in the early stages of development. Sophisticated technology or management skills that usually accompanied FDI were not as critical in these industries, and their marketing also does not require special expertise. This situation changed as the Korean economy entered a new stage of development, and recent amendments in government policy regarding FDI reflect these changes. On top of these factors, relative costs, discussed in previous sections, made debt capital much more attractive to Korean businessmen than equity capital, particularly in the earlier development period. Accordingly, Korean entrepreneurs preferred to take advantage of negative costs by using foreign debt rather than sharing these benefits with foreign business partners.

---

6. During 1982–86, 69.5 percent of US FDI went to these three sectors. This ratio was slightly reduced during 1987–90 to 58.6 percent.

7. The proportion of Japanese FDI in the hotel accommodation sector was 37.2 percent during 1987–90, reduced from 66.5 percent during 1982–86. On the other hand, 36.8 percent of Japanese FDI to Korea was channeled into electronics and electrical equipment, transportation equipment, and chemicals sectors during 1987–90. During the 1982–86 period, these three sectors together received only 15.9 percent of the total Japanese FDI into Korea.

The macroeconomic impact of FDI may be analyzed in terms of its contribution toward macroeconomic goals such as economic growth, a favorable balance of payments, and increased employment. However, in this kind of analysis there are problems in measuring these contributions and, consequently, estimated results often become controversial. In particular, FDI involves important external benefits or positive spillovers into the economy, especially regarding the transfer of technology (broadly defined to include both production-related engineering technology and management know-how). When trying to take such benefits into account, the measurement problem becomes even more formidable (Graham and Krugman 1989).

Certain studies have been made in this area that do shed light on the subject (see appendix, table A.45). A recent study for 1984–86 estimates that total value added by FDI represented an average 1.7 percent of annual GNP for that period. The study also estimates that value added in manufacturing FDI represented only about 4 percent of the manufacturing sector's GNP during that period. At the same time, total production resulting from FDI represented a higher proportion of total production at 7 percent, indicating that FDI-related businesses may have been involved more in assembly-type operations than in direct, high value-added activities. FDI contributed 2.5 percent of annual GNP growth for the period between 1984 and 1986.[8] An earlier study of the 1972–80 period indicates that the annual average contribution of FDI to GNP growth was only 1.3 percent (Cha 1986). Although still small, these estimates seem to show that FDI is having an increasing impact on the nation's economic growth.

Employees supported by FDI represented about 1.4 percent of total employees from 1984 to 1986, and the incremental employment provided through FDI contributed about 1.7 percent to increasing national employment. FDI contributed around 3 percent of incremental employment for the 1972–80 period. This reduced employment contribution can be interpreted as a result of the shift in FDI from labor-intensive to capital- and technology-intensive sectors in the 1980s.

The measurement problem becomes more formidable in calculating the impact of FDI on the nation's balance of payments. Sweeping assumptions are inevitably made, and available studies on the subject are no exception. Therefore, let us consider here only the direct trade activities of the FDI reported in these studies.

As expected, the share of foreign affiliate trade in the nation's total is relatively high. During the 1984–86 period, foreign affiliates' export share was around 11 percent of the national total. The export orientation of FDI was revealed in earlier studies that showed that the export-to-sales

---

8. The survey was conducted by Korea Credit Analysis, Inc., and results were summarized in Ministry of Finance (1991).

**Table 5.7 Exports of Korea and of foreign affiliates in Korea:
geographical distribution, 1984–86** (percentages)

Exports to	Exports of Korea as a whole			Exports of foreign affiliates		
	1984	1985	1986	1984	1985	1986
US	35.8	35.5	40.0	38.7	41.5	36.1
Japan	15.7	15.0	15.6	28.2	27.5	24.8
Other	48.5	49.5	44.4	33.1	31.0	39.1

Source: Ministry of Finance, Korea. 1991. *The Korean Economy and Foreign Capital* (January).

ratio for FDI firms was much higher than for average firms in Korea. The ratio for FDI firms was 27.4 percent in 1971 and 41.5 percent in 1980 while the share for the national average was 6.9 percent and 13.3 percent, respectively, for comparable years. During those three years, foreign affiliates' exports grew faster than national exports as a whole. Exports by Japanese affiliates grew at an annual average rate of 16.6 percent while US affiliate exports grew 11.7 percent during the same period.

Examination of the destination of exports shows that foreign affiliates in general tend to export more to their home country markets. In the case of Japan, the tendency is even more prominent. In 1986, for example, 15.6 percent of the nation's total exports went to Japan while Japanese affiliates in Korea sent 42.7 percent of their exports to Japan. Korea as a whole sent 40 percent of its exports to the US market in 1986 while the US affiliates in Korea exported 66.6 percent to the US market (see tables 5.7 and 5.8).

These aspects of foreign affiliates' exports to the United States and Japan and their impact on Korea's bilateral trade balances with those countries should be studied in greater detail. Korea's increasing trade surplus with the United States at the time and its decreasing trade deficit with Japan in 1986 was partially accounted for by the business activities of those countries' foreign affiliates. This has interesting policy implications for the countries involved. In this context, export requirements for FDI in Korea and special incentives provided to exporting FDI firms need to be reconsidered, as it is not clear if such an arrangement indirectly contributes to trade frictions or hinders rather than helps the economy.

Let us turn to the imports of foreign affiliates. The propensity of FDI firms to import is also higher than for average Korean firms. Based on data from input-output tables and survey results, the same study for the 1971–80 period estimates that foreign affiliates' intermediate-input import dependency was 27.7 percent in 1971 and 33.3 percent in 1980 while the ratio for the Korean economy as a whole was 8.6 percent in 1971 and 14.2 percent in 1980.[9]

---

9. This dependency is defined as the share of intermediate inputs in gross domestic

Table 5.8 Exports of foreign affiliates in Korea: geographical distribution, 1984–86

Home country	1984 Millions of dollars	1984 Percent-ages[a]	1985 Millions of dollars	1985 Percent-ages[a]	1986 Millions of dollars	1986 Percent-ages[a]
US, exporting to						
US	402	64.5	393	69.6	485	66.6
Japan	16	2.6	18	3.2	25	3.4
Other	205	32.9	154	27.2	218	30.0
Japan, exporting to						
US	293	30.5	314	33.6	296	27.0
Japan	362	37.7	384	41.1	462	42.7
Other	305	31.8	237	25.3	323	29.9
Other, exporting to						
US	106	21.7	106	23.0	76	13.5
Japan	207	42.4	137	29.7	102	18.1
Other	175	35.9	218	47.3	386	68.4

a. Proportions of exports to different countries to their total exports.

Sources: Ministry of Finance, Korea. 1991. *The Korean Economy and Foreign Capital* (January).

The raw material imports of foreign affiliates were on the average 9.6 percent of total imports from 1984 to 1986. Again, foreign affiliates tended to import more from their home countries than did the Korean economy as a whole (see tables 5.9, 5.10). However, the US affiliates import more from Japan than they export to Japan, and the Japanese affiliates in Korea export more to the United States than they import from them. The contribution of foreign affiliates to total raw material imports, excluding oil, was 25.4 percent for the period between 1984 and 1986.

In the case of Korea, the primary objective of government FDI policy has been the transfer of technology, except in labor-intensive, off-shore assembly, or sourcing-type activities. The transfer of technology includes the introduction of production-related engineering technology, management and other know-how, and training of local employees. Certainly, filling the domestic savings gap was another consideration. However, this objective was always secondary, and this is supported by the fact that the proportion of FDI in total foreign capital transferred to Korea was relatively small throughout the development decades.

Entire industries that were capital- and technology-intensive and import-substituting would never have gotten off the ground in Korea without FDI capital and technology, particularly in earlier years. Good examples of this are fertilizers, petroleum refining, petrochemicals, and heavy machinery sectors where there were no domestic firms established before the arrival of FDI.

production for the whole economy and refers to total sales rather than gross domestic sales for foreign affiliates.

Table 5.9 Imports of Korea and foreign affiliates in Korea: geographical distribution, 1984–86 (percentages)

Imports from	Korea as a whole			All foreign affiliates in Korea		
	1984	1985	1986	1984	1985	1986
US	22.4	20.8	26.6	19.3	18.3	19.2
Japan	24.9	24.3	34.4	26.3	28.5	42.4
Other	52.7	54.9	39.0	54.4	53.2	38.4

Source: Ministry of Finance, Korea. 1991. *The Korean Economy and Foreign Capital* (January).

The petroleum refining industry in Korea was established with foreign affiliates in a joint-venture arrangement. Currently, however, three of five firms are solely owned by Koreans. A substantial number of former employees of these firms provided necessary construction and operating skills for petrochemical plants established in the later years in Korea. The heavy machinery and petrochemical industries also experienced similar spillover effects during later expansions, and former FDI employees even contributed to plant exports in the petrochemical industry (Koo 1985, 190–213).

Even without a detailed cost-benefit analysis of FDI, it seems reasonable to assume that the first and foremost objective of inviting FDI into those important industrial sectors in Korea has been accomplished successfully so far. However, FDI policy reform was introduced in 1984 with the realization that Korea had reached a stage in which FDI would have to play a more important role and therefore that the promotion of an FDI-friendly environment was essential. With the reform, FDI increased rapidly before slowing substantially in recent years. This issue will be further pursued in chapter 7.

The Role of Foreign Technology

> . . . [T]hat one is a follower and not a leader is a precious advantage. This way one can peek over the shoulder of those ahead to see what they are doing. This inspires a very forward-looking approach in which countries can consciously or unconsciously pattern themselves on those which have gotten somewhat further along the path. . . . [T]he late-developers had the advantage of studying the past progress of other countries which preceded them in economic development. They were able to see how far the front-runners had gotten and, even if they were in no position to copy them yet, this information was still useful. —Jon Woronoff (1986)

Technology consists not only of technical and scientific knowledge and procedural methods, but also organizational and managerial techniques

Table 5.10 Imports of foreign affiliates of different home countries: geographical distribution, 1984–86

Home country	1984 Millions of dollars	1984 Percent-ages[a]	1985 Millions of dollars	1985 Percent-ages[a]	1986 Millions of dollars	1986 Percent-ages[a]
US affiliates' imports from						
US	396	59.4	391	56.6	442	49.9
Japan	106	15.9	101	14.6	174	19.6
Other	165	24.7	199	28.8	270	30.5
Japanese affiliates' imports from						
US	68	8.4	67	7.6	106	8.3
Japan	572	70.9	596	67.6	942	73.6
Other	166	20.6	219	24.8	232	18.1
Other, imports from						
US	92	6.5	65	5.1	68	6.6
Japan	79	5.6	116	9.1	241	23.2
Other	1,237	87.9	1,099	85.9	726	70.1

a. Proportions of foreign affiliates' imports from different countries.

Source: Ministry of Finance, Korea. 1991. *The Korean Economy and Foreign Capital* (January).

to transform inputs into outputs (Dahlman and Sercovich 1984). Technology transfer, therefore, can take place through various means: patents, licenses, engineering data, operating manuals, technical services, management consultancy, and learning by training or by watching.

Technology transfer can also take place through importing capital equipment embodied with specialized technology. Koreans have preferred other arrangements to FDI for foreign technology transfer: assistance from abroad—either from buyers of output or sellers of capital equipment or raw materials—and licensing agreements or joint ventures were the vehicles of choice for obtaining production-related engineering technology. When other alternatives were not available, Koreans purchased the necessary technology to apply by themselves. The last alternative, which was not considered to be very attractive, was to bundle FDI equity participation with technology transfer. As one study (Rhee et al. 1984, 46) aptly commented, "The Koreans thus were selective in the amount of technology they transferred from abroad in relation to the other baggage that came with it." Even when FDI was chosen as a vehicle for transferring technology, Koreans never neglected to localize the technology whenever possible and improve their technological capabilities further.

Based on a data survey of firms in the 1970s, Rhee et al. (1984, 39–50) reported that suppliers of capital equipment and raw materials and buyers of output were the leading channels of foreign technology transfer for all industries, and the importance was, as expected, even higher for traditional industries, where there was already substantial accumulated local technological capability. A similar result was suggested in the author's earlier study with Leroy Jones on entrepreneurial functions. According to the study, technology was the most important benefit that foreign firms could provide to assist Korean entrepreneurs (Jones and SaKong 1980, 189–90).

One of the strengths of the Korean economy since the early 1960s has been the way in which entrepreneurs in export-related sectors are allowed free access to foreign capital equipment and raw materials.

From nearly 30 percent to over 35 percent of imports in recent decades have been capital goods (see appendix, table A.46). The ratio has increased in recent years, reflecting ongoing restructuring toward more technology- and capital-intensive sectors. Because of the emphasis on restructuring, Korean exporters have been able to purchase capital equipment that embodied the latest technology. Sellers' assistance usually included installation, so the Koreans learned the operation process free of charge in most cases. Sometimes, as a part of the purchase agreements, engineers were sent abroad for training. This was a highly important source of foreign technology transfer in Korea (Westphal, Kim, and Dahlman 1985).

Also, buyers of output very often provided technology-related product design, production processes, quality control, and other management know-how to help businesses deliver quality products with appropriate specifications and design in a timely manner. This channel of foreign technology transfer, particularly in earlier years, was also important for Korea. Accordingly, Korea's adoption of an outward-looking development strategy helped entrepreneurs to take advantage of technology transfer at a low cost.[10] These are additional benefits that accrue from the outward-looking development strategy, besides static efficiency gains from trade.

On the other hand, the study also reports that for modern industries where the local technological gap is greatest, technical licensing agreements were the leading channel of foreign technology transfer in Korea (Rhee et al. 1984, 40). Countries that fail to nurture local absorptive capacity cannot make use of cheaper sources of technology transfer. But Korea, with its high level of general education and local R&D efforts, was able to take advantage of such technology transfer at low cost.

As indicated earlier, policies toward foreign technology transfer in general were rather tightly administered in the sense that only large

---

10. For good discussions on this aspect of technology transfer, see Dahlman and Sercovich (1984) and Kim (1989).

technological gaps could be filled by licensing agreements or FDI. Over time, however, as industrial restructuring itself necessitated more foreign technology, the government liberalized technology transfer.

The first of these liberalization measures was introduced in 1978. The government designated industries such as machinery, ship building, electronics, chemicals, and textiles for automatic approval of technological licensing, provided the contractual terms met preannounced criteria: the maximum ratio of royalty payments to sales receipts should not exceed 3 percent, the contract periods should not exceed three years, and royalty prepayments should not exceed $30,000 with total contracted royalties of $100,000. In 1979 further liberalization measures were introduced by relaxing the preannounced conditions and allowing automatic approval for all industries except those in the nuclear and defense sectors. Even these exceptions were lifted altogether in 1980.

A more important reform was introduced in 1984, when technological licensing agreements no longer required government approval but only notification to government authorities. Government authority in dealing with technology imports and with contractual terms and conditions was delegated to designated banks in 1988. However, until 1986, only contracts for importing trademark goods were not permitted.

The number of technical licensing agreements and royalty payments rose dramatically in the 1980s. Of the $6.1 billion in royalty payments from 1962 to 1991, over 90 percent was for technology imported since 1982. This reflects the rapid increase in technology imports since the early 1980s (see appendix, tables A.47 through A.51).

About 51 percent of technology transfer cases were from Japan while 27 percent were from the United States during 1962–91. However, nearly 48 percent of royalty payments went to the US while 31.3 percent went to Japan.

In terms of industrial distribution, 72.8 percent of technology transfers went to the oil refinery, chemical, electrical and electronics, and machinery industries from 1962 to 1991. They represent those sectors that had the greatest technological gap, and for the same reason, FDI was also heavily concentrated in these areas.

Did foreign affiliates in Korea import foreign technology through technical licenses more actively than other Korean firms? One study (H. W. Kim 1990) covering the period up to 1978 suggests active technology imports of foreign affiliates in Korea. It shows that foreign affiliates made 100 percent of petroleum refinery, 35.4 percent of chemical, 36.7 percent of electronics, and 15.5 percent of machinery-sector licensing agreements.

Among technical licensing agreements, the more significant cases are those related to patents, as they tend to involve modern technology. In 1989 47.8 percent of licensing cases were with patents. More than 50 percent of technical licensing agreements in the following sectors included patents: electrical and electronics (61.9 percent), machinery (54.2 percent), and chemicals (50.6 percent). Indeed, modern technology is more critical in these sectors. Proportionally, agreements with US and European partners included more patents than agreements with the Japanese in 1989. About 54 percent of licensing agreements with the United States, 54 percent with West Germany, 39 percent with France, and 36 percent with Japan included patents.

Technical licensing agreements including trademarks were also frequent. In 1989 25 percent of licensing cases included trademarks. Nearly 70 percent of technical licensing agreements in the textile and garment industry included trademarks, as might be expected. They were primarily to acquire famous brand names for domestic sales. It is worth remembering that until the mid-1980s, trademark acquisition was not allowed in Korea.

Was foreign technology transfer to Korea important for development? This is difficult to determine without detailed cost-benefit analysis. However, one can say that those sectors in which technical licensing agreements were concentrated are the sectors currently doing well in exports—for example, machinery and electronics—and in import substitution, particularly oil refineries.

According to one 1985 survey (Kwon 1986), only about 10 percent of imported technology can be considered state-of-the-art. Consequently, one might argue that the older technology that tended to be imported did not contribute much to Korea's general technological advancement. In the past, however, Korea's industrial competitiveness came primarily from combining known and proven technologies with diligent skilled labor and capable managers. Until the catchup process is complete and these advantages are exhausted, such technology greatly contributes to enhancing competitiveness and should be considered beneficial.

How about management, technology, and know-how transfer? Korea was rather secluded throughout its history, and it wasn't until the early 1960s that the Korean economy started to become integrated into the world through trade, foreign direct investment, tourism, and so forth. Management technology and know-how can be transferred through these channels. Particularly, Korea's outward orientation encouraged entrepreneurial contact with outsiders and must have facilitated this kind of technology transfer.

One cannot leave out technical assistance programs provided bilaterally by the United States and multilaterally through overseas education and training programs. Aid administered by the US AID in the late 1950s and early 1960s was different from the Korean reconstruction program of the 1950s in that it emphasized the exchange of experts and short-term training of Koreans in the United States. The AID program sent approximately 1,900 experts to Korea between 1951 and 1972. About 4,000 Koreans went to the United States under the same program.[11] The direct and indirect impacts of these programs should not be underestimated.

Multilateral technical assistance was mostly provided by UN-affiliated organizations, the Colombo plan, and others. From 1951 to 1982, approximately 2,300 foreign experts were sent to Korea, and about 15,000 Koreans participated in training through these organizations. Some of these programs, such as the United Nations Development Programme (UNDP), were specifically designed to build expertise for formulating socioeconomic policies in Korea. Consequently, these programs also must have helped to transfer significant levels of general technology to Korea during the early development period.

The Korean government limited the number of students going abroad to save foreign exchange in the earlier years. However, students majoring in science, engineering, and business administration were treated more favorably in the national screening process than were those in the humanities and social sciences, even in the 1960s. These restrictive policies were liberalized in the late 1970s and again in recent years as the balance of payments situation turned favorable.

The Korean government also has been making conscious efforts to attract foreign-educated Korean students back to Korea. The establishment of the Korea Institute of Science and Technology (KIST) in 1967 not only provided an excellent research environment but also prestige and remuneration for returning scientists. Currently there are 250 scientists and engineers at KIST holding advanced degrees earned abroad. Under the auspices of the Ministry of Science and Technology, there are 21 research institutes with nearly 5,000 researchers altogether.[12]

One important point to be made with respect to these efforts is that they not only directly contributed to enhancing local technological capability but also made cheaper sources of technology transfer available for Korea. In other words, with the enhanced local technology absorptive capacity, Korea could easily take advantage of embodied technology. It is beyond the scope of this study, but the significant impact these efforts made on technology transfer should be fully explored for possible emulation by others.

The Role of Foreign Trade

The overall beneficial effects of foreign trade on an economy are almost impossible to quantify in a meaningful way. In addition to static allo-

---

11. These programs cost approximately $126 million. See Kim (1989).

12. There were 10,337 employees, including administrative and nonresearch staff, in addition to 4,920 researchers at those institutes as of June 1991.

cative efficiency gains from foreign trade, there are all sorts of beneficial elements accompanying foreign trade that are difficult to quantify. Well-known benefits of foreign trade include efficiency gains by achieving economies of scale, higher capacity utilization, X-efficiency gains from exposure to foreign competition, and other externalities provided by markets abroad. In addition, foreign trade plays an even more important role in closing both the domestic savings and foreign-exchange gaps during development. In the case of Korea, during the earlier stages of development, foreign trade contributed both directly and indirectly to closing these gaps by enhancing Korea's credit standing in international capital markets and helping to make necessary borrowing possible.

The Korean trade regime in the 1950s was characterized as biased toward import substitution in nondurable consumer products and their inputs. Foreign exchange rates were kept at a consistently overvalued level, and the highly complicated multiple exchange rate system was maintained.

It is often argued that these policies, particularly the overvalued currency, discouraged exports. As was discussed earlier, however, foreign exchange holdings did provide windfall-gain opportunities through other profit-making avenues such as the import-export link system. In other words, Korean exporters could earn a much higher effective return on foreign exchange generated from exports even in the 1950s. It has already been shown that the effective exchange rate for exports, inclusive of various subsidies, has remained quite stable since the late 1950s.

What was lacking then was the strong leadership commitment to export promotion and nonpecuniary incentives, which reduced uncertainties associated with successful export activities. At the same time, there were plenty of opportunities for windfall gains through "zero-sum" entrepreneurial activities or rent-seeking activities, which are more profitable than socially productive entrepreneurial activities such as exports.

As a result, according to one estimate, exports contributed less than 10 percent to real GNP growth at this early stage. On the other hand, import substitution in the 1950s was relatively more important (see appendix, table A.52). Since the early 1960s, however, the contribution of exports to total output, manufacturing output, and real GNP increased substantially while import substitution gradually played a much smaller role and even contributed negatively in later periods.

These estimates are still partial in the sense that not all the beneficial effects of trade are included in them. They are based on demand-side growth analysis only. However, there are other beneficial effects of trade that increase productivity in the economy as a whole. These supply-side factors certainly interact with demand-side factors as well.

The contribution of total factor productivity gains to national income growth was maintained at a relatively high level during the last three decades (see appendix, table A.53), although it is difficult to determine exactly how much of total factor productivity was affected by foreign trade. It is worth noting, however, that total factor productivity was at its lowest during 1972–82 when the outward-looking development strategy weakened to some extent.[13]

Bilateral Trade Disputes and Their Impact

Thanks primarily to the adoption of an outward-looking development strategy, Korea's export-led growth during the last three decades has been so phenomenal that Korea became a leading member of the group of newly industrializing economies (NIEs) in the 1980s. Korea even experienced current account surpluses in the late 1980s after suffering from chronic balance of payments deficits.

This phenomenal success, however, brought its own problems. As Korea's exports grew fast, its export share in the world naturally increased. Trade disputes and friction with Korea's trading partners were bound to arise. Especially when Korea's major trading partners suffered from severe domestic economic problems and trade deficits, these disputes became serious.

The United States has traditionally been the most important market for Korea's exports. It made up more than one-third of Korea's export markets in the 1980s. As a result, Korea became the seventh largest US trading partner. Furthermore, the composition of Korean exports in the 1980s was different from that of the earlier period, when Korean exports were primarily labor-intensive goods such as textiles, footwear, and so forth. Coming into the 1980s, Korea began to export such capital- and skill-intensive items as automobiles, color television sets, videocassette recorders and personal computers, for which US industries were fighting a losing competitive war with Japan. Korea has recorded bilateral trade surpluses with the United States since 1982.[14]

The United States was suffering from twin deficit problems. As a result, a protectionist mood began to prevail there. Japan became the major target, but Korea was perceived as "the second Japan" by Americans and therefore had to suffer as well from protectionist US policies. The US government started to restrict Korean access to the US market

---

13. A recent empirical study (Greenaway and Nam 1988) found that annual incremental capital to output ratios (ICORs) for outward-oriented economies were lower than those of inward-oriented economies, suggesting that investment productivity was higher for outward-oriented economies.

14. The bilateral trade balance was in favor of the United States for many years before 1982. Starting with a $162.8 million surplus in 1982, Korea recorded its highest surplus, $9.6 billion, in 1987. Since then, the surplus has been reduced rapidly, and currently the balance is again in favor of the United States.

by means of "process protectionism" and "administered protection" policies, and it threatened unilateral retaliation if Korea did not open its markets.[15]

From 1984 to 1989, Korea's total exports to the United States amounted to $95.5 billion. Nearly 30 percent of the total, or $27.1 billion of exports, was subject to US protectionist policies in one form or an other, the largest proportion being voluntary export restraints (VERs) for textiles and steel.[16] Antidumping charges were the most frequently used process protectionist measures against Korean exports during the 1980s. There were 63 initiations of protectionist measures other than VERs against Korean exports from 1980 to 1989, and 25 out of the 63 cases were antidumping charges. Initiations under Section 337 of the Tariff Act of 1930 were also used frequently in relation to infringement of intellectual property rights, particularly in the second half of the 1980s.

Since the middle of the 1980s, the United States started to aggressively use Section 301 of the Trade Act of 1974, which was amended by the 1988 Omnibus Trade and Competitiveness Act, to gain bilateral reciprocity. The US government has invoked Section 301 twice against Korea since 1985, first to gain access to the insurance market and second to get intellectual property rights protection. There were two industry-initiated Section 301 cases, namely tobacco and wine, while the US movie industry threatened to file a petition for Section 301.

In the case of beef, a Section 301 petition was filed, but the issue was transferred to the General Agreement on Tariffs and Trade (GATT). All of these cases, however, were more or less resolved through negotiations without invoking retaliatory measures. Korea, with a number of preemptive trade concessions, has so far also avoided being named a "priority foreign country" under the provisions of Section 301. But the Korean telecommunications policy was designated as a "priority foreign practice," and Korea was included in the "priority watch list" with regard to intellectual property rights protection in 1989. Under the 1988 Omnibus Trade and Competitiveness Act, the US government also registered complaints against what it referred to as Korea's foreign exchange rate manipulation a few times as well.[17]

Important questions to ask in connection with this are how these protectionist measures affected Korea and how much the United States gained through these policies. These issues will be addressed here primarily in qualitative rather than quantitative terms.

---

15. For detailed discussions, see Schott (1989), Nam (forthcoming), Kihwan Kim (1991), and Noland (1991).

16. See Nam (forthcoming) for statistics.

17. It is unclear, however, how exchange rate "manipulation" is distinguished from exchange rate "management," as practiced by the United States and other G-7 countries. See Bergsten (1989), Williamson (1989), and Balassa and Williamson (1987).

Protectionist measures taken to restrict Korean access to the US market since the early 1980s left a critical mark on the psychological makeup of the Korean society. Let us take one of the early antidumping cases, involving the photo album industry. This case was a real shocker for Koreans. Total album exports to the United States amounted to $36 million in 1985, involving 62 small companies. Nearly 70 percent of these companies had between 20 and 99 total employees. These small, family-run companies did not have proper bookkeeping records. The US authorities charged dumping margins based on estimated data provided by the US firms that had filed suit. A shockingly high final margin, 64.81 percent, was then applied to all Korean exporting firms. This high final dumping margin was even more disturbing for Korea because the preliminary margin announced by the US Commerce Department was 4.04 percent. This decision illustrates well the arbitrary nature of such measures and of one aspect of process protectionism.

Even though the macroeconomic impacts of the case on both economies are negligible, its immediate impact on the album industry can easily be imagined. The industry's capacity utilization rate was reduced to 40 percent, and 1,000 employees were immediately discharged. Its emotional impact on the Korean society was even greater. Korean housewives and young students in large cities staged campaigns to buy the products of the affected firms. This campaign was followed by fierce anti-American demonstrations by radical students, who forcefully occupied the US Chamber of Commerce office in Seoul.

In a way, the color television antidumping case of 1983 and the album case of 1985 awakened the nation to the merciless reality of international competition.[18] Koreans suddenly began to realize that the United States was no longer a benevolent big brother, always ready to help Koreans who were trying to make it. Instead, many Koreans began to see the United States as a losing competitor in the international economic arena that unfairly harassed even its closest allies.[19] Up to this point, anti-American slogans often heard in other parts of the world were not familiar to most Koreans. However, such trade-related issues touched the minds of the Korean people differently, and subsequently, ordinary people on the street occasionally expressed anti-American sentiments.

These negative feelings were further aggravated by the United States' insistence that Korea open its markets. Particularly, pressure for the

---

18. Trade unions and color television firms in the United States filed antidumping charges against Korean exporters. The final average dumping margin was determined to be 10.65 percent. Due to this margin, Korean color TV exports to the United States were reduced to $230 million in 1985 from $300 million in 1984.

19. Around this time, many articles to this effect appeared in daily newspapers and weekly journals.

opening of the cigarette market caused violent reactions from many Koreans. The reasons for this phenomenon are manifold. As with other agricultural products, the market involves farmers and their livelihoods. Another important reason has to do with the unfortunate historical legacy of the Korean War. US cigarettes had come to represent many social evils that existed in the nation during the Korean War—smuggling, corruption, illegal activity, immorality, conspicuous consumption, and so forth. Furthermore, Koreans knew of the vigorous antismoking campaigns in the United States.

In any case, one after another, sensitive trade disputes between the two countries and market-opening shockers continued throughout the decade. After the clash over the cigarette market came market openings in service markets including banking, insurance, and securities. The intellectual property rights agreement was another unexpectedly fast adjustment Koreans had to make. Pressure on foreign exchange was also a new policy matter the government had to learn to deal with. Of course, pressures put on these markets and other agricultural products continuously intensified the general sense of ill feeling toward the United States.

These bilateral trade problems caused serious damage to the Korean governmental policy stance, which had been contributing to the maintenance of the liberal global trading system. As discussed in chapter 4, the Korean government unilaterally initiated international liberalization programs beginning in the early 1980s to reduce both tariff and nontariff barriers for its own reasons. Domestic adversaries of such liberalization now gained strong ground for delaying such programs and preventing new reform programs from being initiated. Now they would say, "Let's wait until we are pushed" and "it's better to have something to yield when we are pushed." It became easier for this camp to persuade the general public that the trade reforms were primarily for the benefit of other nations, including the United States. However, such an approach could only damage the Korean economy, as necessary reforms are not only delayed but are also reactive, pushed forward piecemeal based on other nations' needs. The nation needed its own well-sequenced reform programs for its own good.

These same forces pushed the government and the national assembly to emulate trading partners' bad practices of process protectionism. This not only put the nation in a vicious circle of trade conflicts with others but also made it more difficult to initiate trade reform efforts consistent with GATT principles.

What did the United States gain from these policies? No one can deny that US pressure opened most of the affected markets faster and more widely than would otherwise have been the case. It is also difficult to deny that US market-restricting protectionist measures also succeeded in reducing Korean exports of affected items.

But were these "successes" worthwhile for the United States, considering all the problems they caused? That is for US policymakers to decide. From Korea's perspective, even bilateral trade problems are better brought to multilateral forums such as GATT to make the issues less political. Secondly, even at the bilateral level, negotiations should be based on overall programs sequenced appropriately rather than case-by-case solutions for the benefit of both countries. For Koreans, there is every reason to support a multilateral trading system. At the same time, Koreans should realize that their country is no longer perceived by others as a war-torn, helpless nation but rather is seen as a fierce competitor, to be kept under close observation.

The IMF and the World Bank

Korea joined the IMF in 1955, taking advantage of the transitional arrangements of Article XIV, which allows a new member to maintain existing restrictions on payments and transfers for current international transactions. In November 1988, however, Korea formally accepted the full obligations of Article VIII of the IMF's Articles of Agreement by eliminating all remaining restrictions on current international transactions. The IMF resident representative office was closed in July 1987, after 22 years of operation in Korea.[20]

During this period of Korea's active membership, Korea took full advantage of the IMF's surveillance function, financial assistance, and other technical assistance and training services. As of June 1987, Korea's total borrowing from the IMF amounted to 2.5 billion in Special Drawing Rights (SDR). The IMF's financial assistance, regardless of the different borrowing arrangements, has significant impact on the receiving country, much more so than the sheer magnitude of the borrowing indicates. First of all, through financial assistance arrangements, the borrower's international credit standing itself is enhanced, enabling the country to borrow from other sources in times of necessity. Secondly, through lending conditionalities, the borrower is obliged to initiate necessary reforms that would help solve the nation's balance of payments problems and enhance the nation's long-term growth potential. As importantly, the process of financial assistance itself involved serious discussions of macroeconomic policy framework and financial discipline.

Korea made 16 stand-by arrangements with the IMF. Even though Koreans never actually drew on nine of them, their financial impact,

---

20. Until 1965, when the first resident representative office was opened, there was no close, cooperative relationship.

both direct and indirect, was significant, particularly in times of Korea's economic difficulties. An even more important aspect of the IMF's financial assistance for Korea, however, was the serious discussion it engendered on macroeconomic policy and financial discipline. Not only did the Korean government take these talks seriously, it fully used them to garner support for the policies from both politicians and the business community in general. The planning and financial ministries also used IMF discussions to sway other economic ministries with conflicting interests. The opinions of multilateral institutions, with their more objective perspective on domestic problems, can often be useful in selling painful adjustment programs to the public. As Korea's then finance minister, the author summarized this point in remarks made at the closing of the IMF Resident Representative Office in Seoul in July 1987:

> The value of these [financial] agreements went beyond the financial amounts involved. They provided a guiding framework under which conflicting domestic claims on resources could be reconciled with supply. Moreover, by providing an independent affirmation of the Government's resolve to pursue sustainable economic goals with prudent policies, these arrangements facilitated our access to international capital markets by bolstering international confidence in Korea.[21]

Korea joined the World Bank in 1955 and the International Development Agency (IDA) in 1961.[22] Financial assistance began in 1962 with a $14 million IDA credit line. The Bank made its first loan of $5 million to Korea in 1968. As of 31 March 1991, Korea had received 95 bank loans amounting to $6,648.8 million and eight IDA credits of $115.58 million.[23] In fact, it accounts for nearly one-third of Korea's overall public loans. These loans were primarily channeled into four distinctive areas: the social overhead capital sector, that is, improving and extending highways, railways, ports and harbors, and waterways; social development areas, such as education, health, and population control; agricultural development; and private plant and equipment investment through public development finance mechanisms. In addition, Korea received structural adjustment loans in the early 1980s

---

21. These remarks were reprinted in *Finance & Development*, March 1989, 19.

22. Korea joined the International Finance Corporation (IFC) in 1964. As of January 1992, the IFC invested $105 million in 23 Korean corporations. The IFC's gross commitment totaled $249.4 million, but there were cancellations. IFC investments have been primarily made in electronic products, development financing, and capital markets.

23. The total Bank loan amount includes one Third Window loan and total credits that took account of cancellations and refinancing of one IDA credit in a subsequent Bank loan. Korea made prepayment of Bank loans totaling $1.644 billion with its current account surplus in 1987–88.

and financial sector loans to support financial sector liberalization in 1983 and 1985.[24]

The World Bank also provided technical assistance to Korea through its lending operations for projects. In addition, the Bank served as the executing agent for UNDP Planning Assistance Projects for the preparation of Korea's fifth and sixth five-year plans. In addition, meetings of the International Economic Consultative Organization for Korea (IECOK) were held under the auspices of the Bank. IECOK gave Korea the opportunity of presenting a favorable picture of the economy's prospects in order to persuade international lenders to extend loans and thereby improve the credit standing of the nation.[25] Korea also benefited greatly from consultations with IECOK on the choice of the nation's development strategies and policies.

It is well beyond the scope of this study to discuss the World Bank's contribution to Korea's economic development. It must be said, however, that its contribution to the Korean economy exceeds the vast quantitative impact of the loans. Korea, always open to outside advice, fully used the Bank, as it did the IMF, in reassessing its own plans and programs. Indeed, if the common problem with most developing countries is an inappropriate choice of development strategies and macroeconomic management of their economies, Korea must be considered an exceptional country. It seriously listened to the outside voices of such objective multilateral institutions as the Bank and IMF.[26] The Bank summarized the positive and mutually respectful relationship between Korea and itself in this way:

> Korea's openness and adaptability to the winds of change have enabled external financial agencies such as the World Bank to help the country's development efforts effectively. Although the bulk of resources for Korea's development— human and material—has come from Korea itself, external assistance from the Bank and other multilateral and bilateral donors has played a crucial role. The Bank's partnership with Korea has enhanced the normal Bank-client relationship by providing a continuous exchange of ideas, with the Bank drawing on Korea's

---

24. The first structural adjustment loan (SAL) of $250 million was approved in December 1981 and fully disbursed in September 1984. The second SAL of $300 million, approved in November 1983, was also fully disbursed by September 1984. Two financial sector loans of $255 million and $222 million were approved in June 1983 and June 1985, respectively, and a small portion of the second loan is yet to be disbursed.

25. The final meeting of IECOK was held under the chairmanship of the World Bank in July 1984.

26. Of course, there are individual projects implemented against the Bank's recommendation that turned out to be "successful." The most often-cited projects are the Pohang integrated steel mill and the Seoul-Pusan highway projects. There were also various occasions in which the Korean authority and the Bank disagreed on specific policies and the timing of their implementation. However, these were exceptions rather than the rule. Furthermore, Koreans, taking the available wisdom seriously, carefully reevaluated these cases and were more cautious in their implementation.

successful development experience and Korea tapping the Bank's experience in economic policy analysis and planning. On the whole it has been a mutually beneficial partnership. (World Bank 1985, 2–3)

Korea has agreed to "graduate" from World Bank loan operations in 1995.[27] During the phase-out period, Korea is expected to keep Bank loans at a minimum level.

At this juncture of Korea's development and the beginning of a new cooperative era, it seems appropriate to reemphasize the positive role both the World Bank and the IMF played. Even without having detailed, quantitative analyses of the Bank's intermediate- to long-term loans and the IMF's short-term credit facilities and their contributions to Korea's economic development, one can definitely say that Koreans took full advantage of them for their nation's economic development.

As previously discussed, the Korean bureaucrats felt compelled to produce results or to deliver outcomes in terms of good economic performance. As a result, valuable outside advice was never wasted, regardless of whether it was from private or public, or from multilateral or bilateral sources.

At the same time, the Korean government needed a kind of sounding board for its ideas and nonpolitical multilateral institutions to help persuade the public to accept painful economic adjustments. This advice on the macroeconomic management and structural adjustments of the Korean economy undoubtedly served the receptive Koreans well. Thus it is no wonder Korea became a success story of close cooperation between multilateral institutions and a developing nation.

Summary

Korea's economic success of the last three decades is due, to a great extent, to international factors: foreign markets, foreign capital, and imported technology. It is well-known by now that the outward-oriented growth strategy adopted in the early 1960s was successful. The implementation of this strategy, in turn, relied heavily on foreign debt capital. External borrowing was necessary to finance investments in export industries and build necessary social overhead capital. In the 1950s, however, Korea had to rely heavily on foreign aid, which served as the major source of financing the nation's balance of payments deficits. Foreign aid greatly contributed to closing both the nation's savings and foreign-exchange gaps.

Coming into the 1960s, however, the role of foreign aid was diminished drastically while foreign borrowing began to play a critical role in

---

27. Japan and Australia were graduated from the Bank in the 1960s and other OECD nations—Spain and Greece—in the 1970s.

the course of Korea's economic development. Until a few years ago, Korea was the fourth most heavily indebted nation among developing nations. From the early 1960s, Koreans believed that export-led growth and industrialization, financed by foreign debt, would eventually generate debt-servicing capacity and stimulate domestic saving. With this belief, the government actively encouraged foreign borrowing. At the same time, the government tightly monitored the situation from the very beginning to ensure that borrowed capital was put to productive uses, especially in export-related areas.

It is generally believed that Korea was able to use borrowed capital productively as intended. The right development strategy and effective leadership commitment were the most important factors contributing to this positive result. The export-oriented growth strategy, backed by unwavering leadership commitment, successfully promoted exports and growth, and consequently, generated debt-service capacity. Korea was able to reduce its gross foreign debt through prepayment arrangements beginning in 1986, when Korea started to generate a current account surplus.

Compared to foreign borrowing, foreign direct investment played only a minor role in Korea's recent development. There are a few possible explanations for this phenomenon. The recent colonial experience made Koreans generally suspicious about the real motives behind FDI. There still is a lingering suspicion that FDI is really a means to dominate Korean industries. In addition, there were other important factors related to economic policy. The promotion of labor-intensive light manufacturing industries in the early stage of economic development required less sophisticated technology, management, or marketing skills, all of which usually accompany FDI. At the same time, the relative cost structure was such that foreign debt capital was much more attractive to Korean businessmen than foreign equity capital. Consequently, Korean entrepreneurs preferred to take advantage of foreign debt rather than sharing benefits with foreign business partners.

In the case of Korea, the primary objective of the government's FDI policy has been the transfer of technology, and it seems that this objective has been accomplished successfully.

Technology transfer can take place through patents, licenses, FDI, and the import of capital equipment with embodied technology. FDI was the least attractive option to Koreans. Assistance from abroad, either from buyers of output or sellers of capital equipment and raw materials, licensing agreements, or joint ventures were preferred to obtain production-related engineering technology in Korea. The Koreans relied heavily on suppliers of capital equipment and raw materials and on buyers of output to transfer technology to Korean industry. The importance of technology transfer was greatest in those traditional industries where there was already substantial accumulated local technological capability.

When other alternatives were not available, Koreans simply bought technology and applied it by themselves. The last alternative considered was technology transfer bundled with FDI equity participation. When FDI was chosen, however, Koreans localized the technology whenever possible to improve their capabilities further.

Korea today is one of the major trading nations in the world. Since the early 1960s, the contribution of exports to total output, manufacturing output, and real GNP increased substantially compared with earlier periods. On the other hand, contributions made by import substitution were gradually reduced and became negative in later periods. Foreign trade contributed to Korea's development indirectly as well, helping to close both the gaps in domestic savings and foreign exchange by enhancing Korea's credit standing in international capital markets and helping to make necessary borrowing possible.

The United States traditionally has been the most important market for Korea's exports. It provided more than one-third of Korea's export market in the 1980s. Furthermore, Korea began recording bilateral trade surpluses with the United States in 1982. Because the US economy was suffering from twin deficit problems, Korea became one of the major targets for US process protectionism. At the same time, the United States aggressively pressured Korea to open its market, threatening retaliatory measures.

In short, the United States succeeded in hurting Korea's exports to the United States and gained access to Korean markets in which it was interested. But at what cost? Both economic and political costs for both countries were rather high. A better solution may be found in the multilateral settlement process of trade disputes.

Korea's relationships with important multilateral institutions such as the International Bank for Reconstruction and Development (IBRD) and IMF have been highly productive. In addition to financial assistance, Koreans took the advice and consultations of IBRD and IMF seriously, and the Korean government made full use of these discussions to gain the support of politicians and different ministries with conflicting interests.

6

Korea's New Role in the World and Asia-Pacific Economy

When every country turned to protect its national private interest, the world public interest went down the drain, and with it the private interests of all. —Charles P. Kindleberger (1986, 290–91)

Even though South Korea is small in landmass, it looms large in the world economy. Its GNP ranked 15th largest in the world in 1989, and total trade increased from $477 million in 1962 to $153.4 billion in 1991, making Korea the 11th largest trading nation in the world.[1]

As a major trading partner and as a country whose future economic progress depends on foreign trade, Korea has new, important roles to play in preserving a liberal, global economic environment. At the same time, Korea is a "pioneer country" among developing nations in terms of successful economic development, and it can contribute to other countries' development through more active international economic cooperation. In addition, as an important member of the regional economy, Korea can make a positive contribution to the continued prosperity and balanced growth of the region.

In this chapter, Korea's history regarding international economic cooperation is presented. The chapter covers how Korea, as a development pioneer, can help developing nations, and it also discusses economic cooperation with the developing world, including Korea's outgoing foreign direct investment (FDI). Korea's role in Asia-Pacific economic cooperation and Japan's leadership role, which is critical for continued development of the region as well as the rest of the world, are also considered here.

---

1. This ranking excludes the former Soviet Union and all Eastern Bloc nations.

Past International Cooperation

Generally speaking, the history of Korea's international cooperation has been rather short. Following Japanese colonial rule in the 1940s and the devastating Korean War of 1950–53, the country was on the passive, aid-receiving end of international economic cooperation throughout the 1950s. Then came the 1960s, when Korea actively sought developmental cooperation, primarily as a borrower, in the international financial community. With substantial international financing to accommodate its development strategy, Korea during this decade was becoming a more active participant in the international financial and trade community. This trend continued and accelerated in the 1970s.

Korea joined the International Monetary Fund (IMF) and the World Bank in 1955. It became a member of the Asian Development Bank (ADB) from its creation in 1966, and it joined the United Nations Commission on Trade and Development (UNCTAD) and the Colombo Plan. In 1967 Korea joined the GATT and the Geneva Convention of International Commercial Dispute Settlement. From 1962 the Korean government requested that the US Agency for International Development (AID) help it create an international economic cooperative consultative body for Korea. The primary purpose of such an organization was to facilitate Korea's international borrowing for its development. This effort bore fruit only after the first five-year development plan was successfully completed.

In May 1966 the World Bank arranged a preliminary meeting in London for the establishment of the organization by inviting 11 nations other than Korea and representatives of the United Nations Development Programme (UNDP) and IMF as observers. The consultative body, called the International Economic Consultative Organization for Korea, or IECOK, was inaugurated in Paris in December 1966. The inaugurating member nations and other participating multilateral institutions were the United States, Japan, France, Canada, Australia, West Germany, Belgium, Italy, Taiwan, UNDP, IMF, and the World Bank (Economic Planning Board 1982a and b).[2] In the ensuing years, IECOK played an important role in facilitating Korea's borrowing from these advanced nations.

The Korean government made bilateral diplomatic and economic efforts as well. One important effort was the establishment of annual bilateral cabinet-level meetings with many countries. In 1965 the Korea–West Germany Economic Cooperation Agreement and Korea–West Germany Fiscal Aid Agreement were signed. With these agreements, the

---

2. Most of the inaugural member nations and institutions continued to be participants until IECOK consultation officially ended in 1984. However, Taiwan discontinued its participation in the consultation in 1979, and ADB, OECD/Development Assistance Committee, and the International Finance Corporation (IFC) participated in IECOK meetings later on.

first Korea–West Germany Economic Cabinet Meeting was held in Seoul in March 1966. This was followed by the Korea-Japan Economic Cabinet Meeting in 1966 and similar cabinet meetings with Thailand, Taiwan, the Philippines, Vietnam, and India.

Between 1967 and 1971, various trade agreements were completed with many European and African countries. In the 1960s, 21 trade agreements and 310 bilateral agreements were concluded. The establishment of overseas branches for trading companies was encouraged, and at the same time, foreign banks were allowed to operate in Korea, and Korean banks were permitted to open overseas offices. In December 1970 the Foreign Trade Law was amended to liberalize trade to "hostile" nations in order to expand export markets.

Since the early 1970s, the private sector has started to actively initiate programs for economic cooperation with other countries. For example, the Federation of Korean Industries (FKI), in cooperation with other economic associations in Korea, established bilateral private economic cooperation councils with various nations to facilitate bilateral economic and business dialogue among business leaders of respective nations. Such councils were created with Canada in 1972, with European countries including Belgium, Italy, and France in 1974, and with various developing nations, including Saudi Arabia in 1975. In 1977 trade missions, consisting of members from both private and public sectors, visited Scandinavian nations and established private economic cooperative councils with them. Special efforts were also made to promote private technical and financial cooperation with these nations.

In 1975 the official termination of aid from AID and Japanese Claim Funds made economic relations with these nations a partnership rather than a donor-receiver relationship. At the same time, Koreans made conscientious efforts to diversify economic partnerships to other countries besides the United States and Japan. In particular, private entrepreneurs were quite successful in making new business partners in the developing world, covering Africa, Latin America, and Southeast Asia. These private initiatives contributed substantially to Korea's obtaining raw materials and to selling plants and equipment in these nations. As private enterprises advanced to developing nations and Middle Eastern nations, Korea's financial relationships naturally became more international.

The private sector also established the Korea–ASEAN business leaders club in 1979, and in 1982 it established the Korean chapter of the Pacific Basin Economic Council (PBEC) and thereby began to participate more actively in Asia-Pacific economic cooperation. The Korea–US economic cooperation council was established in 1973 and one with Japan in 1981. The Korea-Japan council's special purpose was to facilitate the transfer of modern technology and to help reduce chronic bilateral trade imbalances. Although the council has not yet produced significant visible results, it should accomplish more in the future as both countries' governments provide more support.[3]

As Korea started to generate current account surpluses, its posture in international economic cooperation naturally changed. As discussed in a following section, Korea took the first systematic approach to becoming a bilateral donor for developing nations through the creation of the Economic Development Cooperation Fund (EDCF) in 1986.

More significantly, Korea was starting to make prepayments of its outstanding foreign debt with its newly generated current account surplus at a time when the developing world debt was posing a serious problem and when debt forgiveness and debt rescheduling for these nations caused major concerns within the international financial community.

Even though Korea was the fourth most highly indebted nation in the developing world at the time, neither the IMF's list of 15 highly indebted nations nor US Secretary of State James Baker's list of 17 included Korea, simply because Korea was not expected to have any difficulty servicing its debt. In this regard, it can be argued that Korea contributed to the international financial system's stability by adroitly managing its own finances so as not to become a subject of international financial concern.[4]

Korea's New Role in the World Economy

The New World Order and Korea

The world is entering into a new order. The end of the Cold War has led the world into a period in which economics has become the dominant factor in determining international relations (Bergsten 1990, 96–112; Krause 1990). At the same time, the reduced role of military security as the predominant driver in international relations leaves the way open for vigorous and more frequent airing of economic frictions and disputes.

In the absence of an economic hegemon, major economic powers will jointly have to take responsibility for providing the "public goods" necessary to maintain a stable and prosperous world political economic

---

3. In response to the Korean government's persistent requests for transfer of technology, the Japanese government has consistently responded that such decisions should be left up to the private sector. To the extent that this is true, both governments should actively encourage closer private cooperation.

4. This factor was not usually brought up in international forums for discussing trade, despite the fact that Korea's debt-servicing capacity was directly related to its international trade capacity. This point was articulated in a statement made by the author, then Korean finance minister, at annual meetings of the World Bank and IMF in 1987. In this regard, it is desirable to establish a closer international trade-finance linkage through closer cooperation among relevant international organizations, such as IMF and GATT.

system (Kindleberger 1973). The most important public good is the maintenance of a liberal global economic system obtained through keeping world markets, and hence trade, freely accessible and nondiscriminatory to all trading partners.

The sharing of responsibility through joint economic leadership involves burden-sharing or cost-sharing among major economic powers. Of course, this burden or cost is not confined to direct out-of-pocket expenses. It also includes indirect or implicit costs that collective leadership incurs in providing public goods to maintain a liberal global economic system.[5] For example, market opening involves domestic structural adjustment costs.

What does this new world order mean to Korea? Korea is still a small country in that it cannot affect the outcome of major world events.[6] However, it is not small enough to afford the luxury of irresponsibility. In fact, Korea is becoming a major player, particularly in the area of international trade. Furthermore, because of its unique industrial and trade structure, characterized by large conglomerates, or *chaebols*, which export high-tech products and sophisticated consumer durables that compete directly with products from industrialized economies,[7] Korea is often perceived as larger than life by casual foreign observers.

Consequently, Korea is expected to participate actively in responsibility- and burden-sharing.[8] Korea has benefited greatly from a liberal global trade system and a stable financial environment in the past, and it will have to depend on such an environment in the future. Thus, for its own good, Korea should be ready to adapt to the new world order by actively assuming its share of responsibility and costs. In this connection, it is important for Korea to contribute to the successful completion of the Uruguay Round, or for that matter any multilateral forum aimed at maintaining free world trade.

In addition, Korea must take appropriate positive steps domestically to make necessary structural adjustments. A critical new challenge for Korea is reconciling international demands for responsibility-sharing with domestic political resistance to market opening and sensitivities to necessary but difficult structural adjustments in agriculture and finance.

---

5. For an illustrative discussion on the subject in relation to the recent Gulf War, see Bergsten (1991).

6. Even though Korea is one of the world's major trading nations, its export and import shares in the world were only 2.23 percent and 2.32 percent, respectively, in 1990 (see appendix, table A.6).

7. In fact, Korea is one of only four countries exporting computer chips to the United States.

8. As previously indicated, Korea has participated in burden-sharing to the extent that it has been externally liberalizing its economy on its own initiative. In addition, Korea recently participated in direct international cost-sharing during the Persian Gulf War.

Systemic changes in the global economy also call for Korea to take a fresh approach to international economic cooperation. These changes provide new opportunities for Korea as well. As a pioneer in successful development, Korea is ideally suited to organize closer international cooperation among developing nations. Korea should take advantage of the opportunities presented by the new world order and its improved standing to establish this new leadership role.

Korea as Pioneer

Once economic progress in the pioneer countries is a visible reality, the strength of the desire to imitate, to follow suit, to catch up obviously becomes an important determinant of what will happen among the non-pioneers. —Albert O. Hirschman (1958, 8)

No country from the developing world has joined the ranks of industrially advanced nations since World War II.[9] However, Korea today is on the threshold of doing so. Once Korea makes this transition successfully, its significance as a model for developing economies will necessarily increase.

Korea's recent first-hand experience in development can be helpful in assisting follower nations. Already, Korea has been providing technical assistance to developing nations on a limited scale.[10] The technical assistance programs include training for foreign technicians in Korea, sending Korean experts abroad, providing free technical services for project feasibility studies, and inviting high-ranking government officials to Korea to study through such programs as the International Development Exchange Program (IDEP) sponsored by the Korea Development Institute (KDI).[11] The government's training program and KDI's IDEP in particular have been popular among many follower nations. Currently, however, these programs are being operated on a rather small scale. For instance, there were 580 trainees and 107 participants in both programs in 1990.

Korea recently sent a mini-version of the Peace Corps to some Southeast Asian nations to work in such areas as agriculture and fisheries.[12]

---

9. Some might argue Japan achieved this, but Japan was never really considered as part of the Third World after World War II.

10. The Korean government has been providing a small amount of bilateral grants-in-aid since late 1970s. During 1977–90, $91.4 million of grants-in-aid was provided. Korea also provided technical assistance, amounting to only $72.7 million, during 1985–90 on a case by case basis.

11. Korea provided 44 feasibility studies free of charge during 1985–90 and invited a total of 3,128 foreign trainees to Korea.

12. A total of 40 volunteers were sent abroad during 1990–91.

Such programs should be properly tailored to fit each nation's needs. Korea has abundant human resources, both active and retired, whose services could be widely used by other nations in various specialized fields.

The government of Korea, however, must first offer special incentives for potential providers of relevant services. Especially for active government officials, extra incentives have to be provided to elicit their voluntary services in the developing nations as well as in multilateral institutions. Incentives, of course, should not be confined to remuneration. These services should become part of evaluations for promotion because, in this world of rapid globalization, officials' exposure to world economic affairs will affect job performance. In fact, it is a good policy to require prior service abroad for certain positions in the government.

Korea could also initiate technical assistance programs in cooperation with other pioneer countries and with capital-rich developed nations. At the same time, Korea should coordinate closely with multilateral development institutions, including the UNDP and UNIDO, in order to use Korean experts more widely. To this end, Korea should not only contribute to existing funds such as the World Bank's Consultant Trust Fund but seriously consider the establishment of a Korea International Development Fund, under the auspices of multilateral institutions, that would make use of Korean and other experts.

Currently, multilateral capital cooperation primarily takes the form of capital contributions to the International Bank for Reconstruction and Development (IBRD), EBRD, ADB, and IMF. In this connection, Korea should be allowed to make capital contributions and have voting rights in these institutions that are commensurate with its economic strength.[13] At the same time, international development organizations, in cooperation with the Korean government, should make efforts to more widely use Korea's rich human resources. In fact, in some cases, it is conceivable that Korea's own technical assistance programs could be linked with multilateral technical cooperation projects.

At the same time, multilateral organizations should encourage pioneer countries such as Korea to get more actively involved in international development efforts. Giving proper credit to successful pioneer countries will have the same beneficial effect on the developing world that rewarding honor students has on the whole class.

---

13. Korea's actual quota share at the IMF as of October 1992 is 0.48 percent while Korea's calculated quota share, reflecting its relative economic position in the world, was 1.131 percent at the time of the IMF's Ninth General Review of quota shares in 1988. Because actual quota share for Korea was 0.51 in 1988, it can be said that only 45 percent of Korea's economic capability is reflected in Korea's IMF position in 1988. Similarly, Korea is also underrepresented at the World Bank.

Economic Cooperation with the Developing World

Historically, Korea has been at the receiving end of international economic cooperation. To supplement domestically available resources for investment, foreign capital inducement policies were actively promoted, as discussed previously. As the Korean economy began to experience its current account surpluses and to reach a new stage of development in the mid-1980s, Korea started to take a new stance on international economic cooperation.

A significant turning point in international capital cooperation policy occurred in July 1987 when the Korean government established the EDCF under the auspices of the Ministry of Finance, primarily to facilitate bilateral financial cooperation with needy developing nations.[14] Even though the amount of financial resources involved is still rather small, the EDCF is expected to be used more widely in coming years for developing as well as former planned economies. It could also be used for cofinancing with multilateral institutions.

Another important step was taken in April 1991 when the Korea International Cooperation Agency (KOICA) was established under the Ministry of Foreign Affairs to consolidate developmental assistance projects previously administered by different ministries. The KOICA will cover such projects as grants-in-aid, technical assistance, training foreign personnel, sending Korean experts to developing nations, and training Korean personnel for international cooperation activities.

Table 6.1 shows Korean development assistance trends. Official development assistance (ODA) remains modest, at $89 million in 1990, even though it increased rapidly from $48 million in 1985. The ratio of ODA to GNP stayed at only 0.04 percent in 1990. It is much lower than the 0.7 percent level recommended by the Organization for Economic Cooperation and Development's Development Assistance Committee (DAC) or the DAC nations' average of 0.3 percent. The Korean government is known to have an internal guideline to increase this ratio to around 0.2 percent by 1996. Although low, this level will still be much higher than today's level for OECD non-DAC members of 0.08 percent.[15]

ODA consists of both bilateral and multilateral assistance. Bilateral assistance in turn is made up of grants-in-aid, technical cooperation, and capital cooperation. Grants-in-aid is generally provided with commodities such as motor vehicles, farm equipment, and other machinery, with the exception of financial aid for natural disasters in developing nations. As previously indicated, Korea's technical assistance to date has primarily been in the form of training technicians and government

---

14. For a comprehensive discussion on international cooperation, see Hak Soo Kim (1991).

15. Currently, Greece, Ireland, Luxembourg, Portugal, Spain, and Turkey are non-DAC OECD members.

Table 6.1 Official development assistance, 1985–90 (millions of dollars except where noted)

ODA	1985	1986	1987	1988	1989	1990
Total	48.3	111.5	74.7	62.3	98.5	89.2
Bilateral assistance	14.9	15.0	17.3	19.9	22.9	32.4
Grants-in-aid	8.5	8.5	9.1	11.4	12.6	11.6
Technical cooperation	6.4	6.5	8.2	8.5	8.5	9.1
Economic Development Cooperation Fund	n.a.	n.a.	n.a.	n.a.	1.8	9.9
Other	n.a.	n.a.	n.a.	n.a.	n.a.	1.9
Multilateral assistance	33.4	96.5	57.4	42.4	76.6	56.8
Contribution to multilateral institutions	4.9	4.9	5.8	6.7	8.7	10.3
Capital contribution to multilateral institutions	28.5	91.6	51.6	35.7	66.9	46.5
ODA as a share of GNP	0.05	0.11	0.06	0.04	0.05	0.04

n.a. = not applicable
ODA = official development assistance

Source: Economic Planning Board. 1991. *Statistics of Economic Cooperation with Developing Countries* (May).

officials from developing nations in Korea. Korea will have much more to offer in this area in the future. This is particularly fitting because Korea benefited through this kind of assistance from other more advanced nations.

Another important bilateral development effort involves the EDCF. Currently the EDCF has a rather meager capital base of $270 million, from which only about $10 million was actually drawn in 1990. The EDCF was used to finance such projects as railway modernization in Nigeria, telephone system expansion in the Philippines, and road construction in Sri Lanka. This EDCF-related aid, in conjunction with technical cooperation, should be steadily increased in coming years.

Korea's Outgoing Foreign Direct Investment

Broadly defined, international cooperation should include FDI, in addition to suppliers' credit and other private capital flows. It is rather natural to expect that FDI will not only grow the fastest but will also become proportionally the most important capital cooperation item in coming years. The past trend of FDI already shows this pattern.

The history of Korean investment abroad has been rather short. It began in 1968 with a forestry development project in Indonesia. From 1968 on, outgoing FDI grew at a modest rate. This modest growth continued until 1986 when the nation started to experience a balance of payments surplus (see appendix, tables A.54 and A.55). One exceptional year was 1978, when FDI increased substantially, albeit from a meager base. This large increase was due primarily to a sharp rise in construction-project investment in Middle Eastern countries.

Since 1986, however, outgoing FDI has been growing at a rapid rate. The average annual growth rate for the amount involved from 1987 to 1990 on an approval base, in actual investment, and the accumulated total amount outstanding were 49.9 percent, 80.3 percent, and 39.8 percent, respectively. Even then, Korean outgoing FDI was considered relatively small. For example, its ratio to GNP in 1990 was less than 1 percent and is still much smaller than Korea's incoming FDI.

The rapid increase in Korea's outgoing FDI in recent years reflects two mutually reinforcing forces. First, Korean businesses are participating in the current international trend toward globalization of business operations. They are interested in taking full advantage of host countries' different factor endowments and raw materials. Some are interested in acquiring necessary skills and technologies via FDI. At the same time, they are also interested in avoiding trade barriers. Rapidly rising domestic wages, an appreciating local currency, and the prevailing international mood toward regionalism and protectionism have contributed to pushing Korean firms in this direction.

Second, as Korea experienced a balance of payments surplus in 1986, the Korean government began to liberalize regulations on outgoing FDI. This policy change was effective in increasing FDI outflow because it came when Korean firms for the first time had enough financial resources to participate in global business activities.

Distribution trends by industry and by country of outgoing FDI are worth noting. Almost half of Korea's outgoing FDI, in terms of total outstanding net investment, was to the manufacturing sector concentrated in North America and Southeast Asia. In particular, the recent surge in outgoing FDI was dominated by increased investments in the manufacturing sector (see appendix, table A.56). In 1990, for example, 60.7 percent of the approved FDI (and 57.9 percent of total cases of FDI) were in the manufacturing sector. Even though the total amount of FDI outstanding is not as great, most of the comparable cases of FDI in trade-related areas are also concentrated in the same two geographical areas.

FDI in the manufacturing sector on an approval basis is mainly in the primary metal, metal fabrication (or machinery), and textiles and footwear sectors (see appendix, table A.57). Textile and footwear industry FDI is primarily concentrated in Asia (45 percent of approved cases) and in the Central and South American nations (32 percent of approved cases). Obviously, these cases mostly occur in labor-intensive sectors, and as such, their primary motive is to take advantage of cheaper labor forces in those regions.

Leading Korean electric and electronics firms generated the recent surge in machinery sector FDI, investing primarily in the United States until 1987. During 1988–89, however, FDI in this sector was directed toward other geographic areas while it slowed in the United States. During that period, out of 38 newly approved projects, 24 went to the Asian region, 9 to the European countries, and only 3 went to the United States. It is natural to expect Korea's outgoing FDI to rise in Eastern European nations and China in the near future. Motor vehicle and other transportation equipment FDI is also expected to follow the regional distribution trend set by the electric and electronics industries.

FDI in the primary metal sector began on a small scale in relatively low-technology areas. During the last few years, however, huge stainless steel and hot coil production projects, going mostly to North America, were included on the approved list. The number of such projects is not large, but the amount of investment is substantial because each project requires huge amounts of capital.

There are other important characteristics of Korea's outgoing FDI. In the past few years, both the number of projects and total investments made by small and medium-sized firms have increased substantially. Small and medium-sized firms' share of FDI in 1980 was only 2.8 percent of total cases and 1.8 percent of the total amount. These proportions have increased rapidly in recent years, reaching 32.6 percent and 9.9 percent, respectively, in 1989. These rapid increases reflect, first of all, dramatic changes in Korea's factor market situation, the labor market in particular. Most outgoing investments by small and medium-sized firms are in labor-intensive manufacturing sectors, such as textiles and clothing, footwear, and electronic and automobile parts. The destination of investment, therefore, is predominantly Asia, especially Indonesia and Thailand.

Another interesting aspect of FDI from small and medium-sized companies is that many are making their investments with large, financially stronger Korean firms, general trading companies in particular, thereby taking advantage of these firms' well-established marketing channels. With general trading companies providing financial support, raw materials, and marketing channels, small and medium-sized companies can move their production facilities abroad, where wage levels are still much lower than those that prevail in Korea. Small and medium-sized companies have also been known to move their production bases abroad by means of mergers and acquisitions.[16]

As previously discussed, the upward trend of Korea's outgoing FDI continued until 1990, when the nation experienced a rapid deterioration in its balance of payments, caused primarily by structural factors in the Korean economy—that is, changed factor endowments—rather than cyclical phenomena. One can safely assume that Korea's economic integration into the world economy by means of FDI will continue in coming years.

The Asia-Pacific Economy and Korea

Deepening Regional Interdependencies

The Asia-Pacific region, particularly the Asian-Pacific or Western Pacific, has been the most dynamic economic region in the world in the post-World War II era. Most countries in the region have managed to take full advantage of the liberal global economic environment facilitated by the General Agreement on Tariffs and Trade (GATT) after World War II. Japan was the leader. Throughout the 1960s, Japan grew at an annual average rate of over 10 percent. Then came the so-called Asian newly industrializing economies (NIEs), which followed Japan's lead throughout the 1970s and 1980s (table 6.2). In recent years, the region has started to witness the emergence of a second tier of NIEs, the members of the Association of Southeast Asian Nations (ASEAN).[17]

---

16. For a good discussion on these topics, see *Quarterly Korean EXIM Bank Bulletin*, June 1990.

17. This growth phenomenon in the region is often described as "the flying-geese" pattern of development. This term was first used by Professor Akamasu Kaname in the 1930s in relation to product cycles. Saburo Okita, however, popularized the term in the present context.

Table 6.2 Average annual growth rates of real GDP, 1960–89
(percentages)

Regions	1960–69[a]	1970–79[b]	1980–89
Total, Pacific Basin economies	6.4	6.9	5.3
Total, developing economies	6.5	8.0	6.1
Total, Asian NIEs	6.8	8.3	6.5
Hong Kong	10.0	9.4	7.4
Korea	7.7	9.5	8.2
Taiwan	9.5	10.2	7.5
Singapore	8.9	9.5	7.3
Total, ASEAN[c]	5.8	7.4	5.1
Indonesia	3.4	7.8	5.7
Malaysia	6.5	8.1	5.7
Philippines[d]	4.9	6.1	2.1
Thailand	8.3	7.4	6.9
China[c]	2.9	7.5	8.8
Total, developed economies	6.0	3.7	3.0
Japan	10.9	5.2	4.2
Total, North American economies	4.9	3.7	3.0
Canada	5.6	4.7	3.1
United States	4.1	2.7	2.8
Total, Oceania	4.7	3.0	2.5
Australia	5.3	3.6	3.3
New Zealand	4.1	2.4	1.7
European community	4.8	3.3	2.1
OECD	5.1	3.3	2.8

NIE = newly industrializing economy
OECD = Organization for Economic Cooperation and Development
a. 1960–70 for Hong Kong, Malaysia, and Canada; 1961–69 for Singapore, Taiwan, Indonesia, EC, and OECD.
b. 1971–79 for Malaysia.
c. Real national income.
d. Real GNP.

Sources: Census and Statistics Department, Hong Kong. *Estimates of Gross Domestic Product*, various issues; International Monetary Fund. 1989, 1990, and May 1991. *International Financial Statistics, Yearbook*; Organization for Economic Cooperation and Development (Paris). 1991. *National Accounts: 1960–1989*; Republic of China. 1990. *Statistical Yearbook*; The Economist Intelligence Unit, *Country Reports*, various issues; James, William. 1990. "Basic Directions and Areas for Cooperation: Structural Issues of the Asia-Pacific Economies." A paper presented at Asia-Pacific Economic Forum, June 21–22, Korea Institute for International Economic Policy, Seoul, Korea.

The bright economic future of the region is often highlighted by marking the next century as "the Pacific Century." Certainly the center of economic gravity has been shifting toward the Asia-Pacific from the Europe-Atlantic region since the middle of the current century.

Thanks to dynamic economic growth experienced by the region, Asia-Pacific GDP as a percentage of world GDP increased to 58.9 percent in

1989 from 46.0 percent in 1970.[18] The share of regional trade in world trade also increased to 41.5 percent in 1989 from 33.3 percent in 1970 (table 6.3). These figures contrast sharply with those for the European Community or the nations of the OECD, which are not increasing as fast or are decreasing.

As is well known, the Asia-Pacific region consists of a group of countries diverse in terms of history, culture, religion, language, form of government, and so forth. From an economic perspective, however, what stand out most are the region's diverse factor endowments and very different stages of development. There are resource-rich nations, such as the ASEAN members, Australia, and Canada; advanced technology- and capital-rich nations such as the United States and Japan; and nations with recent industrialization and development experience that are rich in human resources, namely the Asian NIEs.

Dynamic growth in the region in recent years owes much to the adoption of an outward-oriented development strategy by the most rapidly growing economies in the region, i.e., Japan since the 1950s, the Asian NIEs since the 1960s, and China and the ASEAN economies since the 1980s. The strong complementary relationships existing among these economies, together with an outward orientation, has led to deepening interdependencies among these economies.[19] In short, one can say that the openness, dynamic growth, and complementary relationships of these groups of nations inevitably resulted in speedy economic integration of the region (Krause 1990).

In addition, the recent trend of relocating industries through direct investments, particularly by Japan, and the recycling of Japan's trade surplus in the region through ODA has increased interdependencies even further. For the past few years, Japan has been the largest foreign aid donor among the 18 OECD DAC members, although ODA outflow relative to GNP is not the highest among these nations. The Asian region as a whole received nearly 70 percent of Japanese ODA since the mid-1970s, and the share during 1987–88 was 72.3 percent (Okita 1991, 35; Kosai and Matsuyama 1991, 64).

The deepening interdependencies can be seen from both trade and FDI flows in the region. Table 6.4 shows that, by 1989, all economies in the region had 55 to 73 percent of their trade within the region. On the average, intraregional trade in 1989 increased to 65.0 percent of total trade compared with 54.0 percent in 1978.[20]

---

18. Countries included here are the United States, Canada, Japan, Australia, New Zealand, four Asian NIEs, other ASEAN nations, and China.

19. In this connection, it should be pointed out that tourism is another important factor promoting economic integration in the region. See Krause (1990, 7–8).

20. One interesting question often asked in this connection is whether the region is biased

Table 6.3 Pacific Basin GDP and trading volume in the world, 1970–89 (billions of dollars except where noted)

GDP and trading volume	World	Pacific Basin[b]	EC	OECD	Pacific Basin as share of world	EC as share of world	OECD as share of world
GDP							
1970	3,138	1,444.1	681.9	2,105.1	46.0	21.7	67.1
1980	11,790	4,777.6	3,123.4	7,785.7	40.5	26.5	66.0
1989	16,929[a]	9,969.1	4,829.0	14,470.2	58.9	28.5	85.5
Trading volume							
1970	579.7	192.9	241.4	452.2	33.3	41.6	78.0
1980	3,841.9	1,220.2	1,463.8	2,648.8	31.8	38.1	68.9
1989	5,892.4	2,447.6	2,299.4	4,399.5	41.5	39.0	74.7

a. World GDP for 1989 was estimated on the basis of annual growth rates reported in International Monetary Fund. 1990. *World Economic Outlook* (May).

b. The Pacific Basin includes Australia, Canada, People's Republic of China, Hong Kong, Indonesia, Japan, Korea, Malaysia, New Zealand, Philippines, Singapore, Taiwan, Thailand, and the United States. National income was used for China.

Sources: Economic Planning Board. 1989. *Background Paper for APEC Ministerial Meeting* (September); International Monetary Fund. 1989, 1990, and May 1991. *International Financial Statistics, Yearbook; Direction of Trade Statistics*, various issues; Ministry of Finance, Republic of China. 1982. *Monthly Statistics of Exports and Imports*, No. 157 (September); 1990. *Statistical Yearbook of the Republic of China;* 1990. Directorate-General of Budget. *Accounting and Statistics of the Republic of China;* United Nations, Statistical Division, Department of Economic and Social Development. 1983, 1984, and 1987. *Statistical Yearbook;* Organization for Economic Cooperation and Development (Paris). *National Accounts: 1960–1989.* 1991.

Table 6.4 Pacific Basin Intraregional trade[a] (percentages)

Nations, regions	Share of exports going to Asia-Pacific economies		Share of imports coming from Asia-Pacific economies		Share of trade with Asia-Pacific economies	
	1978	1989	1978	1989	1978	1989
Japan	55	68	51	62	53	65
China	56	73	50	63	53	68
Asian NIEs	65	70	70	75	67	73
Korea	63	74	71	71	67	73
ASEAN (4)	75	74	66	77	71	76
North America	47	59	51	62	49	61
US	38	51	43	58	41	55
Oceania	63	67	57	67	60	67
Total, Asia Pacific	54	65	54	66	54	65

NIE = newly industrializing economy
ASEAN = Association of Southeast Asian Nations
a. Figures for New Zealand not included for Taiwan. Figures for Taiwan not included for 1978. Figures for Taiwan not included for Thailand in 1989.

Sources: International Monetary Fund. *Direction of Trade Statistics*, 1982 and 1990. *Yearbook*; Republic of China. 1990. *Statistical Yearbook*; Asia Pacific Economic Cooperation. 1989. *Background Information Paper*, Canberra (November).

Intraregional trade growth for Asia-Pacific countries far exceeded the rate of overall world trade growth. As a consequence, the share of trade of these nations in the world total increased substantially. For example, Japan's, the Asian NIEs', ASEAN's, and China's combined share of world exports and imports was only 14.3 percent and 14.7 percent, respectively, in 1980, but this increased to 21.5 percent and 16.9 percent, respectively, by 1987. Japan's share of exports more than doubled between 1965 and 1987, from 4.9 percent to 9.9 percent in 1987. The Asian NIEs' share more than quadrupled during the period, from 1.6 percent in 1965 to 7.6 percent in 1987.

At the same time, the Asian NIEs' share of imports increased almost as rapidly, from 2.1 percent in 1965 to 6.5 percent in 1987. Japan's share of imports did not increase as much as its share of exports, growing from 4.5 percent in 1965 to only 6.2 percent in 1987 (Okita 1991, 27). It is worth noting the trend of sharply increased trade between ASEAN and the Asian NIEs and between the Asian NIEs and China after 1978.

Intraregional FDI flows have also been growing rapidly in recent years. This surge in FDI occurred mostly in the 1980s, first by the Japanese and later by the Asian NIEs. It is also true that the Asian NIEs first and

toward integration of East Asian economies, leading to an East Asian economic bloc. Intraregional trade among these economies did grow in recent decades. It increased to 40 percent of the total trade of these economies in 1990 and to 30 percent in 1970. This phenomenon has been attributed to the natural force of relatively high overall trade growth attained by these economies (Frankel 1991).

then ASEAN absorbed and benefited from the increased flow of direct investment. The fast appreciation of the Japanese yen and changes in its comparative advantage were the primary factors for Japan's FDI upsurge. Since Japanese FDI is such an important factor in increasing interdependency in the region, it deserves special attention. In an effort to restructure their economy, the Japanese moved skilled labor- and technology-intensive production bases to the Asian NIEs and established labor-intensive production bases in the ASEAN region, while keeping high-tech production bases in Japan.

Japanese FDI has increased rapidly since 1985. The average annual Japanese outgoing FDI during the first half of the 1980s was around $8.6 billion, but it increased to $22.3 billion in 1986 and reached more than $60 billion in 1989 (Komiya and Wakasugi 1991, 54), although the rate of increase in FDI appears to have tapered off since then. The total amount of Japanese FDI during 1986–89 surpassed the total amount of previous Japanese FDI. Japan became the leading nation in outgoing FDI in the world. During this period, 59.3 percent of Japanese FDI went to North America and Asian countries.

Japanese FDI to the United States grew to $53.4 billion by the end of 1988. Japan became the second largest investor in the United States, following only the United Kingdom. Japanese FDI to the Asian NIEs and ASEAN in particular grew very rapidly as well. It grew by nearly 60 percent and 27 percent in 1988 for ASEAN and the Asian NIEs, respectively (Lo, Nakamura, and Song 1989).

Between 1980 and 1985, Japanese FDI outstanding grew at an average annual rate of 21.2 percent, reaching $22.3 billion. Similarly, the Asian NIEs rapidly stepped up their FDI in the ASEAN. Taiwan's and Korea's FDI in ASEAN, for example, grew nearly ninefold and fourfold, respectively.

Even though intraregional FDI has been growing fast, it is still a small proportion of total financial flows and regional capital formation. Nonetheless, FDI has significant effects on future trade and the industrial restructuring of economies in the region. FDI is also significant because it is usually accompanied by technology transfer. The Asian NIEs were the primary recipient of Japanese FDI in the past. Now ASEAN is attracting both Japanese and Asian NIEs' FDI, a significant development in the region.

Asia-Pacific Regional Economic Cooperation

Growing economic interdependencies in the region, as discussed earlier, are bound to produce frictions and disputes. Resolving these problems and enhancing economic cooperation in the region is an important matter. Current account imbalances between Japan and the United States and between the Asian NIEs and the United States in recent years have been aggravating the trade environment in the region. There is a definite need for a mechanism by which such disputes can be resolved and tensions can be diffused. In addition, the growing economic interdependencies among nations in the region necessitate appropriate institutional arrangements by which important economic policies of common interests can be discussed and possibly coordinated (Krause 1991, 10–14).

There have been various calls to establish cooperative bodies for closer economic cooperation in the region. The recently established Asia-Pacific Economic Cooperation (APEC) ministerial forum is an important new step in this direction.[21] This forum is expected to enhance regional economic cooperation and contribute to continued dynamism in the future. Even this forum, however, is not expected to grow into an EC-type economic bloc in the foreseeable future, in view of the region's diverse economic and political make-up.

Recent APEC ministerial meetings endorsed the principle of "open regionalism," which calls for nondiscriminatory economic cooperation between third parties consistent with the GATT system. APEC is expected to evolve into a consultative body whose purpose is to build consensus on a gradually broadening range of economic issues, from trade and investment to tourism. At this point, however, APEC may need to be institutionally strengthened with the establishment of a permanent secretariat and regular summit meetings. The complications in regional economic relations brought on by the end of the Cold War add urgency to this goal.

Deep-seated suspicion and distrust between some of the countries in the region still exists. Accordingly, these countries must get comfortable with regional cooperative initiatives over a long period before they can develop into a tight-knit regional cooperative institution. For this reason, it seems useful to have subregional cooperative efforts as long as they are consistent with APEC principles and, thus, with the GATT.

New Role in Northeast Asia

Geopolitically, South Korea is an ideal catalyst for regional cooperation in the Asia-Pacific area, particularly in the Northeast Asian region, which has great potential for development. The Korean peninsula is located in the center of the Northeast Asian economies, which also include Japan,

---

21. The first APEC ministerial forum was held in Canberra, Australia, in November 1989. APEC originally started with 12 member countries. The three Chinas—mainland China, Taiwan, and Hong Kong—became APEC members at the Seoul meeting held in November 1991.

northeastern China, and the eastern part of Russia.[22] This region shares strong economic complementarities. The end of the Cold War now makes close economic cooperation in this area a real possibility for the first time, and South Korea, the leading member of the Asian NIEs, can play a critical role in this endeavor.[23]

Until mutual trust and respect are established, even well-intended cooperative initiatives on the part of the Japanese will inevitably be viewed as another version of the East Asian Co-prosperity Sphere of the past. It seems natural, therefore, for Japan to make a special effort to earn the respect and trust of the members of the region. One Japanese author recommends, "It will be essential for Japan to face up to the dark side of Japanese modern history and sincerely demonstrate its repentant attitude in public education and in public speeches by its politicians and officials, in order to win trust and respect from Asian neighbors" (Sato 1991). One practical way to achieve this is by cooperating closely with South Korea toward subregional development.

Japan's capital and advanced industrial technology could be supplemented with Korea's middle-level technology and macroeconomic and project-level management experience to make a potent combination. Although Japan's ODA budget quintupled during the last decade, the number of staff in Japanese development assistance agencies did not grow. Insufficient staffing, together with the relative inexperience of the ODA staff and their lack of specialized skills, is known to be the main reason for delays in Japanese ODA disbursement.

Japanese ODA volume per staff is two to three times higher than that of the United States, the United Kingdom, France, or West Germany (Noland 1989, 20–21). This also explains the relatively low level of technical assistance from Japan in terms of the human resources component of ODA. Japan ranked 14th among 18 DAC member countries in 1988 in this area (Sato 1991, 30). Korea, on the other hand, has a substantial

---

22. Narrowly defined, Northeast Asia usually encompasses the Korean peninsula, Japan, the eastern part of China (the three northeastern provinces of Heilungkiang, Kirin, and Liaoning), and the far eastern region of Russia. The region's share of world population and GNP share in the world for 1989 were 5.7 percent and 13.3 percent, respectively (Yeon 1991). Because both Korea and Japan economically depend so heavily on the United States and because the United States as a North Pacific nation has a vital interest in Northeast Asian economic affairs, its inclusion in any meaningful economic cooperative endeavor of the region is inevitable.

23. The Cold War front still exists in the Korean peninsula. Even this front has started to crumble, albeit slowly, making economic cooperation possible between the two Koreas. Unification is the ultimate goal of most Korean people. The process, however, should be a gradual one. Therefore, economic cooperation, at both bilateral and multilateral levels, should be the first objective for both nations. Unless amicable cooperative relations are established between the two Koreas, Northeast Asian cooperation to promote the region's stability and prosperity cannot possibly be achieved.

stock of human resources and expertise in the selection and management of appropriate developmental projects. It stands to reason that by acting together, these two nations could accomplish much more for regional development than they could by acting separately.[24]

This subregional cooperation eventually might well be developed into a new multilateral regional development bank for Northeast Asian countries, specifically to cover the two Koreas, Japan, eastern regions of Russia, northeastern provinces of China, and possibly Mongolia (Yeon 1991). This bank might play an important role in transforming regional nonmarket economies in particular and maintaining regional stability. The abundant natural and human resources available in North Korea, China and Russia, the modern technology and capital provided by Japan, and recent development experience and middle-level technical know-how of South Korea are an ideal combination for building regional development and cooperation.[25]

Through this type of bold initiative, Japan in close cooperation with South Korea, its closest neighbor, would be able to contribute toward regional prosperity. As a world superpower, Japan has to exert leadership on the global stage. This leadership will not be effective unless Japan first gains the trust and respect of its neighbors.

Japan's Expected Leadership Role in the Region

The strong inter- and intraindustrial linkage and rapid inflow of FDI between nations in the Asia-Pacific region deepened the economic interdependencies of the 1980s.[26] The Asia-Pacific region, however, has to make proper structural adjustments in a changed world economic order. In particular, the economic future of Asia-Pacific nations depends heavily on the neighboring economic giant, Japan, especially at a time when the US economy can no longer provide necessary "public goods." Let us briefly discuss the regional expectations for Japan as well as the world's perspective.

It is well known that the income elasticity of Japanese imports is low compared with that of other countries such as the United States and Germany. This is to say that Japanese imports do not increase much even when the Japanese economy expands. The relatively low level of

24. Balassa and Noland (1988, 172) suggest a few other ways to overcome manpower resource constraints within the Japanese government.

25. Along this line , the UNDP-sponsored Tuman River Area Development Programme is under way with the participation in the program management committee of China, Mongolia, Russia, and North and South Korea. Japan began participating as an observer in October 1992. See UNDP press release, 11 October 1992.

26. See Lo, Nakamura, and Song (1989) for analyses of industrial linkages in the Pacific region.

Japanese import elasticity is often attributed to the characteristics of the country's economic structure, which produces almost all necessary parts, intermediate products, and capital goods domestically. These characteristics are often described (by the Japanese) as "full-set economic (or industrial) structure," and this inevitably restricts the "horizontal division of labor," particularly with its Asian neighbors (The Japan Forum on International Relations, Inc. 1986).

Japanese imports of manufactured goods, however, have been increasing quite fast in recent years. Today, more than 50 percent of Japan's imports and over 60 percent of its imports from the Asian region are manufactured goods. Japan's monthly trade with its Asian neighbors surpassed its trade with the United States in late 1989 for the first time, and currently Japan's trade with the Asian NIEs is larger than its trade with the EC.

Japan has recently put emphasis on correcting its "full-set principle" to expand beyond the existing horizontal division of labor. If indeed Japan is broadening the division of labor to include its Asian neighbors, it is natural to expect that intraregional trade in manufactured goods will accelerate. At the same time, this will also accelerate Japanese industrial restructuring by encouraging labor-intensive, low-value-added industries to move to labor-abundant neighboring countries.

Another factor is Japan's new aid policy, announced in Bangkok in January 1987 by Minister Hajime Tamura of the Ministry of International Trade and Industry. Japan's ODA commitment for 1990 came close to $10 billion.[27] Roughly 70 percent of this commitment is for its Asian neighbors. In essence, the new policy is to combine Japanese ODA with private capital flows and trade to help establish Asian export bases, mostly with Japanese subsidiaries or joint ventures. In other words, the new policy would encourage labor-intensive, low-technology industries to move abroad. Products of these industries are to be imported back to Japan. This new policy was applied to ASEAN countries, China, and India in recent years.

It is beyond the scope of this study to explore the extent to which these factors affected the rapid rise in Japanese imports of manufactured goods from its neighbors. The fact, however, is that a substantial proportion of the manufactured goods imported from Asian NIEs and ASEAN are known to be products of Japanese subsidiaries and joint ventures abroad.[28] It is reasonable, therefore, to expect intraregional trade to increase even faster in coming years as Japanese direct investment starts to bear fruit.

---

27. Japan now is the largest foreign aid donor, surpassing the United States.

28. It has been estimated that 90 percent of TV sets, 50 percent of electrical fans, and 70 percent of calculators imported from the Asian NIEs in 1987 were produced by Japanese-owned plants (*Mitsubushi Bank Review*, July 1988).

Through its new policies, Japan begins to manifest the "flying-geese" pattern, with Japan as the lead goose. There is nothing wrong with this as long as the Japanese "gradually transform the V-formation (of flying-geese) to a straight-line pattern with horizontal integration," as late starters catch up with early starters (Okita 1991, 26). Whether this desirable pattern of regional development will occur depends to a large extent on the regional role of Japan.

Unfortunately, however, many in the region believe that the Japanese are not really interested in actively promoting a straight-line pattern. According to one author, "The 'new horizontal division of labor' that Japan wishes to promote in Asia still has a strong vertical component. Despite the use of the term 'horizontal division of labor,' the two-way trade of goods within the same product category is not Japan's primary policy objective" (Arase 1991).

Complaints are often heard from the region that the Japanese are reluctant to transfer high technology to follower nations for fear of the "boomerang effect." If, in fact, this is true, then the V-formation will never turn into a straight-line pattern. Or put another way, latecomers in the region will never be able to catch up with the early starter, Japan, in every field.

When Japanese Prime Minister Kiichi Miyazawa visited Seoul in January 1992, Koreans demanded, as they have many times in the past, that Japan spur technology transfer to help correct the nation's perennial trade deficit with Japan. In 1991 Korea's trade deficit with Japan was $8.8 billion, amounting to 91 percent of Korea's overall trade deficit in that year. Since the two nations normalized diplomatic relations in 1965, Korea's accumulated trade deficit with Japan totaled $66.3 billion while Korea's total trade deficit during the same period (1965–91) was $33.3 billion.[29] Realizing that the trade deficit with Japan is a chronic structural problem, Koreans want Japan to provide technology to help restructure Korean industries.

The Japanese position on this issue has been that Korea's current trade deficit with Japan is a natural result of the country's industrial and trade structure, which relies heavily on Japanese capital and intermediate goods for export production. Furthermore, they argue that the transfer of technology is basically up to the private sector, not for the Japanese government to meddle with. The argument itself seems reasonable enough. Needless to say, the Korean private sector should make more serious efforts to facilitate technology transfer. However, as long as such ideas as the "boomerang effect," the "full-set principle," and the everlasting "V-formation" continue to float around Japanese policy circles and in-

---

29. These deficit figures are based on customs clearance and, accordingly, free-on-board prices for export and cost plus insurance and freight prices for imports.

dustries, weaker economic partners such as Korea will never really be persuaded to trust and respect Japanese leadership.

These nations also complain frequently of remaining Japanese import restrictions, most of which are included in the Structural Impediment Initiatives (SII) talks with the United States. Until these complaints are addressed adequately, Japan will continuously suffer from a "legitimacy deficit" in the region that hampers Japan's ability to exert the kind of economic leadership necessary in the region as well as in the whole world. Even though Japan is the largest aid donor and direct investor, the United States still provides the largest markets for Asians, particularly in manufactured goods from the Asian NIEs. US imports from the Asian NIEs totaled $69.9 billion in 1988 while Japanese imports from these countries came to $27.9 billion. As a matter of fact, their recent economic success owes heavily to the US market.

As the United States corrects its macroeconomic imbalances by reducing its budget and trade deficits, these economies will have to find new markets to maintain their dynamic growth. The Japanese market can be an alternative import-absorber for them. This, too, would represent an important part of the burden-sharing on the part of Japan necessary for the maintenance of the world's and the region's prosperity and stability.

By stimulating domestic demand, providing easier market access, and keeping a stronger yen to fully reflect Japan's economic fundamentals, Japan would induce more imports from abroad, particularly from this region. Japan's reputation as a mercantilistic nation is no easier to erase in this region than in any other part of the world. Hideo Sato (1991, 17) puts it aptly when he states, "the mercantilistic reputation does present a very serious handicap for Japan. . . . Utmost efforts need to be exerted, therefore, in order to erase this image and also to make other countries realize that Japan is a reliable leader committed to reciprocal and multilateral free trade."

Sato points out that even though German cars are highly competitive, the market share of imported foreign cars is 30 percent in Germany compared with 4 percent for imported cars in Japan in recent years. It is critical for Japan to exert leadership in promoting a liberal international trade environment by taking liberalization initiatives at home. Japan's liberalization initiatives will not only contribute toward correcting intraregional trade imbalances but also trans-Pacific trade imbalances in the Asian NIEs indirectly. It will be much easier both politically and economically for these countries to persuade their domestic adversaries of the merits of liberalization when Japan also takes liberalization initiatives in its own market. If Japan and the United States fail to manage their bilateral relationship in this tripolar world, it is unlikely that a viable collective international leadership can be established. In this connection, Japan's Asian neighbors, as well as the whole world, would like to see the US-Japan SII talks bear fruit. Of course, it presumes that the benefits from SII would be shared multilaterally in a most-favored nation fashion. The United States needs to put its own house in order through budget deficit reduction, increased domestic saving, improved productivity, an improved education system, and extended corporate planning horizons.

At the same time, Japan needs to devote more effort to opening up its markets by breaking down structural impediments to free trade, including the rigid distribution system, an unbalanced saving-consumption ratio, and inadequate social overhead capital bases. This would not only help reduce US trade deficits vis-à-vis Japan but also contribute to reducing US deficits vis-à-vis the Asian NIEs as Japan absorbs a substantial amount of imports from these nations.

Japan has been taking various policy initiatives to promote regional economic cooperation. It is still true, however, that there is a strong antipathy toward Japanese dominance in regional affairs. One important reason why countries in this region would like to have US participation in any regional economic cooperative endeavor is that they see the United States as a counterweight to Japan. In a sense, Japan is caught in the dilemma of being damned-if-it-does and damned-if-it-doesn't. For this reason, it is critical for Japan to first earn trust from its neighboring nations by cooperating closely with them.

Summary

The formation of the new world order and Korea's current position in the world economy will present challenges as well as opportunities for Koreans in coming years.

Under the new world order, supported by a collective leadership, economic disputes and conflicts are expected to arise more frequently regarding responsibility-sharing in providing public goods. Even though Korea is not big enough to affect the outcome of major world events, it is not small enough to be neglected in the burden-sharing process. Koreans need to face the challenge of opening their markets more widely and make necessary structural adjustments while reconciling domestic political resistance to change. Korea has benefited greatly from the liberal global economic environment in the past, and it has a vested interest in helping to maintain a freer world trade environment to support its own continued prosperity.

Korea's unique position in the world economy presents it with special opportunities. As a pioneer country among the developing world, Korea has an important role to play in helping follower nations. Korea now has abundant human resources with valuable first-hand experience in development. Technical assistance to the developing world so far has consisted of bringing foreigners to Korea for training. Korea can now afford to send more experts, both public and private, to those nations. Multilateral developmental institutions should make special efforts to use Korean expertise in assisting developing nations. In this connection, their technical assistance programs might very well be interlinked with Korea's own programs. In addition, Korea should be invited to make contributions to those institutions at a level commensurate with its economic capability.

The history of Korea's international cooperation has been rather short. Korea has actively participated in the world financial community as a borrower since the early 1960s. A watershed in the history of Korean international cooperation occurred in 1986 when a developmental fund was established to assist other developing nations. This was the nation's first systematic approach to becoming a donor in the international capital cooperation circle.

With respect to regional cooperation, Korea is geopolitically as well as economically in an ideal position to become a catalyst in promoting regional cooperation, particularly cooperation in Northeast Asia. This region has great potential for fruitful cooperation, as members of the region share strong economic relationships. Thanks to the end of the Cold War, this potential can now be turned into reality. In this process, Korea can play the role of catalyst.

As a regional power, Japan has an important role to play in regional cooperation. Because of unfortunate past historical events, however, even well-intended cooperative initiatives by Japan alone still tend to be viewed with suspicion. One practical approach to solving this problem might be for Japan to cooperate with Korea more closely to promote regional prosperity. Japan's capital and advanced industrial technology, together with Korean middle-level technology and development management know-how, can accomplish a great deal for the region's development and progress that neither could do alone.

This Korea-Japan cooperation might well take the form of a new regional development bank, which could help transform nonmarket economies in the region while maintaining economic stability. It might also serve Japan's interests by establishing a regional basis for mutual trust and respect, laying the groundwork for Japan to exert leadership on a global scale.

The development pattern of the region is often described as a "flying-geese" pattern of development. Only through the active promotion of a horizontal division of labor among economies in the region will the V-formation gradually turn into a straight-line pattern. In this respect again, bold Japanese initiatives toward technology transfer are highly desirable. At the same time, potential recipients in the region should make efforts to facilitate this transfer.

Regional progress and development are possible only through meaningful cooperation. However, this cooperation is only likely to succeed if Japan takes appropriate measures. As the only Asian superpower and the most important regional economy by far, Japan's share of the burden in fostering cooperation is proportionately greater than that of its neighbors.

7

Setting a New Agenda

The most important agenda of the State relate not to those activities which private individuals are already fulfilling, but to those functions which fall outside the sphere of the individual, to those decisions which are made by no one if the State does not make them. The important thing for government is not to do them a little better or a little worse, but to do those things which at present are not done at all. —John Maynard Keynes (1926, 46–47)

As seen from earlier discussions, over the last three decades, Korea achieved the kind of economic development that today's developed nations took almost a century to accomplish. Korea today, however, is at a crossroads. Starting as a typical developing nation in the early 1960s, Korea came a long way to become a leading member of the newly industrializing economies (NIEs) and is now at the threshold of joining the club of the industrially developed. There are already serious discussions both inside and outside Korea about the possibility of joining the Organization for Economic Cooperation and Development (OECD) in the near future.

To be successful in making the transition, however, Korea will have to face important challenges. The main purpose of this chapter is to discuss the different domestic and international settings behind these challenges, focus on a few of the key issues facing Korea today, and discuss policy priorities and a policy agenda for the future.

Changed Domestic and International Settings

Legacies of Past Policies

Plagued with an absolute poverty problem and widespread unemployment in the early 1960s, the relatively literate, culturally and ethnically homogeneous Korean populace was ready to accept a strong and active government committed to curing the nation's economic ills. The government's growth-first rhetoric did not disturb them so long as they could expect the elimination of absolute poverty through gainful employment.

Surrounded by worldly powers and directly confronted with a hostile neighbor, Koreans had to work hard just to survive. At the same time, Koreans had no choice but to live alongside their economically prosperous neighbor, Japan. Most Koreans seemed to believe that there was no reason why they could not do as well as their neighbor if they, too, worked hard. In addition, the lingering, bitter memory of the Korean War and the ensuing hostile environment made them work even harder because they realized their survival depended on the nation's economic growth and prosperity.

As previously discussed, Korea in the early 1960s already had important characteristics conducive to the nation's economic growth and development. The nation's sociocultural standard was already high among developing nations. The Confucian tradition in Korea valued civil service highly, helping to produce quality bureaucrats. Private entrepreneurial energies were there, too. Unfortunately, however, their energies were mostly devoted to rent-seeking activities, or zero-sum entrepreneurial activities. Korean workers in general were already literate and highly disciplined. At the same time, the Korean agricultural sector had a virtually unlimited supply of labor. A majority of the nation's population lived in the rural areas.

What was lacking in the early 1960s was strong leadership commitment to the nation's economic development that would serve as a catalyst for every segment of Korean society to work toward the nation's economic betterment. Koreans are traditionally not only receptive to strong leadership exercised by the government, they expect it. Especially when the nation is plagued with widespread poverty, unemployment, and underdevelopment, such expectations naturally become more intense. In the early 1960s, Korea saw the emergence of a new leadership that was fully committed to economic development goals.

Constrained by being poorly endowed with natural resources, the limited size of markets, and the meager saving potential of the time, the nation had to look outside its borders for capital, technology, and markets. The new leadership, in fact, did look outside. In essence, they saw exports as a means of generating foreign exchange needed for imports of materials and capital equipment to support industrialization.

So the outward-oriented development strategy was adopted, and the strategy was implemented by tilting the existing incentives in favor of socially productive, positive-sum entrepreneurial activities. For effective implementation of the strategy, the government itself took on the role of banker because this function "makes possible the carrying out of new combinations" of a positive-sum nature à la Schumpeter. Turning commercial banks into de facto public enterprises and establishing special banks that were de jure public institutions made it possible in the early

1960s for government to assume the role. Just as important, particularly in the early stages of development, the active enticement of foreign capital, and the government's screening and allocation of borrowed capital, made the government's banking role even more powerful.

Export promotion itself was geared to the government's banker role. Entrepreneurial energies were channeled toward socially productive activities and away from rent-seeking activities through incentives that favored exports. In addition, the foreign exchange system itself was made more simple and convenient for all potential exporters, reducing transaction and opportunity costs of exports. Along with financial incentives for private entrepreneurial activities, the government took on the entrepreneur's role of gap-filler and input-completer[1] by providing necessary services for both current and potential exporters in international markets.

In sum, the Korean government's export promotion policy was implemented, first, by developing the kind of business environment that would facilitate production, investment, and positive entrepreneurial activities as a whole. At the same time, the expanding social infrastructure in physical, institutional, and intellectual areas helped to improve the microeconomic environment for private entrepreneurs. Second, more incentives, both pecuniary and nonpecuniary in nature, were provided to support exports, offsetting existing distortions unfavorable to export activities.

The Korean government took a flexible, pragmatic, nonideological, and highly results-oriented approach in choosing policy tools and adopting development strategies to achieve its goals. In fact, the Korean government liberally took advice from experts and specialists outside the government and, in many cases, from abroad. In the early stages of development, the Korean government relied heavily on foreign consultants under the auspices of multilateral institutions and on foreign-trained Korean experts.

In the early 1970s, with the president's personal blessing, the government established an economic think-tank, the Korea Development Institute (KDI), manned with foreign-trained economists recruited primarily from the United States.[2] In addition, the Korean government sent elite economics bureaucrats abroad for both degrees and short-term training. The training of bureaucrats in modern economic theory and planning techniques undoubtedly facilitated the effective use of outside consultation.

---

1. These functions are the unique characteristics of entrepreneurship. Due to market imperfections or vagueness of inputs for production, entrepreneurs have to fill the "gaps" to provide complete inputs for production. See Leibenstein (1968).

2. The establishment of such institutes certainly contributed to reversing "brain-drain" as well.

This liberal attitude of the Korean government contrasts with many other countries, where the advice of foreign consultants, even from foreign-educated nationals, is not really welcomed. It is also significant to recognize that major economic decision-making positions in the government were almost always filled by economics experts or technocrats rather than political appointees. That tradition has more or less continued until very recently. Major economic ministers and the president's chief economic advisers were either career economist-bureaucrats or professional economists.

In any case, these professionally trained bureaucrats speedily introduced necessary policy measures, incentives, and institutional innovations to achieve national development goals. These government policies and incentives can be summarized as an outward-oriented industrialization strategy that emphasized exports.

Economic growth and industrialization can only be achieved through private entrepreneurial activities in a market-oriented economy. Of course, when the private sector is not deemed appropriate for certain ventures, the Korean government in particular is not hesitant to play the role of entrepreneur cum manager through public enterprises or other policy tools. In the 1960s and 1970s a substantial number of public enterprises were established. As the Korean economy reached different stages of development, some of those public enterprises had been privatized. Continuous privatization and streamlining of public enterprises remains an important policy issue.

Under these circumstances, government policies were characteristically probusiness and proentrepreneur, and particularly proexport. At the same time, in implementing a growth-first strategy through export-led industrialization, policy was biased in favor of large, well-established businesses with proven track records. In the early stages of export promotion, one might justify this strategy because these companies had the organizational and technological economies of the scale necessary to compete against large, efficient foreign competitors. This policy, however, gave rise to economic power concentration—in other words, the *chaebol* problem. At this stage of development, it is critical in this area as well to strike a proper balance between growth and equity.

Another related issue is the direction of future industrial policy. An important question is whether industrial targeting—that is, "picking winners," as was done in promoting the heavy and chemical industries (HCIs)—can be used again. It is important to remember first that the cost of failure from the visible hand of the government in this regard is expected to be high, and second, that industrial targeting could cause trade friction and disputes under the changed international trade environment.

In addition, the probusiness and proentrepreneur policy at the early stage of development resulted in restriction of certain basic labor rights. These restrictions, however, stayed in place too long after the sociopolitical environment had changed, setting the stage for violent reactions. Current conditions call for a new approach to this problem.

Structural adjustments in the 1960s and the early 1970s were relatively simple and easy. There was an unlimited pool of labor in the agricultural sector, and the workers were already quite literate and disciplined, thanks to culture, education, and, in the case of male workers, exposure to military training. Because the export promotion policy resulted in standardized labor-intensive light manufacturing development, not much more additional training was necessary. At the same time, because workers were taken from the already-crowded agricultural sector, structural adjustments were not that difficult to achieve. As a matter of fact, average agricultural productivity improved as disguised unemployment was reduced in the agricultural sector.

However, as second-tier NIEs began to catch up in the mid-1970s when surplus labor was almost exhausted, restructuring industries toward higher value-added and more sophisticated production was deemed necessary.[3] At the same time, after successful implementation of two five-year economic development plans and export-led industrialization, the government gained confidence in its decision-making ability and general economic management capabilities. It was during this period that the Korean government launched its ambitious HCI promotion program, in which government intervention in resource allocation became more direct and intense. The government literally forced structural adjustments toward heavy and chemical industries through a combination of incentives and commands. In many cases, the government talked leading entrepreneurs into launching HCI projects and provided them with fiscal and financial subsidies. The government's strategy of forcing industrial restructuring left the traditional export sectors and other light manufacturing sectors without adequate resources. Thus the large number of small and medium-sized firms in these sectors suffered the most.

Beginning in the mid-1970s, labor shortages began to appear, particularly in the skilled-labor market, due to the overheated economic situation at home and the Middle East construction boom. As a result, overall wages increased fast and inflation accelerated. With rapidly increasing income, many household savers were lured into real estate speculation, and such rent-seeking activities also attracted a substantial proportion of entrepreneurial energies.

It was evident toward the end of the 1970s that there were serious structural imbalances and chronic inflationary problems that had to be corrected for economic progress to continue. Structural imbalances between different-sized firms, between heavy and light industries, be-

---

3. As discussed earlier, the aftermath of the fall of South Vietnam to the Communists and the imminent reduction of US troops stationed in Korea also affected the government's decision to restructure Korean industries.

tween urban and rural sectors, and between different geographical regions—in addition to worsening income distribution—made relative poverty a serious sociopolitical issue for the nation. The nation's development strategy also needed to be reevaluated, as most of these imbalances resulted from governmental policies and growth strategies.

The government's assumption of the banker's role led to serious nonperforming asset (NPA) problems in commercial banks, which were de facto public enterprises. This problem of NPAs became a serious obstacle to banking sector reform and liberalization. Problems caused by industrial targeting and by the government acting as financier surfaced not only in those NPAs but also in the underutilized industrial capacity evident in many targeted sectors. These sectors needed their own structural adjustments.

Coming into the 1980s, the government started to change its role in the economic arena. Industrial targeting was abandoned, and various subsidies and policy loans with subsidized rates were either eliminated or reduced. Import liberalization and tariff reduction programs were introduced to increase efficiency in domestic industries. Government-held shares of commercial banks were sold to the public, and direct operational controls were reduced.

As previously discussed, chronic inflation was a serious problem in the late 1970s. There were discussions about the inevitability of stabilizing the economy in the late 1970s among academic circles and some quarters of the government. As economic stability became the government's top priority in the early 1980s, painful policy measures were introduced. In addition to tight aggregate demand management, administratively controlled prices were liberalized, and antitrust laws were strengthened. Imports were also used to supplement supply shortages of critical commodities.

Primarily as a result of these adjustment efforts, both price stability and stable growth were simultaneously achieved in a few years. By 1986 the Korean economy was running at full steam: GNP grew 12.9 percent, consumer price inflation was stabilized at 2.8 percent, and a current account surplus of $4.6 billion was recorded.[4] The surplus was the first meaningful one in Korea's modern history.[5]

Since 1986 the Korean economy has continued to show outstanding economic performance, with inflation under control, GNP growth in double digits, and a surplus in the balance of payments. This outstanding performance is often attributed to favorable external conditions, known as the three lows: low oil prices, low international interest rates, and

---

4. For a detailed discussion on the Korean economy at that time, see SaKong (1989, 7–17).

5. In 1977 Korea had a small amount of current account surplus, primarily due to temporary remittances from construction activities in the Middle East.

low dollar value vis-à-vis other major currencies. While it is true that the Korean economy benefited from these conditions, what is important is that Korea was ready to take full advantage of them.[6] Painful reforms and timely adjustments enhanced Korea's ability to compete successfully in international markets.

Around this time Koreans were full of optimism. The 1986 Asian Games were hosted successfully, and the country prepared confidently for the 1988 Summer Olympics. With the current account surpluses, the government started to make prepayments of its foreign debt, which had been frequently politicized as a symbol of Korea's economic weakness. At the same time, various economic liberalization measures, both domestic and international, were introduced. Domestically, for example, measures were taken to alleviate commercial banks' NPAs, laying the foundation for financial sector reform. Special efforts were also made to widen the securities market in preparation for external liberalization. The speed of import liberalization and tariff reduction was accelerated, and existing restrictions on current account transactions were eliminated for the most part.

Elevated Expectations and Political Change

Continued economic prosperity and rising optimism about Korea's economic future seemed to elevate people's expectations for economic gain, as well as political and social gains, even further. These expectations forced the announcement of the June 29 Democratization Pledge in 1987. This announcement, which promised a new constitution among other things, marked the beginning of a new era for Korea.

Immediately after the announcement was made, labor disputes and work stoppages erupted. Workers' suppressed demands seemed to explode all around the country simultaneously. Most of the labor strikes were illegal under existing laws, but even then, the government was reluctant to enforce them. Both management and workers were not prepared to deal with the situation properly either.

Consequently, solutions were found in most cases on an ad hoc basis. In the meantime, confrontational management-worker relationships negatively affected the general work ethic and managerial attitudes— the driving forces of the dynamic Korean economy to this point.

In accordance with the revised constitution, new political leadership was installed in February 1988. The government party, however, was not able to gain majority seats in the national assembly in the general election. Three opposition parties competed in trying to satisfy the in-

---

6. Needless to say, given Korea's long-term growth potential, the Korean economy cannot sustain a GNP growth rate at a two-digit level while maintaining price stability without the benefit of unusually favorable external conditions.

satiable demands of voters by pressing the government party to expand income-transfer-type public expenditures while leading the people to believe that those demands could be met without seriously affecting economic stability and growth goals. The government party, being a minority in the national assembly, responded to the voters' popular demands in much the same way. In fact, the nation's new political leadership seemed to take good economic performance for granted and therefore acted as if the Korean economy could in fact satisfy all demands.[7]

With the weakened leadership commitment to economic rationale in such a political environment, the government ended up accommodating many of those demands. The proportion of transfer-income expenditures in the government's budget increased sharply beginning in 1988, from an annual average of 5.1 percent from 1981 to 1987 to 11.1 percent in the period between 1989 and 1991.[8] It rose to 12 percent in 1991. Naturally, public investment in other sectors, including the social overhead capital sector, had to be sacrificed.

For the first time in Korea's recent history, political demands overwhelmed economic decision-making, often exceeding the bounds of economic reality. As a result, the Korean economy started to show growing signs of macroeconomic imbalances and a seriously distorted relative price structure.[9] Nevertheless, purposeful stimulative measures were introduced to counter a moderation of economic growth in 1989, further worsening the inflationary situation.[10]

---

7. The role of technocrats was drastically reduced, and more significantly, their policy-making was no longer much insulated from politics. These changes must reflect both the nation's new political environment and the weakened political leadership commitment to economics. With a strong leadership commitment, however, the situation could have been much different.

8. Farm household subsidies, including rice price support and agricultural debt reduction, increased most drastically.

9. The nation's balance of payments experienced a sharp turnaround in recent years. A $14.2 billion surplus in 1987 turned into a $8.8 billion deficit, or 3.3 percent of GNP, in 1991. The average rate of consumer price inflation for the 1988–91 period was 7.8 percent, increased from 4.8 percent for the 1981–87 period. Even the current inflation has been suppressed, to the extent that energy prices have been administratively kept at lower levels. As of February 1992, the gasoline price in Korea was 26 percent cheaper than the price in the oil-producing United Kingdom. It was cheaper in Korea than in Japan and France by 53.0 percent and 44.0 percent, respectively. Korea's petroleum consumption increased by 24.1 percent in 1990 compared with 5.0 percent in Japan (Economic Planning Board 1992).

10. Certainly, it can be considered an economic policy mistake. In this regard, Cheng and Krause (1991, 23) rightly point out, the worsened economic performance "should not be totally attributed to its [Korea's] political experiment with democracy." With a strong leadership commitment to economics, even such a mistake could have been avoided.

Changed International Environment

The summarized presentation above outlines the basis for the important domestic policy issues and challenges facing Korea today. There are other challenges arising from the changed international environment and Korea's new position in the world. In this regard, Koreans must realize that the world is about to enter into a new order in which economic relations will play a dominant role. Furthermore, world economic leadership to maintain prosperity has to be shared among the major economic powers through cooperation and coordination.

This collective economic leadership in a multipolar world implies burden-sharing and responsibility-sharing. In other words, collective leadership has to provide necessary public goods and share the cost, direct or otherwise. In addition, other important international economic players such as Korea will also be asked to assume their share of responsibility. At this juncture, Korea has to widen its international perspective and has to be ready to adapt to the changing environment appropriately. This, in itself, is a major challenge for Korea.

Korean parents today still talk to their children about the *bori gogei* of their early years. *Bori gogei* can be directly translated as "barley hill." It refers to the difficult springs of earlier years in which food remaining from the previous year's autumn harvest usually ran out and could not be replenished until the summer barley harvest. Consequently, many people starved, and most Koreans experienced hunger and privation.

Today, absolute poverty, as represented by *bori gogei*, has virtually disappeared, and the younger generation only reads or hears about the *bori gogei* from books or stories told by their elders. Within the span of a single generation, Koreans saw their economy move from a developing to a newly industrializing status. Now they are about to see their economy attain an industrially advanced status. Yet the Korean mind-set has not kept up with the nation's material advancement. While this can be a blessing, it can also prove a hindrance when it comes to adapting to a changing environment appropriately.

Koreans on the whole still have a rather narrow perspective on international matters as well. Most Koreans still maintain a highly mercantilistic mentality. One has to remember that, until recently, Korea was one of the most heavily indebted nations in the developing world, having suffered from chronic balance of payments deficits for many years. Because Korea's economic achievement in the last three decades had been based on a strategy of active export promotion, Koreans became used to thinking that increasing exports and achieving balance of payments surpluses in themselves were the ultimate national goals and social virtues. Thus it may take time and effort to persuade the Korean people of the desirability of market opening and import liberalization.

The Korean government recognizes the need to work toward changing some of these attitudes. In order to do so, the government set up the Presidential Commission on Economic Restructuring in 1988 to organize public debates and build consensus.[11] The commission has primarily dealt with issues regarding the nation's internationalization, industrial restructuring, and equity. Yet, this commission has not been able to draw the level of attention needed to accomplish its goal of building new consensus on these issues. This in part reflects the prevailing sociopolitical climate in Korea regarding these issues. Undoubtedly, the *bori gogei* and mercantilistic mentality still prevails in Korea, rendering the task of internationalization formidable.

Indeed, Korea today is at an awkward place in the international economic community. It is rapidly pursued by its immediate follower nations in many industrial sectors where it has been enjoying comparative advantages while still struggling to move up the ladder of industrial development. Furthermore, the end of the Cold War will naturally tend to push most countries to reorient their priorities toward economics and to put watchful eyes on others (Bergsten 1992, 3–24). For Korea to be successful in making its transition to an industrially advanced status, it is urgent that it adapt smoothly to the new environment with new strategies in a timely fashion.

In addition to systemic world changes, endogenous changes in the Korean economic system call for new international strategies. Korea has become a major player in international trade. These changes in Korea's position in the world and in the international environment call for Korea to take on a new role with new obligations. In addition, Korea has much to offer to the world, particularly to developing nations, as a "pioneer" country. However, this status will be maintained and respected only when Korea sustains economic prosperity and successfully joins the ranks of the industrially developed.

The end of the Cold War has special implications for Korea. The Korean peninsula has been on the front lines of the Cold War. The two Koreas now have legitimate hopes that peaceful national unification can be achieved. It is important in this connection, however, to draw Koreans' attention to one critical lesson to be learned from the recent German experience. The unification of two parts of a nation with different economic systems and different living standards not only requires ingenious preparation but also a great deal of money. Unless economically well-prepared, the golden opportunity of the nation's unification could be wasted.

---

11. This commission is similar to Japan's Maekawa Commission. See Presidential Commission on Economic Restructuring (1988).

Major Policy Issues and Challenges

Given the different and difficult domestic and international settings described above, Korea now has to face new challenges and set new policy priorities for its successful transition to the ranks of the industrially developed. A newly elected government is expected to be inaugurated in early 1993. It will be charged with the great responsibility of facing these challenges, some of which will demand immediate response and others requiring longer term strategies.

In short, the Korean economy today is bigger, more complex, more open, and further integrated into the world economy than ever before. These factors tend to reduce the effectiveness of certain policy instruments that might lead to more frequent and costlier government failures. At the same time, as Korean private entrepreneurs and businesses become more experienced and, in some cases, become world-class competitors, they will be able to carry out innovative activities in many areas where public assistance was previously needed.

Consequently, the agenda for the government today should be substantially different from that of the past, and the way the economy is managed has to be changed accordingly. Unlike earlier periods, the government can and should rely more on private initiatives to raise overall economic efficiency and to minimize the social costs of government failures. With this background, let us now highlight critical policy issues and discuss a policy agenda for the future.

Renewed Leadership Commitment with Economics as a National Priority

Korea is at a critical juncture, where a renewed strong leadership commitment to economics is needed to prevent the Korean economy from slowly but persistently losing its competitive advantage. With this commitment reestablished, the government should first convince the Korean people and their political leaders of the necessity for reorienting national policy priorities toward economics.

As always, the most effective way to convince Koreans is to put the Korean economy in an international perspective. While Koreans are taking good economic performance for granted, many other follower nations have begun to set their national priorities aright and have started to move their economies forward again. They have been vigorously liberalizing their economies and opening their markets to trade and foreign investment. As these nations gain momentum while Korea stumbles, the same trick of compound interest rates of economic growth, from which Korea benefited greatly in the past, might very well frustrate Koreans in coming years unless they do something about it soon.[12]

---

12. Imagine China becoming the world's largest economy within 15 years, measured on

It is therefore important for the government to communicate effectively with the people about how the world has been changing, how the changes are going to affect Korea, where Korea stands today in the world economic arena, and what its options are. It would be especially effective to point out that even the nation's peaceful unification depends on a solid economic foundation more than anything else.

North Korea, with a population of over 21 million, is estimated to have had a per capita income of $1,095 in 1990 compared with South Korea's $5,659 in the same year. The South has a population of 42.8 million, twice that of the North, but its GNP in 1990, at $237.9 billion, was roughly 10 times greater than the North's $23.5 billion. The gap between the two Koreas' consumption and social overhead capital is even wider than the gap between their respective per capita income. For example, KDI estimates that the level of consumer welfare[13] in 1990 in the North, at $471, is one-seventh that of the South, at $3,263. This gap is even greater than the difference between the South's current level of welfare per capita and its level 30 years ago.[14] Similar wide gaps exist in other areas such as telecommunications and other infrastructure. It is beyond the scope of this study to explore the best strategy for the two Koreas' unification.[15] However, it is worthwhile to draw Koreans' attention to the potential magnitude of the cost of unification.

Considering the wide gap that exists between the two Koreas' economic structures and individual living standards, sudden unification beginning in year 2001 and achieved in the subsequent four years, for example, is estimated to cost about 8.2 to 8.6 percent of the South's gross regional product (GRP) in order to bring the per capita income of the North up to a level equivalent to about half of that of the South.[16] Extending the time horizon out a bit, the cost is estimated to be 3.5 to 3.7 percent of the South's GDP if unification is achieved between 2001 and 2010 (Korea Development Institute 1991).

These estimates only consider expenditures for the North Korean economy, and therefore, additional resources should be put aside for

a purchasing power parity basis and provided that the current high rate of growth for the Chinese economy continues (Summers 1992).

13. Consumer welfare is estimated as the sum of both individual and social consumption.

14. In 1990 dollars, it was $652 for the South in 1960.

15. There are different opinions regarding the speed of unification, for example. Some argue for a gradual approach to unification while others prefer a sudden unification. See Bae (1992).

16. This is based on the assumption that the two Koreas unify in the year 2001. Obviously, if the South continues to grow faster than the North in coming years, the cost for unification will increase as unification is delayed. As the two nations' economic gap is narrowed through, for example, closer economic cooperation, the cost will be reduced accordingly (Bae 1992).

the South Korean economy itself before unification takes place. In this connection, the two Koreas might well jointly plan to use their "peace dividends" for this purpose. In addition, the brunt of the unification burden will fall on South Korea, and therefore, it needs to consider other means of mobilizing resources for unification, such as a unification tax or unification bond. The bottom line is that it is urgent for Korea to reorient its priorities toward economics to provide a solid foundation for unification.

As previously indicated, in response to popular demands supported by competing political parties, the government has during the last few years nearly abandoned the disciplined macroeconomic policy stance it has maintained since the early 1980s. Not only has the proportion of income-transfer expenditure increased, a substantial amount of national resources have ended up in politically motivated large public works and enormous housing projects.[17] This has rapidly pushed the general wage level and land prices up even higher.[18] Labor unions reacted to this bubble economy by demanding wages that exceeded productivity gains.[19] Entrepreneurs took advantage of prevalent rent-providing opportunities by engaging in real estate speculation and financial arbitrage.

Only with a strong leadership commitment and a national emphasis on economics can a more disciplined macroeconomic policy stance be restored. Unless the government sets policy priorities correctly and leads the way, other tough policy decisions cannot be effectively implemented.

In today's political environment, the government has to make even more strenuous efforts to reach consensus on economic policy. In this regard, regular public economic forums should be used fully. Participants in these forums should include politicians, farmers, business lead-

---

17. As indicated in chapter 4, the ratio of housing investment to GNP mostly remained at less than 5 percent in the earlier period, when the nation's priority was on investment in directly productive sectors and on achieving macroeconomic stabilization. The nation's housing investment was restricted primarily by controlling land supply for housing and limiting credit availability for housing purchases. As a result, the housing shortage became a political issue in the late 1980s. The government reacted by sharply increasing housing investments in the early 1990s to 8 percent of GNP in 1990 and more than 9 percent of GNP in 1991. This sudden shift of resources into the housing sector further aggravated both inflation and urban concentration, as most of new housing units built were concentrated in the Seoul metropolitan area.

18. As the housing price also rose, actual housing production units stayed about the same level as before, even with the higher proportion of GNP allocated for housing (Renaud 1992, 17).

19. During 1988–91, wages in the manufacturing sector went up by 20.5 percent per year while average productivity gains were 6.7 percent for the same period. Consequently, the unit labor cost for the manufacturing sector increased by 14.8 percent. During the three years of 1988–90, Korea's unit labor cost increased by 49.3 percent while it actually decreased in Japan by 9.9 percent and increased by 12.9 percent in Taiwan for the same period (Economic Planning Board 1992).

ers, union leaders, academics, journalists, and representatives from other interest groups in addition to top economic policymakers. In this connection, a Presidential Council on Setting National Policy Priorities might well be established to educate the public and to build consensus.

The government's role in setting a clear vision of the nation's economic future should be strengthened. In this connection, it would be desirable to continue preparing intermediate-range economic and social development plans for the nation. However, more emphasis should be put on the process rather than on the plan itself. The planning process also should provide opportunities for communicating with and educating the public.

The national primacy of economics and leadership commitment to it should also be manifested in the consistency and predictability of major economic policy directions, which in turn will facilitate policy implementation.[20] Frequent changes of the major players in the government not only reduce policy consistency and predictability, they also negatively affect credibility, thereby hampering implementation.[21]

Appropriate Industrial Policy and Financial Sector Reform

The term industrial policy is often used to refer to a policy of "picking winners," although it should be viewed broadly so as to include all government policy affecting the nation's industrial output and its composition.[22] Despite the fact that Korea abandoned picking-the-winners industrial policy some time ago, there are still some who argue that Korea still needs such a policy.

There are legitimate arguments against such a policy. First of all, the Korean private sector today is better prepared to pick possible winners than the government in most cases. In a world in which the trend toward globalization is accelerating, large private firms often have greater access to relevant information on technologies and markets than the government does.

---

20. Both technocrats' and bureaucrats' integrity can be better protected from political influences when the national primacy of economics and strong leadership commitment are in place.

21. The average tenure of key economic policymakers in the current government—about one year—has been much shorter than the tenures of their counterparts in previous governments.

22. Some call it either "general" industrial policy or "adaptive" industrial policy (Lindbeck 1981, 391–405; Diebold 1980). In today's Korean context, the term industrial policy is often used to include policies concerning *chaebols*. However, the issue of *chaebol* versus small and medium-sized firms has more to do with the nation's industrial organization—that is, the issue of who produces the nation's output rather than an issue of industrial composition.

Secondly, "picking the winner" implies an obligation on the part of the government to bail out a business if the venture runs into difficulty. In other words, the government becomes an implicit risk partner. This naturally creates a "moral hazard" problem for those businesses. In fact, a substantial portion of the Korean commercial banks' NPAs originate from the government's past targeting of overseas construction, ocean shipping, and heavy and chemical industries.

As noted before, the Korean government paid a high price for such industrial policies in terms of the explicit costs of alleviating the overhang of NPAs. As will be discussed in a following section, the alleviation policy involved subsidized loans to commercial banks from the central bank and tax privileges for banks and firms taking over these troubled firms.

In addition to these apparent costs, there were other implicit social costs involved as well. The NPA overhang delayed the liberalization of the financial sector, banks in particular. They also caused X-inefficiencies for bank management, as improved profitability through better management was more than offset by larger losses due to those nonperforming assets. In the mid-1980s, as will be explained later, the government tried to address this issue, but managed solutions were sought at high sociopolitical costs. Indeed, the price paid for the past industrial policy has been excessive.

Korea still needs an appropriate industrial policy, however. First of all, it is necessary to facilitate structural adjustments. In this connection, the government's role in supporting market mechanisms should be further emphasized. The role should include eliminating distortions in both product and factor markets and providing incentives to draw resources away from declining industries.

Other types of functional promotion policies for industrial development should not be excluded. However, these policies should not be targeted toward any particular products or firms but should provide both fiscal and financial incentives for R&D efforts to stimulate entrepreneurs' general competence in identifying and developing new technologies. "Technology policy" belongs in this category in that its goal is "to identify and nurture technologies that cut across industries or that undergird the competitive position of different sectors" (Young 1992, 45–46). In essence, these functional industrial policies are aimed at reducing technology-related market failures.[23]

To facilitate effective implementation of these policies, the government should first concentrate on providing a market-friendly environment for private initiatives. In this connection, the importance of a stable and consistent macroeconomic policy and a favorable microeconomic environment for socially productive, private entrepre-

23. For a detailed discussion on the subject, see Leipziger and Petri (1992).

neurial activities should be reemphasized. Rent-seeking entrepreneurial energies can be shifted into socially productive activities only with macroeconomic stability and with an appropriate relative-price and incentive structure in place.

The development of the Korean financial sector was repressed throughout the rapid growth era. This repression was further deepened when Korea opted to "pick winners." Accordingly, Korean commercial banks in particular, burdened with the legacies of past industrial policy, have not entirely been exposed to competition, even from domestic nonbank financial intermediaries. Interest rates in the banking market have been mostly controlled.

As previously discussed, the Korean government made a major effort to alleviate the NPA problem and thereby to lay a foundation for liberalizing the sector. This accomplished, an effort was made to liberalize interest rates in 1988, but due primarily to shifts in key economic players, the policy was never implemented as originally intended. Even though the timing now is much worse, it is not only necessary, it is urgent to liberalize interest rates as a prerequisite to fostering domestic competition, which in turn must occur before Korean banks can be fully exposed to severe international competition.

To effectively compete against tougher international or global competitors, the nation's financial sector itself has to be efficient. Therefore, it is critical for the overall efficiency of the Korean economy. It is primarily for Korea's own good. Of course, there are external reasons for liberalization as well. The completion of the Uruguay Round of trade negotiations, currently bogged down with agricultural disputes between the European Community and the United States, will put pressure on the sector to open up to international competition.

Regardless of the outcome of the Uruguay Round, however, bilateral trade pressures are also expected to be directed toward the financial sector. Since February 1990, the governments of Korea and the United States have been holding financial policy talks. The primary purpose of the talks is to deal with market access problems of US financial institutions and the progress of Korea's financial sector liberalization. The keen interest of the United States in these issues was highlighted during a summit meeting of the two national leaders in January 1992. The Europeans and Japanese are also waiting in line for access to the Korean financial market.

Korea's stock market is still rather underdeveloped. The government has taken steps to widen and deepen the market by stimulating both supply and demand with fiscal and financial incentives. The securities industry itself is not very developed; it, too, needs to be prepared to face outside competition. Appropriate legal and institutional foundations should also be established before opening up the industry fully.

In the meantime, the government should keep to the preannounced schedule for capital market opening announced in 1988.[24]

The financial sector liberalization should be implemented based on two interrelated principles: it should be conducted with a package approach, and the implementation procedure should proceed on a preannounced schedule. Rather than liberalizing the sector ad hoc, pushed by pressure from others, it should be implemented according to a carefully prepared liberalization package tailored to Korea's own needs. Of course, it is all for the better if trading partners' demand for reciprocal market opening can be accommodated in the process.

A gradual approach to financial market liberalization reduces the risk of failure or backsliding. The liberalization package needs to be implemented in accordance with a preannounced schedule. Needless to say, a gradual approach should not become an excuse for delaying liberalization. Adhering to a schedule would enhance the predictability and the credibility of the Korean government in domestic and international business circles. This in turn will enhance businesses' confidence in the Korean economy. The immediate challenge, however, is to persuade domestic political opponents of the need to liberalize while getting potential foreign competitors to realize the importance of endurance and patience.

One important issue along this line is national treatment. Currently, foreign financial institutions enjoy favorable treatment in some respects; in others, they are subject to more restrictions than their Korean counterparts. There are various historical reasons for this. For example, when the nation was suffering from chronic current account deficits, foreign financial institutions were allowed to take on certain kinds of business, for example, fixed-margin currency swap arrangements. At the same time, due to the underdevelopment of Korean financial institutions, foreign institutions were restricted from participating in other kinds of business activities. What should be done now is to level the field for competition between financial institutions by gradually reducing both privileges and restrictions—that is, to ensure national treatment.

Soon, Korean financial institutions will have to compete against formidable international financial giants. To win the competition, they, too, will need all kinds of economies: technical economies of scale, organizational economies of scale, economies of scope. In this connection, the

---

24. This intermediate-term liberalization program was announced with two purposes. First of all, Korea needed an intermediate-term liberalization plan for its securities market. Secondly, major trading partners, the United States in particular, were very much interested in immediate access to the market. With such a properly sequenced liberalization package, it is easier to reassure these trading partners, even when the speed or extent of liberalization is not fully satisfactory to them at the time.

bank ownership concentration and banking market segmentation issues have to be carefully reevaluated.

Currently, the Banking Law sets a ceiling of 8 percent bank share ownership by any single shareholder. This clause was introduced primarily to prevent *chaebols* from owning any of the nationwide commercial banks. Considering the possible conflicts of interest that could arise if industrial *chaebols* could own and control banks, this clause appears reasonable. On the other hand, it is bound to create a minority-majority shareholder situation for banks. Even for banks, it is desirable in principle to allow a majority shareholder to have effective control when banks' operations are fully liberalized.

An alternative that would reconcile both aspects is to eliminate the 8 percent ceiling for shareholders other than industrial *chaebols* as financial sector liberalization progresses. In this connection, it seems inevitable to allow financial groups to emerge and specialize in financial services. They should, however, be separated from industrial *chaebols*. Of course, their equity shares must be widely and publicly disbursed. This issue will be further discussed in the following section on *chaebols*.

Another remaining policy decision relates to financial market desegmentation. What should Korea do about the current world trend toward so-called universal banking? As the NPAs overhang problem subsides and bank interest rates are liberalized, Korean commercial banks are expected to become genuine commercial banks. During the learning process, it seems reasonable to have the "specialization first" policy continued. As international financial integration and globalization trends continue, however, it is inevitable that Korean banks eventually will have to conform to the world trend.

Chaebols and New Government-Business Relations

The *chaebol* is one of the most controversial issues in Korea today. Most *chaebol* founders in Korea are very capable and innovative entrepreneurs.[25] In fact, many of them have proved themselves to be world-class. It is natural, therefore, to expect that *chaebol* companies would grow faster than their competitors, just as the best companies in countries around the world have.

Critics contend, however, that growth in these companies was unfairly accelerated by government subsidies and other privileges. In the process, other competitors, small and medium-sized companies in particular, were not on a level playing field. To make things worse, these critics point to the fact that the *chaebols*' rapidly growing asset portfolios are owned and controlled by a few individuals and their family members. Consequently, they argue, the fruits of future growth will not be widely

---

25. For *chaebol* case studies, see Jones and SaKong (1987, 343–64).

shared, and concentration of economic wealth will be further intensified. The problem may get worse if concentrated economic power wields influence over government policy.

It is well known that Korean *chaebols* are highly diversified horizontally. To the extent that they have benefited from organizational economies of scale by reducing the required entrepreneurship per unit of output, the Korean economy must also have gained. On the other hand, however, their positions are so dominant—either monopolistic or oligopolistic—in many of Korea's industries that they cause economic inefficiencies of all sorts. In particular, financially weak small and medium-sized companies have to suffer just to survive in these sectors.

In short, the *chaebol* issue today has two interrelated aspects, in addition to the traditional economic efficiency problem: legitimacy and distributional equity. The legitimacy issue originates from the perceived unfairness or injustice associated with the *chaebols'* emergence and growth. The distributional equity issue arises from the concentration of economic power, which is a consequence of the *chaebols'* rapid growth.

There are two sources of unjustifiable *chaebol* growth that are mentioned most frequently in Korea today. First of all, the *chaebol* legitimacy problem arises from *chaebols* having grown by virtue of privileged access to bank loans. In the absence of a well-functioning capital market, the bank loan market was and still is the most important source of corporate funds. Under this situation, well-established large companies naturally tend to crowd out financially weak small and medium-sized borrowers. Particularly during the HCI promotion era, as was discussed earlier, large *chaebol* firms participating in HCI projects gained greater access not only to cheaper policy loans but also to general bank loans, even during times of credit rationing. On this grounds, critics conclude they grew at the expense of others: the weak and the taxpayers.

It is well known that most big *chaebol* firms have higher debt-to-equity ratios than their smaller competitors.[26] This, in turn, tends to intensify the legitimacy question and create other economic problems. More often than not, the high degree of leverage for large firms becomes a factor for automatically feeding more loans into them to make "the bicycle keep running" even in bad times. In times of difficulties, the "too big to fail" or "too important not to save" argument usually wins, creating a serious moral hazard problem. As a matter of fact, this kind of practice toward *chaebols* contributed to aggravating the legitimacy aspect of *chaebols* even further.

In addition, the high financial leverage of big *chaebol* firms is a potentially destabilizing factor for the overall economy. *Chaebol* firms are highly interdependent financially, through cross-equity shareholdings, cross-loan guarantees, and so on. Consequently, one *chaebol* firm's financial

---

26. For a good discussion on the high leverage issue, see E. H. Kim (1990, 341–57).

trouble could easily develop into a group disaster. This, in turn, could create a serious problem for the nation's banking sector and the nation's financial system as a whole.

Secondly, the *chaebols'* problem with legitimacy often arises from their real estate holdings. *Chaebols* are very often accused of gaining much from "nonbusiness" real estate holdings. In fact, the Korean government occasionally took measures to force *chaebols* to sell off a part of those holdings. Whether or not *chaebols* had any speculative motives for holding real estate, there is no doubt that they gained substantially from rapidly rising real estate prices to the extent that they have held much large real estate.[27] The general perception is, therefore, that they got richer with socially unproductive, rent-seeking activities.

The legitimacy issue and the distributional equity issue are interrelated for *chaebols* to the extent that their ever-growing asset portfolios are held by a few individuals and their family members. If, in fact, *chaebol* firms' equity shares were widely held, the distributional equity issue would be substantially mitigated simply because even wealth transfers that lacked legitimacy could be shared by the general public.

While most big *chaebol* companies are listed on the Korea Stock Exchange, only 30 percent of the firms of the top 30 *chaebols* (or less than 60 percent of the total paid-in capital for the 30 *chaebols*) went public. Even for those that went public, the majority of their equity shares are still held by original owners or their family members or both. As of April 1992, 46.1 percent of total paid-in capital of the top 30 groups was held by a majority individual shareholder (usually the founder or the second-generation owner), his relatives, and *chaebol* companies. Their share ranges from 65.5 percent to 37.7 percent, averaging over 50 percent for the top five *chaebols*.[28]

The traditional economic efficiency problem is still a concern, as chaebol firms' industrial concentration is substantial,[29] and interindustrial cross-subsidization among *chaebol* firms through such means as cross-equity shareholdings and cross-loan guarantees are widely used. Although this is not the primary concern of today's emotionally charged

---

27. Detailed information on *chaebols'* real estate ownership is not publicly available. However, it is known that land ownership distribution, both individual and corporate, is highly skewed—that is, more skewed than income distribution; the Gini coefficient for land in 1980 was estimated to be 0.85, compared with 0.36 for income. The top 5 percent of landowners own more than 65 percent of the land in Korea.

28. Hyundai, 65.5 percent; Dae Woo, 48.8 percent; Sam Sung, 58.3 percent; Lucky Gold Star, 39.7 percent; Sang Yong, 37.7 percent.

29. In 1987 the number of manufactured commodities shipped by the top 30 *chaebols* was 1,499. *Chaebol* firms had the largest market share in 475 items (or 32 percent of the total), and for 941 items (or two-thirds of the total), *chaebol* firms were among the top three largest shippers (Kyu Uck Lee 1991).

chaebol debate, it also needs to be properly addressed by means of appropriate antitrust and fair trade laws.

Based on the discussions above, it is clear that future *chaebol* policy should specifically focus on three aspects of the issue: legitimacy, distributional equity, and economic efficiency.

For both the legitimacy and distributional equity aspects of the issue, the policy of encouraging *chaebol* firms to disburse their equity shares widely should be continued, albeit gradually. In the process, however, majority shareholders should be properly protected from losing management control. Equity shares with nonvoting rights might well be used to this effect.

In dealing with *chaebols*, their growth and diversification *per se* should not be condemned, particularly if they grew and diversified with their own money. Korean firms must compete against companies from all over the world, in many cases against international business giants or affiliated firms of big international conglomerates. Considering the relative scale of Korean *chaebols* in the world, it therefore seems desirable for *chaebols* to concentrate in their specialized areas.

As previously indicated, the Banking Law sets a ceiling of 8 percent bank share ownership, and as a result, Korean *chaebols* today cannot own any nationwide commercial banks. Considering the chronic excess demand for bank loans and the *chaebol* firms' dominance in various industrial fields, the policy of restricting industrial *chaebols* from owning and controlling commercial banks can be justified.

Most *chaebols* today, however, have expanded into financial fields, including provincial banks, insurance companies, securities companies, and short-term finance companies. Industrial *chaebols* should be encouraged to remain in relevant industrial fields only. Therefore, unless they choose to specialize chiefly in financial fields, they should be encouraged to leave the field for others.

For growth and diversification to be legitimate, special favors such as fiscal subsidies, privileged access to cheaper sources of capital, and special bail-out policies for *chaebols* should be eliminated. At the same time, proper instruments for dealing with the concentration of economic power—strict fair trade and antitrust laws, for example—should be invoked as needed. Even though large size and diversification *per se* are not bad, their impacts on competition and distributional equity should be closely scrutinized for proper application of such laws.

Until the banking sector is fully liberalized and other means for protecting small and medium-sized firms are in place, *chaebols'* access to banks, which enables further rapid growth and diversification, has to be limited in one way or the other. In this regard, the current credit supervision system, which restricts both *chaebols'* access to cheaper bank funds and their use of them, can be justified. Even today, if *chaebols* choose not (or can afford not) to use bank loans, they are not subject to the restriction.

In 1991, however, the basket system of bank credit supervision was amended to exclude loans extended to "mainline businesses" of big *chaebols* from bank credit ceiling calculations. Considering the high proportion of loans to these mainline businesses—40 to 50 percent of all bank loans to these *chaebols*—and the fungibility of money, this measure eventually will increase the overall bank loan proportion to these groups. The government is known to have taken this measure for the short-term purpose of stimulating investments. As such, it needs to be reevaluated as the cyclical necessity disappears.

As financial sector liberalization proceeds, the credit supervision system itself needs to be reevaluated. Improvement of the weak corporate financial structure of *chaebols* should be encouraged in the long run by fostering efficient equity markets and through an improved tax regime that is not biased toward equity financing. The current policy of limiting cross-shareholding and cross-loan guarantees should be continued and tightened over time.

It is also important to have stricter rules for bailing out distressed firms. Just as financial institutions became dependent on the government under the government-led growth strategy, business firms, larger ones in particular, still tend to look for assistance from the government in times of difficulty. Yet once the government takes its hands out of business affairs, the "too big to fail" doctrine will also lose ground. With financial sector reform and an appropriate financial infrastructure in place—for example, deposit insurance schemes and efficient capital markets—the market will have to deal with firm-level problems. Even under these conditions, of course, the government will still have to deal with industrywide structural problems through appropriate policies.

The salient feature of the Korean government-business relationship has been government's domination of the relationship. In short, the Korean government's control over commercial banks was the basis for such a relationship. In the absence of well-developed capital markets, Korean business firms had to rely heavily on commercial banks. At the same time, the government encouraged private businesses to use relatively cheap bank loans for the nation's export-led industrialization. An inevitable result was a high debt-to-equity ratio for most Korean businesses. This made Korean businesses more vulnerable to the public financier. It is no wonder that Korean *chaebols* are so keenly interested in owning financial institutions.

As previously indicated, considering both the domestic and international changes taking place in the economic environment, the Korean government has no choice but to relinquish its financier's role and liberalize the nation's financial sector. Besides, Korean businesses are going to have more and more alternatives to domestic bank financing. Accordingly, a new government-business relationship will have to emerge.

It is important for the nation's continued progress that Korea establishes a productive government-business relationship. Under this new relationship, the nation's financial sector will have to take over the financier's role from the government. Consequently, it is critical for Korea to establish a cooperative financier-business relationship first. Such a highly cooperative relationship is found in both Japan and Germany.[30] At this time, however, it would be difficult for Korea to emulate these models. The separation of industrial groups from financial groups in terms of their ownership ought to be the policy direction for Korea today. After Korean *chaebols* become widely held and the nation's financial sector is fully liberalized, however, the current Japanese or German model might be worth considering. In the meantime, the Korean government might encourage banks to use a system closer to the "prime bank" model for industrial firms without entering ownership relationships. The government will have to rely more heavily on the bank supervisory function to ensure a cooperative and productive financier-business relationship.

In essence, the new relationship must become more balanced between the government and private businesses. This in no way indicates, however, a weaker leadership role for the government. A stronger leadership role is expected from the government in providing a clear vision of economic direction, stable macroeconomic policy stance, and a favorable microeconomic environment for productive entrepreneurial activities. The government also has to make strenuous efforts to build economic policy consensus. It should frequently use not only public forums, open seminars, and hearings but also consultative councils and special commissions set up for the government.

Structural Adjustments and Competitiveness

Economic development requires continual structural adjustment. To the extent that Korea developed rapidly during the past three decades, structural adjustments have been successful. The current task of making structural adjustments is more formidable, not only because the Korean economy is at a more advanced development stage, but also because it is more open internationally.

---

30. Shortsightedness or "short-termism" is a buzzword for the current structural problems of the US economy. To overcome this problem, a noted economist recently proposed that a new relationship between industrial firms and financial institutions be established. He went so far as to propose creation of a business group like that of Japan and Germany (Thurow 1992; see also Competitiveness Policy Council 1992).

In this awkward stage of development, the Korean economy is being squeezed on two fronts: while Korea loses its competitive advantages in labor and middle-level, technology-intensive, lower-cost products, it now faces difficulties in establishing competitive edges in differentiated products that are capital- and technology-intensive. Differentiated, high-value-added products require constant product and process innovation and dynamic responses to market changes in addition to manufacturing excellence.

Korea now needs a new competitive strategy to facilitate economic adjustment toward a more sophisticated industrial structure. The new strategy should promote an advantage based on output quality to replace the past input-cost advantage for Korean products.

Technology and innovation are at the core of this strategy. In this connection, a strong technology policy, as an important part of a functional industrial policy, is necessary. First of all, this technology policy should assist and encourage Korean firms to adopt an efficient R&D strategy. At this stage of development, the Korean strategy should put more emphasis on commercial follow-through than on scientific breakthroughs.

Considering the relatively small R&D capability of Korean firms, R&D networking, not only among Korean firms but with foreign partners as well, is worth encouraging.[31] In the meantime, it is important to provide incentives for private R&D activities to raise the nation's R&D expenditure, together with increased public expenditure for R&D activities. The expenditure as a percentage of GNP has to be raised to reach a level comparable to today's developed nations within a few years.

The long-term R&D strategy should be supplemented by active FDI inducement for transfer of advanced manufacturing technology as well as for marketing and customer services. As discussed in chapter 5, FDI in general and manufacturing FDI in particular increased rapidly beginning in 1986. Unfortunately, however, the trend was soon reversed. Furthermore, FDI in high-tech fields, for which tax privileges are currently provided, has been sharply reduced since 1989. In 1988 56 percent of FDI (in value terms) was in the manufacturing sector in areas designated as high-tech. The proportion was drastically reduced to 25.1 percent in 1989 and down to only 6.6 percent in 1991.[32]

---

31. Korea's overall R&D expenditure in 1990 amounted to $4.5 billion, less than General Motors' 1988 R&D spending of $4.7 billion. Seventy-four percent of expenditures were made by private firms. Korea's R&D expenditure was 1.91 percent of GNP in 1990. It was 2.69 percent for Japan in 1989 and 2.74 percent for the United States in 1990 (Sung 1992).

32. In terms of FDI cases, the proportion was reduced to 2 percent in 1991, down from 19.6 percent in 1988.

Various economic cost factors could have contributed to the decreasing trend of FDI: for example, rapidly increasing wages, high land prices, and frequent and prolonged labor disputes. However, significant administrative and legal barriers to FDI still exist. It is critical for Korea to promote an FDI-friendly environment, especially in high-tech fields. More importantly, Korean entrepreneurs should learn how to work with foreign business partners. Korea should make every effort to benefit from the business globalization trend in building its own national competitive foundation.

The chronic trade deficit with Japan, which has been increasing in recent years, is evidence of Korea's vulnerable competitive position. In 1988 the deficit was $3.9 billion. It increased to $5.9 billion in 1990 and to $8.8 billion in 1991. Only a new, technology-oriented competitive strategy can help solve the problem.

From 1987 to 1990 Korea's accumulated trade deficit with Japan amounted to $19.1 billion. On the other hand, during the same period, the trade balance in basic materials, parts, and machineries with Japan was $35.2 billion in favor of Japan.[33] This reflects Korea's unique industrial structure and weak competitive base. Korea imports intermediate and capital goods from Japan, and it assembles and processes those semifinished products to export to other markets, primarily the United States, by taking advantage of a competitive edge based on input costs.[34]

Even this situation, undesirable as it is, cannot last long because Korea no longer has input cost advantages in these products. The result could be a reduced deficit with Japan, but at the cost of substantial losses in Korea's overall exports. Koreans cannot afford this, a fact that underscores the urgent need for a sensible national competitive strategy.

Structural adjustments for the agricultural sector remain a big challenge. Regardless of the outcome of the Uruguay Round of trade negotiations, it is in Korea's interest to make necessary but difficult structural adjustments for the agricultural sector according to Korea's own schedule.

Nearly 20 percent of Korean workers are still employed in the agricultural sector. Just 20 years ago, this proportion was over 50 percent. This means that workers in the nonagricultural sector still have strong emotional ties, if not direct family connections, with the agricultural

---

33. During 1982 to June 1991, Korea's deficit for basic material, parts, and machinery trade with Japan was $62.3 billion while its total trade deficit with Japan was $40.1 billion (Park 1991, 54).

34. The Korean export promotion incentive system is partly responsible for this situation to the extent that the system is based on gross and not net value of exports. There have been no particular incentives given for the production of intermediate inputs and not many for the production of capital equipment.

sector. This in itself compounds the political difficulties of restructuring the sector. What makes things more difficult is the composition of rural household income. Currently, over 50 percent of rural household income still comes from agricultural activities, unlike neighboring Taiwan or Japan, where well over 80 percent of rural income is from nonfarm activities. The real challenge is to accelerate industrial relocation toward rural areas to help increase opportunities for rural households to earn nonfarm income and to absorb displaced agricultural workers.

Investments in social overhead capital in rural areas must be expanded to accelerate industrial relocation. At the same time, governmental support for industrial training and job placement for displaced farmers should also be provided to facilitate the necessary adjustments for the agricultural sector. The sector needs to be made competitive through commercialized scientific farming and specialization. These necessary measures should be supported through a structural adjustment facilitating fund for a limited period.

Korea must make smooth structural adjustments while persuading important trading partners to allow Korea to take a gradual approach to opening markets for important agricultural products. At the same time, the government has to convince farmers that it will use resources released in the reduction of income-transfer-based agricultural supports for structural adjustment of the sector.

Relative Poverty and Income Distribution

Distributional equity is a key policy issue in Korea today. Despite the improving trend of recent income distribution statistics, there is a widespread perception that Korea's income distribution is worsening. The worsening income distribution, whether real or perceived, must be given priority.

It could be that actual income distribution in recent years has in fact worsened. Another possibility is that published income distribution statistics do not accurately portray the actual distributional situation in Korea. Still another possibility is that a gap between actual and perceived income distribution may exist and has widened in recent years (SaKong 1990).

There have been claims that published statistics seriously underestimate income inequality in Korea primarily due to biases in coverage (Yoo 1990; Hong 1991). The first coverage problem concerns the exclusion of certain households from Korea's household income survey—the very rich, the very poor, self-employed businessmen, medical doctors, lawyers, nonfarm households in rural areas, and farm households in urban areas. Another problem arises from incomplete coverage of certain categories of income, such as capital gains, inheritance, and property income. An additional source of bias toward equality is the fact that the basic income-distribution data report only the mean income of each income bracket rather than the individual family income for each income bracket.

The incomplete coverage of capital gains from real estate could be the most serious source of bias in recent years.[35] As Korea in recent years experienced unprecedented rapid real estate price increases, including prices for housing, the incomplete coverage of capital gains from real estate, both realized and unrealized,[36] seriously distorts the statistics. To the extent that real estate ownership is concentrated among the higher income brackets, the incomplete coverage of capital gains could skew the statistics toward greater than actual equality.

Korea's private land ownership is known to be highly concentrated. About 3 percent of the economically active population owned over 65 percent of total private land as of June 1989. Among landowners, the upper 5 percent and 10 percent, owned 65.2 percent and 76.9 percent, respectively (Kang 1989; Hong 1991). According to estimated Gini coefficients, land ownership is much more concentrated than income in Korea, i.e., 0.85 for land compared with 0.36 for income (Hong 1991, 5).[37]

On the other hand, the price of land in recent years has been rising much faster than overall inflation. From 1987 to 1990, average land prices went up nearly 24 percent per annum while the GNP deflator rose less than 6 percent annually during the same period. Consequently, capital gains for landowners, both realized and unrealized, could have been substantial. According to one estimate, for example, capital gains as a percentage of GNP were somewhere between 54 and 199 percent in 1989, depending on which land value figures one uses (Hong 1991, table 1).

In short, income distribution statistics that exclude all or part of capital gains from real estate distort actual income distribution in favor of equality to a large extent. In this connection, an interesting recent study (Leipziger 1992) attempts to integrate estimates on the distribution of wealth, both financial and real, with available income distribution data. Preliminary results of the study show a considerably more skewed dis-

---

35. The exclusion of capital gains from equity share transactions is another source of bias in the income distribution statistics. The magnitude is estimated to be smaller, however. Capital gains from equity shares of unlisted companies became subject to a proportional tax in 1991.

36. Hong (1991) estimates that about 5 percent is actually realized.

37. Financial asset ownership is also known to be more skewed than income distribution. The estimated Gini coefficient for financial assets (based on a Bank of Korea survey) was 0.56 as compared with 0.36 for household income distribution in 1988. According to a KDI survey, the Gini coefficient for financial asset ownership was even higher, i.e., 0.77 while the coefficient for income distribution based on the same survey was 0.40 in 1988 (Kang 1989, 76; Kwon 1992, 14).

tribution of income than that in published statistics for 1988, supporting the argument of a built-in equality bias in the official statistics.

Despite improving income-distribution statistics covering the most recent years, policymakers should take the worsening income distribution argument seriously, and corrective measures must be taken. In the meantime, government should cooperate closely with relevant research institutes in an effort to make household surveys for income distribution as realistic as possible. At the same time, a serious attempt should also be made to use realistic household wealth surveys to improve the quality of income distribution statistics. The government should realize that the its credibility is at stake.

In addition to the possibility of actually worsening income distribution, it is likely that the perceived income distribution gap has also widened in recent years. People who cannot afford to take advantage of capital gains might very well feel that they are even poorer and more deprived. In particular, recent rapid increases in housing prices must have left non-house-owners feeling further deprived. The proportion of house-owning households in urban areas has steadily decreased to less than 50 percent while housing prices increased substantially in recent years: for example, the price for apartments went up by 51.4 percent between 1985 and 1989 (Korea Research Institute for Human Settlements 1991).

When the large number of non-house-owners saw the dimming possibility of owning houses while their counterparts were making substantial capital gains from owning their homes, their perception of relative deprivation or social injustice must have been further intensified. As a consequence, while capital gains directly contribute to worsening actual income distribution, the perceived income distribution gap between the rich and the poor became even greater, making the income distribution issue socially and politically more acute.

The perceived gap in income distribution may have widened even further in recent years because of a surge in unrealistic expectations. When absolute poverty disappears from society, relative poverty usually becomes a key social concern. In particular, if a society was persuaded to stick with economic growth objectives long enough and actually achieved phenomenal growth while eliminating absolute poverty, as Korea did, people's unwarranted expectation for reaching economic nirvana would become widespread sooner or later. To a great extent, these feelings may have come to a head recently because of Korea's current transitional phase of development, both economic and political.

Furthermore, given Korea's relatively high per capita income, people's tolerance for what is seen as worsening income distribution or any distributional injustice, actual or perceived, wears thin fast. They no longer feel gratified by others' success, as they did in earlier stages of development. As Albert Hirschman suggested (1973, 544–66), when Korea, an extremely homogeneous nation, reaches this stage of intolerance, social conflicts may become even more acute, and people's frustration may become even further exaggerated. Korea seems to have reached this stage.

Rapid political changes may have reduced the tolerance level further while accentuating existing imbalances. Recent violent labor disputes, farmers' demonstrations, regional animosities, and the general mood of social discontent are signs of growing intolerance and a call for new policy priorities.

Disparities among not only income classes but also industries, different sizes of firms, and regions need to be addressed as well. The widespread feeling of relative poverty, both actual and perceived, presents formidable challenges.

Future policies should address this issue. First of all, the government should do more in providing basic needs for the poorer segment of society: educational assistance and vocational training, low-cost housing, basic health care, and public transportation for needy households. At the same time, the quality and scope of Korea's social welfare system, including newly introduced medical insurance and national pension schemes, must be continuously improved and expanded.

Korea's current tax burden ratio is still below 20 percent, and therefore, ways can be found to increase the ratio without too much additional burden on ordinary taxpayers. However, there is a danger of overcommitment, of going beyond the nation's financing capability.

An improved system of land taxes can be a convenient alternative to raising tax revenue. Korea's overall ratio of property tax to GNP is relatively low compared with other countries. Even though Korea's land value as a percentage of GNP in 1989 was nearly 1,000 percent while it was only 62 percent for the United States and 350 percent for Japan in 1988, property tax revenue as a percentage of GNP in 1989 for Korea was only 0.5 percent, compared with 3.1 percent in 1988 for the United States and 3.4 percent in 1988 for Japan (Wontack Hong, personal communication to the author). Despite relatively high nominal tax rates for capital gains earned from land sales in Korea, the effective tax rates are still negligible due to the unrealistic land value assessment system.[38] Capital gains tax revenue of land sales relative to GNP in 1989 was a meager 0.31 percent for Korea, compared, for example, with 2.6 percent in 1988 for Taiwan.[39] It is therefore important to introduce a more realistic land evaluation system while nominal property and capital gains tax rates can actually be reduced to encourage compliance.

It is also important to eliminate opportunities for making unearned income from land ownership or speculation; this will help improve in-

---

38. Officially assessed land prices were only around 33 percent in 1988.

39. Figures provided by Professor Wontack Hong.

come distributional gaps of both kinds. In this regard, an effective tax system for both land holding and land transaction based on a proper land evaluation system should be put in place.[40] Korea is a land-scarce nation, and as a result, incentives for real estate hoarding and speculation always exist.

It is often argued, however, that Korea's land (and housing) scarcity and the high price of property have been worsened by complex and extensive public regulations and other interventions restricting supply responses (Hoffman and Struyk, forthcoming). Considering the importance of the issue, it seems worthwhile to set up a special presidential commission to review all the existing laws and regulations and the system of land development and to suggest improvements.

From the distributional equity perspective, another important area for tax reform is the financial asset market. Legacies of the growth-first development era are still apparent in this market. Interest and dividend income are subject to a flat withholding income tax rather than a progressive global income tax so that much lower rates can be applied to earnings from financial assets.[41]

The introduction of the controversial so-called "real name" system of financial asset holding, together with an integrated income tax scheme, would greatly contribute to mitigating the distributional inequality among financial asset holders. For this reason, in addition to others, it is important to implement the real-name system, as the Korean economy prepares to absorb its immediate impact and necessary institutional arrangements such as a real-name system for real estate holders are made in advance.

Financial savings are much more desirable than real-asset holdings. Capital gains from trading equity shares of listed companies are not taxed because the promotion of the equity capital market has been an important policy goal in Korea. However, to the extent that financial asset ownership is highly skewed, these taxation policies would affect household income distribution unfavorably.

Financial savings are encouraged primarily to channel the mobilized funds into productive industrial uses. The promotion of the capital mar-

---

40. To this end, the Korean government has introduced various reform measures, which have been under consideration for some time in Korea. They include an improved land-value evaluation scheme for tax purposes, a global land tax system, taxes on unrealized capital gains, a levy on gains from land price increases of land development, and so forth (Hong 1991).

41. Currently, the withholding tax rate is 20 percent of interest and dividends from financial assets under a "real name." With a surcharge of 1.5 percent—that is, the resident tax—the rate goes up to 21.5 percent. On the other hand, the global income tax rate is progressive, up to 50 percent. The withholding rate goes up to 60 percent if the income is from financial assets under a fictitious name. With the surcharge, the rate becomes 64.5 percent.

ket has the same primary purpose. In addition, the equity market in particular is promoted to help improve Korea's weak corporate financial structure. These goals are still valid. Privileges provided to this end, however, should not be so great as to induce even industrialists to engage in arbitrage. Striking a balance between growth and equity objectives is the key in this area.

In terms of reform sequencing, the financial asset market is second only to the real estate market as a target for prevention of undesirable diversion of financial resources. The approach should be based on a gradualism well-articulated in advance. In the process, as always, interests of the relatively poor (for whom distributional reform measures are necessary) should be properly protected. In other words, the immediate goal should be to reduce distributional inequality among financial asset owners.

The relative poverty issue is not confined to different income classes. The same issue exists between different-sized firms, namely, *chaebols* versus small and medium-sized companies. Appropriate policies concerning economic power concentration, or *chaebols*, are justified on this ground as well. The income disparity between urban and rural households and between different regions should also be narrowed by increasing income earning opportunities in nonfarming activities for rural households and disadvantaged regions. Current policies of encouraging industrial firms to move to rural and economically distressed areas and of expanding regionally balanced investments in social infrastructure should be continued to achieve these goals.

In dealing with the relative poverty issue, the need to strike a proper balance between sustained, stable growth and distributional equity, and to avoid irresponsible political responses to people's rapidly rising, unrealistic expectations, cannot be overemphasized. Policymakers must remind the Korean people of the several countries that have been frustrated at the threshold of industrial development simply because their policymakers failed to make hard choices.

Worker-Management Relationships

Korea's recent agonizing labor disputes naturally force attention on the establishment of a productive worker-management system. More importantly from a long-term perspective, productive industrial relations can be an important source of productivity improvement and thus an important element of a nation's competitive base, as is evidenced by the Japanese and German experiences (Kochan 1992). Korea is now at the stage where a competitive strategy based on differentiated output quality must be pursued, and the key to the success of such a strategy is appropriate human resources development and productive industrial relations.

Existing labor laws were amended rather hastily beginning in 1987 without careful studies or wide-ranging expert consultation (Kihwan Kim 1990). Consequently, there is much room for improvement. Detailed recommendations for improvements regarding these laws are well beyond this author's expertise and, thus, the scope of this study.[42] It is, however, more than clear that the social cost of not having an adequate industrial relations system and industrial peace are so high that adequate social investment should be made in this regard. Both sides will have to learn that collective bargaining is give-and-take—that is, intended to reconcile differences for mutual benefit. They also should learn how to respect the rules of the game while the government reorients the traditional paternalistic attitude toward workers and maintains fair and neutral law enforcement.

An immediate important task for the government is to create a favorable environment in which a cooperative social partnership among government, business, and workers can be promoted. Most urgently, to this end there should be a conscious government effort to integrate in-depth economic analyses of industrial relations issues into the decision-making behind the nation's macroeconomic policies and intermediate plans more closely. Closer interactions between concerned ministries and policy research institutions should facilitate the effort.

The importance of cooperative, tripartite information-sharing cannot be overemphasized. The nation's economic strategies and policy goals should always be well-articulated for businesses and workers. They must be able to see that government's policy goals are consistent with their own long-term interests. Of course, it is more important for employers to persuade their workers that only through company prosperity can their own welfare be enhanced. However, only when the employers' point is proven in action will workers be persuaded and motivated to work hard for their companies.

Educational Reform and Human Resources Development

Many have rightly emphasized the superior general level of education as the most important base for Korea's successful economic development. As previously indicated, Korea's new competitive strategy in this age of information and globalization calls for more active human resources development and a higher quality education. Koreans are still fervent believers in education, and there is strong demand for quality education.[43] The government should make every effort not to waste this valuable Korean attribute.

---

42. For policy recommendations, see Park (1990) and Linddauer (1990).

43. Unlike some other nations, Korea has never experienced a major problem of dropouts in middle or high school. Serious social problems frequently arise from the difficulties students face in seeking admission to higher educational institutions.

Up until recently, Korea had to devote more than one-third of its annual budget to defense. Consequently, other areas, including public education, were constrained. The government should carefully plan to use future "peace dividends" (as they arise) as an additional source of investment in education and human resources development. Korea's future survival and enhanced position in the world now depend more on economics than ever before. It is therefore logical for Korea to earmark part of resources released from the nation's defense budget cut for general investment in human capital formation, which is the competitive base for the Korean economy.

At the same time, both public and private educational institutions should be allowed to use private financial resources to augment the limited public resources for quality education. This option is almost closed in Korea today. For example, Korea does not permit wealthy parents to make financial donations to universities in exchange for their children's admission.

It is widely believed that worse-off parents in general would oppose such a scheme. Would they still oppose it if it is implemented in such a way so that their children do not get hurt but actually benefit from the financial resources mobilized from wealthy parents?[44] For example, the system could be set up so that the resources can only be used for scholarships for poor students and research grants for professors. While private resources can be used for improving higher education, limited public tax money can be concentrated on upgrading the quality of primary education. Only through education can children avoid the inheritance of poverty and can the nation successfully compete in international markets.

Needless to say, the purpose of education goes beyond the scope of economics. However, it is important to have a system of education that adequately supplies the human resources needs of a changing industrial structure. The overall educational reform of the future should fully reflect Korea's new economic competitive strategy.

More incentives should also be provided to the industry for vocational training of workers, and existing laws and regulations regarding vocational training should be effectively implemented.[45] Vocational training is necessary for both upgrading the workers' skills and getting new skills

---

44. The system should be so designed that the number of extra admissions should in no way adversely affect ordinary admissions based on academic merit.

45. The Special Law for Vocational Training of 1974 required firms with 200 or more workers to provide basic training periodically. This law and the Law for Vocational Training of 1967 was integrated into the Basic Law for Vocational Training in 1976. According to this new law, firms with 300 (currently 150) or more workers were required to train a certain proportion of their full-time employees regularly. If firms choose not to meet the legal requirements, they are subject to a vocational training levy.

for shifting jobs. With vocational training, the economy benefits through the enhanced national economic competitive base, and so do the workers because their income-earning capacity is improved. Therefore, vocational training programs should be properly incorporated into the nation's adaptive industrial policy, as well as its industrial relations system.

Active Participation in International Cooperation

As previously indicated, the new world order will require major economic players to depend more heavily on international economic cooperation. As an important international economic player, Korea needs to participate more actively in various international economic organizations and forums where major policies are coordinated and discussed.

Currently, there are discussions both within Korea and among OECD nations about the possibility of Korea joining the OECD. Admission to that organization in itself is neither proof nor guarantee of Korea's advancement to the ranks of the industrially developed. It is, however, a good indication of the importance others attach to the Korean economy and of the potential as well as the willingness on the part of Koreans to participate in world economic affairs.

Korea has to overcome important challenges before graduating from developing nation status. Joining the OECD might be a way to hasten necessary structural adjustments. As a member of the OECD, Korea would be required to make certain obligatory adjustments, such as liberalizing capital account transactions and providing assistance to the developing world—both of which should be carried out anyway.

In addition, Korea could gain valuable opportunities for sharing information regarding world economic and technological advances and the future policy direction of major economic players and technological leaders. There are concerns that Korea, as a small member, would not only lose its autonomy in economic policy but also be forced to accept the terms of major OECD nations. In response, one may ask whether Korea will be able to avoid this situation by not joining the organization.

Conclusion

With such big challenges looming ahead, and faced with a very different and difficult political and economic environment, the obvious question is whether the Korean people and government will be able to respond and adjust successfully. It is not going to be easy, but if history is any guide, Koreans will learn fast. The Korean people and particularly Korean politicians will realize that they can no longer take good economic performance for granted, as they have in recent years. They will soon realize that political development itself may be harmed if the economy does not continue to prosper.

More important for Koreans is the fact that in this rapidly changing post–Cold War era, unification is now a real possibility. The two Germanies' recent unification vividly illustrates the fact that success depends on a solid economic foundation more than anything else. Korea will learn from the German experience.

Already, there is widespread public concern about the economy. In fact, one major political issue of the recent general election held in March 1992 was economics. However, it will take time to reestablish policy priorities and new working relationships between the national assembly and the administration, government and business, management and workers. Nevertheless, this process should not take longer than a few years. In a long-term perspective, therefore, optimism still is the watchword for Korea's future.

8

Summary and Conclusions

The economic success of the East Asian newly industrializing economies (NIEs)—that is, Korea, Taiwan, Hong Kong, and Singapore—has been drawing much attention not only from economists but from other social scientists in recent years. As a result, much has already been written on the "four little dragons," mostly to find major attributable factors for their success and useful lessons for other follower nations. The recent rapid political changes and necessary economic reforms of the former Soviet Union and Eastern Bloc nations are expected to create even more interest in these economies.

This study was begun with two distinct objectives in mind: first, to deal with the past to see what lessons can be drawn, and second, to examine Korea's new challenges. Korea is at a critical juncture in its economic development, and there are important new challenges to be faced before it can join the ranks of industrially developed nations. At the same time, Korea, as an important international economic player, must assume appropriate new roles and take advantage of emerging opportunities, as was discussed in the last chapter.

Initial Conditions and the Role of Government

Korea made a surprisingly successful transition from an agrarian, underdeveloped economy to a newly industrializing economy in a relatively short period. It may become the first nation from the developing world, with the possible exception of Taiwan and Singapore, to join the ranks of industrially advanced nations since World War II.[1]

---

1. As pointed out in chapter 2, there are different views regarding when Japan joined the

Korea did have favorable initial conditions for development when it started its rapid growth in the early 1960s. Among them were the relatively high sociocultural standard,[2] literate and motivated work forces, and latent entrepreneurial energies. The foundation for the first stage of import substitution was established in the 1950s. What was lacking, however, was an incentive mechanism by which Korea's favorable factors could interact to produce a desirable economic outcome. As a consequence, existing entrepreneurial energies were primarily engaged in socially unproductive but privately productive rent-seeking entrepreneurial activities, such as acquisition of import licenses and foreign currency at cheaper exchange rates available under a complicated multiple exchange rate system.

With the emergence of a new political leadership, which made a strong commitment to the nation's economic development, the government began to play an active role in economic affairs. The bureaucracy, operating within a hierarchical, Confucian culture, felt compelled to produce results. Consequently, it welcomed advice from many quarters, be it from multilateral institutions or domestic academic circles.

Outward-Looking Development Strategy and Its Implementation

Korea adopted an outward-looking development strategy at a time when import substitution based on an inward-looking development strategy was still popular among developing nations. Various institutional mechanisms, including a complicated multiple exchange rate system, were revamped.

In addition to strong pecuniary incentives, various nonpecuniary incentives, such as social recognition on "Export Day" for those who achieved a high level of exports, were provided to encourage export activities and to overcome widespread export pessimism. Through the government's entrepreneurial gap-filling activities, such as filling the business information gap through the Korean Trade Promotion Corporation (KOTRA), private entrepreneurial energies were channeled into export activities. One important aspect of these incentives and other governmental assistance for exports was that it was industry-neutral—that is, all exports were treated equally, regardless of industrial origin.

Korea's outward-oriented development strategy, mostly based on industry-neutral incentives for exports, succeeded beyond expectations

---

industrially advanced group of nations. In any case, Japan was not really considered to belong to the developing world after World War II.

2. The sociocultural development standard may be viewed in terms of the extent of literacy, the character of basic social organization, the importance of the indigenous middle class, the extent of social mobility, and so on.

throughout the 1960s and into the early 1970s. The government's effective policy implementation, backed by strong leadership commitment to the nation's development, was a critical factor for Korea's success. The approaches to Korea's policy implementation could be succinctly characterized as pragmatic, flexible, and nonideological. The Korean government's attitude was, "If the market works, fine. Otherwise, let's make it work." In so doing, it used a wide range of policy instruments, from highly discretionary commands to pure price incentives.

The Confucian cultural heritage did play a role in Korea's development. In particular, it affected policy formulation and implementation. Given a strong leadership commitment, in a society where hierarchical loyalty and civil service are highly valued, bureaucratic energies were effectively focused on national priorities. The results-oriented pragmatism of Korean bureaucrats and their ability to show nonideological flexibility at the policy implementation level emanate from this cultural heritage. In addition, the high value placed on social harmony facilitates entrepreneurial responses, given other incentives. This, in turn, increases the effectiveness of policy implementation.

Many have argued that a Confucian cultural heritage actually hindered economic development. However, given strong leadership commitment, it can become an enabling factor. This was true in Korea, where an appropriate strategy, based on "getting prices right," was implemented. One may conclude that favorable cultural characteristics may count for little in economic terms in the absence of other important factors.

An outward-looking development strategy is often defined as either "export promotion" or "trade liberalization." Export promotion strategy is characterized as giving roughly equal or positive incentives to both exports and import substitution; trade liberalization is described as a strategy that gives negligible incentives to both export and import substitution. Generally, quantifiable incentives are considered in both cases.

In the case of Korea, the outward-looking development strategy was implemented primarily through export promotion. In the Korean context, nonpecuniary incentives and the government's entrepreneurial gap-filling activities, along with "getting prices right," were the most important factors in promoting exports, particularly in the earlier period.

Korea's policy regime changed substantially in the early 1970s when the ambitious heavy and chemical industry (HCI) promotion drive was launched.[3] This drive was initiated to direct Korea's export commodity structure toward higher-value-added production and at the same time to promote defense industries that would strengthen national security. The drive was implemented through industry-specific and sometimes firm-specific incentives. The promoted industries were protected from

3. The heavy and chemical industries included iron and steel, nonferrous metal, general machinery, shipbuilding, petrochemicals, and electrical equipment.

foreign competition. This new emphasis on promoting target industries led some to consider shifting toward import substitution. However, the "export-first" policy, within the framework of an outward-looking development strategy broadly defined, was never abandoned in Korea. One might consider that the strategy was shifted to a less extreme export promotion strategy in the 1970s.

Economic Setback and Its Background

Korea's development is often characterized as government-led. The strategy itself was essentially based on the government's direct involvement in financial resource allocation. The government replaced the banker's role in screening and evaluating projects with governmental directives, particularly in implementing the HCI promotion drive. The financial market repression not only distorted the nation's resource allocation, the sector itself was left underdeveloped. After growing nearly 10 percent per year for almost two decades, the Korean economy in the latter part of the 1970s was already too big and too complicated to countenance such an underdeveloped financial system. Furthermore, the private sector became much more sophisticated and thus was able to assume some roles the government had been playing.

The Korean economy toward the end of the 1970s was suffering from seriously lopsided resource allocation, rapidly growing chaebols with high leverage, chronic inflation, slowing exports, and worsening international competitiveness. This endogenously problem-ridden economy was hit by a series of exogenous shocks in 1979–80: the second oil shock, a disastrous rice harvest, and the death of President Park. As a result, the Korean economy suffered a serious setback in 1980.

Stabilization Efforts

After the assassination of President Park, the newly established government had to deal with problems of stabilization and structural adjustments to ensure Korea's sustained growth. The new government immediately committed to the goal of economic stabilization. The previous development strategy of "growth at any cost" was replaced by the strategy of "stability at any price." The Korean government itself tried hard to set an example through disciplined fiscal management. In doing so, the government took highly unpopular actions before the nation's general election, freezing the budget, civil servant salaries, and the government purchase price of rice from farmers. These measures undoubtedly contributed to making the government's intention and commitment more credible.

At the same time, the government waged a strong campaign to persuade the Korean people of the necessity of burden-sharing by all economic units. While the government, through "zero-based budgeting," was trying to restrain its own budgetary expansion, wage earners were urged to accept smaller wage hikes, farmers were to accept fewer subsidies, businesses were to refrain from price increases, and households were to spend less and save more. The long-run benefits of price stability were widely propagated through various economic education forums.

Strong and comprehensive disinflationary measures, combined with the government's credible commitment, were quite successful in breaking the built-in inflationary trend within a rather short period. Again, the strong leadership commitment to price stabilization was instrumental in promoting strong bureaucratic action to implement the policies. In 1982 the rate of inflation was reduced to single digits for the first time in 20 years.

The successful Korean stabilization efforts suggest a few points that are critical to price stabilization policy. First of all, in order to fight persistent and chronic inflationary psychology, it is imperative to start the whole effort with a credible political leadership commitment to the nation's stabilization goal. To make the commitment credible, the government oftentimes may have to take politically unpopular and painfully drastic measures. It is therefore crucial for the government to make special efforts to gather a consensus and solicit cooperation from all segments of the society.

Secondly, to make the government's burden-sharing campaign more persuasive, the government must first set an example of its commitment through disciplined fiscal measures.

Important Domestic Liberalization Measures

An essential part of Korea's government-led development strategy was based on severe financial sector repression. Commercial banks were reduced to the position of rationing agents rather than profit-seeking financial institutions. Consequently, financial sector liberalization, especially liberalization of the banking sector, was the most urgent reform area necessary for a new development strategy, which would rely a great deal on private initiatives.

One of the most important constraints in deregulating interest rates and promoting competition among financial institutions, however, was the heavy burden of non-performing assets (NPAs) of commercial banks. The Korean government in the mid-1980s took measures to alleviate the NPA overhang problem at substantial economic and political cost. Undoubtedly, these measures had a short-term objective of stabilizing the financial sector, but they had another important objective in laying a foundation for liberalization of the financial sector.

Another important reform was introduced in the public enterprise sector, which has been playing a critical role both quantitatively and qualitatively in the Korean economy. The essence of the reform was to give more autonomy to public enterprises, in addition to introducing an *ex post* performance evaluation system as well as an incentive bonus scheme. A salient feature of the reform involved personnel management of public enterprises. It legally blocked external recruitment of middle and higher level managers of public enterprises to give more promotion opportunities for lower- and middle-level enterprise managers.

The main goal of this public enterprise reform was to make enterprises more efficient in achieving given objectives by providing better incentives, a revised bonus system, promotional opportunities, appropriate signals for managers to work toward, and autonomy with *ex post* accountability by eliminating redundant administrative controls and regulations.

Other important reforms included deregulation of administrative controls and strengthening antitrust and fair trade laws. Import liberalization and tariff reduction programs introduced then were also expected to contribute to promoting the economic efficiency of oligopolistic and monopolistic firms, in addition to achieving other important goals.

External Liberalization

Korea took a gradual approach to external reforms. While severely restricting capital account transactions, it also began gradually to liberalize current account transactions—that is, commodity imports—in the mid-1970s. In 1978, an ambitious intermediate-term import liberalization plan was announced, but the plan was suspended due to unexpected exogenous disturbances such as the second oil shock. Import liberalization resumed in 1981 when the economy began to recover from these shocks. To minimize the impact of sudden liberalization, a preannounced schedule and an import-surveillance system were introduced.

The preannounced schedule was designed primarily to reduce the uncertainty for firms involved and to give them time to adjust. Potential trading partners also have benefited from the scheme by being able to prepare for market openings. By implementing the policy according to the schedule, the government also enhanced its credibility.

A gradual import liberalization schedule was announced again in 1984, and it was extended in 1985 to cover the period between 1986 and 1989. The pace of import liberalization has been accelerated since 1986, when Korea started to generate current account surpluses.

Along with these import liberalization plans, the tariff reduction schedule was also preannounced in early 1983 and again in 1988. Controls on current account and capital account transactions were also gradually lifted in the early 1980s, and these decontrols were accelerated in 1986. Korea formally announced the acceptance of full obligation to IMF Article VIII in 1988 and decided to give up the privileges of the GATT Article XVIII, Section B as of January 1990. In addition, a five-year capital market liberalization plan was also announced in 1988. As domestic interest liberalization measures were introduced, the system of market-determined foreign exchange rates gradually improved, beginning in the late 1980s.

International Factors in Korea's Development

Considering its poor natural resource endowment, limited market size, and the availability of foreign capital and proven technology, Korea had to look outward to break the vicious circle of underdevelopment. Korea's success in the last three decades owes greatly to such international factors as foreign markets, foreign capital, and imported technology.

Unemployed and underemployed workers, albeit literate and disciplined, had to be absorbed in the manufacturing sector, so foreign markets had to be found. In the absence of a domestic savings base, however, investment in manufacturing industries for exports and social infrastructure had to be financed by foreign capital. In the 1950s, the role of foreign aid was important in closing the nation's savings and foreign exchange gaps. However, coming into 1960s, foreign borrowing started to become important in closing these gaps. The productive use of borrowed capital was ensured by tight monitoring schemes. The appropriate development strategy and effective leadership commitment were bases for those monitoring schemes to successfully generate debt-servicing capacity.

Perhaps Korea is an exception among developing nations, which traditionally have relied little on foreign direct investment (FDI). Korea's recent colonial experience seemed to make Koreans generally suspicious about the motives behind FDI, especially Japanese FDI. More importantly, Korea's unique relative capital cost structure favored borrowing capital, which made Korean businesses prefer foreign debt as well.

Now Korea is at a different stage of development in which sophisticated technologies must be imported to upgrade its industrial structure. These technologies are usually bundled with FDI. Consequently, Korea has been liberalizing its regulations to encourage businesses to rely more on FDI. The recent FDI trend, however, indicates that more needs to be done in this connection.

Korea's outward-looking development strategy efficiently facilitated technology transfer. Assistance from buyers of Korean products and sellers of capital equipment and raw materials has been an important channel of technology transfer in Korea. Being a late industrializing nation pursuing an outward-looking development strategy, Korea undoubtedly enjoyed more advantages from "learning by watching" in both engineering and managerial advances than did those countries that pursued inward-looking strategies.

Korea's phenomenal success brought its own problems. As Korea's export market grew fast, its export share in the world naturally increased rapidly. Trade disputes and frictions with major trading partners were bound to arise. The United States, traditionally the most important market for Korean exports, provided more than one-third of the market for Korea's exports in the 1980s. Furthermore, Korea began to record a trade surplus vis-à-vis the United States in 1982, when the US was suffering from its twin deficit problem. Korea became one of the major targets for US policies to restrict access to the US market while increasing bilateral pressure for market opening and currency appreciation.

To some extent, the United States did "succeed" in restricting Korean access to the US markets and forcing the Korean markets to open up sooner than they otherwise would have. But at what cost? In fact, economic and political costs for both countries were rather high. The antidumping case of Korean album exports to the United States and US pressure to open the Korean cigarette market are cases in point (see discussion, chapter 5). Despite relatively small amounts of money involved, these cases generated a high level of anti-American sentiment. From Korea's perspective, it is much better to have its own external liberalization programs, tailored to its own needs, before being pushed into liberalization policies by others. A better solution could have been found within the multilateral process of dispute settlement.

Korea is about to graduate from the World Bank's loan assistance program. Its relationship with important multilateral institutions such as the International Bank for Reconstruction and Development and the International Monetary Fund during the last three decades of rapid development have been quite productive. In addition to valuable financial assistance, Koreans took these institutions' guidance and consultations seriously; the Korean government fully used its discussions with them not only to formulate better policies but to persuade politicians and ministries with differing views to accept new policies. Korea is now at the stage where it is able to contribute to these institutions to assist in world development.

Korea's New Role in the World and Regional Economy

Under the new world economic order, Korea is expected actively to share responsibility for maintaining world economic stability and prosperity. In particular, Korea is expected to play an important role in preserving a liberal global economic environment. In order to work toward this goal, Korea should accelerate both domestic and international liberalization.

Korea has benefited greatly from a liberal global trading system and a stable financial environment, and it will have to depend on such an environment in the future. Thus, for its own good, it is important for Korea to make positive contributions toward the successful completion of the Uruguay Round or, for that matter, any multilateral forum aimed at maintaining and enhancing worldwide free trade.

At the same time, Korea as a "pioneer country" has an obligation to provide positive contributions for follower nations of the developing world through active economic cooperation. Korea's recent establishment of the Economic Development Cooperation Fund for the purpose of assisting developing nations is an important first step in this direction. For the time being, however, Korea has more to offer in the area of technical assistance through use of its abundant human resources. The most recent first-hand experiences of managing developmental efforts at both the macroeconomic and project level can be used in assisting follower nations. In this regard, Korea's technical assistance programs might very well be interlinked with programs at various multilateral institutions.

As an important regional economic power, Korea has roles to play for the region's continued prosperity. The Northeast Asian region could be an ideal place for applying Korea's developmental experiences and tested middle-level industrial technology. If this effort is closely complemented by Japan's capital and advanced technology, the region's overall development (and its reorientation toward markets in the case of formerly nonmarket economies), will be successfully promoted. Korea should also actively promote the principle of "open regionalism" in the Pacific Rim. This principle has been endorsed by a promising regional cooperative body, Asia Pacific Economic Cooperation (APEC). Korea should work to ensure that APEC becomes a better institutionalized, cooperative body for promoting regional stability and prosperity.

As an important international economic player, Korea needs to participate more actively in major international organizations and forums where important policies are discussed and coordinated. By doing so, Korea could take advantage of valuable opportunities for sharing information on world economic and technological advances and on future policy directions of major economic and technological leaders.

Korea has to make difficult structural adjustments before it can join the ranks of the industrially developed. These politically difficult but necessary adjustments could be implemented faster and possibly easier in a multilateral context. Korean membership in the Organization for Economic Cooperation and Development (OECD) might serve this purpose as well.

Major Policy Issues and Challenges

Renewed Leadership Commitment and Priority Setting

Both internal and external environmental changes dictate that Korea have a renewed leadership commitment to economics. It is critical that Korea not allow its economy to continue losing its competitive advantage. Only with a strong leadership commitment to economics and a national consensus on the primacy of economics can a more disciplined macroeconomic policy stance be restored. Such a stance requires maximum insulation of economic policymaking from political influences. If the government fails to give top priority to economics and does not set an example, other tough policy choices will not be possible. Without economic preparedness, even the valuable unification opportunity may be wasted.

The government now has to try even harder to persuade the general public and politicians to accept tough economic policy choices. Regular public forums should be used fully to build consensus on these policies. A presidential council that sets national priority on economics might well be established for consensus-gathering as well as for public education. The government's leadership role also should be strengthened in order to provide a clear vision of the nation's economic future. The primacy of economics and the leadership commitment to it should be reflected in the consistency and predictability of major economic policy directions, and this consistency, in turn, will facilitate policy implementation.

Appropriate Industrial Policy and Financial Sector Reform

The term industrial policy should be viewed broadly so as to include all government policy affecting the nation's industrial output and its composition. However, the term is often used to refer to industrial policy based solely on "picking winners." Korea paid a high price for such an industrial targeting policy in the heavy and chemical industry (HCI) promotion of the 1970s. In addition to various explicit costs, with the government as an implicit business risk bearer, the moral hazard problem for both concerned firms and banks caused additional economic costs.

Korea still needs an appropriate industrial policy. An adaptive industrial policy must be implemented to facilitate the necessary structural adjustments, particularly to draw resources away from declining industries. Other functional policies such as "technology policy" should be included. These policies should not be targeted toward any particular products or firms but should provide incentives for promoting certain functions, such as technology development.

To facilitate effective implementation of such industrial policies, the government should first concentrate on providing a market-friendly environment for private initiatives. It should emphasize the importance of a stable and consistent macroeconomic policy and a favorable microeconomic environment for socially productive, private entrepreneurial activities.

The legacy of Korea's government-led development strategy of the past is still pervasive throughout the Korean financial sector. This is not surprising, considering that the government-led development in Korea was implemented primarily through governmental control of the financial sector. Consequently, the government's role as financier was the most important factor in Korea's unique government-business relationship. It is essential, therefore, to liberalize the financial sector first, to redefine the role of the government in the Korean economy, and to establish a new government-business relationship.

The development of the Korean financial sector was heavily repressed throughout the rapid growth era. The problem of overhang of nonperforming assets became a major obstacle for liberalization of Korea's financial sector, though the Korean government did take measures to alleviate the problem in the mid-1980s.

To effectively compete against tough international competitors, it is crucial to make the nation's financial sector efficient through liberalization. This liberalization should be implemented based on two interrelated principles: it should be based on a package approach, and a gradual implementation procedure with a preannounced schedule should be used. Rather than liberalizing the sector ad hoc and at others' insistence, liberalization should be carried out according to a carefully prepared program tailored to Korea's own needs.

A gradual approach to financial sector liberalization reduces the risk of failure or backsliding. Adhering to a preannounced schedule should enhance the predictability and credibility of the Korean government in domestic and international business circles. This in turn will bolster business confidence in the Korean economy.

Currently, the Banking Law prohibits any single shareholder from owning more than 8 percent of outstanding bank shares. This clause was introduced primarily to prevent *chaebols* from owning and controlling nationwide commercial banks. It is, however, bound to create a minority-majority shareholder situation. Even for banks, it is desirable in principle to allow a majority shareholder because it then becomes possible to have effective control and maintain responsible management when bank operations are fully liberalized.

An alternative that would reconcile both concerns is to eliminate the 8 percent ceiling for shareholders, except for industrial *chaebols*, as financial sector liberalization progresses. It seems inevitable that financial groups will emerge and specialize in financial services. They should, however, be kept separate from industrial *chaebols*. Of course, the equity shares of these groups must be widely disbursed.

As the NPA overhang problem is gradually mitigated and bank interest rates are liberalized, Korean commercial banks are expected to become genuine banks. A policy of ensuring that banks focus on their area of specialization—rather than immediately combining to form diversified financial services conglomerates—seems reasonable at the outset.

Chaebols and a New Government-Business Relationship

The *chaebol* issue is one of the most controversial in Korea today. Essentially, the *chaebols* are characterized by two interrelated problems, in addition to the traditional economic efficiency problem: legitimacy and distributional equity. The legitimacy issue stems from perceived or actual unfairness or injustice involved in the emergence and growth of *chaebols*. The latter arises from the concentration of economic power, which is a consequence of the *chaebols'* rapid growth.

The legitimacy problem arises primarily from *chaebols'* privileged access to the bank loan market. Another source of contention is the *chaebols'* real estate holdings. In other words, the general perception is that they grew fast at the expense of others—the weak and taxpayers in general—and that they got richer through socially unproductive, rent-seeking activities.

Problems of legitimacy aggravate those of distributional equity to the extent that the *chaebols'* ever-growing portfolio of assets is concentrated in the hands of a few individuals and their family members. If the equity shares of *chaebols* were widely held, the distributional equity issue would be substantially resolved because even "illegitimate" wealth transfer could be shared by the general public.

Today's *chaebol* issue has a traditional economic efficiency aspect as well, since the industrial concentration of *chaebols* is substantial and interindustrial cross-subsidization among *chaebol* firms through cross-equity shareholdings and cross-loan guarantees is widely practiced. Although it is not the prime concern in today's emotionally charged debate over *chaebols*, this issue should be dealt with through relevant antitrust and fair trade laws.

For both legitimacy and distributional equity reasons, the policy of encouraging *chaebols* to disburse their equity shares widely should be continued. In the process, however, it is important that majority shareholders should be properly protected from losing management control. Nonvoting shares may be used to this effect.

In dealing with *chaebols*, it is important to support the principle that growth and diversification *per se* should not be condemned, particularly if the *chaebols* grew and became diversified with their own funds. Korean firms have to compete against companies from all over the world, in many cases against international business giants and affiliated firms of large international conglomerates. Considering the relative scale of *chaebols*, however, it seems desirable for them to concentrate in their specialized fields. For *chaebol* growth and diversification to be legitimized, special favors such as fiscal subsidies, privileged access to cheaper sources of financing, and special bail-out policies should be eliminated. At the same time, antitrust and fair trade laws should be strengthened and strictly applied to deal with the concentration of economic power issue. Until the banking sector is fully liberalized and other means of protecting small and medium-sized firms are in place, *chaebols'* access to banks has to be limited in one way or an other.

A salient feature of Korea's government-business relationship of the past was the government's domination of the relationship. In short, the Korean government's control of commercial banks was the basis for such a relationship. In the absence of well-developed capital markets, Korean businesses had to rely heavily on commercial banks. At the same time, the government encouraged private businesses to use relatively cheap bank loans for the nation's export-led industrialization. An inevitable result was a high debt-to-equity ratio for most Korean businesses. This made Korean businesses more vulnerable to the public financier. No wonder Korean *chaebols* are so keenly interested in owning financial institutions.

As previously indicated, considering both domestic and international economic environmental changes taking place, the Korean government has no choice but to relinquish its financier's role and liberalize the nation's financial sector. Besides, Korean businesses are going to have more and more alternatives to domestic bank financing. Therefore, a new government-business relationship will have to emerge.

Because the nation's financial sector will have to assume the real financier's role, Korea must establish a cooperative financier-business relationship first. In essence, the new relationship will become more balanced between the government and private businesses. This indicates in no way, however, a weaker leadership role for the government. A strong government role is needed to provide a clear vision of the future direction of the economy, a stable macroeconomic policy environment, and a favorable microeconomic environment for productive entrepreneurial activities. The government also has to make strenuous efforts at consensus-building, using not only public forums, open seminars, and hearings but also various consultative councils and special commissions set up for the government.

Structural Adjustments and a Competitive Economy

Korea is caught between two competitive fronts. While it loses its competitive advantages in labor-intensive and middle-level, technology-intensive products, Korea now faces difficulties in establishing a competitive edge in capital- and technology-intensive differentiated products. Differentiated, high-value-added products require constant product and process innovation and dynamic responses to market changes in addition to manufacturing excellence.

Korea now needs a new competitive strategy to facilitate economic adjustment toward a more sophisticated industrial structure. In essence, the new strategy should be based on technology and innovation. The strategy must promote a competitive advantage based on differentiation of output quality to replace the past input-cost-based advantage for Korean products. To this end, a strong technology policy, placing more emphasis on commercial followthrough than on scientific breakthroughs, should be implemented, as has been done by Japan but not by the United States. This policy should assist and encourage private firms to adopt an efficient R&D strategy, and at the same time, it should be supplemented by active inducement of FDI for transfer of technology, and for marketing and customer services.

The structural adjustment of the agricultural sector is a big challenge for Korea. The sector still employs nearly 20 percent of Korean workers. Furthermore, over 50 percent of rural household income is still derived from agricultural activities. The real challenge, therefore, is how to accelerate industrial relocation to rural areas to help increase rural households' opportunities for earning nonfarm income and to absorb displaced agricultural workers.

Investments in social overhead capital in rural areas must be extended to accelerate industrial relocation. At the same time, governmental supports for industrial training and job placement for displaced farmers should also be provided to facilitate structural adjustment of the sector. To facilitate speedier adjustment and agricultural productivity improvement, the government might establish a structural adjustment facilitating fund for the agricultural sector for a limited period.

Enhancing Distributive Equity

Despite the apparent trend toward favorable income distribution up until very recent years, distributional issues have lately been drawing a great deal of attention in Korea. It could be that actual income distribution in recent years has, in fact, worsened. Another possibility is that published income distribution statistics do not accurately portray the actual distributional situation in Korea. Still another possibility is that a gap between actual and perceived income distribution may exist and has widened in recent years. Some believe published statistics seriously underestimate income inequality in Korea, primarily due to problems of biased coverage in the data collection. The incomplete coverage of capital gains of real estate could be the most serious source of bias because Korea has experienced unprecedented and rapid real estate price increases in recent years. Given Korea's highly skewed land ownership, the exclusion of capital gains would bias the statistics toward equality.

The government should take the worsening income distribution argument seriously and put corrective measures in place. At the same time, it is important for the government to make the income and wealth distribution survey as accurate as possible. The credibility of the government is at stake.

In addition to the possibility of actual worsening income distribution, it is also likely that the perceived income distribution gap has also widened in recent years. People who cannot take advantage of capital gains might very well feel more deprived. In particular, recent rapid increases in housing prices must have left non-house-owners feeling further disadvantaged. The proportion of house-owning households in urban areas has dropped to less than 50 percent while housing prices have increased substantially in recent years.

The gap may be perceived as widening even further in recent years because of a surge in unrealistic expectations. When absolute poverty disappears from society, relative poverty usually becomes a key social concern. Furthermore, given Korea's higher per capita income level, people's tolerance for what is seen as worsening income distribution—or any distributional injustice, actual or perceived—deteriorates fast. They no longer feel gratified by watching others "make it," as they did at earlier stages of development.

In addition, rapid political changes may have reduced the tolerance level further while accentuating existing imbalances. Recently experienced violent labor disputes, wild farmers' demonstrations, regional animosities, and the general mood of social discontent are signs of growing intolerance and the call for new policy priorities.

Disparities among not only income classes but also industries, different sizes of firms, and regions need to be addressed properly. The widespread perception of relative poverty among Korean people today presents formidable challenges. The government should take measures to deal with the situation. First of all, it should do more to provide for the basic needs of the poorer segments of society, through educational assistance and vocational training, low-cost housing, basic health care, and public transportation. The quality and scope of Korea's social welfare system, including newly introduced medical insurance and national pension schemes, must be continuously improved and expanded.

Korea's current tax burden ratio is still below 20 percent, and thus it is possible to increase the ratio without creating too heavy a burden on ordinary taxpayers. To finance these expenditures, an improved system of land taxes can be a convenient alternative to raising tax revenue. Korea's overall ratio of property tax to GNP is relatively lower than that of other countries.

Despite relatively high nominal tax rates for capital gains earned from land sales in Korea, the effective tax rates are still negligible due to the unrealistic land value assessment system. It is, therefore, important to introduce a more realistic land evaluation system while nominal property and capital gains tax rates can be reduced to encourage compliance.

It is also important to eliminate opportunities for making unearned income from land ownership or speculation. This will help narrow income distributional gaps of both kinds. In this regard, an effective tax system for both land holding and land transaction based on a proper land evaluation system should always be in place. Korea is a land-scarce nation, and as a result there are always incentives for real estate hoarding and speculation.

It is often argued, however, that the scarcity and high price of property have been exacerbated by complex and extensive public regulations and other interventions restricting supply responses. Considering the importance of the issue, it seems worthwhile to set up a special presidential commission to review all the existing laws and regulations and the system of land development.

From the distributional equity perspective, another important area for tax reform is the financial asset market. Legacies of the growth-first development era are still in place in this market. Obviously, financial savings are much more desirable than real-asset holdings. Capital gains from trading equity shares of listed companies are not taxed because the promotion of the equity capital market has been an important policy goal in Korea. However, to the extent that financial-assets ownership is highly skewed, these taxation policies would affect household income distribution unfavorably.

Financial savings are encouraged primarily to channel mobilized funds into productive industrial uses. The promotion of the capital market has the same primary purpose. In addition, the equity market in particular is promoted to help improve Korea's weak corporate financial structure. These goals are still valid in Korea. Privileges provided to this end, however, should not be so great that they induce industrialists to engage in arbitrage. Striking a balance between growth and equity objectives is the key in this area.

Reform of the financial asset market should come on the heels of real estate market reform, which will prevent the undesirable diversion of financial resources into real estate. The approach should be based on a gradualism well-articulated in advance. In the process, as always, interests of the relatively poor (for whom distributional reform measures are necessary) should be properly protected. In other words, the immediate goal should be to reduce distributional inequality among financial asset owners. In this connection, it is important to introduce the real-name system of financial asset holding as the Korean economy prepares to absorb its immediate impacts.

The relative poverty issue is not confined to different income classes. The same issue exists between different-sized firms, namely, *chaebols* versus small and medium-sized companies. Appropriate policies to remedy economic power concentration of *chaebols* are justified on this ground as well. The income disparity between urban and rural households, and between different regions, should also be narrowed by increasing income-earning opportunities for rural households and disadvantaged regions in nonfarming activities. The current policies of encouraging industrial firms to move to rural and economically distressed areas and expanding regionally balanced investments in social infrastructure should be continued in this regard.

In dealing with the relative poverty issue, it is critical to strike a proper balance between sustained, stable growth and distributional equity and to avoid irresponsible political responses to rapidly rising expectations. It is important for Koreans to remember that there are countries frustrated at the threshold of the industrially developed stage simply because they did not choose difficult options but resorted to populistic solutions.

Establishing a Productive Worker-Management Relationship

A productive industrial relations system is an important element of a nation's competitive base, as evidenced by the Japanese and German experiences. Korea has reached the stage where a competitive strategy based on quality differentiation rather than on price has to be pursued. Such a strategy can succeed only with appropriate human resources development and productive industrial relations.

Under the suppressed industrial relations system, both workers and managers lacked opportunities for learning how to find workable solutions to industrial relations issues bilaterally. First of all, both sides will have to learn how to engage in collective bargaining.

An important immediate task for the government is to create a favorable environment in which a cooperative social partnership among government, business, and workers can be promoted. In this regard, it is critical to have a cooperative, tripartite information-sharing system. The government must clearly articulate the nation's economic strategies and policy goals for businesses and workers. Employers will have to prove that only through company prosperity will the welfare of workers be enhanced.

Educational Reform and Human Resources Development

Many have rightly pointed out that Korea's phenomenal economic success owed a great deal to its superior general level of education. Korea's new competitive strategy calls for more active human resources development and higher-quality education. Koreans are still fervent believers in education, and there is a strong demand for quality education. The government should not allow this valuable attribute of the Korean people to be wasted.

Korea's future survival and enhanced position in the world now depend more on economics than ever before. It is natural, therefore, for Korea to earmark part of the "peace dividends" released from the defense budget for investment in human capital formation, which is the competitive foundation for the Korean economy. It is also important that both public and private educational institutions be allowed to use private financial resources to augment limited public resources for quality education.

It should also be emphasized that the overall educational reform of the future should fully reflect Korea's new economic competitive strategy. The system of education should properly accommodate the needs of a changing industrial structure.

More incentives should be provided to the private sector for the vocational training of workers, and existing laws and regulations regarding vocational training should be effectively implemented. Vocational training programs should be properly incorporated into the nation's adaptive industrial policy as well as the industrial relations system.

Concluding Remarks

Korea's future depends on how Koreans face these critical challenges. It is not going to be easy, but if history is any guide, Koreans will learn fast and adapt to the new situation quickly.

The Korean economy in recent years has been showing macroeconomic imbalances and structural abnormalities. Chaotically rapid political evolution and shifts in national policy priorities have prevented Koreans from putting in place needed structural adjustments to adapt to changing domestic and international environments. Prevailing populistic demands not only forced the government to put off politically unpopular structural adjustments but to accommodate some of these demands. For the first time in recent Korean history, Koreans have allowed politics to dominate economics.

However, this situation will not prevail for long in Korea. Koreans already have begun to realize that even the nation's unification depends on its economic capability, as is well illustrated by the recent German unification experience. Therefore, it will not be too long before the primacy of economics is reestablished. In an intermediate- to long-term perspective, therefore, optimism still is the watchword for Korea's future.

Appendices

Table A.1 Real GDP per capita for selected nations in 1985 international prices, 1962–88 (dollars)

Year	Selected Asian developing nations					Selected Latin American nations			Selected industrialized nations			
	Korea	Sri Lanka	Malaysia	Thailand	Philippines	Argentina	Brazil	Mexico	Japan	UK	W. Germany	US
1962	958	1,442	1,950	1,037	1,274	3,459	2,045	2,915	3,249	6,504	6,422	10,418
1967	1,300	1,367	2,204	1,310	1,395	3,897	2,079	3,632	4,998	7,438	7,258	12,381
1972	1,893	1,395	2,680	1,463	1,556	4,459	3,048	4,255	7,381	8,388	9,095	13,645
1977	2,860	1,384	3,570	1,855	1,865	4,658	4,045	4,756	8,518	9,227	10,140	14,677
1982	3,278	1,701	4,931	2,183	2,116	4,092	4,110	5,794	10,058	9,737	10,903	14,968
1987	4,699	1,959	4,288	2,594	1,820	4,193	4,441	5,005	11,620	11,495	12,124	17,735
1988ᵃ	5,156	2,012	4,727	2,879	1,947	4,030	4,438	4,996	12,209	11,982	12,604	18,339

a. 1988 figures of Brazil and Sri Lanka are projected by utilizing 1985 national GDP data from International Monetary Fund, *Interná* various issues.

Source: Summers, R. and A. Heston. May 1991. "The Penn World Table (Mark 5): An Expanded Set of International Con *Quarterly Journal of Economics*, 327–68 (Supplement).

Table A.2 Industry share of GDP for selected countries, 1960–90 (percentages)

	Korea			India			Mexico[f]			Japan		
	Manufac- turing	Indus- try 1[a]	Indus- try 2[b]	Manufac- turing	Indus- try 1	Indus- try 2	Manufac- turing	Indus- try 1	Indus- try 2	Manufac- turing	Indus- try 1	Indus- try 2
1960	13.78	20.07	24.72	13.28	19.08	23.65	19.20	29.20	32.50	32.87	42.49	51.06
1965	18.02	24.77	28.79	13.84	20.04	24.78	20.81	31.11	34.00	32.15	42.47	51.10
1970	21.16	29.16	35.89	13.78	20.16	24.18	23.65	32.66	37.39	36.00	46.67	53.55
1975	26.18	33.56	39.49	15.05	21.45	25.57	23.45	33.18	38.91	30.20	42.41	48.84
1980	29.58	41.33	49.02	15.94	23.29	27.51	22.17	32.73	39.13	29.24	41.92	48.08
1985	28.19	40.93	49.15	16.60	25.98	31.32	23.41	33.35	40.03	29.77	40.86	47.04
1987	30.33	42.91	51.10	17.05	26.55	32.37	25.79	35.89	43.05	29.05	40.55	46.76
1990	n.a.	n.a.	n.a.	n.a.	n.a.	n.a.	24.60	31.8[c]	38.9[d]	n.a.	n.a.	n.a.

	UK[g]			W. Germany			US		
	Manufac- turing	Indus- try 1	Indus- try 2	Manufac- turing	Indus- try 1	Indus- try 2	Manufac- turing	Indus- try 1	Indus- try 2
1960	32.13	42.74	50.40	40.20	53.26	59.46	28.57	38.11	44.66
1965	29.90	40.79	48.19	40.14	53.13	58.89	28.71	37.80	44.23
1970	28.75	38.19	49.83	38.42	49.42	55.06	25.69	34.69	41.09
1975	26.07	36.41	43.78	34.48	44.14	50.14	22.74	32.94	39.24
1980	23.24	36.66	42.88	32.65	42.75	48.54	21.81	33.56	40.01
1985	20.87	34.90	40.95	31.88	40.73	46.53	22.10	20.98	37.26
1987	20.87	31.76	38.04	32.18	40.7[e]	46.35[e]	19.28	29.22	35.35
1990	24.30	36.9[c]	44.2[d]	n.a.	n.a.	n.a.	n.a.	n.a.	n.a.

n.a. = not available
a. Industry 1 includes mining, manufacturing, construction, electricity, gas, and water as per Kuznets' industry definition.
b. Industry 2 includes industry 1, transportation, storage, and communication as per UN industry definition.
c. Gas, water, and electricity are only partially included.
d. No storage is included.
e. Data for gas, water, electricity, and mining are from 1986.
f. 1989 data are used for 1990 Mexico.
g. 1988 data are used for 1990 UK. No mining is included for 1990 UK.

Sources: UN. 1978, 1986, and 1987. National Accounting Statistics; The Economist Intelligence Unit. 1991. Country Reports, No. 1.

Table A.3 Sectoral growth rates, 1971–91 (percentages)

Year	Agriculture, forestry, and fishing	Mining and manufacturing	Other
1971	3.0	15.9	9.4
1972	2.4	11.6	4.4
1973	7.3	27.7	11.4
1974	6.5	15.3	6.3
1975	3.9	12.2	5.3
1976	9.8	21.6	11.0
1977	2.8	14.9	10.6
1978	−9.8	19.9	12.8
1979	7.0	9.5	6.1
1980	−19.1	−1.0	−0.3
1981	14.3	9.4	1.9
1982	7.4	5.4	7.8
1983	7.7	15.0	12.7
1984	−1.5	16.8	8.1
1985	3.8	7.0	7.8
1986	4.6	18.0	12.0
1987	−6.8	18.2	14.1
1988	8.0	13.1	12.8
1989	−1.1	3.5	10.3
1990	−5.1	8.7	12.0
1991	−0.8	8.4	9.6

Source: Economic Planning Board. *Major Statistics of the Korean Economy*, various issues.

Table A.4 GNP and trade, 1962–1991

	GNP	Exports	Imports	Total trade	Exports as a share of GNP	Imports as a share of GNP	Total trade as a share of GNP
		(in hundred millions of dollars)				(percentages)	
1962	23.0	0.5	4.2	4.7	2.4	18.3	20.6
1963	27.0	0.9	5.6	6.5	3.3	20.7	24.1
1964	29.0	1.2	4.0	5.2	4.1	13.8	17.9
1965	30.0	1.8	4.6	6.4	6.0	15.3	21.3
1966	37.0	2.5	7.2	9.7	6.8	19.5	26.2
Average 1962–66					**4.5**	**17.5**	**22.0**
1967	43.0	3.2	10.0	13.2	7.4	23.3	30.7
1968	52.0	4.6	14.6	19.2	8.8	28.1	36.9
1969	66.0	6.2	18.2	24.4	9.4	27.6	37.0
1970	81.0	8.4	19.8	28.2	9.9	24.4	34.6
1971	95.0	10.7	23.9	34.6	11.6	25.2	36.8
Average 1967–71					**9.4**	**25.7**	**35.2**
1972	107.0	16.2	25.2	41.1	15.0	23.6	38.3
1973	135.0	32.3	42.4	74.7	23.7	31.4	54.8
1974	188.0	44.6	68.5	113.1	23.9	36.4	60.6
1975	209.0	50.8	72.7	123.5	24.4	34.8	59.3
1976	287.0	77.2	87.7	164.9	26.8	30.6	57.5
Average 1972–76					**22.8**	**31.3**	**54.1**

1977	368.0	100.5	108.1	208.6	27.2	29.4	56.5
1978	515.0	127.1	149.7	276.8	24.7	29.1	53.8
1979	615.0	150.6	203.4	354.0	24.6	33.1	57.7
1980	605.0	175.1	222.9	398.0	28.9	36.8	65.8
1981	668.0	212.5	261.3	473.8	31.9	39.1	71.0
Average 1977–81					**27.5**	**33.5**	**61.0**
1982	713.0	218.5	242.5	461.0	30.7	34.0	64.8
1983	795.0	244.5	261.9	506.4	30.7	32.9	63.6
1984	870.0	292.4	306.3	598.7	33.6	35.2	68.7
1985	897.0	302.8	311.4	614.2	33.8	34.7	68.5
1986	1,027.0	347.1	315.8	662.9	33.8	30.7	64.6
Average 1982–86					**32.5**	**33.5**	**66.0**
1987	1,289.0	472.8	410.2	883.0	36.7	31.8	68.5
1988	1,728.0	607.0	518.1	1,125.1	35.1	30.0	65.1
1989	2,112.0	623.8	614.6	1,238.4	29.5	29.3	58.9
1990	2,422.0	650.2	698.4	1,348.6	26.8	28.8	55.7
1991	2,808.0	718.7	815.2	1,533.9	25.6	29.0	54.6
Average 1987–91					**30.7**	**29.8**	**60.6**
Overall Average 1962–81					**21.2**	**28.6**	**49.8**

Sources: Bank of Korea. 1982. *Economic Statistics Yearbook*; National Statistical Office. 1992. *Major Statistics of the Korean Economy*; Bank of Korea. 1991. *National Accounts*.

Table A.5 Average annual growth rates of trade, 1962–90 (percentages)

Year	Exports				Imports			
	Korea	World	US	Japan	Korea	World	US	Japan
1962	34.1	4.5	3.9	16.1	33.5	5.2	11.6	−3.0
1963	58.2	9.6	6.9	10.9	32.7	8.7	4.7	19.5
1964	36.9	11.8	14.5	22.4	−27.9	11.7	9.1	17.8
1965	47.1	8.8	3.9	26.6	14.6	8.9	14.2	2.9
1966	42.9	9.6	10.0	15.7	54.6	10.1	19.5	16.6
Average 1962–66	**43.8**	**8.9**	**7.8**	**18.3**	**21.5**	**8.9**	**11.8**	**10.8**
1967	28.0	5.0	5.3	6.8	39.1	4.6	3.8	22.5
1968	42.2	11.8	10.1	24.2	46.9	11.0	23.0	11.4
1969	36.7	14.3	9.6	23.3	24.7	13.8	8.6	15.7
1970	34.2	14.6	14.3	20.8	8.8	14.9	10.1	25.7
1971	27.9	12.7	2.1	24.9	20.7	11.4	14.0	4.8
Average 1967–71	**33.8**	**11.7**	**8.3**	**20.0**	**28.0**	**11.1**	**11.9**	**16.0**
1972	52.1	19.5	13.0	20.6	5.3	17.4	21.8	20.5
1973	98.6	38.6	44.0	27.3	68.1	37.9	24.4	60.9
1974	38.3	49.4	40.4	49.8	61.6	47.1	51.5	61.4
1975	13.9	3.0	9.5	0.6	6.2	3.8	−4.5	−6.6
1976	51.8	13.7	7.3	20.6	20.6	13.2	25.1	12.2
Average 1972–76	**50.9**	**24.8**	**22.8**	**23.8**	**32.4**	**23.9**	**23.7**	**29.7**

1977	30.2	13.1	5.5	20.5	23.2	14.5	21.1	9.9
1978	26.5	15.7	18.4	21.1	38.5	16.1	16.0	12.0
1979	18.4	27.6	27.8	4.2	35.8	25.7	19.4	37.5
1980	16.3	20.7	21.0	27.5	9.6	22.9	15.6	28.6
1981	21.4	−1.7	5.8	16.1	17.2	−0.8	6.4	1.1
Average 1977–81	**22.6**	**15.1**	**15.7**	**17.9**	**24.9**	**15.7**	**15.7**	**17.8**
1982	2.8	−8.0	−9.3	−8.7	−7.2	−6.6	−6.8	−8.0
1983	11.9	−3.5	−5.0	6.2	8.0	−2.9	5.9	−3.8
1984	19.6	7.6	8.9	14.1	16.9	6.5	28.3	7.7
1985	3.5	1.3	−2.3	5.6	1.6	0.8	1.8	−4.2
1986	14.6	10.1	3.8	19.0	1.4	9.3	8.5	−2.3
Average 1982–86	**10.5**	**1.5**	**−0.8**	**7.2**	**4.1**	**1.4**	**7.5**	**−2.1**
1987	36.2	18.0	11.9	9.7	29.9	17.8		
1988	28.4	14.4	26.9	14.5	26.3	13.9		
1989	2.8	7.7	12.9	3.4	18.6	8.0		
1990	4.2	n.a.	8.3	5.0	11.4	n.a.		
Average 1987–90	**17.9**	**13.4**	**15.0**	**8.2**	**21.6**	**13.2**		
Average 1962–90	**30.3**	**12.5**	**11.4**	**16.2**	**22.1**	**12.3**		

n.a. = not available

Source: International Monetary Fund. 1990 and April 1991. *International Financial Statistics.* Reprinted with permission.

(handwritten note: next page, too)

229

Table A.6　US, Japan, Korea: Shares of world trade, 1962–90
(percentages)

Year	Exports			Imports		
	US	Japan	Korea	US	Japan	Korea
1962	16.31	3.82	0.04	12.96	4.10	0.31
1963	15.92	3.87	0.06	12.48	4.51	0.38
1964	16.31	4.24	0.08	12.19	4.76	0.24
1965	15.58	4.93	0.10	12.79	4.50	0.25
1966	15.64	5.21	0.13	13.90	4.76	0.36
Average 1962–66	**15.95**	**4.41**	**0.08**	**12.86**	**4.53**	**0.30**
1967	15.69	5.30	0.16	13.78	5.58	0.48
1968	15.46	5.89	0.21	15.27	5.60	0.63
1969	14.83	6.35	0.25	14.57	5.69	0.69
1970	14.78	6.69	0.30	13.96	6.22	0.65
1971	13.39	7.42	0.33	14.29	5.85	0.71
Average 1967–71	**14.83**	**6.33**	**0.25**	**14.37**	**5.79**	**0.63**
1972	12.66	7.48	0.42	14.82	6.01	0.64
1973	13.14	6.87	0.60	13.37	7.01	0.77
1974	12.36	6.89	0.55	13.76	7.69	0.85
1975	13.13	6.73	0.61	12.68	6.94	0.87
1976	12.39	7.14	0.83	13.99	6.85	0.93
Average 1972–76	**12.74**	**7.02**	**0.60**	**13.76**	**6.90**	**0.81**
1977	11.55	7.60	0.94	14.80	6.58	1.00
1978	11.82	7.96	1.03	14.78	6.35	1.19
1979	11.84	6.50	0.96	14.05	6.94	1.27
1980	11.86	6.86	0.92	13.21	7.27	1.15
1981	12.77	8.10	1.14	14.17	7.41	1.35
Average 1977–81	**11.97**	**7.02**	**1.00**	**14.20**	**6.91**	**1.19**
1982	12.59	8.05	1.27	14.14	7.30	1.35
1983	12.20	8.72	1.45	15.43	7.23	1.50
1984	12.55	9.51	1.64	18.60	7.31	1.65
1985	12.10	9.80	1.68	18.77	6.95	1.66
1986	11.34	10.53	1.73	18.49	6.17	1.53
Average 1982–86	**12.16**	**9.32**	**1.55**	**17.09**	**6.99**	**1.54**
1987	10.75	9.78	1.65	17.42	6.20	1.68
1988	11.95	9.82	2.25	16.57	6.75	1.87
1989	12.49	9.40	2.14	16.45	7.00	2.05
1990[a]	13.52	9.87	2.23	n.a.	7.86	2.32
Average 1987–90	**12.18**	**9.72**	**2.07**	**16.81**	**6.95**	**1.98**
Overall Average 1962–90	**13.34**	**7.29**	**0.89**	**14.70**	**6.32**	**1.05**

n.a. = not available
a. 1990 data are based on the 1989 world total.

Source: International Monetary Fund. 1990 and May 1991. *International Financial Statistics.* Reprinted with permission.

Table A.7 Industrial composition of exports (1967–91)

	1967	1972	1977	1982	1987	1991
Total exports (millions of dollars)	3,320	1,624	10,047	21,853	47,281	71,870
Primary goods						
millions of dollars	88.0	196.0	1,386.0	1,727.0	2,814.0	3,326.0
share of total exports	27.5	12.1	13.8	7.9	5.9	4.6
Manufactured goods						
millions of dollars	232.0	1,428.0	8,661.0	20,126.0	44,467.0	68,544.0
share of total exports	72.5	87.9	86.2	92.1	94.1	95.4
Heavy products[a]						
millions of dollars	29.0	361.9	3,415.9	10,618.2	24,466.0	43,059.0
share of total manufactured goods	12.5	25.3	39.4	52.8	55.0	62.8
Light products[b]						
millions of dollars	203.3	1,066.0	5,244.6	9,507.9	20,001.0	25,485.0
share of total manufactured goods	87.5	74.7	60.6	47.2	45.0	37.2

a. Includes primary metal manufacturing, metal products and machinery, electric or electronic products, etc.
b. Includes food, beverages and tobacco, textiles and leather, lumber and wood products, footwear, etc.

Sources: Ministry of Commerce and Industry, Korea; Korea Foreign Trade Association. *Trade Yearbook,* various issues.

Table A.8 Top 10 exports, 1961–91

1961			1970			[illegible]		
Export	Millions of dollars	Percentages	Export	Millions of dollars	Percentages	Export	Millions of dollars	Percentages
1. iron ore	5.3	13.0	textiles & garments	341.1	40.8	textiles & garments	[illegible]	[illegible]
2. tungsten	5.1	12.6	plywood	91.9	11.0	electronic products	[illegible]	[illegible]
3. raw silk	2.7	6.7	wigs	90.1	10.8	steel products	[illegible]	[illegible]
4. anthracite	2.4	5.8	iron ore	49.3	5.9	plywood	[illegible]	[illegible]
5. squid	2.3	5.5	electronic products	29.2	3.5	footwear	[illegible]	[illegible]
6. other fish	1.9	4.5	confectionary	19.5	2.3	deep-sea fish	[illegible]	[illegible]
7. graphite	1.7	4.2	footwear	17.3	2.1	ships	[illegible]	[illegible]
8. plywood	1.4	3.3	tobacco and products	13.5	1.6	metal products	[illegible]	[illegible]
9. grain	1.4	3.3	steel products	13.4	1.5	petroleum products	[illegible]	[illegible]
10. animal fur	1.2	3.0	metal products	12.2	1.5	synthetic resin prod[illegible]	[illegible]	[illegible]
Total	25.3	62.0		660.6	77.1		3,552.9	69.9
Nation's total export	40.9	100.0		835.2	100.0		6,081.0	100.0

1980			1985			1991		
Export	Millions of dollars	Percentages	Export	Millions of dollars	Percentages	Export	Millions of dollars	Percentages
1. textiles	5,014	28.6	textiles & garments	7,004	23.1	electronic products	20,157	28.0
2. electronic products	2,004	11.4	ships	5,040	16.6	textiles & garments	15,478	21.5
3. steel products	1,854	10.6	electronic products	4,285	14.1	steel products	4,509	6.3
4. footwear	904	5.2	steel products	582	8.5	ships	4,124	5.7
5. ships	618	3.5	footwear	571	5.2	footwear	3,836	5.3
6. synthetic resin products	571	3.3	petroleum products	914	3.0	chemical products	2,989	4.2
7. metal products	433	2.5	automobile parts	768	2.3	general machinery	2,338	3.3
8. plywood	352	2.0	synthetic resin products	741	2.4	automobiles	2,315	3.2
9. deep-sea fish	352	2.0	elastic products	609	2.0	fishing products	1,643	2.3
10. electric products	324	1.9	metal products	538	1.7	petroleum products	1,451	2.0
Total	12,426	71.0		24,053	79.4		58,840	81.9
Nation's total export	17,505	100.0		30,283	100.0		71,870	100.0

Source: Korea Foreign Trade Association. *Trade Yearbook*, various issues.

Table A.9 Exports by major countries, 1965–91

Year	Total exports (millions of dollars)	US Millions of dollars	US Percentages	Japan Millions of dollars	Japan Percentages	Europe Millions of dollars	Europe Percentages	Other Asia Millions of dollars	Other Asia Percentages	Other Millions of dollars	Other Percentages
1965	175.1	61.7	35.2	44.6	25.5	21.4	12.2	41.2	23.5	6.2	3.5
1970	835.2	395.2	47.3	234.3	28.1	76.3	9.1	81.7	9.8	47.7	5.7
1975	5,081.0	1,536.3	30.2	1,292.9	25.4	936.7	18.4	760.0	15.0	555.1	10.9
1980	17,504.9	4,606.6	26.3	3,039.4	17.4	3,115.6	17.8	4,279.9	24.4	2,463.3	14.1
1985	30,283.1	10,754.1	35.5	4,543.4	15.0	4,297.3	14.2	5,683.2	18.8	5,005.1	16.5
1986[a]	34,714.5	13,880.0	40.0	5,425.7	15.6	5,216.9	15.0	5,760.5	16.6	4,431.4	12.8
1987	47,280.9	18,310.8	38.7	8,436.8	17.8	7,848.6	16.6	7,482.1	15.8	5,202.7	11.0
1988	60,696.4	21,404.1	35.3	12,004.1	19.8	9,657.1	15.9	10,911.3	18.0	6,719.8	11.1
1989	62,377.2	20,639.0	33.1	13,456.8	21.6	8,838.1	14.2	11,689.5	18.7	7,753.8	12.4
1990	65,015.7	19,360.0	29.8	12,637.9	19.4	10,846.9	16.7	13,076.5	20.1	9,094.4	14.0
1991	71,870.1	18,559.3	25.8	12,355.8	17.2	12,632.5	17.6	19,121.1	26.6	9,201.4	12.8

a. Repaired vessels are excluded in 1986 and thereafter.

Source: Korea Foreign Trade Association. Trade Yearbook, various issues.

Table A.10 Imports by major countries, 1965–91

Year	Total imports (millions of dollars)	US Millions of dollars	Percent- ages	Japan Millions of dollars	Percent- ages	Europe Millions of dollars	Percent- ages	Other Asia Millions of dollars	Percent- ages	Other Millions of dollars	Percent- ages
1965	463.4	182.3	39.3	175.0	37.8	40.6	8.8	53.2	11.5	12.3	2.7
1970	1,984.0	584.8	29.5	809.3	40.8	217.7	11.0	318.6	16.1	53.5	2.7
1975	7,274.0	1,881.1	25.9	2,433.6	33.5	606.1	8.3	1,875.8	25.8	477.9	6.6
1980	22,291.7	4,890.2	21.9	5,857.8	26.3	1,905.0	8.5	7,436.1	33.4	2,202.5	9.9
1985	31,135.7	6,489.3	20.8	7,560.4	24.3	4,026.8	12.9	6,632.5	21.3	6,426.6	20.6
1986a	31,583.9	6,544.7	20.7	10,869.3	34.4	3,908.6	12.4	4,973.0	15.7	5,288.3	16.7
1987	41,019.8	8,758.2	21.4	13,656.6	33.3	5,480.6	13.4	6,807.2	16.6	6,317.1	15.4
1988	51,810.6	12,756.7	24.6	15,928.9	30.7	7,021.8	13.6	8,029.8	15.5	8,073.5	15.6
1989	61,464.8	15,910.7	25.9	17,448.6	28.4	7,627.9	12.4	10,335.3	16.8	10,142.3	16.5
1990	69,843.7	16,942.5	24.3	18,573.9	26.6	9,912.6	14.2	12,876.9	18.4	11,537.8	16.5
1991	81,524.9	18,894.4	23.2	21,120.1	25.9	12,689.5	15.6	19,775.0	24.3	9,045.9	11.1

a. Repaired vessels are excluded in 1986 and thereafter.

Source: Korea Foreign Trade Association. Trade Yearbook, various issues.

Table A.11 Health-related indicators

	Physicians (population per)		Nursing personnel (population per)		Daily calorie supply (per capita)		Infant mortality rate (per thousand live births)		Life expectancy	
	1965	1984	1965	1984	1965	1986	1965	1989	1965	1989
Korea	2,680	1,160	2,970	580	2,254	2,878	62	23	47	70
India	4,880	2,520	6,500	1,700	2,103	2,104	150	95	46	59
Sri Lanka	5,820	5,520	3,220	1,290	2,164	2,319	63	20	64	71
Thailand	7,160	6,290	4,970	710	2,134	2,287	88	28	55	66
Philippines	n.a.	6,700	1,140	2,740	1,896	2,255	72	42	56	64
Argentina	600	370	610	980	3,207	3,118	58	30	67	71
Brazil	2,500	1,080	3,100	1,210	2,415	2,709	104	59	57	66
Mexico	2,080	1,240	980	880	2,570	3,135	82	40	60	69
Japan	970	660	410	180	2,679	2,848	18	4	70	79
France	830	320	380	110	3,218	3,310	22	7	71	77
UK	870	n.a.	200	120	3,350	3,252	20	9	71	76
US	670	470	310	70	3,236	3,666	25	10	70	76

n.a. = not available

Source: World Bank, *World Development Report 1991* and *World Tables*, vol. 2, 3rd ed., 1983. Data used with permission.

Table A.12 School enrollment of secondary and tertiary schools[a], 1960–88 (percentages)

Year	Korea secondary	Korea tertiary	India secondary	India tertiary	Sri Lanka secondary	Sri Lanka tertiary	Thailand secondary	Thailand tertiary	Philippines secondary	Philippines tertiary	Argentina secondary	Argentina tertiary
1960	27	5	20	3	27	1	2	2	26	13	23	11
1965	35	6	27	5	35	2	14	2	41	19	28	14
1967	34	n.a.	n.a.	n.a.	n.a.	n.a.	13	n.a.	n.a.	n.a.	39	n.a.
1970	42	8	26	6	47	1	17	2	46	20	44	14
1972	47	8	26[b]	9[b]	52	n.a.	23[b]	2	51	22	48	17
1975	56	10	28	9	48	1	25	4	54	18	54	27
1977	64	11	27	8	42	1	28	5	61	24	56	29
1980	76	16	32	n.a.	55	3	29	13	65	28	56	22
1982	82	24	35	9	57	4	29	22	66	27	59	25
1985	89	32	38	6	63	4	30	20	64	31	71	36
1987	88	36	39	n.a.	66	4	28	20	68	29	74	39
1988	89	38	41	n.a.	n.a.	n.a.	28	n.a.	71	28	n.a.	n.a.

Year	Brazil secondary	Brazil tertiary	Mexico secondary	Mexico tertiary	Japan secondary	Japan tertiary	France secondary	France tertiary	UK secondary	UK tertiary	US secondary	US tertiary
1960	11	2	11	n.a.	74	10	46	10	66	9	86	32
1965	16	2	17	4	82	13	56	18	66	12	n.a.	40
1967	20	n.a.	18	n.a.	85	n.a.	62	n.a.	n.a.	n.a.	97	n.a.
1970	26	5	22	6	86	17	74	20	73	14	100	50
1972	35	8	29[b]	9[b]	92	19	81	17	77	11	96	51
1975	26	11	33	11	92	25	82	25	82	19	92	57
1977	32	13	39	11	93	32	83	26	83	19	n.a.	56
1980	34	12	46	14	93	31	85	26	83	20	89	56
1982	34	12	53	15	95	30	88	27	86	19	94	58
1985	36	11	53	16	95	29	90	30	84	22	97	58
1987	39	11	53	16	95	30	92	31	83	22	98	60
1988	38	11	53	15	95	30	94	35	n.a.	n.a.	n.a.	n.a.

n.a. = not available

a. Primary school enrollment in most sample countries is almost 100 percent. Adult literacy rate is almost 99 percent. It was 71 percent in 1960 and 93 percent in 1979 in Korea.

b. Data are from 1973.

Sources: The World Bank, World Development Report, various issues and World Tables, 1988 and 1989; United Nations Educational, Scientific, and

Table A.13 Countries with which Korea established diplomatic relations in the 1960s

Area	Country	Establishment date
Asia/Oceania	Australia	31 October 1961
	Japan	18 December 1965
	Maldives	30 November 1967
	New Zealand	26 March 1962
America	Argentina	15 February 1962
	Bolivia	25 April 1965
	Canada	14 January 1963
	Chile	12 June 1962
	Colombia	10 March 1962
	Costa Rica	15 August 1962
	Dominican Republic	6 June 1962
	Ecuador	5 October 1962
	El Salvador	30 August 1962
	Guatemala	24 October 1962
	Guyana	13 June 1962
	Haiti	22 September 1962
	Honduras	1 April 1962
	Jamaica	13 October 1962
	Mexico	26 January 1962
	Nicaragua	26 January 1962
	Panama	30 September 1962
	Paraguay	15 June 1962
	Peru	1 April 1963
	Uruguay	17 October 1964
	Venezuela	29 April 1965
Europe	Austria	18 September 1963
	Belgium	2 May 1961
	Greece	5 April 1961
	Iceland	10 October 1962
	Luxembourg	16 March 1962
	Malta	2 April 1965
	Netherlands	4 April 1961
	Portugal	15 April 1961
	Vatican City	11 December 1963
Mid-East	Iran	23 October 1962
	Israel	9 April 1962
	Jordan	26 July 1962
	Morocco	6 July 1962
	Saudi Arabia	16 October 1962
	Tunisia	31 March 1969
Africa	Botswana	18 April 1968
	Burkina Faso	20 April 1962
	Cameroon	10 August 1961
	Central Africa	5 September 1963
	Chad	6 August 1961
	Cote d'Ivoire	23 July 1961
	Ethiopia	23 December 1963
	Gabon	1 October 1962
	Gambia	21 April 1965
	Kenya	7 February 1964
	Lesotho	7 December 1962
	Liberia	18 March 1964
	Madagascar	25 June 1962
	Malawi	9 March 1965
	Niger	27 July 1961
	Rwanda	21 March 1963
	Senegal	19 October 1962
	Sierra Leone	25 June 1962
	Swaziland	19 November 1968
	Uganda	26 March 1963
	Zaire	1 April 1963

Table A.14 Major export-promotion incentives

	Duration
	April 1950–1973
	January 1962–1973
come tax by 50 ۰orts	January 1961–December 1972
۰wance for fixed ۰t production in ۰۰۰۰۰۰۰، ۰۰۰۰۰۰، ۰۰۰ ۰۰turing	January 1961–1973
Tax credit for foreign market development expenditures	August 1969–1973
Foreign market development reserve system expanded	1973
Overseas business loss reserve system established	1973
Overseas investment loss reserve system established	1973
Tariff incentives	
Tariff exemptions on capital equipment for export production	March 1964–December 1973
Tariff payments on an installment basis for capital equipment used in export production	January 1974–
Tariff exemptions on raw material imports for export production	April 1961–June 1975
Tariff drawback on imported raw material used for export production	July 1975
Wastage allowance	July 1965–
Deferred payment system for tariff	July 1975–October 1988
Financial incentives	
Financing for export sales	February 1948–July 1955
Export shipment financing	June 1950–July 1955
Export promotion fund financed by counterpart fund	November 1959–January 1964
Financing imports of materials to be used in export production	October 1961–February 1972
Export credits (trade credit before 1961)	June 1950–
Financing suppliers of U.S. offshore military procurement	September 1962–
Fund to promote the export industry	July 1964–September 1969
Fund to convert small- and medium-size firms into export industries	February 1964–

Types of incentives	Duration
Fund to prepare exports of agricultural and fishery products	September 1969–
Foreign currency loans	May 1967–
Financing exports on credits	October 1969–
Automatic export financing ceiling for large exporters	1976–
Overall export financing system introduced	October 1985–
Differentiated export financing for large versus small and medium companies	October 1986–
Other promotion schemes	
Foreign exchange deposit system	June 1949–January 1961
Trading license based on export performance	January 1953
An export bonus with preferential foreign exchange	1951–May 1961
Payment of export subsidy	1954–1955 and 1960–1965
Discount on railroad freight rates	1958–
Monopoly rights on exports of specific items to specific areas	April 1960–November 1980
Creation of exporters associations for various export products	September 1961–
Financing KOTRA	March 1962–
Export-import link system	November 1962–March 1965 1966–
Discount on electricity rates	1965–1976
Waiver issuance for shipping	1965–
Local L/C system	March 1965–
Differential treatment of traders based on export performance	February 1967–
Export insurance	January 1969
General trading company	May 1975
Export-import bank	June 1976–
Special loan privileges for small and medium exporters' raw material imports	August 1987–
Export financing for big corporations discontinued	February 1988–

Source: Hong, Wontak. 1979. *Trade, Distortions and Employment Growth in Korea.* Seoul: KDI Press, and various official documents for the later period.

Table A.15   Foreign-exchange market distortions, 1955–75 (current won per dollar)

Year	Official rate[a]	Distortion premium[b]	Tariffs and taxes[c]	Demand price	Distortion factor[e]
1955	31.3	48.1	5.9	85.3	2.72
1956	50.0	52.9	7.0	109.9	2.20
1957	50.0	58.9	9.4	118.3	2.37
1958	50.0	64.0	20.3	134.3	2.69
1959	50.0	84.7	47.8	182.5	3.65
1960	63.8	83.9	52.0	199.7	3.13
1961	127.5	n.a.	30.8	222.5[d]	1.74
1962	130.0	n.a.	28.8	245.2[d]	1.89
1963	130.0	39.8	21.0	268.0[d]	2.06
1964	214.3	39.7	36.8	290.8	1.36
1965	266.5	0.0	41.0	307.5	1.15
1966	272.2	0.0	37.2	309.4	1.14
1967	272.5	0.0	39.0	311.5	1.14
1968	276.8	0.0	46.9	323.7	1.17
1969	286.8	0.0	38.7	325.5	1.13
1970	310.1	0.0	40.6	350.7	1.13
1971	346.1	0.0	34.4	380.5	1.10
1972	391.8	0.0	37.0	428.8	1.09
1973	398.4	0.0	29.1	427.5	1.07
1974	406.0	0.0	27.7	433.7	1.07
1975	484.0	0.0	34.8	518.8	1.07

n.a. = not applicable

a. Twelve-month average from Hong, Wontak. 1976. *Factor Supply and Factor Intensity of Trade in Korea*, 140.

b. Estimate of windfall profit accruing to importer with privileged access to foreign exchange at official rate. From 1955 through mid-1961, and again in 1963 and 1964, there was a competitive market for foreign exchange earned by exporters. The resulting exchange premiums are taken from C. R. Frank, K. S. Kim, and L. E. Westphal. 1975. *Foreign Trade Regimes and Economic Development: South Korea*, 70–71. From mid-1964 on, a series of devaluations maintained a reasonable approximation to an equilibrium rate. Parity rates calculated by Frank, Kim, and Westphal (1975, 235) and Wontack Hong (1976, 141) show, if anything, undervaluation rather than overvaluation. A thin black market has existed with a very stable premium of about 30 won per dollar from 1965 through 1975 with the exception of the post-Vietnam psychological scare. The stability of this premium at an absolute rather than a relative rate, as well as its small size, suggests that it is largely a risk premium in an illegal market. We conclude that disequilibrium premiums after 1964 are virtually zero.

c. Estimates of tariffs (including foreign-exchange tax prior to 1962) per dollar of final consumption imports. Average rates per dollar were first calculated from the Bank of Korea *Economic Statistics Yearbook* and multiplied by an estimate of the ratio of actual consumer goods rates to the average. For the 1964–1967 and 1967–1972 tariff regimes the estimates are derived from Frank, Kim, and Westphal (1975, 61). For earlier years the estimates are based on highly subjective examinations of legal rates, and for later years on collections by Standard International Trade Classification codes, which do not distinguish end users. The resulting estimates are indicative only of broad orders of magnitude.

d. Confusion accompanying a plethora of reforms in the early years of the Park military government made the data for these years unreliable. Accordingly, we substituted a linear extrapolation.

e. Demand price divided by official rate.

Source: Jones, Leroy P. and Il SaKong. 1980. *Government, Business, and Entrepreneurship in Economic Development: The Korean Case.* Cambridge: Harvard University Press.

Table A.16 Effective exchange rates: nominal and adjusted for purchasing power parity (PPP), 1958–79 (won per dollar, except where noted)

Year	Nominal exchange rate			Wholesale price index (1985 = 100)		Official rate	PPP–adjusted exchange rate				
	Official rate	Effective rate[a]		South Korea	Major trade partners[b]		Effective rate			Gross effective rate for exports to imports	Net rate for exports to imports
		Exports	Imports				Exports	Exports, gross rate[c]	Imports		
1958	50.0	115.2	64.4	39.9	96.8	121.4	279.6	279.6	156.6	1.8	1.8
1959	50.0	136.0	82.8	40.8	97.5	119.5	324.9	n.a.	197.9	n.a.	1.6
1960	62.5	147.6	100.2	45.2	98.0	135.6	320.1	n.a.	217.4	n.a.	1.5
1961	127.5	150.6	147.0	51.2	98.4	244.9	289.3	n.a.	282.2	n.a.	1.0
1962	130.0	141.7	146.4	56.0	97.7	226.7	247.1	264.2	255.5	1.0	1.0
1963	130.0	177.5	148.1	67.5	98.4	189.5	258.8	276.1	215.9	1.3	1.2
1964	214.3	263.7	247.0	90.9	98.6	232.5	286.1	305.3	268.0	1.1	1.1
1965	265.4	275.3	293.1	100.0	100.0	265.4	275.3	304.6	293.1	1.0	0.9
1966	271.3	283.8	296.4	108.8	102.8	256.4	268.2	305.1	280.4	1.1	1.0
1967	270.7	290.7	296.2	115.8	103.9	242.8	260.8	298.8	265.4	1.1	1.0
1968	276.6	294.8	302.5	125.2	105.5	233.2	248.5	298.7	255.0	1.2	1.0
1969	288.2	306.6	312.7	133.7	108.7	234.3	249.3	299.4	254.5	1.2	1.0
1970	310.7	331.5	336.4	145.9	112.7	239.9	255.9	307.9	260.0	1.2	1.0
1971	347.7	370.5	369.5	158.5	115.5	253.5	270.1	328.6	269.7	1.2	1.0

table continued next page

Table A.16 Effective exchange rates: nominal and adjusted for purchasing power parity (PPP), 1958–79 (won per dollar, except where noted) Continued

Year	Nominal exchange rate Official rate	Nominal exchange rate Effective rate[a] Exports	Nominal exchange rate Effective rate[a] Imports	Wholesale price index (1985 = 100) South Korea	Wholesale price index (1985 = 100) Major trade partners[b]	PPP–adjusted exchange rate Official rate	PPP–adjusted exchange rate Effective rate Exports	PPP–adjusted exchange rate Effective rate Exports, gross rate[c]	PPP–adjusted exchange rate Effective rate Imports	PPP–adjusted exchange rate Gross effective rate for exports to imports	PPP–adjusted exchange rate Net rate for exports to imports
1972	391.8	404.3	415.2	160.7	126.8	275.0	283.1	348.9	290.2	1.2	1.0
1973	398.3	407.0	417.7	193.3	155.6	320.6	327.6	396.5	332.5	1.2	1.0
1974	407.0	415.6	425.5	274.7	188.4	279.2	285.1	338.4	288.1	1.2	1.0
1975	485.0	497.9	509.9	347.4	197.0	275.0	282.3	320.9	286.6	1.1	1.0
1976	485.0	493.7	516.6	389.2	207.8	258.9	263.6		275.8		1.0
1977	485.0	493.8	520.7	424.3	226.4	258.8	263.5		277.8		0.9
1978	485.0	494.5	527.9	474.0	258.9	264.9	270.1		288.3		0.9
1979	485.0	496.5	521.0	562.8	285.7	246.2	252.0		264.5		1.0

n.a. = not available

a. The effective exchange rate for exports includes exchange premiums resulting from multiple exchange rates, direct cash subsidies, direct tax reductions, and interest rate subsidies per dollar of exports, but excludes indirect tax and tariff exemptions. The effective rate for imports includes actual tariffs and tariff-equivalent barriers per dollar of imports but excludes the quantitative restrictions on imports.

b. An average of the wholesale price indexes of the United States and Japan (Japanese prices converted into US dollars), weighted by South Korea's annual trade volume with the respective countries.

c. "Gross" effective exchange rates for exports include indirect tax and tariff exemptions.

Sources: Kim, Kwang Suk. 1985. "Lessons from South Korea's Experience with Industrialization," in Corbo, V., A. Krueger, and F. Ossa (eds.), *Export Oriented Development Strategies: The Success of Five Newly Industrialized Countries.* Boulder and London: Westview Press. Westphal, Larry E. and Kwang Suk Kim. 1982. "Korea," in Bela Balassa and Associates (eds.), *Development Strategies in Semi-industrial Economies.* Baltimore and London: Johns Hopkins University Press.

Table A.17 Relative incentive rates on export and domestic sales in Korea, 1978 (percentages)

	Effective subsidy rate for export sales		Effective protection rate for domestic sales		Effective incentive rate for total sales	
	Balassa[a]	Corden[a]	Balassa	Corden	Balassa	Corden
Agriculture, forestry, and fishing	15.9	15.1	77.1	73.4	72.6	69.1
Mining and energy	11.4	10.6	−25.7	−23.8	−23.6	−21.8
Primary production, total	15.3	14.5	61.9	58.7	58.6	55.5
Processed food	31.7	16.7	−29.4	−16.0	−23.0	−12.6
Beverage and tobacco	13.2	10.8	28.0	22.8	27.8	22.6
Construction materials	19.1	15.1	−15.0	−11.9	−10.5	−8.4
Intermediate products I	23.6	17.1	−37.9	−27.4	−31.4	−22.7
Intermediate products II	26.3	17.6	7.9	5.3	12.0	8.1
Nondurable consumer goods	17.3	12.1	31.5	21.9	24.0	16.7
Consumer durables	38.0	23.1	131.2	81.0	83.2	51.2
Machinery	24.4	16.9	47.4	33.2	43.2	30.3
Transport equipment	26.1	19.6	135.4	73.8	87.2	48.7
Manufacturing, total	22.8	15.8	5.3	3.7	9.7	6.7
All industries	17.9	13.9	30.6	24.1	27.8	21.9
Primary production plus processed food	15.6	14.0	55.5	50.0	52.3	47.1
Manufacturing, excluding beverage and tobacco	23.6	16.2	2.7	1.9	8.2	5.6
Manufacturing, excluding beverage and tobacco and processed food	22.9	15.9	5.1	3.5	10.0	7.0
All industries, excluding beverage and tobacco	18.1	14.0	30.8	24.2	27.9	21.9

a. These names indicate alternative estimation procedures: see Balassa, Bela and Associates. 1982. *Development Strategies in Semi-Industrial Economies*. Baltimore: Johns Hopkins University Press, for an explanation of the distinction.

Source: Nam, Chong-Hyun. 1990. "Export Promotion Strategy and Economic Development in Korea." In Chris Milner, ed., *Export Promotion Strategies*, New York: New York University Press.

Table A.18 Interest rates on bank loans and inflation rates, 1971–91 (percentages)

Year	General loan	Export	Policy loans (lending rates) Machinery Promotion Fund	National Investment Fund	Curb market rate	GNP deflator
1971	22.0	6.0	n.a.	n.a.	46.4	12.9
1972	15.5	6.0	n.a.	n.a.	37.0	16.3
1973	15.5	7.0	10.0	n.a.	33.4	12.1
1974	15.5	9.0	12.0	12.0	40.6	30.4
1975	15.5	9.0	12.0	12.0	41.3	24.6
1976	18.0	8.0	13.0	14.0	40.5	21.2
1977	16.0	8.0	13.0	14.0	38.1	16.6
1978	19.0	9.0	15.0	16.0	39.3	22.8
1979	19.0	9.0	15.0	16.0	42.4	19.6
1980	20.0	15.0	20.0	22.0	44.9	24.0
1981	17.0	15.0	11.0	16.5–17.5	35.3	16.4
1982[a]	10.0	10.0	10.0	10.0	32.8	7.1
1983	10.0	10.0	10.0	10.0	25.8	5.0
1984	10.0–11.5	10.0	10.0–11.5	10.0–11.5	24.8	3.9
1985	10.0–11.5	10.0	10.0–11.5	10.0–11.5	24.0	4.2
1986	10.0–11.5	10.0	10.0–11.5	10.0–11.5	23.1	2.8
1987	10.0–11.5	10.0	10.0–11.5	10.0–11.5	22.9	3.5
1988	10.0–13.0	10.0	10.0–11.5	10.0–11.5	22.7	5.9
1989	10.0–12.5	10.0	10.0–11.5	10.0–11.5	23.7	5.2
1990	10.0–12.5	10.0	10.0–11.5	10.0–11.5	20.6	10.6
1991	10.0–12.5	10.5	10.0–11.5	10.0–11.5	21.4	10.9

n.a. = not applicable

Sources: Bank of Korea. 1992. *Principal Economic Indicators* (June); *Monthly Bulletin*, various issues; National Statistical Office. 1992. *Korean Economic Indicators* (March).

Table A.19 Average cost of borrowing, 1972–91 (percentages)

	1972	1973	1974	1975	1976	1977	1978	1979	1980	1981	1982	1983	1984	1985	1986	1987	1988	1989	1990	1991
Heavy and chemical industries (A)	10.53	8.65	10.38	10.24	10.14	11.50	10.09	12.51	17.58	17.49	15.29	12.93	14.39	12.74	11.97	12.06	12.66	13.53	12.54	12.69
Light industries (B)	13.31	10.90	10.59	12.16	13.70	14.29	15.85	16.62	20.05	19.64	16.93	14.63	14.46	14.77	13.53	13.40	13.59	13.77	13.06	13.53
(C) = (B) − (A)	2.78	2.25	0.21	1.92	3.56	2.79	5.76	4.11	2.47	2.15	1.64	1.70	0.07	2.03	1.56	1.34	0.93	0.24	0.52	0.84

Source: Bank of Korea. Financial Statements Analysis, various issues.

Table A.20 Structural change in manufacturing, 1970–89 (percentage share in manufacturing output)

	Gross output						Value added						Employment					
	1970	1975	1980	1983	1985	1989	1970	1975	1980	1983	1985	1989	1970	1975	1980	1983	1985	1989
Light industry	70.5	58.5	48.4	44.2	43.5	39.6	64.0	55.6	48.6	46.1	44.0	39.4	74.2	70.3	63.6	58.6	48.4	44.7
Food, beverage, and tobacco	39.5	28.6	21.2	19.2	18.0	15.0	31.0	24.1	22.0	20.0	17.5	15.4	20.2	14.6	13.4	13.5	6.9	6.1
Textiles and leather	17.6	19.6	16.5	14.0	15.1	14.4	19.0	21.1	17.4	13.2	13.9	12.2	32.3	41.1	34.1	29.3	30.2	27.9
Lumber and wood products	3.5	2.4	2.0	1.8	1.5	1.4	3.5	1.9	1.4	1.4	1.3	1.3	4.8	3.1	3.2	2.7	2.5	2.2
Paper printing and publishing	3.5	2.8	3.1	3.6	3.6	3.7	2.0	5.0	3.9	4.1	4.3	4.5	4.8	4.2	4.1	4.5	4.4	3.9
Nonmetallic mineral manufacturing	3.5	3.0	3.7	3.6	3.6	3.3	5.5	5.0	5.0	4.7	5.0	4.5	4.8	3.6	4.1	4.1	0.6	1.1
Miscellaneous manufacturing	3.0	2.2	2.0	2.0	1.6	1.8	5.0	3.4	2.8	2.7	2.0	1.6	7.3	3.6	5.1	5.0	3.8	3.4
HCI products	29.5	41.5	51.6	55.8	56.5	60.4	36.0	44.4	51.4	53.9	56.0	60.6	25.8	29.7	36.4	41.4	51.6	55.3
Chemicals and chemical products	14.6	21.4	24.7	23.6	22.2	18.5	20.0	22.6	23.8	21.4	20.5	19.6	9.7	9.9	11.5	12.2	17.0	14.0
Primary metal manufacturing	5.0	6.7	10.0	10.0	11.1	10.0	3.5	3.8	6.0	6.1	7.6	8.3	3.2	2.6	3.2	4.1	1.9	2.2
Metal products, machinery	9.9	13.3	16.9	22.4	23.3	31.9	12.5	18.0	21.6	26.8	27.8	32.7	12.9	17.2	21.7	25.2	32.7	39.1
Total manufacturing	100.0	100.0	100.0	100.0	100.0	100.0	100.0	100.0	100.0	100.0	100.0	100.0	100.0	100.0	100.0	100.0	100.0	100.0

HCI = heavy and chemical industry.

Source: Bank of Korea. *Input-Output Tables*, various issues.

Table A.21 Chaebols' value-added share of the nation's GDP, 1973–89 (percentages)

Chaebols in rank-ordered groups	1973			1974	1975			1976	1977	1978		
	GDP	Nonagriculture	Manufacturing	GDP	GDP	Nonagriculture	Manufacturing	GDP	GDP	GDP	Nonagriculture	Manufacturing
Top 5	3.5	4.8	8.8	3.8	4.7	6.4	12.6	5.1	8.2	8.1	10.7	18.4
Top 10	5.1	7.3	13.9	5.6	7.1	9.7	18.9	7.2	10.6	10.9	14.4	23.4
Top 20	7.1	10.0	21.8	7.8	9.8	13.3	28.9	9.4	13.3	14.0	18.5	33.2
Top 46	9.8	13.8	31.8	10.3	12.3	16.9	36.5	12.3	16.3	17.1	22.6	43.0

Chaebols in rank-ordered groups	1979	1980	1981[a]	1982	1983	1984	1985	1986	1987	1988	1989
	GDP	GDP	GDP	GDP	GDP	GDP	GDP	GDP	GDP	GDP	GDP
Top 5	n.a.	n.a.	n.a.	n.a.	n.a.	n.a.	n.a.	n.a.	n.a.	n.a.	n.a.
Top 10	n.a.	n.a.	20.4	23.0	21.9	24.2	24.1	23.6	23.4	23.3	22.7
Top 20	n.a.	n.a.	26.3	29.3	27.6	29.6	29.5	28.9	28.5	27.3	26.7
Top 30	n.a.	n.a.	30.8	33.2	31.6	33.5	33.1	32.4	31.9	30.4	29.6
Top 46	16.6	19.5	24.0	n.a.	n.a.	n.a.	n.a.	n.a.	n.a.	n.a.	n.a.

n.a. = not available

a. For 1981–1989, chaebols' manufacturing GDP shares are reported for the top 10, 20, and 30. Consequently, they are higher than SaKong's estimates for 1981.

Sources: For 1973–1978, SaKong, Il. 1980. "Economic Growth and Concentration of Economic Power," Korea Development Review. (March); for 1979–1981 top 46, SaKong's updated data are used; for 1981–1989 top 10, 20, and 30, recent Korea Development Institute estimates are used.

Table A.22 Chaebols' share of employment and shipment, 1977–87 (percentages)

Top Chaebols	Employment			Shipment share		
	1977	1982	1987	1977	1982	1987
Top 5	9.1	8.4	9.9	15.7	22.6	22.0
Top 10	12.5	12.2	11.9	21.2	30.2	28.2
Top 15	14.4	14.5	14.0	25.6	33.9	31.6
Top 20	17.4	16.0	15.1	29.3	36.6	33.9
Top 25	18.9	17.1	16.3	31.9	38.8	35.8
Top 30	20.5	18.6	17.6	34.1	40.7	37.3

Source: Lee, Kyu-Uck and Jae-Hyung Lee. 1980. *Business Group and Concentration of Economic Power*, Seoul: KDI Press, (in Korean).

Table A.23 Industrial distribution of chaebols' value added, 1978 (percentages)

Sector	Top chaebols			
	1–5	1–10	1–20	1–46
Agriculture, forestry, fishing	0.14	0.10	0.14	0.12
Mining and quarrying	0.88	0.66	0.62	0.51
Manufacturing	54.05	51.31	56.65	59.91
Construction	17.54	24.73	20.77	19.85
Electricity, gas, water	0.11	0.08	0.07	0.05
Transport, storage, communication	9.90	9.24	7.92	6.69
Trade, restaurants, hotels	4.11	3.26	4.58	4.05
Finance, insurance, real estate	9.53	7.52	6.45	6.34
Services, ownership of dwellings	3.74	3.10	2.90	2.48
Total	100.0	100.0	100.0	100.0

Source: Jones, Leroy P. 1987. "Jaebul and the Concentration of Economic Power in Korean Development: Issues, Evidence, and Alternatives." In Il SaKong, ed., *Macroeconomic Policy and Industrial Development Issues.* Seoul: KDI Press.

Table A.24 Chaebols' share of value added by industries, 1978 (percentages)

Sector	Top chaebol groups:				
	1–46	1–5	6–10	11–20	21–46
Agriculture, forestry, fishing	0.08	0.05	0.00	0.03	0.00
Mining and quarrying	5.54	4.56	0.00	0.98	0.00
Manufacturing	42.98	18.39	5.03	9.82	9.74
Construction	37.01	15.51	13.84	2.38	5.28
Electricity, gas, water	0.64	0.64	0.00	0.00	0.00
Transport, storage, communication	17.92	12.57	3.18	1.64	0.53
Trade, restaurants, hotels	4.63	2.22	0.15	1.92	0.34
Finance, insurance, real estate	32.17	22.96	1.34	2.57	5.30
Services, ownership of dwellings	2.87	2.06	0.23	0.47	0.11
Total	17.11	8.12	2.77	3.13	3.09

Source: Jones, Leroy P. 1987. "Jaebul and the Concentration of Economic Power in Korean Development: Issues, Evidence, and Alternatives." In Il SaKong, ed., *Macroeconomic Policy and Industrial Development Issues.* Seoul: KDI Press.

Table A.25   Chaebols' share of heavy and chemical industries, 1978 (percentages)

Groups	Heavy and chemical industries[a]	Light industries
1–5	31.7	5.7
6–10	9.0	1.2
11–20	11.6	8.2
21–46	7.4	11.9
1–46	59.7	27.0
Share of industries, total manufacturing	48.9	51.1

a. Heavy and chemical industries, defined according to Korean usage, includes pulp and paper products (341); chemicals, petroleum, coal, rubber, and plastic products (35); nonmetallic mineral products (36); basic metals (37); fabricated metal products, machinery, and equipment (78). Light industries is defined as the remainder: i.e., food, beverages, and tobacco (31); textiles, wearing apparel, and leather (32); wood and wood products (33); printing and publishing (342); other manufacturing (39).

Source: Jones, Leroy P. 1987. "Jaebul and the Concentration of Economic Power in Korean Development: Issues, Evidence, and Alternatives." In Il SaKong, ed., *Macroeconomic Policy and Industrial Development Issues.* Seoul: KDI Press.

Table A.26   Chaebols' share of value added in manufacturing industries, 1978 (percentages)

Industry	Chaebols' share
Food, beverages, and tobacco	24.9
Textiles, wearing apparel, and leather	34.3
Wood and wood products	73.2
Paper and paper products, printing, publishing	9.2
Chemicals, petroleum, coal, rubber, plastic	38.0
Nonmetallic mineral products	70.1
Basic metal industries	22.8
Fabricated metal products, machinery, and equipment	82.7
Other	15.4
Average	43.0

a. Chaebol data is at factor costs, but a two-digit breakdown is available only at market prices. The two-digit breakdown at factor cost was derived based on an assumption that the ratio of factor to market prices was the same for each subgroup.

Source: Jones, Leroy P. 1987. "Jaebol and the Concentration of Economic Power in Korean Development: Issues, Evidence, and Alternatives." In Il SaKong, ed., *Macroeconomic Policy and Industrial Development Issues.* Seoul: KDI Press.

Table A.27 Chaebols' share of shipment in manufacturing industries, 1987 (percentages)

Top chaebols	Food, beverages, and tobacco	Textile, wearing apparel, and leather	Wood and wood products	Paper and paper products, printing, and publishing	Chemicals, petroleum, coal, rubber, and plastic products	Nonmetallic mineral products	Basic metal products	Fabricated metal products, machinery and equipment	Other
Top 5	4.9	6.3	2.8	5.6	27.4	6.3	9.9	40.9	1.4
Top 10	6.0	10.2	6.0	13.3	37.0	19.5	22.0	46.4	1.4
Top 15	18.3	13.5	6.0	17.0	40.6	20.9	26.5	47.1	1.4
Top 20	22.6	13.5	6.0	17.1	46.2	21.9	31.4	47.8	1.4
Top 25	23.8	18.2	6.2	17.1	46.3	23.0	39.2	48.7	1.4
Top 30	26.2	20.4	6.2	17.2	49.0	28.9	39.2	49.2	1.5

Source: Lee, Kyu-Uck and Jae Hyung Lee. 1990. *Business Group and the Concentration of Economic Power.* Seoul: KDI Press.

Table A.28 Composition of inflation by cost factor, 1971–82
(percentages)

Cost factors	1971–73	1974–75	1976–78	1979–80	1981–82
Import costs	5.9	15.1	0.5	11.6	4.6
Unit import value	2.7	12.1	0.1	8.3	0.6
Exchange rate	3.2	3.0	0.4	3.3	4.0
Cost of productive factors	5.2	9.2	11.8	14.3	8.2
Wages	5.5	9.0	11.9	12.6	9.5
Demand pressure	−0.3	−0.9	1.7	−4.6	−2.2
Agricultural prices	2.7	3.7	4.2	1.6	1.5
Other	0.0	−0.1	0.0	−0.3	0.1
Actual price increases	13.5	27.0	18.2	22.6	12.2

Source: Nam, Sang-Woo. 1991. "The Comprehensive Stabilization Program," in Lee-Jay Cho and Yoon Hyung Kim (eds.), *Economic Development in the Republic of Korea: A Policy Perspective.* Honolulu: University of Hawaii Press.

Table A.29 Monthly wage levels by industry, occupation, and education 1971–90 (percentages, average for each of the three groups = 100)

	1971	1972	1976	1977	1978	1979	1980	1981	1982	1983	1984	1985	1986	1987	1988	1989	1990
Industry																	
Mining	107.0	103.9	105.9	123.0	126.6	119.3	124.1	125.9	119.8	118.2	113.8	111.0	111.3	107.2	104.7	105.8	105.0
Manufacturing	80.7	78.3	85.4	84.5	85.1	86.0	84.6	84.7	84.8	84.7	84.6	83.8	83.9	85.0	88.6	91.2	92.0
Electricity, gas, and water	230.0	210.7	221.6	204.0	191.1	141.6	131.9	135.8	147.9	142.3	146.3	152.8	168.8	159.1	153.1	133.4	145.3
Construction	129.5	132.4	187.4	193.8	189.0	185.3	166.7	150.7	154.9	144.3	136.8	142.1	133.3	130.7	121.6	125.4	130.2
Wholesale, retail, restaurants, hotels	106.1	104.7	115.8	113.1	110.7	113.8	116.6	112.3	115.4	113.2	113.7	111.4	110.3	110.5	105.4	101.6	103.2
Transport, storage, communications	103.4	111.7	110.5	108.3	112.9	116.1	120.4	120.7	116.7	111.1	114.6	113.1	110.9	111.6	115.1	106.6	100.9
Finance, insurance, real estate, business service	214.7	218.0	177.6	179.7	173.4	144.7	132.4	131.9	131.0	131.6	136.0	138.1	135.2	127.4	119.4	113.0	114.4
Community, social, personal services	141.1	147.0	157.4	170.3	155.6	140.2	148.3	151.9	148.2	150.0	144.6	143.4	145.7	152.1	137.2	130.8	121.7
Occupation																	
Professional, technical workers	179.9	193.8	211.5	203.2	203.1	184.5	176.4	167.3	173.3	168.9	167.8	166.6	163.1	169.0	153.6	144.9	138.4
Administrative, managerial workers	270.9	296.7	343.6	328.7	324.8	318.4	290.3	272.4	254.8	252.9	250.4	253.0	238.6	233.4	224.4	211.8	206.2
Clerical and related workers	151.6	142.4	161.2	154.2	136.6	128.4	117.5	117.6	114.5	110.7	110.4	110.2	108.7	106.8	106.1	103.9	103.2
Sales workers	90.2	105.6	81.4	97.9	94.5	84.0	72.1	75.5	91.9	96.1	95.9	100.2	95.8	90.7	89.9	84.4	82.3
Service workers	69.2	72.6	74.4	74.8	74.2	75.1	76.5	76.7	76.9	75.4	76.6	75.3	73.5	74.0	78.1	73.4	73.8
Production and related workers	78.1	80.5	72.5	74.9	75.3	79.1	78.4	79.5	78.2	77.9	79.2	78.7	79.3	80.8	83.8	85.3	85.7
Education																	
Middle school graduates and under	88.3	77.9	67.2	69.6	70.1	71.0	71.9	71.9	71.2	71.5	72.5	72.0	76.7	77.9	79.6	80.8	81.2
High school graduates	131.2	115.6	113.7	114.9	112.3	107.7	104.5	104.2	101.8	98.6	97.3	96.4	93.3	92.1	92.9	92.7	92.6
Junior college graduates	n.a.	n.a.	165.2	169.5	167.5	159.0	152.9	149.3	133.0	137.4	128.2	125.2	119.6	115.7	112.2	109.9	108.1
College, university graduates and over	229.9	210.7	261.2	264.9	259.3	248.6	238.7	234.5	225.6	223.0	220.6	318.5	195.7	192.7	177.4	169.0	161.8
Total female/male ratio	n.a.	45.1	43.9	43.9	43.4	42.3	42.9	44.5	44.0	45.2	45.9	46.7	49.6	50.9	52.0	54.1	55.0

n.a. = not available

Source: Korean Ministry of Labor. *Report on Occupational Wage Surveys*, various issues.

Table A.30   Wages, public utility rates, and rice purchase price, 1970–90 (percentages)

Year	Civil servant's salary	Industrial worker's wage	Rice purchase price	Public utility rates
1970	n.a.	n.a.	35.9	n.a.
1971	14.0	15.4	25.0	n.a.
1972	19.0	17.5	13.0	n.a.
1973	24.0	11.5	15.1	n.a.
1974	48.0	31.9	38.5	n.a.
1975	28.0	29.5	23.7	n.a.
1976	55.0	35.5	19.0	4.3
1977	25.0	32.1	12.1	7.7
1978	26.0	35.0	15.4	6.5
1979	23.0	28.3	22.0	23.8
1980	22.0	23.4	25.0	27.0
1981	17.0	20.7	14.0	21.9
1982	9.9	15.8	7.3	7.9
1983	7.6	11.0	0.0	2.8
1984	2.7	8.7	3.0	2.6
1985	5.2	9.2	5.0	3.9
1986	9.6	8.2	6.0	3.3
1987	8.0	10.0	14.0	2.0
1988	11.0	15.5	16.0	5.9
1989	14.0	20.9	12.0	3.4
1990	13.8	n.a.	5.0	6.1

n.a. = not available

Sources: Economic Planning Board. 1991. *Price-Related Statistics* (June); Ministry of Agriculture, Fishery and Forestry, *Major Statistics*, various issues; National Statistical Office, *Korean Economic Indicators*, various issues.

Table A.31 Korea, Taiwan, Singapore, and Hong Kong: manufacturing unit labor costs, 1976–82 (1975 = 100)

	Korea	Taiwan	Singapore[a]	Hong Kong
Nominal wage				
1976	134.7	116.8	104.7	115.9
1979	311.4	188.1	128.6	170.1
1982	526.6	297.0	191.1	240.4
Labor productivity[b]				
1976	101.0	106.9	103.0	107.0[c]
1979	131.2	136.7	114.2	119.6[c]
1982	148.2	157.4	128.9	133.7[c]
Unit labor costs in national currency				
1976	133.4	109.3	101.7	108.3
1979	237.3	137.6	112.6	142.2
1982	355.3	188.7	148.3	179.8
Exchange rates per dollar				
1976	100.0	100.0	104.2	99.3
1979	100.0	94.9	92.7	101.3
1982	151.1	103.0	90.2	122.9
Unit labor costs in dollars				
1976	133.4	109.3	97.6	109.1
1979	237.3	145.0	122.8	140.4
1982	235.1	183.2	164.4	146.3

a. All industries.
b. Value added per worker.
c. GDP over total employment in all but the construction industry.

Source: Nam, Sang-Woo. 1991. "The Comprehensive Stabilization Program," in Lee-Jay Cho and Yoon Hyung Kim (eds.), *Economic Development in the Republic of Korea: A Policy Perspective*, 234. Honolulu: University of Hawaii Press.

Table A.32 Real effective exchange rates, 1980–83 (end of 1980 = 100)

End of month	Nominal exchange rate (won/dollars)	Indexes			
		Nominal exchange rate	Effective exchange rate[a]	Relative price[b]	Real effective exchange rate[c]
12/80	659.9	100.0	100.0	100.0	100.0
6/81	685.1	103.8	96.2	106.1	90.7
12/81	700.5	106.2	100.0	106.5	93.9
6/82	740.8	112.3	97.8	106.3	91.8
12/82	748.8	113.5	102.1	106.9	95.5
6/83	776.7	117.7	103.6	105.9	97.8
9/83	789.3	119.6	105.2	105.6	99.7
12/83	795.5	120.5	105.7	n.a.	n.a.

n.a. = not available

a. Effective exchange rate $= \sum_i w_i \left(\dfrac{\text{won per dollar}}{\text{basket currency } i \text{ per dollar}} \right)$ Basket currencies include those of Korea's seven major trading partners. The weight given to currency $i(w_i)$ is based on its relative trade volume: United States 0.424, Japan 0.397, West Germany 0.067, United Kingdom 0.039, Canada 0.032, France 0.022, and the Netherlands 0.020.

b. Relative price $= \dfrac{WPI \text{ (Korea)}}{\sum_i wi \, (w_i \, WPI_i)}$

c. Real effective exchange rate $= \dfrac{\text{effective exchange rate}}{\text{relative price}}$

Source: Nam, Chong-Hyun. 1990. "Export Promotion Strategy and Economic Development in Korea," in Chris Milner (ed.), Export Promotion Strategies. New York: New York University Press.

Table A.33 Growth of the money supply, 1965–91 (percentages)

	1965	1966	1967	1968	1969	1970	1971	1972	1973	1974	1975	1976	1977	1978
Growth rates														
M1	34.2	29.7	44.5	44.6	41.7	22.1	16.4	45.1	40.6	29.5	25.0	30.7	40.7	24.9
M2	52.7	61.7	61.7	72.0	61.4	27.4	20.8	33.8	36.4	24.0	28.2	33.5	39.7	35.0
M3	n.a.	n.a.	n.a.	n.a.	n.a.	n.a.	n.a.	31.8	42.0	27.2	28.4	35.6	42.0	35.9
M1 as a share of GNP	8.1	8.2	9.6	10.8	20.1	1.1	10.5	12.4	13.6	12.4	11.7	11.1	12.2	11.3
M2 as a share of GNP	12.1	15.1	19.8	26.4	56.1	3.2	31.8	34.6	36.8	32.3	31.1	30.2	33.0	33.0
M3 as a share of GNP	n.a.	n.a.	n.a.	n.a.	n.a.	n.a.	37.4	40.2	44.5	40.0	38.5	38.0	42.2	42.5
Deposits														
Bank deposit share	n.a.	n.a.	n.a.	n.a.	n.a.	n.a.	81.9	86.2	79.6	77.4	77.5	74.7	73.3	71.0
NBFI deposit share	n.a.	n.a.	n.a.	n.a.	n.a.	n.a.	18.1	14.8	20.5	22.6	22.5	25.3	26.7	29.0

	1979	1980	1981	1982	1983	1984	1985	1986	1987	1988	1989	1990	1991
Growth rates													
M1	20.7	16.3	4.6	45.6	17.0	0.5	10.8	16.6	14.7	20.2	17.9	11.0	36.8
M2	24.6	26.9	25.0	27.0	15.2	7.7	15.6	18.4	19.1	21.5	19.8	17.2	21.9
M3	31.0	33.1	30.5	33.2	21.6	20.1	21.1	29.1	30.2	28.4	27.6	28.6	23.3
M1 as a share of GNP	10.6	10.4	8.7	11.1	11.0	9.7	9.7	9.7	9.5	9.6	10.1	9.3	10.6
M2 as a share of GNP	32.1	34.1	34.4	38.1	37.2	35.3	36.6	37.3	38.0	38.8	41.4	40.1	40.6
M3 as a share of GNP	43.4	48.5	51.1	59.3	61.0	64.5	70.1	78.0	86.8	95.4	108.5	115.4	118.4
Deposits													
Bank deposit share	68.9	65.4	61.7	58.9	55.3	50.8	48.9	44.6	41.0	38.2	35.4	34.3	34.1
NBFI deposit share	31.1	34.6	38.3	41.1	44.7	49.2	51.1	55.4	59.0	61.8	64.6	65.7	65.9

NBFI = nonbank financial institutions
n.a. = not available

Source: Bank of Korea. *Economics Statistics Yearbook; National Accounts,* and *Monthly Bulletin,* various issues.

Table A.34 Foreign economic aid and relief goods received, 1945–60 (thousands of dollars)

Year	United States					Other			Total
	GARIOA	ECA	ICA	PL480	Total	CRIK	UNKRA	Total	
1945	4,934				4,934				4,934
1946	49,506				49,506				49,506
1947	175,372				175,372				175,372
1948	179,593				179,593				179,593
1949	92,703	23,806			116,509				116,509
1950		49,330			49,330	9,376		9,376	58,706
1951		31,972			31,972	74,448	122	74,570	106,542
1952		3,824			3,824	155,334	1,969	157,303	161,129
1953		232	5,571		5,803	158,787	29,580	188,367	194,170
1954			82,437		82,437	50,191	21,297	71,488	153,925
1955			205,815		205,815	8,711	22,181	30,892	236,707
1956			271,049	32,955	304,004	311	22,370	22,681	326,685
1957			323,267	45,522	368,789		14,103	14,103	382,892
1958			265,629	47,896	313,525		7,747	7,747	321,272
1959			208,297	11,436	219,733		2,471	2,471	222,204
1960			225,239	19,913	245,150		244	244	245,394
Total	502,108	109,164	1,587,302	157,722	2,356,296	457,268	122,084	579,242	2,935,538
Percentages					80.3			19.7	100

GARIOA = Government Appropriations for Relief in Occupied Areas
ECA = Economic Cooperation Administration
ICA = International Cooperation Administration
CRIK = Civil Relief in Korea
UNKRA = United Nations Korea Reconstruction Agency
PL = Public law

Sources: Bank of Korea. 1955. *Economic Statistics Yearbook*; Economic Planning Board. 1962. *Korea Statistical Yearbook*.

Table A.35 Foreign debt outstanding, 1960–91 (millions of dollars except where noted)

	Foreign debt	Intermediate to long term		Short term		Total external assets	Net foreign debt	Foreign debt to GNP		Debt service ratios	
Year	Total	Millions of dollars	Percentages	Millions of dollars	Percentages			Total	Net	I	II[a]
1960	83	82	98.8	1	1.2	n.a.	n.a.	3.9	n.a.	0.4	n.a.
1961	83	83	100.0	n.a.	n.a.	n.a.	n.a.	3.9	n.a.	0.4	n.a.
1962	89	89	100.0	n.a.	n.a.	n.a.	n.a.	3.8	n.a.	0.7	n.a.
1963	157	135	86.0	22	14.0	n.a.	n.a.	5.8	n.a.	0.9	n.a.
1964	177	167	94.4	10	5.6	n.a.	n.a.	6.1	n.a.	2.6	n.a.
1965	206	203	98.5	3	1.5	n.a.	n.a.	6.9	n.a.	5.0	n.a.
1966	392	385	98.2	7	1.8	n.a.	n.a.	10.7	n.a.	2.9	n.a.
1967	645	579	89.8	66	10.2	n.a.	n.a.	15.1	n.a.	5.2	n.a.
1968	1,199	1,110	92.6	89	7.4	n.a.	n.a.	22.9	n.a.	5.2	n.a.
1969	1,800	1,606	89.2	194	10.8	n.a.	n.a.	27.2	n.a.	7.8	n.a.
1970	2,245	1,872	83.4	393	16.6	675	1,570	28.1	20.1	18.2	n.a.
1971	2,922	2,443	83.6	479	16.4	n.a.	n.a.	31.2	n.a.	20.4	n.a.
1972	3,587	2,947	82.2	640	17.8	1,497	2,760	33.9	20.4	18.4	n.a.
1973	4,257	3,556	83.5	701	16.5	n.a.	n.a.	31.5	20.4	14.2	n.a.
1974	5,933	4,694	79.1	1,239	20.9	n.a.	n.a.	32.0	n.a.	11.2	n.a.
1975	8,443	6,034	71.5	2,409	28.5	1,693	6,750	40.5	32.3	12.0	n.a.

Year											
1976	10,520	7,475	71.1	3,045	28.9	n.a.	n.a.	36.7	n.a.	10.6	n.a.
1977	12,649	8,934	70.6	3,715	29.4	5,049	7,600	33.8	20.6	10.2	n.a.
1978	14,823	11,672	78.7	3,151	21.3	5,286	9,537	28.5	18.5	12.1	n.a.
1979	20,287	14,831	73.1	5,456	26.9	6,294	13,993	32.5	22.8	13.6	16.0
1980	27,170	17,794	65.5	9,376	34.5	7,539	19,631	44.4	32.4	13.3	18.5
1981	32,433	22,206	68.5	10,227	31.5	7,963	24,470	49.0	36.6	14.3	20.1
1982	37,083	24,656	66.5	12,427	33.5	8,778	28,305	52.0	39.7	16.2	20.6
1983	40,378	28,263	70.0	12,115	30.0	9,504	30,874	50.8	38.8	15.7	18.8
1984	43,053	31,628	73.5	11,425	26.5	10,108	32,945	49.5	37.9	16.5	20.1
1985	46,762	36,030	77.0	10,732	23.0	11,222	35,540	52.1	39.6	18.7	21.7
1986	44,510	35,254	79.2	9,256	20.8	12,008	32,502	42.3	31.7	20.8	22.6
1987	35,568	26,277	73.9	9,291	26.1	13,156	22,412	27.6	19.4	29.6	30.8
1988	31,150	21,370	68.6	9,780	31.4	23,874	7,276	18.0	4.2	13.8	14.1
1989	29,368	18,548	63.2	10,820	36.8	26,357	3,011	13.9	1.4	9.7	10.9
1990	31,700	17,345	54.7	14,355	45.3	26,846	4,854	13.3	2.0	8.0	9.4
1991	39,135	21,898	56.0	17,237	44.0	27,186	11,949	13.9	4.3	4.6	6.0

n.a. = not available
a. Debt Service Ratio II includes short-term interest payments.

Sources: Economic Planning Board. 1985. *White Paper on Foreign Debt*; Bank of Korea. "Foreign Debt-Related Materials"; Korea Chamber of Commerce. 1985. *Efficient Foreign Debt Management and Increasing Domestic Saving* (December).

Table A.36 Foreign debt by borrower, maturity, and interest payment terms, 1979–91

Foreign debt	1979 Millions of dollars	1979 Percentages	1980 Millions of dollars	1980 Percentages	1981 Millions of dollars	1981 Percentages	1982 Millions of dollars	1982 Percentages	1983 Millions of dollars	1983 Percentages	1984 Millions of dollars	1984 Percentages	1985 Millions of dollars	1985 Percentages
Total	20,287	100	27,170	100	32,433	100	37,083	100	40,378	100	43,053	100	46,762	100
Borrower														
Public	5,251	25.9	6,505	23.9	7,862	24.2	9,342	25.2	10,292	25.5	11,056	25.7	11,376	24.3
Private	8,415	41.5	11,058	40.7	11,278	34.8	11,000	29.7	12,144	30.1	11,304	26.2	11,163	23.9
Banks	6,621	32.6	9,607	35.4	13,293	41.0	16,741	45.1	17,942	44.4	20,693	48.1	24,223	51.8
Maturity														
Short-term	5,456	26.9	9,376	34.5	10,227	31.5	12,427	33.5	12,115	30.0	11,425	26.5	10,732	23.0
Intermediate to long-term	14,831	73.1	17,794	65.5	22,206	68.5	24,656	66.5	28,263	70.0	31,628	73.5	36,030	77.0
Interest payment term														
Fixed	8,510	41.9	9,230	34.0	11,060	34.1	12,160	32.8	12,770	31.6	13,451	31.2	14,332	30.6
Variable	11,780	58.1	17,940	66.0	21,370	65.9	24,920	67.2	27,610	68.4	29,602	68.8	32,430	69.4

	1986		1987		1988		1989		1990		1991	
	Millions of dollars	Percent-ages	Millions of dollars	Percent-ages	Millions of dollars	Percent-ages	Millions of dollars	Percent-ages	Millions of dollars	Percent-ages	Millions of dollars	Percent-ages
Total	44,510	100	35,568	100	31,150	100	29,372	100	31,700	100	39,135	100
Borrower												
Public	11,250	25.3	9,852	27.7	8,717	28.0	7,646	26.0	6,829	21.5	6,208	15.9
Private	10,391	23.3	9,354	26.3	8,973	28.8	9,209	31.4	11,356	35.8	11,701	29.9
Banks	22,869	51.4	16,362	46.0	13,460	43.2	12,517	42.6	13,515	42.6	21,226	54.2
Maturity												
Short-term	9,256	20.8	9,291	26.1	9,780	31.4	10,948	37.3	14,342	45.2	17,237	44.0
Intermediate to long-term	35,254	79.2	26,277	73.9	21,370	68.6	18,424	62.7	17,358	54.8	21,898	56.0
Interest payment term												
Fixed	15,780	35.5	n.a.	n.a.	n.a.	n.a.	n.a.	n.a.	n.a.	n.a.	n.a.	n.a.
Variable	28,730	64.5	n.a.	n.a.	n.a.	n.a.	n.a.	n.a.	n.a.	n.a.	n.a.	n.a.

n.a. = not available

Sources: Economic Planning Board. 1985. *White Paper on Foreign Debt*; Bank of Korea. "Foreign Debt-Related Materials"; Korea Chamber of Commerce. 1985. *Efficient Foreign Debt Management and Increasing Domestic Saving* (December).

Table A.37 Uses of foreign debt capital, 1961–91 (hundred millions of dollars)

	1961	1962	1963	1964	1965	1966	1967	1968	1969	1970	1971	1972	1973	1974	1975
Total foreign debt	0.8	0.9	1.6	1.8	2.1	2.9	6.5	12.0	18.0	22.5	29.2	35.9	42.6	59.3	84.4
Change from previous year	0.0	0.1	0.7	0.2	0.3	0.8	3.6	5.5	6.0	4.5	6.7	6.7	6.7	16.7	25.1
Contents of foreign debt increase															
To replenish BOP deficit	−0.3	0.6	1.4	0.3	0.0	1.0	1.7	4.2	5.6	6.3	8.4	3.4	2.9	19.9	20.1
BOP deficit	−0.3	0.6	1.4	0.3	−0.1	1.0	1.9	4.4	5.5	6.2	8.5	3.7	3.1	22.2	18.9
Errors and omissions	0.0	0.0	0.0	0.0	0.1	0.0	−0.2	−0.2	0.1	0.1	−0.1	−0.3	−0.3	−0.3	1.2
To increase foreign assets															
Foreign reserve	0.3	−0.4	−0.4	0.0	0.1	1.0	1.1	0.4	1.6	0.3	−0.5	1.6	3.4	0.2	4.9

	1976	1977	1978	1979	1980	1981	1982	1983	1984	1985	1986	1987	1988	1989	1990	1991
Total foreign debt	105.2	126.5	148.2	202.9	271.7	324.3	370.8	403.8	430.5	467.6	445.1	355.7	311.5	293.7	317.0	391.3
Change from previous year	20.8	21.3	21.7	55.0	68.8	52.6	46.5	33.0	26.7	37.1	−22.5	−89.4	−44.2	−17.8	23.3	74.3
Contents of foreign debt increase																
To replenish BOP deficit	5.5	0.2	14.0	45.0	57.0	50.6	39.5	25.5	22.6	17.7	−40.8	−110.4	−135.7	−57.5	41.6	79.7
BOP deficit	3.1	−0.1	10.9	42.0	53.0	46.5	26.5	16.1	13.7	8.9	−46.2	−98.5	−141.6	−50.5	21.8	87.3
Errors and omissions	2.4	0.3	3.1	3.0	4.0	4.1	13.0	9.4	8.9	8.8	5.4	−11.9	5.9	−7.0	19.8	−7.6
To increase foreign assets	14.0	13.5	2.4	10.0	12.5	4.2	8.1	7.4	5.9	11.2	7.9	11.5	107.2	24.8	4.9	3.4
Foreign reserve	n.a.	n.a.	6.3	8.0	9.0	3.2	0.9	−0.7	7.4	1.0	2.1	12.4	88.4	28.7	−4.2	−10.9
Deferred export	n.a.	n.a.	1.2	1.0	2.0	−0.6	3.5	6.8	−1.8	9.4	4.1	−4.2	−2.5	1.4	−5.0	−8.4
Other asset	n.a.	n.a.	−5.1	1.0	1.5	1.6	3.7	1.3	0.3	0.8	1.7	3.3	21.3	−5.3	14.1	22.7
Other	n.a.	n.a.	5.4	0.0	−0.7	−2.2	−1.1	0.1	−1.8	8.2	10.4	9.5	−15.7	14.9	−23.2	−8.7
Net foreign debt	n.a.	76.0	95.4	140.0	196.3	244.7	283.1	308.7	329.5	355.4	325.0	224.1	72.7	30.1	48.5	119.5
Change from previous year[a]	n.a.	n.a.	19.4	45.0	56.3	48.4	38.4	25.6	20.8	25.9	−30.4	−100.9	−151.4	−42.6	18.4	71.0

BOP = balance of payments
n.a. = not available
a. Equals debt capital used to replenish the BOP deficit plus other.

Sources: Economic Planning Board. 1985. *White Paper on Foreign Debt*; Bank of Korea. "Foreign Debt-Related Materials"; Korea Chamber of Commerce. 1985. *Efficient Foreign Debt Management and Increasing Domestic Saving* (December).

Table A.38 Real interest rates for domestic and foreign loans, 1965–70 (percentages)

Interest rates	1965	1966	1967	1968	1969	1970
Nominal interest rate on domestic bank loan[a]	18.5	26.0	26.0	25.8	24.0	24.0
Real interest rate on domestic bank loan[b]	7.2	14.7	14.7	14.5	12.7	12.7
Real interest rate on foreign loan[b]	−2.3	−2.4	−2.0	−2.2	−1.0	−1.1

a. Commercial bank prime lending rate.
b. Real interest rate was calculated with average GNP deflator for the period of 1965–70.

Source: Frank, Charles R., Jr., Kwang Suk Kim and Larry Westphal. 1975. *Foreign Trade Regimes and Economic Development: South Korea*, vol. VII, NBER. New York: Columbia University Press.

Table A.39 Major economic indicators after first oil shock, 1972–90

Indicators	1972	1973	1974	1975	1976	1977	1978	1979	1980	1981
Real GNP growth rate	5.1	13.2	8.1	6.4	13.1	9.8	9.8	7.2	-3.7	5.9
Gross domestic investment (millions of dollars)	2,244	3,404	5,064	6,108	7,795	10,661	16,613	23,301	19,873	20,548
Rate of change	3.7	54.0	48.8	20.6	27.6	36.8	55.8	40.3	7.0	15.9
Share in GNP	21.3	25.6	32.3	29.2	27.1	29.0	33.5	36.6	32.8	30.7
Heavy & chemical share in manufacturing investment	36.1	39.9	48.1	45.9	47.0	49.2	50.5	52.1	51.2	52.1
Exports growth rate	52.1	98.6	38.3	13.9	51.8	30.2	26.5	18.4	16.3	21.4
Imports growth rate	5.3	68.1	61.6	6.2	20.6	23.2	38.5	35.8	9.6	17.2
Share of oil imports in total imports[a]	8.2	6.5	14.1	17.5	18.3	17.8	14.6	15.2	25.3	24.4
Current account balance (millions of dollars)	-371	-309	-2,023	-1,887	-314	12	-1,085	-4,151	-5,321	-4,646
Construction earning									1,751	2,974
Interest payments on foreign debt	161	213	321	452	516	734	1,028	1,513	2,655	3,631
Total foreign debt (millions of dollars)	3,587	4,257	5,933	8,443	10,520	12,649	14,823	20,287	27,170	32,433
Ratio to GNP	33.9	31.5	32.0	40.5	36.7	33.8	28.5	32.5	44.4	49.0
CPI, rate of increase	11.7	3.2	24.3	25.3	15.3	10.2	14.4	18.3	28.7	21.6
WPI, rate of increase	13.9	6.9	42.1	26.5	12.1	9.0	11.7	18.8	38.9	20.4
GNP deflator, rate of increase (annual average change)	16.7	13.6	30.5	25.2	21.2	16.6	22.8	19.6	24.0	16.9
M1 growth rate[b]	26.1	51.8	23.6	25.4	30.7	38.7	32.2	18.0	17.2	13.4
M2 growth rate	24.2	38.8	26.1	27.0	29.2	37.0	39.3	26.8	25.8	27.4
Budget deficit[c] (millions of dollars)	-410	-68	-405	-417	-397	-653	-620	-126	-1,398	-2,327
Ratio to GNP	3.88	0.50	2.19	2.01	1.39	1.78	1.25	1.77	2.32	3.51

Indicators	1982	1983	1984	1985	1986	1987	1988	1989	1990
Real GNP growth rate	7.2	12.6	9.3	7.0	12.9	13.0	12.4	6.8	9.0
Gross domestic investment (millions of dollars)	21,288	23,668	26,882	27,210	30,048	38,835	53,606	73,155	63,822
Rate of change	11.2	18.0	18.0	9.3	11.9	20.6	22.7	25.3	37.1
Share in GNP	29.8	29.7	30.9	30.3	29.2	30.1	31.1	34.8	37.4
Heavy & chemical share in manufacturing investment	52.8	55.1	56.1	56.7	57.4	57.0	60.5	61.8	61.6
Exports growth rate	2.8	11.9	19.6	3.6	14.6	36.2	28.4	2.8	4.2
Imports growth rate	-7.2	8.0	16.9	1.6	1.4	29.9	26.3	18.6	13.6
Share of oil imports in total imports[a]	25.1	21.3	18.8	17.9	10.6	9.0	7.1	8.0	9.1
Current account balance (millions of dollars)	-2,650	-1,606	-1,373	-887	4,617	9,854	14,161	5,055	-2,179
Construction earning	2,452	1,890	1,710	985	635	1,004	361	239	353
Interest payments on foreign debt	3,823	3,356	3,744	3,687	3,720	3,236	2,931	2,560	2,417
Total foreign debt (millions of dollars)	37,083	40,378	43,053	46,762	35,568	31,150	29,368	29,372	31,700
Ratio to GNP	53.5	53.1	52.2	55.9	30.0	20.0	14.0	18.8	18.6

table continued next page

Table A.39 Major economic indicators after first oil shock, 1982–90 Continued

Indicators	1982	1983	1984	1985	1986	1987	1988	1989	1990
CPI, rate of increase	7.1	3.4	2.3	2.5	2.8	3.0	7.1	5.7	8.6
WPI, rate of increase	4.7	0.2	0.7	0.9	-1.5	0.5	2.7	1.5	4.2
GNP deflator, rate of increase (annual average change)	7.1	5.0	3.9	4.2	2.7	3.4	5.9	4.7	8.9
M1 growth rate[b]	24.2	25.9	9.9	3.2	10.6	19.5	15.5	14.1	18.1
M2 growth rate	28.1	19.5	10.7	11.8	16.8	18.8	18.8	18.4	21.2
Budget deficit[c] (millions of dollars)	-2,265	-855	-1,044	-1,083.9	-97.6	581.1	2,746.5	424.4	-1,540.1[d]
Ratio to GNP	3.26	1.12	1.20	1.21	0.09	0.45	1.59	0.20	0.65[d]

CPI = consumer price index
WPI = wholesale price index
a. Crude oil imports.
b. Based on end of period figures.
c. As defined in *International Financial Statistics*.
d. Provisional.

Sources: Economic Planning Board. *Major Statistics of Korean Economy*, various issues; International Monetary Fund. 1989 and May 1991. *IFS Yearbook*; The Bank of Korea. 1990. *National Accounts*; DRI/McGraw-Hill. 1991. *World Markets Executive Summary*, vol. I.

Table A.40 Foreign direct investment and total outstanding on an approval basis, 1962–91

Year	New investment		Equity increase		Total approval		Outstanding[a]	
	Number of cases	Thousands of dollars	Number of cases	Thousands of dollars	Number of cases	Thousands of dollars	Number of cases	Thousands of dollars
1962–66	39	46,465	3	946	42	47,411	39	47,593
1967–71	350	169,131	65	49,489	415	218,620	367	226,168
1972–76	851	610,510	409	268,915	1,260	879,425	850	894,692
1977–81	244	288,794	352	431,855	596	720,649	780	1,455,091
1982–86	565	686,863	383	1,080,866	948	1,767,729	1,143	2,867,915
1987–91	1,624	2,757,876	960	2,877,090	2,584	5,634,966	2,295	7,967,092
1987	363	556,826	188	506,501	551	1,063,327	1,443	3,899,541
1988	342	583,118	189	699,614	531	1,282,732	1,696	4,994,442
1989	336	426,599	175	663,680	511	1,090,279	1,959	6,048,302
1990	296	336,625	185	465,907	481	802,532	2,122	6,734,896
1991	287	854,708	223	541,388	510	1,396,096	2,295	7,967,092
Total	3,673	4,559,639	2,172	4,709,161	5,845	9,268,800	2,295	7,967,092

a. Outstanding represents the total approval plus other forms of capital increase minus capital decrease and cancellation.

Source: Ministry of Finance, Korea. *Foreign Direct Investment Trend*, various issues.

Table A.41 Foreign direct investment by country of origin on an approval basis, 1962–90

Year	Japan		US		Europe		Other		Total
	Thousands of dollars	Percentages	Thousands of dollars	Percentages	Thousands of dollars	Percentages	Thousands of dollars	Percentages	Thousands of dollars
1962–66	8,329	17.6	24,984	52.7	10,841	22.9	3,257	6.9	47,411
1967–71	89,688	41.0	95,340	43.6	9,891	4.5	23,701	10.8	218,620
1972–76	627,059	71.3	134,955	15.3	38,775	4.4	78,636	8.9	879,425
1977–81	300,851	41.7	235,660	32.7	95,311	13.2	88,827	12.3	720,649
1982–86	876,190	49.6	581,623	32.9	191,735	10.8	118,181	6.7	1,767,729
1987–91	2,116,817	37.6	1,482,364	26.3	1,695,162	30.0	340,623	6.0	5,634,966
1987	497,014	46.7	255,140	24.0	210,484	19.8	100,689	9.5	1,063,327
1988	696,244	54.3	284,401	22.2	242,926	18.9	59,161	4.6	1,282,732
1989	461,528	42.3	328,792	30.2	211,913	19.4	88,046	8.1	1,090,279
1990	235,792	29.4	317,465	39.6	206,709	25.8	42,566	5.3	802,532
1991	226,239	16.2	296,566	21.2	823,130	59.0	50,161	3.6	1,396,096
Total	4,018,934	43.4	2,554,926	27.6	2,041,715	22.0	653,225	7.0	9,268,800

Source: Ministry of Finance, Korea. Financial Statistics, various issues.

Table A.42 Home country distribution of cumulative FDI, 1962–90

Year	Japan		US		Europe		Other		Total
	Number of projects	Percentage	Number of projects	Percentage	Number of projects	Percentage	Number of projects	Percentage	Number of projects
1962–66	5	12.8	25	64.1	4	10.3	5	12.8	39
1967–71	241	66.9	85	23.6	10	2.8	24	6.7	360
1972–76	739	85.2	78	9.0	24	2.8	26	3.0	867
1977–81	132	52.6	67	26.7	38	15.1	14	5.6	251
1982–86	276	47.7	168	29.0	86	14.9	49	8.5	579
1987–91	786	46.9	464	27.7	282	16.8	145	8.6	1,677
1987	207	55.5	93	24.9	40	10.7	33	8.8	373
1988	177	50.3	104	29.5	52	14.8	19	5.4	352
1989	145	41.5	97	27.8	70	20.1	37	10.6	349
1990	145	47.4	84	27.5	53	17.3	24	7.8	306
1991	112	37.7	86	29.0	67	22.5	32	10.8	297
Total	2,179	57.8	887	23.5	444	11.7	263	7.0	3,773

FDI = foreign direct investment

Source: Ministry of Finance, Korea. *Financial Statistics,* various issues.

Table A.43 Industrial distribution of FDI by country on an approval basis, as of 1991

Sector	Japan Thousands of dollars	Japan Percentages	US Thousands of dollars	US Percentages	Europe[a] Thousands of dollars	Europe[a] Percentages	Other Thousands of dollars	Other Percentages	Total Thousands of dollars
Agriculture									
Fisheries and forestry	9,801	27.8	21,926	62.4	1,230	3.5	2,208	6.3	35,165
Mining	10,840	67.0	370	2.3	4,756	29.4	209	1.3	16,175
Manufacturing	2,081,762	33.6	2,087,019	33.6	1,577,343	25.4	460,395	7.4	6,206,519
Food	95,443	25.5	86,543	23.2	166,784	44.6	24,939	6.7	373,709
Textiles	233,672	84.2	13,655	4.9	13,829	5.0	16,239	5.9	277,395
Chemical	394,259	28.2	572,399	41.0	363,720	26.0	67,334	4.8	1,397,712
Pharmaceuticals	26,159	9.0	131,649	45.5	118,985	41.1	12,672	4.4	287,465
Fertilizer	6,107	12.5	13,214	27.1	10,500	21.5	19,000	38.9	48,821
Petroleum refining	2,256	0.3	78,880	12.1	526,035	80.4	47,127	7.2	654,298
Metal	107,212	57.4	51,806	27.7	6,735	3.6	21,190	11.3	186,943
Machinery	239,802	40.7	138,947	23.6	170,156	28.8	41,085	6.9	589,990
Electrical, electronics	569,782	42.9	504,838	38.0	107,552	8.1	145,671	11.0	1,327,843
Transport equipment	284,149	37.0	436,455	56.8	24,578	3.2	22,886	3.0	768,068
Other	122,921	42.1	58,633	20.0	68,469	23.4	42,252	14.5	292,275
Service	1,916,531	63.7	445,611	14.8	331,753	11.0	317,046	10.5	3,010,941
Financial services	238,332	31.0	248,394	32.3	178,007	23.2	103,605	13.5	768,338
Trading, sales	28,578	12.6	78,889	34.7	88,243	38.9	31,419	13.8	227,129
Hotels	1,512,042	87.0	20,236	1.2	48,718	2.8	157,593	9.0	1,738,589
Other	137,579	49.7	98,092	35.4	16,785	6.1	24,429	8.8	276,885
Total	4,018,934	43.3	2,554,926	27.6	1,915,082	20.7	779,858	8.4	9,268,800

FDI = foreign direct investment

a. Europe includes only major European countries investing in Korea: Germany, United Kingdom, France, Netherlands, and Switzerland. Other European countries are included under the heading "Other."

Source: Ministry of Finance. Financial Statistics, various issues.

Table A.44 FDI by sector on an approval basis, 1962–91

Sector	1962–66 Thousands of dollars	1962–66 Percentages	1967–71 Thousands of dollars	1967–71 Percentages	1972–76 Thousands of dollars	1972–76 Percentages	1977–81 Thousands of dollars	1977–81 Percentages	1982–86 Thousands of dollars	1982–86 Percentages	1987–91 Thousands of dollars	1987–91 Percentages	Total Thousands of dollars	Total Percentages
Agriculture														
Fisheries and forestry	128	0.3	1,968	0.9	7,986	0.9	4,726	0.7	5,611	0.3	14,746	0.3	35,165	0.4
Mining	0	0.0	312	0.1	4,278	0.5	1,695	0.2	4,261	0.3	5,629	0.1	16,175	0.2
Manufacturing	46,760	98.6	184,681	84.5	676,168	76.9	482,161	66.9	927,926	52.5	3,888,823	69.0	6,206,519	67.0
Food	3,420	7.2	2,290	1.0	17,709	2.0	35,025	4.9	85,255	4.8	230,010	4.1	373,709	4.0
Textiles	1,120	2.4	21,402	9.8	167,087	19.0	4,981	0.7	16,882	0.9	66,123	1.2	277,395	3.0
Chemical	370	0.8	23,736	10.9	172,013	19.6	140,738	19.5	118,009	6.7	942,846	16.7	1,397,712	15.1
Pharmaceuticals	371	0.8	3,303	1.6	2,497	0.3	14,521	2.0	75,018	4.2	193,755	3.4	289,465	3.1
Fertilizer	24,500	51.7	0	0.0	21,325	2.4	1,500	0.2	1,282	0.1	214	0.0	48,821	0.5
Petroleum refining	5,000	10.5	37,747	17.3	32,460	3.7	9,515	1.3	5,266	0.3	564,310	10.0	654,298	7.1
Metal	0	0.0	17,725	8.1	46,274	5.3	36,097	5.0	21,562	1.2	65,265	1.2	186,943	2.0
Machinery	3,319	7.0	17,681	8.1	40,522	4.6	58,081	8.0	53,850	3.1	416,507	7.4	589,990	6.4
Electrical, electronics	6,710	14.1	38,569	17.6	104,160	11.8	124,394	17.3	250,351	14.2	803,659	14.3	1,327,843	14.3
Transport equipment	190	0.4	4,060	1.8	39,552	4.5	38,645	5.4	255,290	14.4	430,331	7.6	768,068	8.3
Other	1,760	3.7	18,168	8.3	32,569	3.7	18,664	2.6	45,311	2.6	175,803	3.1	292,275	3.2
Service	523	1.1	31,659	14.5	190,993	21.7	232,067	32.2	829,931	46.9	1,725,768	30.6	3,010,941	32.4
Financial services	0	0.0	2,921	1.4	10,441	1.2	93,787	13.0	67,242	3.8	593,947	10.5	768,338	8.3
Trading, sales	0	0.0	42	0.0	10	0.0	358	0.1	21,263	1.2	205,456	3.6	227,129	2.4
Hotels	500	1.0	7,294	3.3	160,763	18.3	71,314	9.9	871,852	38.0	826,866	14.7	1,738,589	18.7
Other	23	0.1	21,402	9.8	19,779	2.2	66,608	9.2	69,574	3.9	99,499	1.8	267,885	3.0
Total	47,411	100.0	218,620	100.0	879,425	100.0	720,649	100.0	1,787,729	100.0	5,634,966	100.0	9,268,800	100.0

Source: Ministry of Finance. *Financial Statistics*, various issues.

Table A.45   Foreign direct investment: its importance in the economy, 1971–86[a] (percentages)

Foreign direct investment	1971	1975	1980	1971–81	1984	1985	1986
Value added of all foreign affiliates							
As a share of GNP	n.a.	n.a.	n.a.	n.a.	1.6	1.7	1.8
In the manufacturing sector, as a share of the sector's GNP	n.a.	n.a.	n.a.	n.a.	3.7	4.0	4.0
Production of foreign affiliates in manufacturing as a share of the sector's total production	n.a.	n.a.	n.a.	n.a.	7.0	7.0	n.a.
Change in foreign affiliate value added as a share of incremental GNP	1.9[b]	1.3	1.2	1.3	n.a.	2.5[c]	n.a.
Foreign affiliate employees							
As a share of total employment	n.a.	n.a.	n.a.	n.a.	1.4	1.3	1.4
In the manufacturing sector, as a share of total manufacturing employment	n.a.	n.a.	n.a.	n.a.	5.3	5.0	5.2
Change in foreign affiliate employment as a share of change in total employment	1.6[b]	0.7	n.a.	3.0	n.a.	1.7[c]	n.a.
Foreign affiliate exports							
As a share of total exports	5.1	13.0	19.0	n.a.	10.3	9.8	11.0
In manufacturing, as a share of total manufacturing exports	7.5	15.8	19.2	n.a.	n.a.	n.a.	n.a.

Raw material imports of foreign affiliates							
As a share of all raw material imports	4.4	10.6	10.5	n.a.	9.4	9.2	10.1
In the manufacturing sector, as a share of total manufacturing imports	5.4	12.2	12.8	n.a.	n.a.	n.a.	n.a.
Less crude imports, as a share of total raw material imports less crude oil	n.a.	n.a.	n.a.	n.a.	7.1	7.4	9.3
Exports of foreign affiliates as a share of all sales	27.4	n.a.	41.5	n.a.	n.a.	n.a.	n.a.
Imported intermediate inputs of all foreign affiliates							
As a share of sales	27.7	n.a.	33.3	n.a.	n.a.	n.a.	n.a.
As a share of GDP	6.9	n.a.	13.3	n.a.	n.a.	n.a.	n.a.

n.a. = not available

a. Figures for 1971–80 are provided in Cha (1986) and those for 1984, 1985, and 1986 are from survey results of the Korea Credit Analysis, Inc., reported in the Ministry of Finance (1991).
b. Figures for 1972.
c. Average for 1984–86.

Sources: Dong Se Cha. 1986. *Impacts of Foreign Capital.* Seoul: KIEL; Ministry of Finance. 1991. *The Korean Economy and Foreign Capital Imported* (January).

Table A.46 Imports of capital goods based on customs clearance, 1970–91 (millions of dollars except where noted)

| Year | Imports of capital goods | Total imports | Gross fixed capital formation | Imports of capital goods (percentages) | |
				As a share of total imports	As a share of gross fixed capital formation
1970	589.5	1,984.0	2,240.2	29.7	26.3
1971	685.4	2,394.3	2,213.2	28.6	31.0
1972	762.0	2,522.0	2,217.4	30.2	34.4
1973	1,158.8	4,240.3	3,257.7	27.3	35.6
1974	1,848.6	6,851.8	5,109.3	27.0	36.2
1975	1,909.2	7,274.4	5,663.2	26.2	33.7
1976	2,427.4	8,773.6	7,415.1	27.7	32.7
1977	3,008.1	10,810.5	10,536.8	27.8	28.6
1978	5,080.3	14,971.9	16,341.7	33.9	31.1
1979	6,314.0	20,338.6	21,850.6	31.0	28.9
1980	5,125.0	22,291.7	20,126.7	23.0	25.5
1981	6,158.2	26,131.4	19,493.5	23.6	31.6
1982	6,232.7	24,250.8	21,127.0	25.7	29.5
1983	7,814.7	26,192.2	24,065.5	29.8	32.4
1984	10,106.3	30,631.4	26,053.0	33.0	38.8
1985	11,040.3	31,135.7	26,248.2	35.5	42.1
1986[a]	11,340.2	31,583.9	29,489.3	35.9	38.5
1987	14,552.4	41,019.8	37,846.5	35.5	38.5
1988	19,033.4	51,810.6	51,068.2	36.7	37.3
1989	22,370.4	61,464.8	67,405.0	36.4	33.2
1990	25,451.3	69,843.7	89,001.4[b]	36.4	28.6
1991	30,092.0	81,524.9	107,403.0[b]	36.9	28.0

a. From 1986 on, repaired vessels are excluded.
b. Preliminary figure.

Source: National Statistical Office, Korea. 1991. *Major Statistics of the Korean Economy.*

Table A.47 Payments for importing foreign technology by country, 1962–91

Year	US Millions of dollars	US Percentage	Japan Millions of dollars	Japan Percentage	West Germany Millions of dollars	West Germany Percentage	France Millions of dollars	France Percentage	Others Millions of dollars	Others Percentage	Total Millions of dollars
1962–76	29.7	26.1	63.7	56.1	8.2	7.2	1.6	1.4	10.4	9.2	113.6
1977–81	159.2	35.3	139.8	31.0	14.0	3.1	14.3	3.2	124.1	27.5	451.4
1982–86	602.7	50.9	323.7	27.3	49.0	4.1	34.7	2.9	174.8	14.8	1,184.9
1987–91	2,121.6	48.7	1,382.0	31.7	212.6	4.9	184.0	4.2	459.1	10.5	4,359.3
1987	239.9	45.8	181.4	34.6	18.6	4.9	25.1	4.8	58.7	11.2	523.7
1988	330.0	48.8	214.7	31.7	22.1	3.3	47.9	7.1	61.6	9.1	676.3
1989	415.7	46.8	273.9	30.8	52.8	5.9	39.9	4.5	106.3	12.0	888.6
1990	514.1	47.3	341.4	31.4	59.3	5.5	29.9	2.8	142.3	13.1	1,087.0
1991	621.9	52.5	370.6	31.3	59.8	5.1	41.2	3.5	90.2	7.6	1,183.7
Total 1962–91	2,913.2	47.7	1,909.2	31.3	283.8	4.6	234.6	3.8	768.4	12.6	6,109.2

Source: Ministry of Finance. Technology Import Statistics, various issues.

Table A.48 Foreign technology imports by country of origin, 1962–91 (number of cases)

Year	Japan	US	W. Germany	UK	France	Switzerland	Italy	Other	Total
1962–76	494	164	23	21	7	11	4	28	752
1977–81	631	302	70	49	39	26	14	94	1,225
1982–86	1,074	515	122	73	82	28	29	155	2,078
1987–91	1,613	1,010	210	119	179	54	80	206	3,471
1987	307	180	35	21	40	7	11	36	637
1988	354	200	49	20	47	10	25	46	751
1989	343	244	37	23	41	15	17	43	763
1990	333	221	55	28	25	16	17	43	738
1991	276	165	34	27	26	6	10	38	582
Total	3,812	1,991	425	262	307	119	127	483	7,526
Percentages	50.6	26.5	5.6	3.5	4.1	1.6	1.7	6.4	100.0

Source: Ministry of Finance. *Financial Statistics*, various issues.

Table A.49 Payments for foreign technology imports by sector, 1962–91

Sector	1962–66		1967–71		1972–76		1977–81		1982–86		1987–91		Total	
	Thousands of dollars	Percentage	Thousands of dollars	Percentage	Thousands of dollars	Percentage	Thousands of dollars	Percentage	Thousands of dollars	Percentage	Thousands of dollars	Percentage	Thousands of dollars	Percentage
Electrical, electronics	80.0	10.3	1,972.0	12.1	10,749.8	11.1	47,461.6	10.5	315,244.4	26.6	1,763,210.3	40.4	2,138,718.1	35.0
Machinery	0.0	0.0	1,119.0	6.9	13,447.5	13.9	89,329.1	19.8	238,328.3	20.1	935,287.3	21.5	1,277,511.2	20.9
Chemical and oil refining	340.4	43.8	7,537.9	46.4	24,753.1	25.6	147,275.3	32.6	149,046.0	12.6	702,038.8	16.1	1,030,991.5	16.9
Textiles	148.0	19.0	809.9	5.0	8,406.8	8.7	18,277.9	4.0	21,994.6	1.9	69,354.7	1.6	118,991.9	2.0
Metal	0.0	0.0	998.3	6.1	22,907.8	23.7	31,976.4	7.1	36,933.7	3.1	45,061.7	1.0	137,877.9	2.2
Electricity	0.0	0.0	1,113.2	6.8	1,645.8	1.7	25,416.0	5.6	173,792.1	14.7	422,883.6	9.7	624,850.7	10.2
Other	208.9	26.9	2,707.4	16.7	14,596.7	15.1	91,655.2	20.3	249,603.9	21.1	421,583.7	9.7	780,355.8	12.8
Total	777.3	100.0	16,257.7	100.0	96,507.5	100.0	451,391.5	100.0	1,184,943.0	100.0	4,359,420.1	100.0	6,109,297.1	100.0

Source: Ministry of Finance. Technology Import Statistics, various issues.

Table A.50 Foreign technology imports by sector, 1962–91 (number of cases except where noted)

Sector	1962–76	1977–81	1982–86	1987–90	1987	1988	1989	1990	1991	Total	Percentage
Electrical, electronics	180	226	501	826	164	212	231	219	180	1,913	25.4
Machinery, shipbuilding	191	448	640	712	161	195	168	188	156	2,147	28.5
Chemical and oil refining	176	225	372	584	135	161	150	138	101	1,458	19.4
Textiles	38	41	127	189	37	52	56	44	37	432	5.8
Metal	74	105	112	101	31	26	23	21	15	407	5.4
Food, agriculture	21	35	116	87	26	16	26	19	17	276	3.7
Ceramics, cement	21	34	50	93	25	20	22	26	14	212	2.8
Other	51	111	160	297	58	69	87	83	62	681	9.0
Total	752	1,225	2,078	2,889	637	751	763	738	582	7,526	100.0

Source: Ministry of Finance. Technology Import Statistics, various issues.

Table A.51 Foreign technology imports by sector and origin, as of 1991 (number of cases except where noted)

Sector	Japan	US	W. Germany	UK	France	Switzerland	Italy	Other	Total
Electrical, electronics	931	715	80	18	30	14	12	111	1,911
Machinery, shipbuilding	1,242	365	159	105	54	34	30	165	2,154
Chemical and oil refining	718	391	101	62	65	25	17	83	1,462
Textiles	147	85	12	18	102	17	25	26	432
Metal	234	77	24	24	7	6	3	30	405
Food, agriculture	128	96	9	8	9	8	1	16	275
Ceramics, cement	122	41	13	11	10	2	3	9	211
Other	291	221	28	14	30	13	36	43	676
Total	3,813	1,991	426	260	307	119	127	483	7,526
Percentage	50.7	26.4	5.7	3.4	4.1	1.6	1.7	6.4	100.0

Source: Ministry of Finance. *Technology Import Statistics*, various issues.

Table A.52a–d Exports and import substitution (percentages)

Table A.52a Contributions to GNP growth

	1955–60	1960–65	1965–70	1970–75	1975–80	1980–85
Exports	9.6	12.8	13.9	26.2	34.9	29.3
Import substitution	1.9	1.4	–18.2	–1.6	–11.8	3.6

Table A.52b Contributions to manufacturing output growth

	1955–63	1963–70	1970–73	1970–75	1975–80	1980–83
Exports	10.0	21.9	55.7	27.3	27.3	32.9
Import substitution	21.4	–1.8	–3.2	–1.3	1.7	3.7

Table A.52c Contributions to total output growth

	1953–60		1960–63		1963–66		1966–68	
	Total	Direct contributions to manufacturing output growth	Total	Direct contributions to manufacturing output growth	Total	Direct contributions to manufacturing output growth	Total	Direct contributions to manufacturing output growth
Exports	12.9	5.1	6.3	6.2	31.4	29.4	21.3	13.0
Import substitution	10.2	24.2	–6.9	0.9	8.9	14.4	–6.6	–0.1

Table A.52d Direct contributions to growth of manufacturing outputs

	1953–61	1962–66	1967–71	1972–74
Exports	–0.2	11.3	17.4	30.9
Import substitution	18.6	–4.2	–8.8	–6.2

Sources: World Bank. 1987. *Korea: Managing the Industrial Transition*, vols. I and II; Frank, Charles R. Jr., Kwang Suk Kim, and Larry Westphal. 1975. *Foreign Trade Regimes and Economic Development: South Korea.* New York: Columbia University Press; Suh, Suk Tai. 1977. "Foreign Aid; Foreign Capital Inflows and Industrialization in Korea: 1945–75," KDI Working Paper 77/2; Bank of Korea. 1989. *Monthly Bulletin* (August). In Korean.

Table A.53 Supply-side sources of growth, 1963–88 (percentages)

	1963–88	1963–72	1972–82	1979–88
National income	100.0	100.0	100.0	100.0
Labor	38.2	33.3	37.9	36.8
Capital	17.7	13.9	26.2	23.5
Total factor productivity	44.1	52.9	35.9	39.6

Sources: World Bank. 1987. *Korea: Managing the Industrial Transition*, vol. I; Hong, Sung Duck. 1991. *Sources of Factor Productivity Growth of the Korean Economy*. Seoul: Korea Development Institute (January). In Korean.

Table A.54 Foreign direct investment (outgoing), 1968–90

Years	Total approval		Actual investment (A)		Withdrawal (B)		Net investment (A−B)		Accumulated net investment	
	Number of cases	Thousands of dollars	Number of cases	Thousands of dollars	Number of cases	Thousands of dollars	Number of cases	Thousands of dollars	Number of cases	Thousands of dollars
1968–71	29	20,178	19	14,314	0	950	19	13,364	19	13,364
1972	15	2,739	13	5,115	0	348	13	4,767	32	18,131
1973	18	16,609	11	3,907	1	190	10	3,717	42	21,848
1974	31	15,278	19	18,149	2	104	17	18,045	59	39,893
1975	32	12,027	20	14,171	9	4,470	11	9,701	70	49,594
1976	39	17,800	46	8,220	16	1,277	30	6,943	100	56,537
1977	61	17,484	53	17,795	7	5,464	46	12,331	146	68,868
1978	90	46,522	86	43,418	12	4,657	74	38,761	220	107,629
1979	51	102,412	52	22,772	3	3,952	49	18,820	269	126,449
1980	45	22,816	44	21,095	26	5,639	18	15,456	287	141,905
1981	65	108,432	45	40,077	11	8,380	34	31,697	321	173,602
1982	54	121,636	50	129,375	19	13,413	31	115,962	352	289,564
1983	67	83,240	60	113,163	11	9,344	49	103,819	401	393,383
1984	50	70,472	46	56,974	15	5,661	31	51,313	432	444,696
1985	44	219,857	40	117,822	29	86,330	11	31,492	443	476,188
1986	74	358,504	50	171,999	18	14,846	32	157,153	475	633,341
1987	109	356,235	91	397,235	32	64,520	59	332,715	534	966,056
1988	253	479,593	165	212,919	31	59,813	134	153,106	668	1,119,162
1989	369	926,935	254	492,496	23	167,514	231	324,982	899	1,444,144
1990	515	1,600,000	368	1,020,000	23	129,144	345	890,856	1,244	2,335,000
Total	2,011	4,598,769	1,532	2,921,016	288	586,016	1,244	2,335,000	1,244	2,335,000

Source: Bank of Korea. *Economic Statistics Yearbook,* various issues.

Table A.55 Annual growth rate of Korea's outgoing FDI, 1987–90
(percentages)

Annual growth rates of FDI	1987	1988	1989	1990	Average 1987–90
On approval basis					
Number of cases	47.3	132.1	45.8	39.6	66.2
Amount	− 0.8	34.8	93.1	72.6	49.9
In actual investment					
Number of cases	82.0	81.3	53.9	44.9	65.5
Amount	130.8	− 45.8	128.8	107.3	80.3
In accumulated net investment					
Number of cases	12.4	25.1	34.6	38.4	27.6
Amount	52.6	15.8	29.0	61.7	39.8

FDI = foreign direct investment

Source: Bank of Korea. Economic Statistics Yearbook, various issues.

Table A.56 Accumulated total net foreign investment by region and industry as of December 1990

	Southeast Asia		Middle East		North America		South and Central America		Europe	
	Number of cases	Millions of dollars	Number of cases	Millions of dollars	Number of cases	Millions of dollars	Number of cases	Millions of dollars	Number of cases	Millions of dollars
Mining	3	205.5	1	19.0	7	101.8	0	0.0	2	44.3
Forestry	6	32.1	0	0.0	1	1.1	0	0.0	0	0.0
Fishery	7	3.7	0	0.0	11	26.3	25	56.9	0	0.0
Manufacturing	295	374.2	7	17.4	82	528.1	61	53.2	26	66.3
Construction	21	9.5	16	16.9	17	22.4	0	0.0	0	0.0
Transportation and storage	15	3.5	1	0.2	15	2.0	2	0.4	4	0.6
Trade	151	47.1	1	0.1	212	319.1	6	3.3	61	36.0
Other	24	39.1	8	2.5	49	104.7	10	7.1	5	4.6
Total	522	714.7	34	56.1	394	1,105.5	104	120.9	98	151.8
As share of total FDI outstanding		30.6		2.4		47.3		5.2		6.5

	Africa		Oceania		Total		Total as share of total FDI outstanding
	Number of cases	Millions of dollars	Number of cases	Millions of dollars	Number of cases	Millions of dollars	
Mining	2	13.6	6	62.4	21	446.7	19.1
Forestry	0	0.0	4	44.5	11	77.6	3.3
Fishery	2	0.1	3	0.8	48	87.8	3.8
Manufacturing	9	11.3	20	10.6	500	1,061.2	45.4
Construction	4	1.5	3	1.7	61	51.9	2.2
Transportation and storage	0	0.0	0	0.0	37	6.6	0.3
Trade	5	2.1	14	2.6	450	410.3	17.6
Other	3	16.5	17	18.7	116	193.3	8.3
Total	25	45.1	67	141.3	1,244	2,335.4	
As share of total FDI outstanding		1.9		6.1			100.0

FDI = foreign direct investment

Source: Economic Planning Board, 1991, Statistics on Economic Cooperation with Developing Countries (May).

Table A.57 Total FDI approval in manufacturing: distribution by region and industry, as of 1989

Industry	Southeast Asia		Middle East		North America		Central and South America		Europe	
	Number of cases	Thousands of dollars	Number of cases	Thousands of dollars	Number of cases	Thousands of dollars	Number of cases	Thousands of dollars	Number of cases	Thousands of dollars
Food and beverages	9	31,717	2	568	7	7,259	2	498	0	0
Textiles and footwear	74	84,597	1	263	18	24,310	52	47,607	2	400
Wood products and furniture	13	11,056	0	0	2	2,973	0	0	0	0
Paper and printing	2	1,545	0	0	5	19,548	0	0	1	279
Petrochemicals	28	36,615	2	18,541	7	6,186	3	1,980	2	24,640
Nonferrous metals	10	32,815	1	1,520	3	2,050	0	0	0	0
Primary metals	4	2,025	1	2,130	4	303,801	0	0	0	0
Machinery	45	63,530	0	0	22	106,240	1	173	13	26,975
Other manufacturing	50	25,474	0	0	5	2,725	0	0	2	1,940
Total	235	289,374	7	23,022	73	475,092	58	50,258	20	54,234
Regional distribution (percentages)		31.6		2.5		51.8		5.5		5.9

table continued next page

Table A.57 Total FDI approval in manufacturing: distribution by region and industry, as of 1989 Continued

Industry	Africa		Oceania		Total		
	Number of cases	Thousands of dollars	Number of cases	Thousands of dollars	Number of cases	Thousands of dollars	Industrial distribution (percentages)
Food and beverages	1	72	1	300	22	40,414	4.4
Textiles and footwear	2	1,355	15	8,571	164	167,103	18.2
Wood products and furniture	0	0	1	500	16	14,529	1.6
Paper and printing	0	0	0	0	8	21,372	2.3
Petrochemicals	2	7,700	1	177	45	95,839	10.5
Nonferrous metals	2	323	0	0	16	36,708	4.0
Primary metals	1	271	0	0	10	308,227	33.6
Machinery	2	3,150	2	1,244	85	201,312	22.0
Other manufacturing	1	400	3	282	61	30,821	3.4
Total	11	13,271	23	11,074	427	916,325	
Regional distribution (percentages)		1.4		1.2			100

FDI = foreign direct investment

Source: Bank of Korea. 1990. *Foreign Direct Investment Statistics Yearbook.*

References

Adelman, Irma, and Cynthia Morris. 1967. *Society, Politics, and Economic Development: A Quantitative Approach*. Baltimore: The Johns Hopkins University Press.

Amsden, Alice. 1989. *Asia's Next Giant: South Korea and Late Industrialization*. Oxford (UK): Oxford University Press.

Arase, D. 1991. "Japan's Emerging Role in the Asian-Pacific." Paper presented at the Conference on US-Japan Relations at Claremont McKenna College (March 15).

Asia Pacific Economic Cooperation. 1989. "Background Information Paper." Canberra. Mimeo (November).

Bae, Jin-Young. 1992. "Speed and Timing of Economic Integration: Unification Cost Approach." Mimeo (August).

Bai, Moo-Ki. 1982. "The Turning Point in the Korean Economy." *Developing Economies*, vol. 20.

Balassa, Bela. 1988. "The Lessons of East Asian Development: An Overview." *Economic Development and Cultural Change*, vol. 36, no.3, (April, supplement).

Balassa, Bela, and Associates. 1982. *Development Strategies in Semi-industrial Economies*. A World Bank Research Publication. Baltimore: The Johns Hopkins University Press.

Balassa, Bela, and Marcus Noland. 1988. *Japan in the World Economy*. Washington, D.C.: Institute for International Economics.

Balassa, Bela, and John Williamson. 1987. *Adjusting to Success: Balance of Payments in the East Asian NICs*. POLICY ANALYSES IN INTERNATIONAL ECONOMICS 17. Washington, D.C.: Institute for International Economics (June).

Berger, Peter L. 1988. "An East Asian Development Model?" In Peter L. Berger and Hsin-Huang Michael Hsiao, eds., *In Search of an East Asian Development Model*. New Brunswick and Oxford (UK): Transaction Books.

Bergsten, C. Fred. 1988. *America in the World Economy: A Strategy for the 1990s*. Washington, D.C.: Institute for International Economics.

Bergsten, C. Fred. 1989. "Currency Manipulation? The Case of Korea." Statement before the Subcommittee on International Trade, Committee on Finance, US Senate (May 12).

Bergsten, C. Fred. 1990. "The World Economy after the Cold War." *Foreign Affairs* (Summer) 96–112.

Bergsten, C. Fred. 1991. "Burdensharing in the Gulf and Beyond." Statement before the Committee on Ways and Means, US House of Representatives (March 14).

Bergsten, C. Fred. 1992. "The Primacy of Economics." *Foreign Policy* (Summer) 3–24.

Bhagwati, J. N. 1986. "Rethinking Trade Strategy." In J. Lewis and U. Kallab, eds., *Development Strategies Reconsidered*. Washington, D.C.: Overseas Development Council.

Bognanno, Mario F. 1987. "Collective Bargaining in Korea: Laws, Practices, and Recommendations for Reform." In Il SaKong, ed., *Human Resources and Social Development Issues*. Seoul: Korea Development Institute.

Bognanno, Mario F. 1988. "Korea's Industrial Relations at the Turning Point." Korea Development Institute Working Paper No. 8816 (December). Seoul: KDI.

Brown, Gilbert T. 1973. *Korean Pricing Policies and Economic Development in the 1960s*. Baltimore and London: The Johns Hopkins University Press.

Brown, William A., and Redvers Opie. 1953. *American Foreign Assistance*. Washington, D.C.: The Brookings Institution.

Bruno, Michael. 1988. "Opening Up: Liberalization with Stabilization." In Rudiger Dornbusch, F. Helmers, and C. H. Leslie, eds., *The Open Economy*. EDI Series in Economic Development. London: Oxford University Press.

Cha, Dong Se. 1986. *An Analysis of Foreign Capital Transfer*. Seoul: Korea Institute of Economics and Technology. In Korean.

Chenery, Hollis B., S. Shishido, and T. Watanabe. 1962. "The Patterns of Japanese Growth, 1914–1954." *Econometrica* (January).

Chenery, Hollis B., and Moshe Syrquin. 1986. "The Semi-industrial Countries." In H. Chenery, S. Robinson, and M. Syrquin, eds., *Industrialization and Growth: A Comparative Study*. London: Oxford University Press.

Cheng, Tun-jen, and Lawrence B. Krause. 1991. "Democracy and Development: With Special Attention to Korea." *Journal of Northeast Asian Studies*, vol. 10, no. 3 (Summer).

Cho, Soon Sung. 1967. *Korea in World Politics, 1940–1950: An Evaluation of American Responsibility*. Berkeley: University of California Press.

Choo, Hakchung. 1992. "Income Distribution and Distributive Equity in Korea." Seoul: Korea Development Institute. Mimeo.

Cole, David C., and Princeton N. Lyman. 1971. *Korean Development: The Interplay of Politics and Economics*. Cambridge, MA: Harvard University Press.

Competitiveness Policy Council. 1992. *Building A Competitive America, First Annual Report to the President and Congress* (March). Washington, D.C.: CPC.

Dahlman, Carl J., and Francisco C. Sercovich. 1984. "Local Development and Exports of Technology: The Comparative Advantage of Argentina, Brazil, India, the Republic of Korea, and Mexico." World Bank Staff Working Paper No. 667.

Diebold, William Jr. 1980. *Industrial Policy as an International Issue*. New York: McGraw-Hill.

Economic Planning Board. 1982a. *Economic Policy of the Development Era*. Seoul: Economic Planning Board. In Korean.

Economic Planning Board. 1982b. *The World Bank Group and IECOK*. Seoul: Economic Planning Board. In Korean.

Economic Planning Board. 1982c. *The Twenty-Year History of the Economic Planning Board*. Seoul: EPB. In Korean.

Economic Planning Board. 1985. *White Paper on Foreign Debt*. Seoul: Economic Planning Board.

Economic Planning Board. 1989. "Background Paper for APEC Ministerial Meeting." Seoul: Economic Planning Board. Mimeo.

Economic Planning Board. 1992. *Current Status and Policy Issues*. Seoul: Economic Planning Board (April).

Frank, Charles R., Kwang S. Kim, and Larry E. Westphal. 1975. *Foreign Trade Regimes & Economic Development: South Korea*, vol. 7, National Bureau of Economic Research. New York: Columbia University Press.

Frankel, Jeffrey. 1991. "Is a Yen Bloc Forming in Pacific Asia?" Essay for the AMEX Bank Review Prize Winners' Forum (14 November). Mimeo.

Gerschenkron, Alexander. 1962. *Economic Backwardness in Historical Perspective.* Cambridge, MA: Harvard University Press.

Graham, Edward M., and Paul R. Krugman. 1989. *Foreign Direct Investment in the United States.* Washington, D.C.: Institute for International Economics.

Greenaway, David, and Chong Hyun Nam. 1988. "Industrialization and Macroeconomic Performance in Developing Countries under Alternative Trade Strategies." *Kyklos,* vol. 41, no. 3: 419–35.

Habakkuk, J. 1971. "The Entrepreneur and Economic Development." In I. Livingston, ed., *Economic Policy for Development.* Penguin Books.

Hicks, George. 1989. "The Four Little Dragons: An Enthusiast's Reading Guide." *Asian Pacific Economic Literature,* vol. 3, no. 2 (September): 35–49.

Hirschman, Albert O. 1958. *The Strategy of Development.* New Haven: Yale University Press.

Hirschman, Albert O. 1973. "The Changing Tolerance for Income Inequality in the Course of Economic Development." *Quarterly Journal of Economics* (November).

Hoffman, Michael, L., and Raymond J. Struyk. N.d. *More Land at Lower Prices: the Deregulation Alternative.* In Lee-Jay Cho and Yoon Hyung Kim, eds., *Korea's Political Economy: International Perspective.* Honolulu: University of Hawaii Press. Forthcoming.

Hofheinz, Roy, Jr., and Kent E. Calder. 1982. *The East Asia Edge.* New York: Basic Books.

Hong, Wontak. 1979. *Trade, Distortions and Employment Growth in Korea.* Seoul: Korea Development Institute Press.

Hong, Wontak. 1991. "Export-Oriented Growth and Equity in Korea." Paper presented at the National Bureau of Economic Research Second Annual East Asian Seminar on Economics held at Taipei, Taiwan, 19–21 June.

Hoselitz, Bert F. 1957. "Economic Growth and Development: Noneconomic Factors in Economic Development." *American Economic Review* 47, no.2 (May).

Japan Forum of International Relations, Inc. 1988. "The Policy Recommendations on the Structural Adjustment of Economies of Japan, US, and Asian NICs" (March).

Jones, Leroy P., and Il SaKong. 1980. *Government, Business, and Entrepreneurship in Economic Development: The Korean Case.* Cambridge, MA: Harvard University Press.

Jones, Leroy P. 1987. "Jaebul and the Concentration of Economic Power in Korean Development: Issues, Evidence and Alternatives." In Il SaKong, ed., *Macroeconomic Policy and Industrial Development Issues.* Seoul: Korea Development Institute Press.

Jones, Leroy P. N.d. *Government Policies Toward Big-Business Groups in South Korea in the 1990s.* In Lee-Jay Cho and Yoon Hyung Kim, eds., *Korea's Political Economy: International Perspective.* Honolulu: University of Hawaii Press. Forthcoming.

Kahn, Herman. 1979. *World Economic Development: 1979 and Beyond.* London: Croom Helm.

Kang, Bong Kyun. 1989. "Economic Development Strategy and Income Distribution in Korea." Korea Development Institute Policy Research Material 89-06. Seoul: KDI (June). In Korean.

Keynes, John Maynard. 1926. *The End of Laissez-Faire.* London: Leonard & Virginia Woolf.

Kim, E. Han. 1990. "Financing Korean Corporations: Evidence and Theory." In Jene K. Kwon, ed., *Korean Economic Development.* New York: Greenwood Press.

Kim, Hak Soo. 1991. *Korea's International Economic Cooperation: Policy Issues and Recommendations.* Seoul: Korea Institute for International Economic Policy (KIEP).

Kim, Hyung Wook. 1990. "A Study of Foreign Direct Investment and Technology Import." Mimeo. In Korean.

Kim, Kihwan. 1989. "Foreign Technology and Korea's Economic Development." Paper presented at a joint Korea-Hungary seminar on economic development in Budapest (September).

Kim, Kihwan. 1991. "The Political Economy of US-Korea Trade Friction in the 1980s: A Korean Perspective." Paper presented at the Hoover Conference on US-Korea Economic Relations (5–7 December), Stanford, CA.

Kim, Kwang Suk. 1982. *Long-term Variation of Nominal and Effective Rates of Protection.* Seoul: Korea Development Institute.

Kim, Kwang Suk. 1985. "Lessons from South Korea's Experience with Industrialization." In V. Corbo, A. Krueger, and F. Ossa, eds., *Export Oriented Development Strategies: The Success of Five Newly Industrialized Countries.* Boulder (CO) and London: Westview Press.

Kim, Kwang Suk. 1988. "Economic Impacts of Import Liberalization in Korea." Proceedings of the Korea Development Institute/CHIER Joint Seminar on Industrial Policies of the Republic of Korea and the Republic of China, held in Seoul, Korea (8–9 February).

Kim, Kwang Suk. 1991. "The 1964–65 Exchange Rate Reform, Export-Promotion Measures, and Import-Liberalization Program." In Lee-Jay Cho and Yoon Hyung Kim, eds., *Economic Development in the Republic of Korea: A Policy Perspective.* Honolulu: University of Hawaii Press.

Kim, Pyung Joo. 1990. *Financial Institutions: Past, Present, and Future.* Honolulu: East-West Center (December).

Kindleberger, Charles P. 1973. *The World in Depression, 1929–1939.* Berkeley, CA: University of California Press.

Kindleberger, Charles P. 1986. *The World in Depression, 1929–1939.* Revised and enlarged edition. Berkeley, Los Angeles, and London: University of California Press.

Klein, Lawrence R. 1986. "Foreword." In Lawrence J. Lau, ed., *Models of Development: A Comparative Study of Economic Growth in South Korea and Taiwan.* San Francisco: Institute for Contemporary Studies Press.

Kochan, Thomas A. 1992. "Industrial Relations and Human Resources Policy in Korea: Options for Continued Reform." In Lee-Jay Cho and Yoon Hyung Kim, eds., *Korea's Political Economy: International Perspective.* Honolulu: University of Hawaii Press.

Koh, Harold. 1975. "The Early History of US Economic Assistance to the Republic of Korea, 1945–1955." Cambridge, MA: Harvard Institute for International Development (September). Mimeo.

Komiya, Ryutaro, and Ryuhei Wakasugi. 1991. "Japan's Foreign Direct Investment." In *The Annals of the American Academy of Political and Social Science.* Philadelphia: American Academy of Political and Social Science (January).

Koo, Bohn Young. 1985. "The Role of Direct Investment in Korea's Recent Economic Growth." In Walter Galenson, ed., *Foreign Trade and Investment: Economic Development in the Newly Industrializing Asian Countries.* Madison: University of Wisconsin Press.

Koopmans, Tjalling C., and John Michael Montias. 1971. "On the Description and Comparison of Economic Systems." In Alexander Eckstein, ed., *Comparison of Economic Systems: Theoretical and Methodological Approaches.* Berkeley: University of California Press.

Korea Chamber of Commerce. 1985. *Efficient Foreign Debt Management and Increasing Domestic Saving.* Seoul: Korea Chamber of Commerce (December).

Korea Development Institute. 1981a. *Materials for Economic Stabilization Policies,* vol. 1. Seoul: KDI.

Korea Development Institute. 1981b. *Policy Recommendations for Improving the Performance of Government-Invested Enterprises.* Seoul: KDI.

Korea Development Institute. 1991. *Summary Report: Establishing Economic Relations between the South and North Korea.* Seoul: KDI (September).

Korea Research Institute for Human Settlements. 1991. *Quarterly Construction Economic Review* (December).

Kosai, Yutaka, and Kenji Matsuyama. 1991. "Japanese Economic Cooperation." *The Annals of the American Academy of Political and Social Science.* Philadelphia: American Academy of Political and Social Science (January).

Krause, Lawrence. 1990. "The Asia-Pacific Economy During the 1990s: Dynamism, Interdependence, and Horizon in Economic Cooperation." Keynote address for Asia-Pacific

Economic Cooperation Forum. Seoul: Korea Institute for International Economic Policy (21–22 June).

Krause, Lawrence. 1991. "Pacific Economic Regionalism and the United States." In *Impact of Recent Economic Developments on U.S.-Korean Relations & the Pacific Basin.* Academic Studies Series, vol. 1. Washington, D.C.: the Korea Economic Institute of America.

Krueger, Anne O. 1974. "The Political Economy of the Rent-Seeking Society." *American Economic Review,* vol. 64, no. 3 (June).

Krueger, Anne O. 1979. *The Developmental Role of the Foreign Sector and Aid.* Cambridge, MA: Harvard University Press.

Kubo, Yuji, Jaime De Melo, and Sherman Robinson. 1986. "Trade Strategies and Growth Episodes." In Hollis Chenery, Sherman Robinson, and Moshe Syrquin, eds., *Industrialization and Growth: A Comparative Study.* London: Oxford University Press.

Kuznets, Simon. 1955. "Economic Growth and Income Inequality." *American Economic Review* (March).

Kuznets, Simon. 1966. *Modern Economic Growth.* New Haven: Yale University Press.

Kuznets, Simon. 1971. *Economic Growth of Nations: Total Output and Production Structure.* Cambridge, MA: Belknap Press of Harvard University Press.

Kwack, Tae Won. 1985. *Tax Depreciation System and Corporate Investment Behavior.* Seoul: Korea Development Institute.

Kwon, Soonwon. 1992. "A Survey of the Quality of Life in ESCAP Region." Korea Development Institute Working Paper No. 9211 (April): 14.

Kwon, Won-Kee. 1986. "Korea's Technological Innovation Policy and Effectiveness of R&D Investment." Unpublished Ph.D. dissertation, Hanyang University. In Korean.

Lee, Hahn-Been. 1968. *Korea: Time, Change, and Administration.* Honolulu: University of Hawaii East-West Center Press.

Lee, Kyu-Uck. 1991. "Concentration of Economic Power." Seoul: Korea Development Institute. Mimeo. In Korean.

Lee, Kyu-Uck, and Jae-Hyung Lee. 1990. *Business Group and Concentration of Economic Power.* Seoul: Korea Development Institute Press. In Korean.

Lee, Suk-Chae. 1991. "The Heavy and Chemical Industrial Promotion Plan (1973–1979)." In Lee-Jay Cho and Yoon Hyung Kim, eds., *Economic Development in the Republic of Korea: A Policy Perspective.* Honolulu: The University of Hawaii Press.

Lee, Young Ki. 1990. "Conglomeration and Business Concentration in Korea." In Jene K. Kwon, ed., *Korean Economic Development.* New York: Greenwood Press.

Leff, Nathaniel A. 1978. "Industrial Organization and Entrepreneurship in the Developing Country: The Economic Groups." *Economic Development and Cultural Change* (July).

Leibenstein, Harvey. 1963. *Economic Backwardness and Economic Growth.* New York: John Wiley & Sons.

Leibenstein, Harvey. 1968. "Entrepreneurship and Development." *American Economic Review* 5 (May).

Leipziger, Danny M. 1992. "Korea: Issues of Distribution." Paper prepared for the University of California–San Diego Symposium on Social Issues in Korea, La Jolla, California (25–27 June).

Leipziger, Danny M., and Peter Petri. 1989. "Korean Incentive Policies towards Industry and Agriculture." In Jeffery G. Williamson and Vadiraj R. Panchamukhi, eds., *The Balance between Industry and Agriculture.* New York: St. Martin's Press.

Leipziger, Danny M., and Peter Petri. N.d. "Korean Industrial Policy: Legacies of the Past and Directions for the Future." In Lee-Jay Cho and Yoon Hyung Kim, eds., *Korea's Political Economy: International Perspective.* Honolulu: University of Hawaii Press. Forthcoming.

Leudde-Neurath, Richard. 1984. "Import Controls and Export-Oriented Development: A Reexamination of the South Korean Case, 1962–1982." Unpublished Ph.D. dissertation, University of Sussex.

Levey, F., and R. C. Michel. 1991. *The Economic Future of America's Family Income and Wealth Trends.* Washington, D.C.: The Urban Institute Press.

Lewis, W. Arthur. 1980. "The Slowing Down of the Engine of Growth." *American Economic Review* 70, no. 4 (September) 555–64.

Lindbeck, Assar. 1981. "Industrial Policy as an Issue in the Economic Environment." *The World Economy* 4, no. 4 (December).

Linddauer, David L. 1990. "Labor Relations in Korea: the Role of the 'Crisis.' " In *Impact of Recent Economic Developments on U.S.-Korean Relations & the Pacific Basin.* Academic Studies Series, vol. 1. Washington, D.C.: Korea Economic Institute of America.

Lo, Fu-chen, Yoichi Nakamura, and Byung-Nak Song. 1989. "Multipolar World Economy and the Asian-Pacific Interdependencies in 1990s." Paper prepared for the Bangkok Conference on the Future of Asia-Pacific Economies (FAPE III) Bangkok, Thailand (8–10 November).

Mason, Edward S., Mahn Je Kim, Dwight H. Perkins, Kwang Suk Kim, David C. Cole with Leroy Jones, Il SaKong, Donald R. Snodgrass, and Noel McGinn. 1980. *The Economic and Social Modernization of the Republic of Korea.* Cambridge, MA: Harvard University Press.

McCune, George. 1950. *Korea Today.* Cambridge, MA: Harvard University Press.

Ministry of Finance. 1991. *The Korean Economy and Foreign Capital* (January). Seoul: Ministry of Finance. In Korean.

Ministry of International Trade and Industry, Japan. 1988. *White Paper on International Trade.* Tokyo: Ministry of International Trade and Industry.

Nam, Chong-Hyun. 1985. "Trade Policy and Economic Development in Korea." Discussion Paper No. 9. Seoul: Korea University (April).

Nam, Chong-Hyun. 1990. "Export Promotion Strategy and Economic Development in Korea." In Chris Milner, ed., *Export Promotion Strategies.* New York: New York University Press.

Nam, Chong-Hyun. N.d. "Protectionist US Trade Policy and Korean Export." In Takatoshi Ito and Anne O. Krueger, eds., *NBER-East Asia Seminar on Economics, Volume 2: Trade and Protectionism.* Chicago: Chicago University Press. Forthcoming.

Nam, Sang-Woo. 1991. "The Comprehensive Stabilization Program." In Lee-Jay Cho and Yoon Hyung Kim, eds., *Economic Development in the Republic of Korea: A Policy Perspective.* Honolulu: University of Hawaii Press.

Nam, Sang-Woo. 1992. "Liberalization of Korean Financial Market." Seoul: Korea Development Institute (May). Mimeo.

Noland, Marcus. 1989. "Learning How to Give." *Look Japan* (December): 20–21.

Noland, Marcus. 1990. *Pacific Basin Developing Countries: Prospects for the Future.* Washington, D.C.: Institute for International Economics.

Noland, Marcus. 1991. "The Origins of US-Korea Trade Frictions." Paper presented at the Hoover Conference on US-Korea Economic Relations (5–7 December).

Nolon, B. 1987. *Income Distribution and the Macroeconomy.* Cambridge (UK): Cambridge University Press.

Okita, Saburo. 1991. "Japan's Role in Asia-Pacific Cooperation." *The Annals of the American Academy of Political and Social Science*, vol. 513. Philadelphia: American Academy of Political and Social Science (January).

O'Malley, William J. 1988. "Culture and Industrialization." In Helen Hughes, ed., *Achieving Industrialization in East Asia.* Cambridge (UK): Cambridge University Press.

Papanek, Gustav. 1988. "The New Asian Capitalism: An Economic Portrait." In Peter L. Berger and Hsin-Huang M. Hsiao, eds., *In Search of an East Asian Development Model.* New Brunswick: Transaction Books.

Park, Chung Hee. 1967. Presidential Message to the Nation (January). In Korean.

Park, Chung Hee. 1970. *The Country, Revolution, and I.* Seoul.

Park, Jun-Kyung. 1991. "The Industrial Environment of the 1990s and Directions for Industrial Policy." *KDI Quarterly Outlook*, Korea Development Institute (4 April). In Korean.

Park, Se-Il. 1990. "Industrial Relations Policy in Korea: Its Features and Problems." In Jene K. Kwon, ed., *Korean Development*. New York: Greenwood Press.

Park, Yung Chul. 1986. "Foreign Debt, Balance of Payments, and Growth Prospects: The Case of Korea, 1965–88." *World Development* 14, no. 8.

Presidential Commission on Economic Restructuring. 1988. *Realigning Korea's National Priorities for Economic Advance*. Seoul.

Renaud, Bertrand. 1992. "Confronting a Distorted Housing Market: Can Korean Policies Break with the Past?" Paper presented at the Korea-US Symposium on Korean Social Issues, Graduate School of International Relations and Pacific Studies, University of California at San Diego (26–27 June).

Rhee, Yung Whee, Bruce Ross-Larson, and Gary Pursell. 1984. *Korea's Competitive Edge: Managing the Entry into World Markets*. Baltimore and London: The Johns Hopkins University Press.

Riedel, James. 1984. "Trade as the Engine of Growth in Developing Countries." *Economic Journal* 94 (March) 56–73.

SaKong, Il. 1980a. "Economic Growth and Concentration of Economic Power." *Korea Development Review*, Korea Development Institute, (March). In Korean.

SaKong, Il. 1980b. "Macroeconomic Aspects of the Public Enterprise Sector." In Chong Kee Park, ed., *Macroeconomic and Industrial Development in Korea*. Seoul: Korea Development Institute.

SaKong, Il. 1981. "Development Strategy and Finance in Korea." In Korea Investment and Finance Co., ed., *Economic Development and Finance in Korea*. Seoul: Korea Investment and Finance Co. In Korean.

SaKong, Il. 1987. "Korea: Il Sakong." *Summary Proceedings: 1987 Annual Meetings of the Board of Governors*. Washington, D.C.: IBRD, IFC, and IDA (29 September–1 October): 127–31.

SaKong, Il. 1989. "The International Economic Position of Korea." In Thomas O. Bayard and Soogil Young, eds., *Economic Relations between the United States and Korea: Conflict or Cooperation?* Washington, D.C.: Institute for International Economics.

SaKong, Il. 1990a. "Korea: At a Crossroads." *International Economic Insights* (November/December): 10–14. Washington, D.C.: Institute for International Economics.

SaKong, Il. 1990b. "Indicative Planning in Korea: Discussion." *Journal of Comparative Economics* (December).

SaKong, Il, and Dae Hee Song. 1982. *Recommendations for the Government-Invested Enterprise Sector Reform*. Seoul: Korea Development Institute. In Korean.

Sato, Hideo. 1991. "Japan as an Emerging Power in the World Economy." Mimeo.

Schott, Jeffrey J. 1989. "US Trade Policy: General Trends and Implications for US-Korean Trade Relations." In Thomas O. Bayard and Soogil Young, eds., *Economic Relations Between the United States and Korea: Conflict or Cooperation?* Washington, D.C.: Institute for International Economics.

Schumpeter, Joseph A. 1934. *The Theory of Economic Development*. Reprint. New Brunswick (US), London (UK), and Oxford (UK): Transaction Books, 1983.

Song, Byung-Nak. 1990. *The Rise of the Korean Economy*. Oxford (UK): Oxford University Press.

Suh, Suk Tai. 1977. "Foreign Aid, Foreign Capital Inflows, and Industrialization in Korea: 1945–75." Korea Development Institute Working Paper 77/2.

Summers, Lawrence H. 1992. "The Economics of the 1990s: Back to the Future." G7 Council policy paper, prepared for the Third Special Session, New York (28–29 May).

Summers, R., and A. Heston. 1991. "The Penn World Table (Mark 5): An Expanded Set of International Comparisons, 1950–1988." *Quarterly Journal of Economics* no. 425 (May) 327–68 (Supplement).

Sung, So-Mi. 1992. "Current Status of Industrial R&D and Its Policy Implications." Korea Development Institute (April). Mimeo. In Korean.

Thurow, Lester. 1992. *Head to Head*. New York: William Morrow and Company, Inc.

Timmer, Peter C. 1973. "Choice of Technique in Rice Milling in Java." *Bulletin of Indonesian Economic Studies* 9 (2).

Trela, Irene, and John Whalley. 1990. *Taxes, Outward Orientation, and Growth Performance in Korea*. The World Bank Conference on Tax Policy in Developing Countries, Washington, D.C. (28–30 March).

United Nations Development Programme. 1992. "Northeast Asian Nations Sign Agreement Launching Tuman River Development." Press Release (11 October).

US Department of State and the Economic Cooperation Administration. 1950. "Economic Aid to the Republic of Korea, ECA Recovery Program for FY 1950." Washington, D.C.: US Department of Date and Economic Cooperation Administration. Mimeo.

US Senate. 1947. "Korea: Report to the President submitted by Lt. Gen. Albert C. Wedemeyer" (September).

Wade, Robert. 1988. "The Role of Government in Overcoming Market Failure: Taiwan, Republic of Korea, and Japan." In Helen Hughes, ed., *Achieving Industrialization in East Asia*. Cambridge (UK): Cambridge University Press.

Weber, Max. 1951. *The Religion of China: Confucianism and Taoism*. New York: The Free Press.

Westphal, Larry E. 1990. "Industrial Policy in an Export-Propelled Economy: Lessons from South Korea's Experience." *The Journal of Economic Perspectives* 4 (Summer) 41–59.

Westphal, Larry E. 1977. "Industrial Policy and Development." World Bank Staff Working Paper No. 263 (August).

Westphal, Larry E., and Kwang Suk Kim. 1982. "Korea." In Bela Balassa and Associates, ed., *Development Strategies in Semi-Industrial Economies*. Baltimore: The Johns Hopkins University Press.

Westphal, Larry E., Linsu Kim, and Carl J. Dahlman. 1985. "Reflections on the Republic of Korea's Acquisition of Technological Capability." In Nathan Rosenberg and Claudio Frischtak, eds., *International Technology Transfer: Concepts, Measures, and Comparisons*. New York: Praeger.

Williamson, John. 1989. "Exchange Rate Policy in Hong Kong, Korea, and Taiwan." Statement before the Subcommittee on International Trade, Committee on Finance, US Senate (May 12).

World Bank. 1987. *Korea: Managing the Industrial Transition*, vols. 1 and 2 (*The Conduct of Industrial Policy* and *Selected Topics and Case Studies*). Washington, D.C.: World Bank.

Woronoff, Jon. 1986. *Asia's Miracle Economies*. New York: M.E. Sharpe Inc.

Yeon, Hacheong. 1991. "Prospects for North-South Korean Economic Relations and the Evolving Role of Korea in Continental Northeast Asian Economic Development." In Jang-Won Suh, ed., *Northeast Asian Economic Cooperation*. Seoul: Korea Institute for International Economic Policy.

Yoo, Jong Goo. 1990. "Income Distribution in Korea." In Jene K. Kwon, ed., *Korean Economic Development*. New York: Greenwood Press.

Yoo, Jungho. 1989. *The Korean Experience with an Industrial Targeting Policy*. Seoul: Korea Development Institute (May).

Yoo, Jungho. 1990. "The Trilateral Trade Relations among the Asian NIEs and the US and Japan." Korea Development Institute Working Paper No.9005. Seoul: KDI (April).

Yoo, Seong-Min. 1992. "The Ownership Structure of Big Business Conglomerates and Its Implication." *Korea Development Review* (Spring).

Young, John A. 1992. "A Technology Policy for America." *International Economic Insights* (March/April) 44–46. Washington, D.C.: Institute for International Economics.

Young, Soogil. 1989. "Trade Policy Problems of the Republic of Korea and the Uruguay Round." Korea Development Institute Working Paper No. 8913. Seoul: KDI (April).

Young, Soogil, and Jungho Yoo. 1982. *The Basic Role of Industrial Policy and a Reform Proposal for the Protection Regime in Korea*. Seoul: Korea Development Institute (December).

Index

Other Publications from the
Institute for International Economics

POLICY ANALYSES IN INTERNATIONAL ECONOMICS Series

1   **The Lending Policies of the International Monetary Fund**
John Williamson/*August 1982*
          ISBN paper 0-88132-000-5   72 pp.

2   **"Reciprocity": A New Approach to World Trade Policy?**
William R. Cline/*September 1982*
          ISBN paper 0-88132-001-3   41 pp.

3   **Trade Policy in the 1980s**
C. Fred Bergsten and William R. Cline/*November 1982*
(out of print)   ISBN paper 0-88132-002-1   84 pp.
Partially reproduced in the book *Trade Policy in the 1980s.*

4   **International Debt and the Stability of the World Economy**
William R. Cline/*September 1983*
          ISBN paper 0-88132-010-2   134 pp.

5   **The Exchange Rate System**
John Williamson/*September 1983, rev. June 1985*
(out of print)   ISBN paper 0-88132-034-X   61 pp.

6   **Economic Sanctions in Support of Foreign Policy Goals**
Gary Clyde Hufbauer and Jeffrey J. Schott/*October 1983*
          ISBN paper 0-88132-014-5   109 pp.

7   **A New SDR Allocation?**
John Williamson/*March 1984*
          ISBN paper 0-88132-028-5   61 pp.

8   **An International Standard for Monetary Stabilization**
Ronald I. McKinnon/*March 1984*
(out of print)   ISBN paper 0-88132-018-8   108 pp.

9   **The Yen/Dollar Agreement: Liberalizing Japanese Capital Markets**
Jeffrey A. Frankel/*December 1984*
          ISBN paper 0-88132-035-8   86 pp.

10   **Bank Lending to Developing Countries: The Policy Alternatives**
C. Fred Bergsten, William R. Cline, and John Williamson/*April 1985*
          ISBN paper 0-88132-032-3   221 pp.

11   **Trading for Growth: The Next Round of Trade Negotiations**
Gary Clyde Hufbauer and Jeffrey J. Schott/*September 1985*
          ISBN paper 0-88132-033-1   109 pp.

12   **Financial Intermediation Beyond the Debt Crisis**
Donald R. Lessard and John Williamson/*September 1985*
          ISBN paper 0-88132-021-8   130 pp.

13   **The United States–Japan Economic Problem**
C. Fred Bergsten and William R. Cline/*October 1985, rev. January 1987*
          ISBN paper 0-88132-060-9   180 pp.

14   **Deficits and the Dollar: The World Economy at Risk**
Stephen Marris/*December 1985, rev. November 1987*
          ISBN paper 0-88132-067-6   415 pp.

BOOKS

Pacific Basin Developing Countries: Prospects for the Future
Marcus Noland/*January 1991*

ISBN cloth 0-88132-141-9	250 pp.
ISBN paper 0-88132-081-1	250 pp.

Currency Convertibility in Eastern Europe
John Williamson, editor/*September 1991*

ISBN cloth 0-88132-144-3	396 pp.
ISBN paper 0-88132-128-1	396 pp.

Foreign Direct Investment in the United States
Edward M. Graham and Paul R. Krugman/*1989, rev. October 1991*

ISBN paper 0-88132-139-7	200 pp.

International Adjustment and Financing: The Lessons of 1985–1991
C. Fred Bergsten, editor/*January 1992*

ISBN cloth 0-88132-142-7	336 pp.
ISBN paper 0-88132-112-5	336 pp.

North American Free Trade: Issues and Recommendations
Gary Clyde Hufbauer and Jeffrey J. Schott/*April 1992*

ISBN cloth 0-88132-145-1	392 pp.
ISBN paper 0-88132-120-6	392 pp.

American Trade Politics
I. M. Destler/*1986, rev. June 1992*

ISBN cloth 0-88132-164-8	400 pp.
ISBN paper 0-88132-188-5	400 pp.

Narrowing the U.S. Current Account Deficit: A Sectoral Assessment
Allen J. Lenz/*June 1992*

ISBN cloth 0-88132-148-6	640 pp.
ISBN paper 0-88132-103-6	640 pp.

The Economics of Global Warming
William R. Cline/*June 1992*

ISBN cloth 0-88132-150-8	420 pp.
ISBN paper 0-88132-132-X	420 pp.

U.S. Taxation of International Income: Blueprint for Reform
Gary Clyde Hufbauer, assisted by Joanna M. van Rooij/*October 1992*

ISBN cloth 0-88132-178-8	304 pp.
ISBN paper 0-88132-134-6	304 pp.

Who's Bashing Whom? Trade Conflict in High-Technology Industries
Laura D'Andrea Tyson/*November 1992*

ISBN cloth 0-88132-151-6	352 pp.
ISBN paper 0-88132-106-0	352 pp.

Korea in the World Economy
Il SaKong/*January 1993*

ISBN cloth 0-88132-184-2	328 pp.
ISBN paper 0-88132-106-0	328 pp.

SPECIAL REPORTS

1 Promoting World Recovery: A Statement on Global Economic Strategy
by Twenty-six Economists from Fourteen Countries/*December 1982*

(out of print)	ISBN paper 0-88132-013-7	45 pp.

FORTHCOMING

A World Savings Shortage?
Paul R. Krugman

Sizing Up U.S. Export Disincentives
J. David Richardson

The Globalization of Industry and National Governments
C. Fred Bergsten and Edward M. Graham

Trade and the Environment: Setting the Rules
John Whalley and Peter Uimonen

The Effects of Foreign-Exchange Intervention
Kathryn Dominguez and Jeffrey A. Frankel

The Future of the World Trading System
John Whalley

Adjusting to Volatile Energy Prices
Philip K. Verleger, Jr.

Downsizing Defense: The New Global Agenda
Ellen L. Frost

The United States as a Debtor Country
C. Fred Bergsten and Shafiqul Islam

International Monetary Policymaking in the United States, Germany, and Japan
C. Randall Henning